PURSUING TRUTH

A volume in the series

Cushwa Center Studies of Catholicism in Twentieth-Century America
edited by R. Scott Appleby, University of Notre Dame

For a list of books in the series, visit our website at cornellpress.cornell.edu.

PURSUING TRUTH

How Gender Shaped
Catholic Education at the
College of Notre Dame of Maryland

MARY J. OATES

CORNELL UNIVERSITY PRESS
Ithaca and London

Thanks to generous funding from the Cushwa Center for the Study of American Catholicism at the University of Notre Dame and Notre Dame of Maryland University, the ebook editions of this book are available as open access volumes through the Cornell Open initiative.

First published 2021 by Cornell University Press

Library of Congress Cataloging-in-Publication Data

Names: Oates, Mary J., author.
Title: Pursuing truth : how gender shaped Catholic education at the College of Notre Dame of Maryland / Mary J. Oates
Description: Ithaca [New York] : Cornell University Press, 2021. | Series: Cushwa Center studies of Catholicism in twentieth-century America | Includes bibliographical references and index.
Identifiers: LCCN 2020036542 (print) | LCCN 2020036543 (ebook) | ISBN 9781501753794 (paperback) | ISBN 9781501753800 (pdf) | ISBN 9781501753817 (epub)
Subjects: LCSH: College of Notre Dame of Maryland—History—20th century. | Catholic women—Education (Higher)—Maryland—Baltimore—History—20th century. | Catholic women's colleges—Maryland—Baltimore—History—20th century.
Classification: LCC LD7251.B3842 O37 2021 (print) | LCC LD7251.B3842 (ebook) | DDC 378.752/6—dc23
LC record available at https://lccn.loc.gov/2020036542
LC ebook record available at https://lccn.loc.gov/2020036543

In memory of my father
Thomas Francis Oates
1905–1994

CONTENTS

ACKNOWLEDGMENTS

This book was advanced significantly by a major grant from the Spencer Foundation. Much-appreciated financial support also came from the College of Notre Dame Travel Grants, a Regis College Kaneb Small Grant, and the Cushwa Center for the Study of American Catholicism at the University of Notre Dame and Notre Dame of Maryland University.

I would like to thank the following individuals for their support and encouragement throughout my work on this project: Scott Appleby, Dorothy Brown, Carol Coburn, Kathleen Sprows Cummings, Dorothy Cunningham, Kathleen Feeley, Mary Adele Geishecker, Suellen Hoy, Jennifer Kinniff, Katherine Magno, Margaret McGuinness, Jean McManus, Jean Mulloy, Rosemarie Nassif, Walter Nugent, Catherine R. Osborne, Harold Petersen, Mary Pat Seurkamp, Josephine Trueschler, and Marylou Yam. I also want to express my thanks to the editorial team at Cornell University Press, including Michael McGandy, Clare Kirkpatrick Jones, Mary Kate Murphy, Eric Levy, and Lisa DeBoer.

Thank you also to my fellow sisters in the Congregation of the Sisters of St. Joseph of Boston, especially Margaret Wallace, and thank you to all the School Sisters of Notre Dame who graciously assisted in my research, especially Eileen O'Dea.

My strongest supporters have always been my family: my brother, Rev. Thomas Oates; and my sisters, Clare Oates, Dorothy Doyle, Eileen Latimer, the late Patricia Coates, and their families. My gratitude to them is immense.

PURSUING TRUTH

Introduction
Women's Education and the College of Notre Dame of Maryland

> Boundaries ought to be crossed. National boundaries, of course; but first of all boundaries of the imagination and sensibility, which wall us in when we think we are so free.
>
> —Marie-Alain Couturier, OP, *Sacred Art*

The status and role of women are incontestably among the most crucial issues facing society today. Yet historians have given little attention to the efforts of women in the nation's largest religious denomination, Roman Catholicism, to take their place as the equals of men over the past century. In seeking that story, the commitment of the Catholic Church to the mission of higher education is of fundamental importance. Women's education inarguably played a critical role in the history of American Catholicism and of American women and their families during the twentieth century. This book views that history through the lens of the College of Notre Dame of Maryland—since 2011, Notre Dame of Maryland University. The college's 1895 founding in Baltimore opened a new chapter in higher education when it became the first Catholic college in the United States to award the four-year baccalaureate degree to women.[1] This book explores women's struggle for equal access to Catholic higher education during the twentieth century and analyzes their responses to challenges from the Catholic Church, higher educational associations, students, established Protestant churches, and secular society.

The "Seven Sisters"—Barnard, Bryn Mawr, Mount Holyoke, Radcliffe, Smith, Vassar, and Wellesley—have traditionally received more attention in the scholarly literature on higher education than other institutions that admitted women, and historians of Catholic higher education in the United

FIGURE 1. Student at the Annex Cornerstone, showing "Notre Dame A.D. 1895." Photo by Margaret Steinhagen, NDMA.

States have tended to focus heavily on colleges established by and for men.[2] Significant scholarship on Catholic women's colleges has developed very slowly,[3] and otherwise exhaustive articles on women's education insufficiently acknowledge their very existence.[4] In this context, *Catholic Women's Colleges* (2002), edited by Tracy Schier and Cynthia Russett, remains the most valuable addition to a sparse literature.[5] This book therefore intends to add a significant corrective to the literature on women's higher education, even as it demonstrates that Catholic women's colleges modeled themselves simultaneously on and against the elite secular and Protestant women's colleges.

The College of Notre Dame of Maryland and other Catholic women's colleges rejected traditional views of women's subordinate place in public and private life and offered their graduates new opportunities to participate as equals in every sector of US society. Moreover, by contesting women's narrow professional and social horizons from within a church that had few public forums where women could be heard, they influenced millions, not simply their own students. And despite ongoing religious tensions between Protestant and Catholic Americans, over time Catholic women's colleges helped create a more tolerant and democratic nation by affording new educational opportunities to women of every faith, social class, and race.

Catholic women's colleges are of particular interest to the history of higher education because, to a far greater extent than their Protestant and secular counterparts, they were founded, governed, staffed, and financed primarily by women. This was not entirely a result of Catholic men's indifference to the cause of women's education. For centuries, women's religious orders had been the only viable agencies through which female members of a patriarchal church could undertake projects of such scope. The talents and voluntary lifetime commitments of their members were major assets of these tightly organized and enduring female orders. During the nineteenth century many women's religious orders began to become highly specialized in professional work, especially in the fields of education and medicine, and to offer Catholic women unique opportunities to unite as influential actors in church and society. Despite the restrictions of cloister and custom, the orders expanded steadily in number and membership from the mid-nineteenth century until the 1960s. For thousands of young women, the benefits of convent life more than compensated for the loss of those offered by the most common alternative life path, marriage and family.

Because of their dedication, slim personal expenses, and experience with collective projects, women's orders were able to overcome one of the chief constraints facing early founders of female colleges: how to fund their work. Wealthy lay patrons were few, bishops and clergy typically offered only verbal support at best, and ordinary parishioners, overwhelmingly working- and lower-middle-class, did not give high priority to church-supported colleges for women. For much of their histories, Catholic women's colleges received their most significant financial support from their founding sisterhoods. A Catholic women's college was a community-wide project. All members of the order, whatever their employment, shared in the sacrifices required for its development. The funds to establish a college and educate sisters for its faculty typically came from an order's collective savings, from borrowing against convent property and tuition-paying schools it owned, and from the small stipends received by sisters staffing parish schools. As a result of this common endeavor, the collective presence of sister-faculty and administrators was always notable. A large convent, with its attached chapel, typically distinguished the campus of nearly every Catholic women's college.

By 1910 there were 14 Catholic women's colleges, and by 1967 they numbered 120.[6] While Catholic women's colleges varied in geographic location, social class of students, and curricular focus, in essential areas they had much in common. All were Roman Catholic in affiliation; religious orders of women had established and supported most of them; and they maintained important collaborative and competitive connections. All were quite small at their foundation, and many remained so. And although a deeply religious spirit marked these institutions, they were founded to advance the cause of higher education for women in general, and they welcomed students of all faiths. The history of the College of Notre Dame of Maryland provides an excellent opening through which to explore the foremost issues faced by these institutions in the twentieth-century United States.[7]

Notre Dame of Maryland's story reveals how major religious, social, and economic forces affected American Catholic women during the twentieth century—and how these women, in turn, affected the course of history. It sheds light on their initiatives and strategies, successes, and failures as they confronted secular and ecclesiastical challenges to developing Catholic higher education for their sex. It also reveals women's intellectual growth and emancipation from male control, from social mores favoring the home, and from limited professional opportunities. The college's development provides new perspectives on how higher education and religion widened the intellectual horizons, professional influence, and social power of American women. Contrary to a conventional wisdom that sees the decades before the Second Vatican Council as a time of harmonious cooperation among Catholics, the College of Notre Dame was a center of political and religious controversy from its inception. Its archives reveal a complex story of boundary crossings, the interaction of multiple cultures, and female enterprise and power, showing how placement and displacement within changing social, political, and ecclesial contexts enlarged the map of educational opportunity for women in the United States.

The question of whether higher education was desirable for women was still a topic of debate among late-nineteenth-century Catholics. Opponents argued that the college experience might encourage middle-class women to seek professional careers, elect to remain single, or, should they marry, have few or no children. Should such choices become popular, they would pose serious threats to the social fabric of church and home. Yet as long as Catholic colleges remained male preserves, episcopal pronouncements that women were compromising their religious faith by attending secular institutions rang hollow. It was this state of affairs that the Congregation of the School Sisters of Notre Dame (SSNDs) determined to address when, in 1895, they established the College of Notre Dame of Maryland in Baltimore.

The SSNDs had been founded in Bavaria, Germany, in 1833 "for the education of female youth," and opened their first school in North America in Baltimore in 1847, after which they soon established a female preparatory boarding school. In 1873, they opened a collegiate institute on a spacious campus in Govanstown, Baltimore County, about two miles from the city center. The College of Notre Dame of Maryland opened on the same property in 1895. In its early years, administrators and faculties of established Catholic men's colleges, with a few exceptions, paid little attention to the women's college. This initial aloofness left the founding sisters free to experiment, and they seized the opportunity. Rejecting prevailing clerical ideas that women's college curriculum ought to prepare them for their future domestic responsibilities, the sisters aimed to integrate the pedagogical ideas of leading mainstream women educators with their own distinctive principles of female education. Theirs would be a liberal arts college offering women the same intellectual and professional opportunities available to their male peers. Despite myriad changes and challenges over the last 125 years, this vision continues to imbue the university today.

Sources, Terminology, and Organization

The major primary sources for the history of the College of Notre Dame of Maryland are located in the archives of Notre Dame of Maryland University, a depository rich and comprehensive in topical and chronological coverage. The archives, currently held at Loyola Notre Dame Library, hold the official records of the college and its precursor, the Collegiate Institute, as well as correspondence and papers of trustees, administrators, and faculty, a significant collection of oral histories and diaries, and records of student clubs and publications. These resources shed light on a complex academic and social world. They reveal how the college met significant public challenges from church officials, mainstream educators, and public critics over the course of the twentieth century.

Any history focused on Catholic women religious faces a number of vocabulary problems. Following common usage, I employ the terms "nun" and "sister" interchangeably, although their definitions differ in canon law. (Officially, sisters take simple vows and belong to religious communities dedicated to public service in the wider society, while nuns, who take solemn vows, lead lives of prayer in strictly cloistered orders.) Similarly, I use the terms "congregation," "order," "community," and "sisterhood" synonymously. As for named individuals, until the 1960s most congregations bestowed religious names on members; thereafter they were free to use their legal names. For accuracy and consistency, I identify individual sisters by surnames (when known) and professional titles, and employ religious titles, such as "Sister" or "Mother," when appropriate.

To enable comparison of Catholic and secular approaches to women's higher education in the context of cultural, social, political, and religious changes in twentieth-century America, the book follows a chronological framework. I address several major themes: interactions with mainstream America; how organization enabled female power; gender dialectics in a patriarchal church; and the questions of race and class in a "democratic" women's college.

Chapter 1 analyzes prevailing church attitudes toward women's higher education and mainstream attitudes toward the Catholic Church in late-nineteenth-century America. It surveys the development in Baltimore of the Collegiate Institute for Young Ladies by the School Sisters of Notre Dame from 1873 to 1895, including the acquisition of property and buildings by the order, the educational philosophy of the school's administrators and faculty, and the academic and extracurricular experiences of its students. A commitment to gender equity as well as religious conviction persuaded the SSNDs to found a college for women in 1895. Catholic colleges at this time admitted only men, and Catholic women were attending public and private colleges and universities in growing numbers. This development, as well as political expediency, prompted the dean of the US hierarchy, James Cardinal Gibbons, to approve the sisters' proposal to establish a women's college.

The burden of financing and staffing the new college rested with the religious order. Gibbons, the archbishop of Baltimore under whose direct supervision the college existed, allowed it to open but offered no tangible support, and there were few lay patrons. Chapter 2, therefore, investigates the governance, financing, and staffing of the new college. Members of the first governing board, administrators, and most full-time faculty were sisters, a female and religious dominance that was to influence the college's development in important ways. Until a sufficient number of sisters held advanced degrees, the college's founder and first dean, Sister Meletia Foley, relied on faculty from local universities, especially Johns Hopkins and the University of Maryland, to supplement, as part-time professors, her small full-time faculty. The diverse teaching styles and scholarly attributes of the early faculty, full- and part-time, lay and religious, are explored in this chapter.

Economic and political forces in this period deeply influenced the culture of the college and triggered significant changes in student demographics and campus life. Chapter 3 explores the opening of the College of Notre Dame to class and racial diversity. It analyzes several critical challenges, including tensions related to class differences among white students in the 1920s and 1930s, and a protracted controversy in the 1940s over whether the college should admit African American applicants. Although problems related to increasing class diversity within the student body gradually resolved, the college's prized "community spirit" remained conspicuously deficient in the matter of race until the 1950s. Poverty programs and church mission work absorbed generous students in the 1930s and 1940s, but there was little campus interest in the cause of racial equality until well into the civil rights era. Finally, the chapter considers another "diversity" issue on campus—the divide between lay and religious faculty and staff.

Chapter 4 examines the benefits and costs of the college's commitment to offering a strictly liberal arts course of study. It considers the college curriculum and academic traditions, both of which reflected the crucial influence of elite eastern women's colleges. Economic distress in the 1930s prompted many Catholic women's colleges to add professionally oriented curricula. However, beyond introducing a social work major in the 1930s and expanding its science curriculum in the 1940s to prepare students to benefit from new opportunities for women in industry and technology, the College of Notre Dame did not follow this trend. In the 1970s, however, the College of Notre Dame became the nation's second college to develop a Weekend College, now a familiar component of US higher educational institutions. The Weekend College offered employed women and men of average means the opportunity to earn a bachelor's degree from a private liberal arts college. While this radical undertaking met with a vigorous response and attracted a large enrollment, it also brought new challenges. Because employed adults sought professional fields of study, the college for the first time significantly diverged from a strictly liberal arts curriculum. This chapter considers the effects of this decision to extend the scope of the college's intellectual and social mission.

As a result of its adherence to the liberal arts, the college's enrollment and endowment lagged behind those of rival Catholic women's colleges that accommodated growing demand for vocationally oriented curricula. This impeded its efforts to meet the standards for recognition by the Association of American Universities. With a small alumnae association and few major lay donors, the college continued to rely heavily on the founding religious order. But the sisterhood alone could not provide an endowment that would enable the expansion needed to benefit from the opportunities of the booming postwar era. The local archbishop's refusal in 1945 to permit the college to undertake a public fundraising drive set the stage for a pivotal decision to look beyond the Catholic community, to state governments and the federal government, for financial support. Seeking governmental support, the college, for the first time, had to demonstrate to the wider American society that its Catholic identity and values did not conflict with its secular mission. Chapter 5 analyzes the impact of two major legal controversies in the 1960s and 1970s that importantly influenced the college's curriculum, faculty, and student experience. In 1963, the College of Notre Dame was one of several Maryland church-related colleges to receive state educational grants. The Horace Mann League, joined by several other citizen groups, brought suit against the state and the colleges on constitutional grounds, claiming that the institutions were "pervasively sectarian." The College of Notre Dame, a defendant in this lawsuit and in *Roemer v. Board of Public Works of Maryland*, a 1970s case on eligibility for Maryland state funding ultimately decided by the US Supreme Court, learned that mainstream perceptions of its religious identity were of central importance, and indeed were vital to its autonomy and success as an institution of higher education.

From its inception in 1895, Notre Dame had modeled its curriculum, academic standards, and collegiate traditions on those of the leading eastern women's colleges. It did not, however, follow them so readily when they gradually relaxed many institutional rules governing student dress, behavior, and campus social life. Casual observers have attributed the recalcitrance of Catholic women's colleges to their control by religious orders. Chapter 6 contends that, contrary to popular belief, the "convent model" was not the major explanation for the slow withdrawal from student oversight. Throughout much of the twentieth century, behavioral regulations at the College of Notre Dame and similar institutions came under the intense and enduring scrutiny of local bishops and clergy. Catholic teachings on sexual morality were more closely linked to female than male public and private behavior, a gender difference that constrained the liberalization of social rules in women's colleges. But as American social mores became more liberal in the 1960s, students rebelled. The civil rights and feminist movements and the reforms in church life introduced by the Second Vatican Council (1962–65) engendered dissent among American Catholics on issues of sexual morality. At the College of Notre Dame, student requests for extended male visitation hours in their residence hall rooms in the early 1970s provoked an explosive battle over the church's moral teachings and students' rights as modern women. This chapter considers how the women's college resolved a major conflict between prevailing social mores and religious values. It asks why nuns, more than lay trustees, administrators, and faculty, became the target of both liberals and conservatives in the controversy, and assesses the order's changing status on the campus.

In the 1960s and 1970s, many Catholic women's colleges merged with local Catholic men's institutions or moved to coeducational status. The College of Notre Dame did neither. Despite intense pressure from hierarchy, clergy, and laymen, its trustees refused to consider persistent overtures to merge with Loyola, a Jesuit men's college on a neighboring campus. This proved to be the most difficult gender battle in the college's long history. The conclusion to the book investigates the college's response to challenges to its autonomy as a women's institution, particularly after Loyola College became coeducational in 1971. Notre Dame's decision to remain an independent women's college demanded extensive changes in curriculum, student body, and organizational structure. Membership in the School Sisters of Notre Dame began to decline seriously in the 1970s, as with most other American sisterhoods. The conclusion reflects on the effects of this important development in the shape of women's higher education under Catholic auspices in the twenty-first century. The order's ability to provide funds and contribute the services of sisters to the college waned, and the large campus presence of sisters, who since 1895 had served as public witnesses to the college's Catholic character, rapidly diminished. Lay administrators and faculty grew in number, and students and faculty became more diverse in class and race as well as religious background. Trustees, administrators, faculty, and leaders of the founding order, like their twentieth-century predecessors, continue to face critical challenges in advancing Catholic higher education for women in the United States.

CHAPTER 1

American Catholics and Female Higher Education

Founding Catholic Women's Colleges

Both the "outsider" status of the Catholic Church in nineteenth-century America and its traditionally conservative position on women's social roles shaped its perspective on women's higher education. Catholic colleges for men were numerous, but no corresponding colleges for women existed. The national hierarchy, for the most part, still considered higher education for women not only unnecessary but possibly dangerous to "true Catholic womanhood." Bishops warned that however "noble" in intellectual accomplishments Protestant women's colleges might be, they were unfriendly toward the Catholic Church and to be viewed with suspicion. Nevertheless, by the 1880s and 1890s, middle-class Catholic women were enrolling in growing numbers in public colleges as well as in private, but non-Catholic, women's colleges.

The hierarchy was not wrong about the presence of anti-Catholic sentiment in Protestant-supported colleges. Until 1898, Wellesley College's founder, Henry Fowle Durant, required that faculty members belong to evangelical Christian churches. Although this policy softened to encompass members of other Protestant denominations, the ban on Catholic faculty persisted. In 1896, college president Julia Irvine, supported by trustee and former president Alice Freeman Palmer, defied it by hiring a Catholic for the French Department over the strong protest of Durant's wife, Pauline. When Irvine proposed to hire a Catholic as choral director of the Beethoven Society, however,

Mrs. Durant appealed to the evangelist Dwight L. Moody, a powerful trustee, who publicly reproached Irvine and her supporters for being willing to "turn the whole college over to the Catholics."[1] And some private colleges made it hard, at times impossible, for Catholic students to fulfill their religious obligations. At the turn of the twentieth century, for example, the Quaker managers of coeducational Swarthmore College, intent on providing a "guarded education," forbade students to attend church services off campus.[2]

The growth of Protestant-supported women's colleges in the late nineteenth century encouraged Catholic sisterhoods to consider developing comparable institutions. For nearly a century, nuns had conducted flourishing boarding academies attracting Protestant as well as Catholic girls. Among the best known was the Georgetown convent school, founded in 1799 by the Sisters of the Visitation in Washington, DC; in 1838 it enrolled one hundred students. By the end of the nineteenth century, it was increasingly clear that secondary-level education was inadequate preparation for careers in the professions, business, government, and social service. Women's orders like the School Sisters of Notre Dame, with their long histories of high standards in education and growing numbers of young entrants, were well-positioned to fill the gap in higher education for Catholic women.

The School Sisters of Notre Dame

Founded in 1597 by the young Frenchwoman Alix LeClerc (1576–1622) and Rev. Peter Fourier, the Congregation of the School Sisters of Notre Dame, originally known as the Canonesses Regular of Saint Augustine, Congregation of Our Lady, operated schools for girls throughout western Europe until the suppression of religious orders during and after the French Revolution and the Napoleonic Wars. In 1833, Caroline Gerhardinger, known by her name in religion as Mother General Theresa of Jesus, restored the order in Munich, Bavaria, and held office as its first general superior until her death in 1879. A strong leader, she vigilantly protected the order's right to govern itself and determine its corporate works. In 1852, while seeking church approbation for the sisters' constitution, she refused to accede to the archbishop of Munich's dictate that a priest head all the motherhouses of the order. "By setting up [clerical] directors in every motherhouse," she insisted, "the School Sisters and all their schools and boarding establishments would be placed under male direction contrary to the good of the sisters and the schools."[3]

Despite intense episcopal pressure, Mother General Theresa held her ground, and by 1859, Rome had approved the constitution. The congregation would have one general superior, and she would be a member of the order.[4] Like all religious communities, the Congregation of the School Sisters of Notre Dame was hierarchical in structure. From the central generalate in Munich, the mother general and her assistants soon governed an international network of provinces. Election of officers took place every six years at a general chapter. In consultation with the generalate, provincial superiors in provincial motherhouses appointed superiors of local convents and assigned them individual sisters. Soon the network was growing rapidly.

In July 1847, only fifteen years after the order's reconstitution, Mother General Theresa escorted five volunteers to the United States to begin the order's work in the New World. After opening a motherhouse in Baltimore, the see city of the Catholic Church's first archdiocese in the United States, she appointed Sister Seraphina von Pronath, the eldest of the group, its superior. The sisters, who had normal school educations and had passed teachers' examinations in Munich, initially conducted classes for girls in neighboring German parish schools. With financial support from King Ludwig I of Bavaria and the Bavarian Louis Mission Society, Gerhardinger spent $18,000 on a three-story brick building on Aisquith Street to serve as a motherhouse for the order and a girls' school. The education of girls was a top priority, she told King Ludwig: "Religious education for the girls is as essential here as their daily bread. . . . Our institute will be the first and only German institute for girls in America."[5]

In 1850, Gerhardinger transferred the US motherhouse from Baltimore to Milwaukee and appointed twenty-six-year-old Josephine Friess, known in religion as Sister Mary Caroline, as North American vicar general. Friess, born in Paris of French and German parentage, was well-educated and astute. At every opportunity, she championed her adopted country's people and culture, and encouraged teachers in the order's many schools to emphasize civic virtues and history. Her favorite song, "Columbia, the Gem of the Ocean," written in 1843, captured her patriotic spirit.[6] Friess and Mother Seraphina von Pronath both recognized that for the order to succeed in the United States, it had to modify its strict cloister rule, which prevented sisters from freely moving outside their convent walls and posed obstacles to fundraising, teaching, and community development work. Friess traveled to the Munich generalate in 1850 to appeal in person for special consideration for US convents. She had some success in the matter of cloister, but her superiors denied her request that sisters be allowed to use English rather than German in community prayers and annual retreats.[7]

By the 1870s, the congregation's rapid growth, as well as the great distances between convents, was making it difficult for Mother Caroline Friess, as vicar for North America, to govern approximately 850 sisters and 90 novices across the United States and, as of 1871, Canada. With the encouragement of Baltimore's archbishop, James Roosevelt Bayley, in 1876 Mother

Theresa Gerhardinger established a provincial motherhouse in Baltimore. Sister Mary Theophila Bauer, Friess's longtime assistant, was appointed superior of the new province in 1877. At this time the Baltimore province numbered 116 sisters, 38 novices, and 30 postulants.[8] The following year, the province admitted another 31 candidates. In 1879, the Munich generalate introduced a commissariat to promote unity among sisters and convents in the two US provinces and "advance mutual aid in the establishment of new houses." Assisted by a vicar general and four councillors, Friess, as commissary general, would now govern all sisters in the US provinces and report directly to the general superior and her council.[9]

In the 1870s, Mother Theophila Bauer again appealed for more relaxation of cloister rules. This time, Mother General Theresa made no concessions. She believed that stricter observance of cloister rules was the best way to combat what she saw as "increasing worldliness" among American nuns. "If the sisters in America are permitted to go out, not only to Church, or funerals and processions, but into stores, out into the country, or even driving, they will become completely secularized," she warned Bauer. Activities like "visits, conversations, entertainments, dramatic performances [are] . . . against the spirit of the order, as are all carriage rides, walks in the country, working in the habit and with men, also going out collecting, playing with little pets: cats or dogs, etc."[10] The cloister rules certainly did not prevent the US provinces from prospering. By 1892, the Congregation of the School Sisters of Notre Dame had become the largest Catholic sisterhood in North America. Its approximately two thousand members educated seventy thousand students in twelve female academies and three hundred parochial schools in the United States and Canada.[11] Two of these schools, both in Baltimore, set the stage for the founding of the College of Notre Dame of Maryland in 1895.

The Collegiate Institute for Young Ladies

In 1863, the order opened a boarding high school for girls adjacent to its Aisquith Street motherhouse. The key figure in the development of the Collegiate Institute for Young Ladies, known as the Institute of Notre Dame, was Louise Wegman (1836–86), a native of Rochester, New York, known in religion as Sister Mary Ildephonsa. An incorporator of the 1864 state charter that empowered the order to conduct schools in Maryland, she became the school's first directress. The school's vigorously American values, curriculum, and educational methods troubled some conservative sisters, who complained to Mother Caroline Fricss in Milwaukee that Wegman was unfit to direct the school: she was a "worldly" young woman who showed insufficient regard for traditional educational methods. While many of their grievances seem petty in retrospect, such as the charge that she allowed students to stage "the-atrical plays at examination time," tensions ran high.[12] In an effort to resolve the matter, Friess asked Mother General Gerhardinger to consider removing Wegman. But Gerhardinger refused, asking Friess pointedly, "By removing Sister Ildephonsa from the Institute will you not lower its standards?"[13]

In 1870, in response to growing public interest in educating girls beyond the high school level, Mother Mary Barbara Weinzierl and Sister Ildephonsa applied to Mother Caroline for permission to purchase property in Gov-anstown, a neighborhood northeast of downtown Baltimore, for a second collegiate institute. They anticipated that a large boarding school would attract Protestant as well as Catholic girls from all sections of the country as well as abroad. Friess, who felt that the order ought to concentrate on parochial schools for the children of working-class families rather than on selective boarding schools for girls from upper-class families, "emphatically refused."[14] However, her superiors in Munich disagreed, approving the proj-ect and instructing her to assist in its financing.

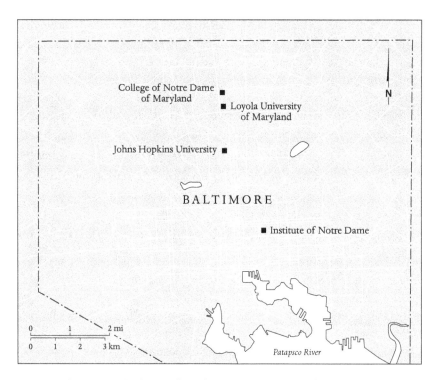

MAP 1. Baltimore, Maryland. The College of Notre Dame of Maryland (now Notre Dame of Mary-land University), as well as Loyola University of Maryland, were once located beyond the city's northern boundary; the SSND motherhouse and the Institute of Notre Dame are on Aisquith Street downtown. Map by William L. Nelson.

The Baltimore sisters moved quickly to acquire over fifty-eight acres of real estate on Charles Street Avenue for the school. On April 17, 1871, they acquired thirty-three acres, at $800 per acre, adjacent to Saint Mary's Catholic Church, and in 1873 purchased a $10,000 seven-acre tract called "Sheridan's Discovery," containing freshwater springs for drinking water. They also secured the neighboring nineteen-acre Troxall estate and Villa Montrose, a large house on the property, for $45,000.[15] In 1878, excavation of a swampy section of Sheridan's Discovery created the Lake of the Lindens, a two-level lake encircled by a carriage drive. The lake featured a bridge spanning the falls between the upper and lower lakes, a boat house, and numerous swans and ducks. A lay sister managed the pump house—as one early student wrote, "fulfilling her monotonous duty in spiritual calm."[16]

Mother Mary Barbara Weinzierl, the Baltimore superior, officially headed the project, assisted by Sister Ildephonsa Wegman, directress of the Aisquith Street school. Wegman took the lead in selecting the school's site, architect, and contractor. Although a noted Baltimore architect, J. Crawford Neilson, designed the school's main building, he apparently had nothing further to do with the project; he does not seem to have visited the site or supervised any construction.[17] Instead the nuns relied entirely on SH & JF Adams, Builders, an established and highly respected local firm that had constructed their Aisquith Street convent school a decade earlier. Samuel Adams assured the sisters that he could get top-quality materials at very low prices and complete the job for $80,000. His commission would be 10 percent of the total cost of the project. In April 1871, the sisters accepted these terms and made a verbal contract with Adams. This was poor judgment, as became evident in December 1872, when Adams informed them that the building's revised cost was $100,000, a figure that ballooned to $150,000 by February 1873. An alarmed Mother Caroline alerted her Munich superiors to the evolving financial crisis.[18]

The sisters, "shocked beyond expression," had few options. The building was too near completion to change contractors, and they had widely advertised that the Notre Dame of Maryland Collegiate Institute for Young Ladies would open the following September. Reluctantly, the order's superiors agreed to borrow up to $30,000 from Adams to ensure that he would complete the building: "We could not see how to do better," the annals record. They also borrowed from the Equitable Society of Baltimore, "creating ground rents on their land as security."[19] When Adams presented his final bill in December 1874, the sisters' lawyer, A. Leo Knott, offered him $10,000 less than he asked. He filed suit, agreeing to arbitration after two years of litigation.[20] The final settlement awarded the sisters $10,000 plus half of Adams's commission, "a very great moral gain in our favor," wrote the convent annalist.[21] However, in the end, the cost of land, architectural services, and building construction totaled nearly $300,000, leaving the order with heavy debt.

Reminiscent of protests in the 1860s against Wegman's leadership at the Institute of Notre Dame, conservative sisters objected that she had made irresponsible financial decisions during the construction of the Charles Street school, that the school's physical scale was pretentious and worldly, and that the building's exterior was too "elaborately ornamented."[22] But Friess recognized that Wegman had aimed to model the school's architecture loosely on the centralized large building favored by early Protestant-supported women's colleges. Wellesley's College Hall, which had opened in 1875, housed "classrooms, dormitories, and administrative offices . . . [as well as] the library, chapel, dining hall, gymnasium and even a large art gallery."[23] Friess ignored Wegman's critics and simply chided her for a few interior features, such as the building's "wide corridors."[24]

Despite construction problems, the Notre Dame of Maryland Preparatory School and Collegiate Institute for Young Ladies on Charles Street opened on schedule on September 23, 1873, with 63 students. It was this school that would become the direct predecessor of the College of Notre Dame. For several years, however, the new school was governed as an annex to the Institute of Notre Dame on Aisquith Street.[25] Boarders from the downtown school moved to Charles Street, and by the end of its first academic year, the new school registered 101 boarding students from "nineteen States and three Continents."[26] Tuition, room, and board charges were $220. Thirty-six sisters, two lay faculty, and five priests made up the staff. Among the nuns were fourteen lay sisters who worked as "housekeepers, infirmarians, and what might be called farm hands [tending cattle, poultry, and bees]."[27]

As directress, Wegman seized every opportunity to publicize the new school. She scored a coup when President Ulysses S. Grant, whose wife's nieces, Bessie Sharp and Betty Dent, were attending the school, agreed to preside at its first commencement on June 14, 1876.[28] To Wegman's delight, the president's appearance brought national attention to the infant Collegiate Institute.[29] The day's events opened at four o'clock in the afternoon with a lavish dinner for the president and Mrs. Grant and about thirty notable citizens, among them Baltimore archbishop James Roosevelt Bayley, Maryland governor John Lee Carroll, Baltimore mayor Ferdinand C. Latrobe, and military dignitaries.[30] At seven o'clock, the three-hour graduation ceremony began with the national anthem as the processional. The entire school of 124 students, dressed in white and representing three continents and nineteen states, sat on the commencement hall stage. Grant awarded diplomas to the seven graduates, as well as prizes, medals, and crowns to meritorious students from all the classes.[31]

Six decades later, a graduate remembered how the ceremonies that day had triumphantly witnessed to the nation's centennial: "Sister Ildefonsa [sic], intensely patriotic, wished to make the day different from any ordinary Commencement."[32] There were, however, conservative nuns who assessed the commencement dinner in honor of Grant as far too extravagant for a convent school.[33] They reproached Wegman for the debt incurred during the school's construction, and interpreted her preference for "American" over German educational methods as disloyalty to the order. It was not unusual for nineteenth-century female administrators of church-related schools to be accused of "worldliness." As late as the 1890s, legendary Bryn Mawr College president M. Carey Thomas faced considerable criticism from "Plain" Quakers for the school's stunning new architecture, furnishings, and landscaping, features they considered to be deplorable departures from traditional Quaker values.[34] Wegman's situation, however, was particularly strained since she resided with her critics in the campus convent.

Given the hierarchical structure of religious communities in the nineteenth century, provincial and local superiors were extremely important in enabling or inhibiting change. They held responsibility for all community projects, and delegated only limited authority to the sisters whom they appointed to head the schools. For Wegman, this proved to be an insurmountable obstacle. Under a cloud within the order, isolated and discouraged, she wrote to Archbishop Bayley on September 26, 1876, to request a dispensation from her religious vows. It was intolerable, she told him, to be "in constant disunion" with her superiors. When she challenged their directives, she felt she was "a disturber of the peace" within the convent, stirring up "disaffection, discord, unhappiness and endless trouble for myself and others."[35] Mother Caroline Friess privately conceded that "much that had been said about Sister Ildephonse [sic] was false and untrue."[36] On July 24, 1877, Wegman left the Collegiate Institute, and the Baltimore sisters never heard from her again.[37] Despite her critics, Wegman had developed a flourishing school with a growing national reputation, and her legacy was vindicated when Sister Meletia Foley, who shared her educational values, succeeded her as the school's directress.

Faculty, Academics, and Religious Life

The Collegiate Institute made advanced academic achievement available to its students from the beginning. From the founding of the Institute of Notre Dame in 1863, directress Ildephonsa Wegman had invited professors from local universities to lecture to students on various subjects. Among the earliest was William E. A. Aikin, MD, a chemistry professor at the University of Maryland Medical School. A graduate of the 1860s remembered his commitment to the new girls' school: "Every week brought the Ven. Prof. Aiken [*sic*] from the University of Maryland."[38] According to a university colleague, he was "a strict Catholic" and "a man of very striking mien. . . . He wore glasses and a wig, and his long flowing white beard gave him a very venerable appearance."[39]

Wegman continued this practice at the Notre Dame of Maryland Collegiate Institute in 1873. A number of Johns Hopkins faculty, notably those in scientific fields, were part-time lecturers at the institute.[40] Robert Dorsey Coale, an 1881 PhD graduate of Johns Hopkins, was "the first student to enter the Johns Hopkins University on its opening in 1876."[41] He succeeded William Aikin as professor of chemistry at the University of Maryland. He also lectured part time at Notre Dame between 1883 and 1891.[42] The writer and scholar Richard Malcolm Johnston, founder of the Penn Lucy School for boys in Baltimore, "gave yearly courses of [weekly] lectures to the senior classes in the Johns Hopkins University and the Notre Dame School at Baltimore."[43] Lucien Odend'hal, prominent in Baltimore music circles and, in 1884, the first director of the Johns Hopkins University glee club, taught at the Collegiate Institute from 1877 until 1895, and then at the college until 1933.[44]

Except for Rev. Dwight E. Lyman, DD (religion), Mademoiselle Conlon (French), and Dr. J. Lopez (Spanish), religious sisters made up the Collegiate Institute's first full-time faculty. Lyman (1818–97), pastor of the Catholic parish in Govanstown, had served as an Episcopalian priest before his 1854 conversion to Catholicism.[45] Sister Meletia Foley, as "assistant matron of the senior circle," taught English, history, and science, and Sister Jeannette Duffy, "assistant matron of the junior circle," instructed in mathematics and astronomy. Sister Evangelista Meyer taught Latin, German, music, and elocution, and Sister Engelberta Heuer taught art. Students could fulfill their foreign language requirement by taking German, French, or "an extended course" in Latin.[46] For an additional fee, they could opt for private lessons in other languages.[47] Although courses in music and art did not carry academic credit, they were popular electives.

Following the practice of southern female seminaries, in the 1870s the Collegiate Institute awarded four "degrees": major and minor mistress of liberal arts and major and minor mistress of English literature.[48] These differed mainly by course of study and level of foreign language mastery. The most demanding, the major mistress of liberal arts, required completion of the liberal arts course, the study of two foreign languages for three years, and a demonstrated ability to speak both fluently. The minor mistress of liberal arts degree required completion of the liberal arts course and two foreign language courses with distinction, plus a demonstrated ability to speak one of these fluently. Students who qualified for a major mistress of English literature degree satisfactorily completed the English language course and three years' work in two foreign languages. Students completing the English language course plus three years' work in one foreign language received the minor mistress of English literature degree.[49]

The Collegiate Institute aimed to provide a rigorous liberal arts curriculum as its cornerstone. However, since parents wanted their daughters to become proficient in the domestic arts, the curriculum also included courses in plain sewing, embroidery, and cooking. "The time thus occupied is not spent in vain, as it enables the pupils to attend wisely and faithfully to what is necessary to the comfort and happiness of home," noted the 1874 catalog.[50] While it may have been popular with parents, neither faculty nor students showed much enthusiasm for the domestic science program. A valedictorian from the 1880s revealed the school's emphases when she called on her peers to "step forth to fight our part in life's arena" and to seek "influence and honor" through "commendable achievements."[51] She made no reference to women's place in the home. By 1893, the Collegiate Institute offered no home economics courses, and just two elective vocational courses, one in elementary bookkeeping, commercial law, and related topics, and another, a "teachers' course," for advanced students interested in becoming schoolteachers.[52]

In its lack of emphasis on "vocational" subjects, the school differed from many female schools of the late nineteenth century. The School Sisters of Notre Dame viewed the domestic arts and other practical subjects as marginal to the central purpose of their preparatory schools and collegiate institutes. Mother Theresa Gerhardinger warned teachers against spending excessive time on vocational subjects: "The children learn trivialities soon enough; they grow to like this sort of thing, and thereby lose their inclination for doing useful and necessary things"—a category that pointedly did not include the domestic arts.[53]

Although a majority of Collegiate Institute students were Roman Catholics, there was always a good representation of Protestants in the student body. The first Jewish student, Harriet Rosenthal, graduated in 1890.[54] In 1876, non-Catholics did not take religion classes, "unless otherwise desired by the parents," but by 1881, they were expected to "attend instructions on Christian Doctrine, unless otherwise stated by the parents."[55] Eighteen-year-old Frances Benjamin Johnston, a non-Catholic and later a leading American photographer, enrolled at the Collegiate Institute in 1882 and received her major mistress of English literature degree in June 1884. Her biographer attests that while at the school, "Johnston was examined on a wide range of subjects" but never took a course in religion.[56] Even so, the school's intensely Catholic atmosphere occasionally disturbed some Protestant parents. In 1887, a Methodist family withdrew their daughter from the school because they felt she "had been unduly influenced to become a Catholic." While administrators denied the charge, the annalist allowed privately that "some of the Sisters had probably been too persistent in speaking upon religious questions and points of doctrine."[57]

Whatever students' religious backgrounds, all were held to the same strict behavioral and sartorial standards. The American public and popular press, secular and ecclesiastical, held long-established views regarding proper female decorum and dress. During the 1870s, students at the institute wore black dresses or black skirts and blouses. The only accessories permitted were a brooch and simple earrings. Rules of student conduct were quasi-conventual, with outside visitors restricted and visits monitored.[58] Every Sunday evening, Directress Wegman presided over an all-school assembly, called "Judgments" by students. After a few opening remarks, she read aloud the names of students whom faculty had observed violating rules of social etiquette as well as school regulations during the preceding week. Students, who knew that Wegman would not mention major moral failings during Judgments, did not fear public shaming on serious matters, which were dealt with privately. For the most part, they enjoyed her inimitable descriptions of the social gaffes of their comrades. A student described a typical 1874 Judgment: "When she commences with her 'all those who' etc. 'stand up,' one rapidly reviewed the week and according to how guilty they might have felt, they knew whether they would be one of the 'stand uppers' or placidly enjoy the evening. After all, whether one stood up or not, it was an adventure."[59] As another put it, "We called it Judgement [sic], but few of us feared it."[60]

From Collegiate Institute to College

The order's leaders in the United States had learned some hard lessons from the conflict that had ultimately overwhelmed Ildephonsa Wegman. The newly appointed superior of the eastern province, Mother Theophila Bauer, relocated the motherhouse from Aisquith Street in downtown Baltimore to the new Collegiate Institute campus on North Charles Street.[61] In 1877, as president of the order's corporation (its board of trustees) and de facto president of the school, Bauer appointed one of the teachers, thirty-year-old Sister Mary Meletia Foley (figure 2), to replace the recently departed Ildephonsa

FIGURE 2. Meletia Foley as a normal school student. Photo from NDMA.

Wegman as directress of studies. Foley (1847–1917), from Wauwatosa, Wisconsin Territory, was the tenth of twelve children born to Irish immigrant farmers. After graduating from Saint Mary's [Collegiate] Institute in Milwaukee, founded by Mother Caroline Friess, she joined the order in 1868. She taught for two years at the Institute of Notre Dame on Aisquith Street before joining the Collegiate Institute faculty on North Charles Street in 1873.

The Collegiate Institute in the 1880s

Theophila Bauer and Meletia Foley strove to develop the school's program and campus according to the professional values they had shared with Ildephonsa Wegman. To enable Foley to work effectively, Bauer released her from some obligatory community duties in the convent horarium, an exceptional privilege that continued when she was appointed dean of the college in 1895. As a result, one of her successors remembered, "on the whole, the [religious] Community saw little of Sister during the school year."[62] Her relative distance from the local community did not diminish her effectiveness, however. Well-liked and more politically astute than her predecessor, Meletia Foley proved to be an effective directress who concentrated on building a school that fulfilled the order's mission to girls: "The system of education pursued is designed to develop the mental, moral, and physical powers of the pupils; to make them refined, accomplished, and useful members of society."[63] The fact that Mother Theophila Bauer collaborated closely with Foley on school matters and approved of her ecumenical ethos and independent spirit discouraged open criticism by sister-faculty of her leadership style or her "too worldly" professional aspirations for students.

In an era when Catholic and Protestant educators rarely interacted, the sisters resolutely pursued ways to forge ties with mainstream educators. The school's proximity to several universities proved a key benefit. Foley's relations with Johns Hopkins administrators and faculty were extraordinarily cordial in the 1870s–90s. Baltimore marveled when Johns Hopkins president Daniel Coit Gilman addressed the Collegiate Institute's graduating class in 1890. According to the *Baltimore Sun*, it was "the first time known in which anyone but a Catholic clergyman has been invited to speak at this or any kindred institution in charge of a religious society of that faith." Certainly it was a rare event for that period in the United States. Gilman gracefully praised the historic role played by female religious orders in the education of women. Although he emphasized that "the whole duties of women were in a different sphere from that of men," he acknowledged that "many ladies, by means of their pen, had acquired fame, and examples were not wanting where females had governed kingdoms with marked ability."[64]

By 1876, with the debt on the Collegiate Institute building still very high at $268,700, concerned Munich superiors had instructed Friess to "sell the whole property . . . for the price the debt came to."[65] Friess, who strongly opposed boarding institutes, moved quickly. The Religious of the Sacred Heart of Jesus had expressed an interest in purchasing the property, but Archbishop of Baltimore James Roosevelt Bayley refused to allow this particular order to work in his archdiocese. With no other immediate offers, Friess halted her efforts to sell the property. But she did not give up hope that another opportunity would soon materialize.[66] Her 1884 response to Baltimore provincial superior Theophila Bauer's proposal to expand the Collegiate Institute was unequivocal: "I have read your plan. It sounds very inviting; however, it is not acceptable. Dear Sister Theophila, now no more boarding schools. . . . Institutes are connected with great outlays of money and need special personnel. Parish schools are more necessary, more serviceable, and the principal work of our congregation. . . . Institutes of today do not conform at all to our work."[67]

Laudatory remarks from James Cardinal Gibbons about the flourishing Collegiate Institute did not impress Friess much, since he never offered any financial support. "It gives me great joy that the Cardinal has praised your Institute," she told Bauer tartly, "but the good man should also present you with a beautiful gift."[68] As long as there was a large debt on the school, Mother Theophila Bauer and Sister Meletia Foley knew that Friess would not allow them to proceed with their plans for a college. Despite Bauer's success in reducing the debt, Friess longed to see the school sold or diverted to other uses. In late 1890, when Cardinal Gibbons informed her that the Religious of the Sacred Heart had again expressed interest in establishing a girls' school near Baltimore, she thought she saw an opportunity. "The thought occurred to me that the Sacred Heart Madames might perhaps buy Govanstown," she wrote to Mother General Margaret of Cortona Wiedemann. Gibbons, unlike his predecessor Bayley, favored this order. He intimated to Friess that he would prefer the Sacred Heart sisters, known for their elite boarding schools for girls, to the School Sisters of Notre Dame. "The Cardinal is in no hurry whatsoever to call for the Madames," Friess relayed to Wiedemann, "but he does think that the taking on of parochial schools would be more agreeable and fitting for us than the maintenance of a first-class Institute." But the idea of selling the school was sure to arouse vehement opposition among the Baltimore Sisters, and by this time the debt on the property was a manageable $60,000, so she admitted to Wiedemann that after all, "I suppose we will have to keep the Institute"—which at this point was well down the road to becoming a college.[69]

Women's Higher Education in the United States

The College of Notre Dame was founded against the backdrop of the late nineteenth-century development of Protestant-backed colleges for women, as well as the admitting of women to coeducational land-grant universities and a few radical liberal arts colleges. Many mainstream college leaders agreed with the Catholic hierarchy's opposition to coeducation. In his 1876 inaugural address at Johns Hopkins University, President Daniel Coit Gilman looked forward to the day when "someone" would establish in Baltimore a female institution like Oxford's Girton Hall. It could "avail itself of the advantages of the Peabody and Hopkins foundations, without obliging the pupils to give up the advantages of a home, or exposing them to the rougher influences . . . still to be found in colleges and universities where young men resort."[70] A decade later, Gilman applauded the recent founding of the Woman's College of Baltimore as "an adequate answer to any suggestion that the University's undergraduate courses should be opened to women students."[71]

In the 1890s, the leaders of US men's colleges and universities, including those supportive of higher education for women, believed that college curricula for both men and women should reflect the fundamentally different roles played by the sexes in home and society. Founders and faculties of elite women's colleges, who strongly disagreed, modeled their curricula on those of elite men's colleges. At Radcliffe College's 1894 commencement, Harvard president Charles W. Eliot predicted that gender-specific curricula would ultimately prevail: "During the last twenty-five years the education of women has been made to resemble as closely as possible the education of men. The standards have been the same. . . . But I think this is only a temporary condition of affairs. It seems altogether probable that the education of women will ultimately differ widely from that of men."[72]

Since the 1870s, Mother Theophila Bauer, Directress Meletia Foley, and the Collegiate Institute faculty had closely followed the development of curricula, academic policies, and social regulations adopted by eastern women's colleges. The 1885 establishment of the Woman's College of Baltimore City (later Goucher College) under the auspices of the Baltimore Conference of the Methodist Episcopal Church, and the 1889 foundation of the Catholic University of America in Washington, DC, reinforced the sisters' conviction that there was a pressing need for a Catholic female college. Protestant denominations had founded numerous women's colleges by the 1890s, but the Catholic Church supported only colleges for men.

The historian Kathleen Sprows Cummings suggests that for an order with a local academy, opening a college in a gradual way was hardly a major event. She supports her view by noting that "in 1895, the School Sisters of Notre Dame turned their Baltimore Institute into the College of Notre Dame without fanfare or celebration. The *Chronicle*, a record of the institute, did not even mention the transition until September 1897, two years after the first college students had been admitted."[73] However, the relative lack of pomp did not mean that the founding of the college was routine. In the 1870s and 1880s, Bauer and Foley faced critical challenges from their superiors to the idea of opening a college. But as one alumna, a historian of the college, later wrote, "the founding of Catholic University galvanized Sister Meletia. If Catholic women were to do graduate work there, they must first have a Catholic college from which to get degrees. . . . [She] said, logically, why not begin one at Notre Dame . . . [which] had a preparatory school—the Academy—which could produce students ready for college work."[74]

The idea of establishing a college faced a number of hurdles, both within and outside the order. Bauer and Foley realized they could not count on major lay donors; wealthy Catholics preferred to support the church's charitable works rather than endow colleges and seminaries. Appeals in the 1880s on behalf of the new Catholic University had been discouraging, and there was little enthusiasm among bishops for a proposed nationwide diocesan collection to benefit that institution.[75] The Baltimore sisters recognized that with a small initial enrollment, tuition revenues would not cover operating expenses. They would have to rely on the order and a few benefactors for funds to acquire property, erect buildings, and hire lay faculty. The order would also have to contribute the services of sisters as faculty and administrators. Some sisters had deep reservations about the project. After all, the order had only recently paid off the large debt incurred in the 1870s to establish the Collegiate Institute. However, most agreed that the cause was compelling. This bridge crossed, the next step was gaining the approval of the hierarchy.

While over 70 percent of late-nineteenth-century US colleges were coeducational, the Catholic Church disapproved of the practice at the college level.[76] Although in 1889, the US bishops had founded the Catholic University of America in Washington, DC, as a graduate institution for clerics, by 1895 it was admitting male lay students to its school of philosophy, graduate school of arts and sciences, and engineering and architectural school. University trustees restricted enrollment to men despite a faculty proposal that women

be accepted.[77] Denied admission to Catholic colleges, women were enrolling in rising numbers not only in public institutions and normal schools but
also in Protestant-affiliated women's colleges. It was the latter trend, rather
than any strong commitment to the intellectual and social advancement
of women, that led the national hierarchy to approve the establishment of
Catholic women's colleges. By the 1890s the success of the Seven Sisters,
and their public endorsement and financial support by prominent male citizens, had made the question of women's higher education reasonable, albeit
somewhat unpalatable, to Catholic Church officials. Social-class goals within
the Catholic community were rising, and Catholic women's colleges promised to tie middle- and upper-class parishioners more closely to the church.

With official church approbation, women religious had been addressing pressing social and educational needs in the United States since the late
eighteenth century. Sisterhoods established and owned many tuition academies for girls and staffed most Catholic elementary and secondary schools
owned by parishes and dioceses. The permanent nature and formal structure
of female religious communities gave their members critical visibility and
status within the Catholic community. Their collective labor and material
resources enabled them to initiate and implement large-scale projects that
were beyond the means of most individual laity. Nuns enabled an immigrant working-class church to finance the immense Catholic educational
and benevolent enterprise that developed across the United States in the
nineteenth and twentieth centuries. At the same time, since schoolteaching,
nursing, child care, and social work were "women's work," sisters posed little
threat to church and societal norms or male hegemony.

But although they were ultimately successful, sisters across the country had
to contend with significant episcopal skepticism about their higher-education
project. When the College of Notre Dame opened in Baltimore in 1895 as an
outgrowth of the Collegiate Institute, the Congregation of the School Sisters
of Notre Dame became the first group to confront the male monopoly over
the church's higher-education sector by opening a college for women. Over
time, many other women's communities took it as their mission to establish
and support similar institutions.[78] The authority of bishops extended to all
Catholic institutions within their dioceses. Women's colleges in the relatively
few dioceses headed by liberal bishops had a major advantage over institutions located in dioceses governed by conservatives. The College of Saint
Catherine in Saint Paul, Minnesota, established in 1905 by the Sisters of Saint
Joseph of Carondelet, is a notable example. The brother of Mother Seraph-
ine Ireland (1842–1930), provincial superior of the Sisters of Saint Joseph of
Carondelet, was Archbishop John Ireland (1838–1918), a liberal church leader

who governed the archdiocese of Saint Paul from the 1880s until his death. He encouraged his sister and her community to open a local women's college, and his critical support, moral and financial, allowed the College of Saint Catherine to experience consistent growth. Women's colleges situated in other dioceses typically faced greater challenges.[79]

Two-thirds of the American hierarchy in the early 1900s were either Irish born or of Irish parentage.[80] Many of these men, as historian Maryann Valiulis writes, shared the view of their counterparts in Ireland that "any attempt by women to leave their domestic confines would wreak havoc not only on the home but on the nation as well."[81] "The great Doctors of the Church affirm unanimously the inferiority of women in the intellectual order," proclaimed Michael O'Kane, OP, of Limerick in 1913. He explained that this "arises from the role nature has destined her to fulfill in the drama of life."[82] His contemporary, the theologian Rev. David Barry, stressed that "woman suffrage is incompatible with the Catholic ideal of the unity of domestic life."[83] Leading US church journals like the *Catholic World* duly reported on prevailing Irish perspectives on the woman question.

Founders and sister-presidents of the first female colleges in the United States, some of Irish birth themselves, faced considerable skepticism from the hierarchy. Among women's colleges founded before 1920, Irish-born nuns headed Trinity College (Washington, DC), the College of Saint Catherine (Minnesota), the College of Saint Angela (New Rochelle, New York), and Marymount College (New York). Despite the German origins of her order, Meletia Foley, founder of the College of Notre Dame of Maryland, was of Irish parentage.[84] Irish influence significantly affected the School Sisters of Notre Dame and the College of Notre Dame, since for over seven decades (1877–1947) only two bishops, both raised in Ireland, governed the Baltimore archdiocese. James Cardinal Gibbons, born in Baltimore, was raised in Ireland until age nineteen. His successor, the Irish-born archbishop Michael Curley, arrived in the United States as a twenty-five-year-old priest. Gibbons, as archbishop of Baltimore, was the first chancellor of the Catholic University of America. (Washington, DC was within the territory of the Archdiocese of Baltimore until 1939.) His staff included the university's first rector, Bishop John J. Keane (1886–96), and his successors, Rev. Thomas J. Conaty, rector, and Rev. Philip J. Garrigan, vice rector, all of Irish heritage.

From his 1877 arrival in Baltimore (the same year as Meletia Foley's appointment as directress), the sisters at the Collegiate Institute endeavored to gain Gibbons's personal interest in the school. He visited the campus frequently to address the students, host visiting dignitaries, and benefit from the expertise of sisters who edited his rough drafts of sermons, articles, and books. The sisters took these opportunities to acquaint him with their ideas about the need for a women's college in his archdiocese.[85] Foley and Bauer also discussed their ideas for a women's college not only with the Collegiate Institute's full-time faculty but also with its cadre of visiting lecturers from local universities. The enthusiasm of mainstream Baltimore educators for a Catholic women's college helped the sisters gain episcopal approval to proceed with the project.[86] The backing of prominent local intellectuals impressed Cardinal Gibbons as well as the order's Munich generalate, although Meletia Foley's strong feminist views continued to confound local clergy: "She maintained that nations were no better than their women and that nations occupy their place in the world, the nations of moral culture and goodness, on account of the virtue and character of their women and particularly of their educated women," remembered Monsignor Patrick C. Gavan, chancellor of the archdiocese from 1902 to 1914, who regularly dealt with Foley. "Woman, and not man, is the strong moral power in the world."[87]

Immediately prior to the founding of the College of Notre Dame, and independent of each other, the Sisters of the Sacred Heart and the Sisters of the Holy Cross had briefly contemplated establishing a "coordinate" college for women in Washington, DC, near the new Catholic University.[88] While university trustees did not oppose the coordinate model, the apostolic delegate viewed it as too much like coeducation.[89] In contrast, when the School Sisters of Notre Dame proposed to open a women's college in Baltimore, safely removed from the Catholic University campus, they gained ecclesiastical approval. The Collegiate Institute of Notre Dame of Maryland, founded in 1873, had operated under an 1864 charter granted by the Maryland legislature "for educational purposes" to its owners, the Congregation of the School Sisters of Notre Dame.[90] (The Institute of Notre Dame on Aisquith Street also operated under this charter.) Now the order applied to the General Assembly of Maryland for a college charter. On April 2, 1896, the 1864 charter was "amended and powers of corporation enlarged" to grant power to the faculty to award bachelor's degrees in the arts and sciences, literature, and music. The amended charter also provided that the college could grant master's and doctor's degrees.[91] Sister Meletia Foley became the college's first dean.

The Collegiate Institute's June 1895 commencement centered entirely on the new college, the first of its kind in the United States, that was to open in September. Students composed and staged "Wisdom's Daughters," an allegory that expressed their intense pride in this radical undertaking. Attired in caps, gowns, and ribbon bows in the colors of ten "prominent educational institutions of the country," the young actresses testified in turn before Minerva, the goddess of wisdom, and her attendants, Science and Virtue, to the merits of the female institutions they represented, among them Wellesley, Bryn Mawr, Vassar, and the Harvard Annex. A paean to the newly founded College of Notre Dame of Maryland concluded the performance: "All united in a final chorus, the theme being the growth of Notre Dame, which, without the foundations and endowments of its more favored sisters, has won for itself enviable reputation in the domain of higher education."[92]

Students in the Collegiate Institute's senior department who were to enroll in the "college class" in September 1895 received freshman-level college credits for courses they had taken during their final year at the institute. In June 1896, the institute awarded its last diplomas, discontinued its "old degrees," and became Notre Dame of Maryland Preparatory School.[93] In recognition of their special status, members of the college class attended the final ceremonies as observers only, and as college freshmen they celebrated with a Class Day, replete, as one student recalled, with the "stupendous innovation" of an all-female evening dance.[94] Over the next three years, the college added sophomore, junior, and senior classes.[95] The North Charles Street campus now comprised a four-year college, a preparatory high school, and a lower school with primary and grammar departments.

On Wednesday, June 14, 1899, James Cardinal Gibbons conferred four bachelor of arts degrees and two bachelor of literature degrees on six young women, the first of their sex to earn bachelor's degrees from a Catholic college in the United States (figure 3).[96] Charles Joseph Bonaparte (1851–1921), grandnephew of Napoleon and a prominent Catholic layman, delivered the college's first commencement address, titled "The Significance of the Bachelor's Degree." He began, "Today and here for the first time in America, a Catholic college for the education of young ladies bestows the bachelor's degree."[97] A graduate of Harvard College and Harvard Law School, and a trustee of the Catholic University, Bonaparte, like his friend Cardinal Gibbons, held conservative views on "women's place" and female suffrage.[98] Following the commencement ceremony, Gibbons hosted "a lunch for the fathers of the graduates," a spectacle of male solidarity that persisted until 1918.[99] In reporting this event the following day, the local *Morning Herald* congratulated the College of Notre Dame for being "in line with an innovation as usual," and for setting a precedent that would soon "be taken up all over the country." A year later, it pronounced the college's academic program to be "as thorough and comprehensive as is offered to men in the best colleges of the country."[100]

FIGURE 3.   First graduates, College of Notre Dame of Maryland, 1899. Standing, right to left: Dora Kilkoff, Nellie Coll. Seated, left to right: Catherine Coll, Louise Power, Mollie Curran, Helen Burr-Brand. Photo from NDMA.

The careers of the pioneer graduates bear out the *Herald*'s statement. Three of them, class valedictorian and Andover, Massachusetts, native Mary Teresa Curran (m. Murphy), BLitt, along with Baltimore sisters Ellen R. Coll, BA, and Catherine W. Coll (m. Crumlish), BA, did not enter the labor force. But Dorothea Kilkoff (m. Butler), BA, a native of Deland, Florida. studied organ at Stetson University before undertaking a thirty-year career in government service.[101] Helen Burr, BA, from Lincoln, Nebraska, studied at the Detroit Institute of Musical Arts and later headed its Harp Department. During her professional career as a performer, composer, and teacher, she played with the Women's String Orchestra of New York, the Detroit Symphony Orchestra, and the Baltimore Symphony Orchestra. Endorsed by the celebrated harpist Carlos Salzedo, she opened a Detroit studio where she offered lessons on the harp for many years. Louise Power, BLitt, from San Francisco, entered the Congregation of the School Sisters of Notre Dame in 1902. As Sister Mary Loyola, she earned an MA in French from Saint John's University, and taught in her order's schools. In 1939, while a French professor at Mount Mary College, Milwaukee, she and Sister Marie Philip, CSJ, a French professor at the College of Saint Catherine in Saint Paul, in an effort to revitalize modern literature through "the culture of Christian civilization," cofounded the Catholic Renascence Society.[102]

Yet despite its successful beginning, publicity for the new College of Notre Dame was not sustained temporally or geographically. The young college immediately faced a significant challenge as episcopal statements regarding Trinity College's imminent opening captured the attention of both the secular and Catholic press.

A New Catholic Women's College: Trinity

Female college graduates had immediately tested the Catholic University of America's male-only policy; about twenty applied yearly for admission to the university's graduate programs beginning in the mid-1890s.[103] The university's chancellor, Cardinal Gibbons, and his clerical board of trustees found themselves under escalating national criticism for barring Catholic women from the university. At this time, Gibbons received an application from the Sisters of Notre Dame de Namur, a well-known teaching order, to establish a girls' preparatory high school within his archdiocese in the Washington area. Joined by Catholic University's rector, Thomas Conaty, and vice rector Philip Garrigan, Gibbons proposed that the sisters instead establish a women's college.[104] Gibbons admitted to Mother Julia McGroarty, SND, the superior of the order, that he and his fellow university officers would benefit directly from the presence of a female college near the university: "Such an institution . . . in the shadow of our great University, will, I am convinced, offer educational opportunities to our young women, which cannot be found elsewhere in the country. It will relieve the University authorities from the embarrassment of refusing women admission, many of whom have already applied for the privilege of following our courses."[105] The *Kentucky Irish American* went further. Trinity College, it declared, would become "the first American Catholic institution to recognize the right of women to higher education."[106]

Conservative opponents, clerical and lay, turned on the Sisters of Notre Dame de Namur. "We did not desire nor seek the work," Mother Julia, the provincial superior, reminded Sister Mary Euphrasia, superior of the order's Washington convent. "Anyone can see we are only the figure-head."[107] Complaints against Gibbons and his supporters flowed to church officials in Rome. Critics took Gibbons's comment that Trinity graduates might someday enroll in the Catholic University graduate school as proof that he endorsed coeducation. To a query from Cardinal Francesco Satolli, prefect of studies in Rome, about the proposed "new female school of higher studies,"

Gibbons replied that coeducation was a nonissue and that other criticisms of the project were "the offspring of ignorance or malice." He also reassured Archbishop Sebastiano Martinelli, the Vatican's apostolic delegate in Washington, DC, that the Trinity project would greatly benefit the church in the United States by dissuading young parishioners from "frequent[ing] Vassar and other anti-Catholic colleges for the study of those higher branches which are not taught in our Catholic academies."[108]

In September 1897, given distorted press accounts about plans for the college, "those immediately concerned," notably "his Eminence the Cardinal-Archbishop of Baltimore and chancellor of the university," approved "an authoritative statement" on the project: "It has been decided to establish in Washington a women's college of the same grade as Vassar, thus giving young women an opportunity for the highest collegiate instruction. . . . It is to be a post-graduate school, and no preparatory department is to be connected with it." Conaty praised the intellectual competence of the Sisters of Notre Dame de Namur and pledged to cooperate with them in everything "consistent with the interests of the university."[109]

Gibbons, the dean of the national hierarchy, was ardently behind the Trinity project, and most of his fellow bishops used their influential pulpits and the church press to advance the great cause. Having a female Catholic college in the nation's capital would greatly boost the reputation of the Catholic Church across the country, they informed their parishioners. New York's auxiliary bishop, John Farley, was typical. In an 1899 *New York Herald* press release, he asked, "Why not establish here in our capital at Washington an institution of learning that will be the admiration of the whole country, Catholic and non-Catholic?" Church newspapers covered the college's construction in great detail and pressed wealthy Catholics to provide the means to ensure that in funding and status it would rival leading Protestant female colleges. The April 30, 1899, edition of the *San Francisco Call* announced that Trinity would be to Catholic University "what Barnard College is to Columbia University and Radcliffe College to Harvard University."[110]

News that a second Catholic women's college was to open within the Baltimore archdiocese came as a rude jolt to trustees and faculty at the College of Notre Dame of Maryland. In June 1897, the *New York Times* announced that Trinity College was to be "the first Catholic college for women in this country."[111] To the distress of the School Sisters of Notre Dame, in the same year, their local newspaper, the *Baltimore Sun*, wrote that "there exists at present no institution under Catholic auspices for the higher education of women."[112] In conversation with one of Trinity's leading planners, Sister Mary Euphrasia Taylor, SND, Cardinal Gibbons referred to Notre Dame as a "Normal School at Govanstown, Maryland," whose students he "would gladly see" enroll at Trinity. He reassured Taylor that he "anticipated no rival College, of the same plane [as Trinity], coming into existence; in the distant future, in Chicago, perhaps, there might arise a College similar."[113] Yet at the same time, he advised Trinity sisters to visit the College of Notre Dame as well as other eastern women's colleges. "Mother Julia [McGroarty] and two Sisters of Notre Dame of Namur called and went through the building," the Notre Dame annalist recorded in July. "They are looking over schools prior to finishing Trinity College."[114] Trinity College opened in the fall of 1900 with eleven regular freshmen, nine special students, and two auditors.[115] Within four years, boosted by Gibbons's support and national publicity, it enrolled eighty-one students.

For the SSNDs, the situation was a painful introduction to church politics. As Catholic University chancellor, Gibbons wanted to defuse the mounting debate over the institution's all-male admissions policy. He saw a solution in the speedy establishment of Trinity College. As a member of Trinity's board of trustees from 1898 until his death in 1921, he used his sweeping national influence, ecclesiastical and political, to advance its enrollment, financial condition, and academic programs.[116] Cardinal Gibbons had given the School Sisters of Notre Dame permission to open a women's college within the Baltimore archdiocese, a prerequisite for opening any church-related institution. Beyond that, his support for the enterprise was minimal. He did not sign a formal legal document witnessing to his approval, and the founding sisters were reluctant to press him for such tangible confirmation. Although a perception lingers among historians that Cardinal Gibbons was one of Notre Dame's major patrons,[117] in fact his sole recorded gift to the college was an autographed photograph of himself, presented on December 6, 1896.[118] He did not publicly acknowledge the College of Notre Dame as the United States' first Catholic women's college, instead referring to it as a collegiate institute or a normal school.[119] At the dedication of College Hall in 1910, he spoke of it only as part of Notre Dame of Maryland, "an ideal school for girls, from kindergarten through College."[120]

As a result of episcopal strategy, the College of Notre Dame of Maryland did not benefit from the momentum that typically accompanies being "first." Following Gibbons's lead, the US hierarchy paid the Baltimore college little attention. Instead, bishops used their influence to promote Trinity College. Proceeds from a widely advertised fundraising lecture by Bishop John Lancaster Spalding of Peoria, Illinois, in January 1899 drew national attention and considerable funds to the institution.[121] In December 1899, six months after the College of Notre Dame had graduated its pioneer class, the Catholic Club in New York City held a major fundraiser for the planned Trinity College. The event's invitational leaflet noted that while women's colleges were spreading nationally, "there is no such institution for Catholic women"—their only options were "Bryn Mawr, Radcliffe, Barnard, Wellesley, Smith or some other well-known women's college not conducted under Catholic auspices."[122] The *Catholic University Bulletin*, reporting on Trinity's solemn dedication in November 1900, again stressed its pride of place: "Hitherto the Catholic Church possessed many excellent schools and academies for the education of young women. There was none, however, that had for its formal aim a post-graduate course of studies and training."[123]

No one in Baltimore publicly criticized Gibbons and his supporters, but there was considerable private sentiment that these men had done the sisters at the College of Notre Dame of Maryland an injustice. "This is written in no spirit of hostility to Trinity College," remarked Rev. Lucian Johnston. "At the same time it is only fair to give due praise to the solid work in collegiate training which has been done for a long while & is now being done by the progressive community in charge of Notre Dame."[124] Publicity about Trinity's progress rendered the College of Notre Dame nearly invisible within the Catholic community. With virtually no press coverage, it was difficult to recruit students nationally. In 1898 Austin O'Malley, MD, an English instructor at Notre Dame University in Indiana, completely ignored the College of Notre Dame in his widely circulated *Catholic World* article "College Work for Catholic Girls." When the Baltimore sisters protested the omission, he replied curtly that he had never heard of the college until "after the article was published."[125]

Yet as we have seen, women's struggle to extend gender agency within the Catholic Church in the United States began with the establishment of the College of Notre Dame. The School Sisters of Notre Dame had crossed a historic line when they defied a conservative tradition to open it. Catholic higher education, until now a prestigious male enclave, had a new, and troubling, gender dimension. In their development, the College of Notre Dame and similar colleges of later foundation were to face some exceptional hurdles. Their efforts at financing and staffing their colleges in the midst of the changing social, financial, religious, and educational environment in the first half of the twentieth century are the subject of the next chapter.

CHAPTER 2

Women Educating Women

Catholic Ways and Means

Pioneer Catholic colleges for women modeled themselves academically on the Seven Sisters, while also building on practices of earlier convent schools like the Notre Dame of Maryland Collegiate Institute. Despite their clear debts to other sectors of higher education, however, Catholic women's colleges departed from Protestant and secular women's colleges, colleges for men, and land-grant institutions in their models of governance and financing. Founded and staffed primarily by women, they faced unique challenges, including establishing both their independence from and a partnership with church authorities; gaining acceptance from mainstream accrediting bodies and other professional college administrators; obtaining suitable credentials for their sister-faculty; and, critical to the whole enterprise, funding land, buildings, and personnel. The School Sisters of Notre Dame and their young college had to meet these challenges in the service of developing a liberal arts curriculum for modern young women.

Governing Catholic Women's Colleges

With the opening of the College of Notre Dame, Catholic nuns entered the world of US higher education for the first time. In mainstream higher-education circles, they were definitely outsiders. While cordial, leaders of mainstream women's colleges did not accept them as professional colleagues.

Administrators and faculty in Catholic men's colleges, meanwhile, saw them as interlopers in a formerly elite male preserve. For its first five years, the Catholic Educational Association, founded in 1899, barred women's college representatives from its meetings. In 1904, it condescended to allow sisters to attend, but only as "interested auditors."[1] No women's college appeared on its list of accredited institutions until 1918. In short, because the governing practices of Catholic women's colleges were radical, in that most responsible posts were held by women, their prestige was low.

Governing boards of Catholic colleges were the corporations of the founding religious orders. Board members selected administrators, approved faculty appointments, made major financial decisions, and oversaw academic programs. Catholic women's colleges frequently invited local bishops to chair their boards of trustees, but the boards themselves remained preponderantly female. Notre Dame's board of trustees, administrators, and full-time faculty were almost entirely female, a feature that, with few exceptions, was to distinguish it and other Catholic women's colleges for much of the twentieth century.[2]

Male representation on boards of trustees of mainstream female colleges remained traditionally high, and men were predictably favored for top administrative posts. Leaders of elite female colleges held the title of either dean or president at the turn of the century. In attendance at Yale's bicentennial celebration in October 1901 were five women "admitted to full standing as college presidents." They were the deans of Barnard and Radcliffe Colleges and the presidents of Wellesley, Mount Holyoke, and Bryn Mawr Colleges.[3] But these posts were often held by men. Scripps College, founded in California in 1926 by a woman for women, chose a man as its first president and offered a majority of its first faculty positions to men.[4] Smith College did not welcome a woman president until the 1970s, Agnes Scott College until the 1980s. Before 1975, no woman had served as treasurer of a Seven Sister college.

Presidents, deans, and treasurers of Catholic women's colleges were usually members of the founding orders, although there were exceptions; from 1904 until 1949, the presidents of the College of New Rochelle (New York) were clerics, and in 1910, New York archbishop John Farley became the first president of the College of Mount Saint Vincent, beginning a tradition of male presidency that lasted until 1956. Typically, however, while the dean was the "operating head" of the college, the superior of the campus convent was its legal president.[5]

Deans of Catholic women's colleges enjoyed considerably less decision-making authority than their mainstream male and female counterparts.

Even without official titles, bishops routinely intervened in the affairs of women's colleges located within their dioceses. While Boston's Cardinal William O'Connell did not sit on the board of trustees of Emmanuel College (est. 1919), he was the *ex officio* president of Regis College (est. 1927). However, he controlled internal decisions at every level in both institutions and ordered sister-administrators to seek his personal authorization "before decisions were made."[6] In contrast, members of the hierarchy rarely served as presidents (even titular) of Catholic men's colleges and were less successful in controlling institutional governance.

Catholic women's college deans faced yet another layer of control, in that their religious superiors constituted the college's board of trustees and the superiors of the campus convents where they resided were also the official presidents of the colleges. As its first dean, Sister Meletia Foley governed the College of Notre Dame from 1895 until 1917. Mother Theophila Bauer, by virtue of her office as superior of the campus convent, was the college president from 1895 until 1904. Her successors, who also held both positions concurrently, were Sisters Florentine Riley (1904–19), Philemon Doyle (1919–29), and Ethelbert Roache (1929–35).[7] After 1935, the order separated the positions of college president and superior of the local convent.

Fifty-four-year-old Florentine Riley, Meletia Foley's good friend and contemporary, became president of the college in 1904. While Dean Foley concentrated on academic matters, faculty and curriculum development, and student campus life, Riley, a woman of proven administrative ability, administered the college's finances and oversaw the development and maintenance of the physical plant and other nonacademic services. An alumna from the 1910s recalled a formidable team: "Sister Meletia never seemed to intrude on her [Riley's] province and all went well."[8] But lay faculty and students in this era found the college's administrative organization baffling. In academic affairs, Foley's successor as dean, Sister Mary I. Dillon, "was the college. . . . She was it," a lay faculty member confidently declared. At the same time, she sensed that Philemon Doyle, the convent superior and college president, "was in charge."[9] Students believed that Dean Dillon and the registrar "really ran the college together," but "then we had a hidden Treasurer who was over in another building, and we had a hidden President, who was over in another building."[10]

When Sister Ethelbert Roache assumed the dual office of local superior and college president in 1929, the duties of each office had become weighty and complex. As college president, it was Roache's duty to reduce the outstanding debt incurred to construct the recently opened Le Clerc gymnasium and auditorium. As local superior she was also responsible for the spiritual and material well-being of approximately 120 sisters in the campus convent. College personnel accounted for only a fraction of this number. Teachers and staff of the campus preparatory, grammar, and primary schools, as well as sisters engaged in domestic service, also resided in the convent. So did candidates preparing to join the order. These young apprentices accounted for about one-quarter of the religious community on campus in the late 1920s.[11]

This governance structure posed challenges for religious sisters on the college faculty. As the superior of the campus convent, Roache held great authority over their personal lives. At the same time, as president of the college, she directed their professional work as teachers and scholars. Conflicts were inevitable as long as a single individual was the local superior as well as the college president. Mother Philemon Doyle, Roache's predecessor, fully appreciated Roache's difficult position. In 1933, as eastern provincial superior, she abolished the policy and assigned Sister Frances Smith to serve as Roache's "adjutant."[12] Two years later, Smith became the first Notre Dame president who was not simultaneously the convent's superior.[13]

Tension may also have arisen between the college's early presidents and its sister-faculty due to their different training. Faculty at the best mainstream women's colleges always held graduate degrees, but the same expectation did not hold for their early administrators. Neither Agnes Irwin, who became Radcliffe's first dean in 1894, nor Caroline Hazard, Wellesley's president from 1899 until 1910, held college degrees.[14] By the time of Notre Dame dean Meletia Foley's death in May 1917, presidents and deans of mainstream women's colleges customarily held graduate degrees. However, no sister at Notre Dame yet held a PhD. Sisters Ignatia O'Connell (1917–22) and Melita Varner (1922–23) jointly fulfilled the dean's responsibilities until 1923 when Sister Mary Immaculata Dillon, who had just earned her PhD at Fordham University, became permanent dean of the college, an office she held for eight years. In 1924, of the seven sisters on Notre Dame's faculty roster, only Dillon held the PhD degree. Three sisters held MAs, and two held BAs. The college president, Mother Philemon Doyle, was not a college graduate.[15] At Catholic women's colleges, administrators generally lagged far behind their secular colleagues in personal academic achievement. For example, Mother Grace Dammann, president of Manhattanville College of the Sacred Heart (New York) between 1930 and 1945, was a Georgetown Visitation Academy graduate, but like Mother Philemon in Baltimore, she did not hold a college degree.[16]

Their Catholic religion, celibate communities, sequestered lifestyle, distinctive garb, and (in some cases) lack of formal higher education presented some difficulties for sister-administrators seeking acceptance as professionals by secular college educators. Far more intractable were their struggles with bishops across the country who opposed the enrollment of nuns in graduate programs in secular universities, insisting that they attend only Catholic institutions. Delegates to the 1914 meeting of the Catholic Educational Association, nearly all male academics, resolved that secular colleges and universities were not "fitting places" for nuns.[17] By the 1920s, a few liberal bishops allowed sisterhoods with motherhouses in their dioceses to send members to secular universities for graduate education.[18] But these exceptions only proved the rule. By the 1950s, US sisterhoods were joining forces to defy episcopal restrictions imposed on them but not on male orders. These gendered confrontations, conducted through the Sister Formation Movement, were determined, widespread, and ultimately successful. Not only did they advance the professional quality of college faculties, but they also laid indispensable groundwork for the women's rights movement within the Catholic Church that commenced in the 1960s.

Women's Orders and Collegiate Economics

As Theophila Bauer and Meletia Foley considered opening a Catholic college for women in the 1890s, they followed news reports of the fate of two colleges in neighboring states in the wake of financial depressions and bank failures. Ingham University in Le Roy, New York, had evolved from a female seminary. Founded in 1835, the seminary became a collegiate institute in 1852 and gained a university charter in 1857. It never recovered from monetary losses incurred during the Panic of 1873, and closed in 1895. Evelyn College, in Princeton, New Jersey, opened in 1887 with no endowment. A severe decline in enrollment and donors during the Panic of 1893 forced its closure in 1897.[19] Avoiding such a fate was a priority for the sisters, but putting a Catholic women's college on firm financial footing was extremely challenging. Little material help was likely to come from church authorities. In order to establish a church-affiliated school, the religious order, male or female, needed to gain the approval of the local bishop. While he typically welcomed such a project, he rarely offered material support for it. Any available episcopal assistance in the form of real estate, buildings, or money was more likely to redound to men's colleges.

Early women's colleges frequently benefited from the philanthropic interest of affiliated churches and wealthy parishioners. Matthew Vassar, for example, liberally supported the college he founded. Rockefeller benefactions allowed Wellesley College, burdened with debt in 1900, not only to retire it but also to build a sizable endowment within a few years.[20] Prospects for similar lay assistance for early Catholic female colleges, however, were poor. Working-class parishioners had little interest in supporting colleges that their own children could not afford to attend, while their affluent coreligionists preferred to send daughters to elite mainstream women's colleges rather than unproven church institutions.

Another possible source of financial aid was wealthy alumnae. In the social milieu of the late nineteenth century, female education was not a philanthropic priority among American women. A few women did, however, begin to give to the colleges that had educated them. An alumnae association for the College of Notre Dame and the campus preparatory school, organized in 1896 by the Collegiate Institute graduates Zerline Stauf '82 and Mary Coale Dugan '79, aimed "to establish and maintain among the students of the school a permanent interest in one another and in the prosperity of their Alma Mater."[21] It got off to a rocky start, however, since graduates of the preparatory school wanted to raise funds to benefit their school, not the tiny new college. Nonetheless, in a spirit of unity, to celebrate "a new era in the life of Notre Dame of Maryland, it having developed in the year 1899 [sic] from a Collegiate Institute into a College," the association pledged to raise $5,000 to endow a permanent scholarship for one student's tuition, room, and board for one year, "in the interest of the higher and Christian education of women."[22]

The college alumnae association attempted for many years to control the disposition of funds it raised by designating them for specific purposes rather than contributing them without restriction to a general endowment fund that would generate income for needs identified by administrators. For example, in the 1910s it established the Sister Maris Stella (Wehage) Memorial Book Fund to honor a popular mathematics professor. In 1924 it raised $10,000 to endow the Sister Mary Meletia Memorial Fund, a lecture series, with the explicit understanding that the college president would consult the association's officers when selecting lecture topics.[23] As a result, in the 1920s, Notre Dame was able to offer only four unendowed $150 tuition scholarships annually, and during the Depression it had to reduce these modest awards further. In 1935 it offered one full and several partial tuition scholarships, and a few small assistantships.[24] At this point, the alumnae association agreed to concentrate its fundraising efforts on student scholarships. The larger alumnae chapters in Baltimore, Washington, and New York took up the cause. Although most of these scholarships were unendowed, they greatly improved the college's ability to attract excellent applicants.

Where, then, were the necessary resources to come from? One place was tuition. The cost to attend secular women's colleges varied by geographic location and institutional prestige. While in 1907 tuition at eastern colleges like Radcliffe and Bryn Mawr was $200, it was only $75 at Randolph-Macon Woman's College (Virginia) and Rockford College (Illinois).[25] Mount Holyoke College charged lower tuition and fees than comparable eastern colleges because it continued to require every student to do up to fifty minutes of institutional housework daily, thus reducing operating costs considerably. By this time, comparable colleges like Wellesley had dropped assigned housework. Others, like Bryn Mawr, had never introduced it.[26]

Without cash endowments, early Catholic women's colleges relied heavily on tuition revenues. Since their students came from middle- and working-class families, tuitions were lower than those of most mainstream colleges. Catholic female colleges did not expect students to do any domestic work beyond caring for their own rooms. At the turn of the century, the College of Notre Dame relied on lay sisters to do much of the domestic and maintenance work.[27] Annual fees for tuition, room, and board at Notre Dame in 1902 totaled $275; tuition alone held at $100 for many years. The College of Saint Angela (New York) charged its boarders $350 in 1904.[28] And while elite men's colleges tended to raise tuition only very slowly (Harvard College's stayed at $150 from 1870 to 1914), charges rose significantly over time at mainstream and Catholic women's colleges alike. In the 1930s Bryn Mawr students paid $775 annually for room and board, while Notre Dame students paid between $550 and $750. Differences depended on the quality of housing selected, with private rooms with baths in choice locations carrying substantial premiums.[29]

Tuition alone, however, could never account for the entire cost of operating a college; those that tried this risky route, like Evelyn College, failed. Consistent financial support needed to come from somewhere, and if not wealthy lay or clerical donors, there was only one real place left to look. Catherine E. Beecher, founder of many Protestant girls' academies and unfriendly toward the Catholic Church, nevertheless admitted ruefully, "It is a remarkable fact that, if we except Roman Catholic nunneries, I know not of even one case in this nation where a woman is supported as an educator by an endowment given by a woman."[30] Beecher had identified the essential financial element in the development of Catholic women's colleges in the twentieth century: the religious order.[31] Colleges like Notre Dame looked mainly to their founding orders for the contributed services of sisters as faculty members and staff, as well as for loans and funds to acquire real estate, erect buildings, and pay the salaries of lay faculty.

Sisters viewed these collective gifts as feminist expressions of religious philanthropy. "Endowments have not been received," Mary Dillon admitted in 1919, "but each member of the community has brought her offering of personal fortune be it great or small;—and thus Notre Dame stands a monument of women's spirit of sacrifice."[32] As the number of young Americans joining religious orders grew steadily for much of the twentieth century, superiors were confident that there would be sufficient young sister-faculty prepared to succeed retiring generations. College presidents and deans were able to rely heavily on these "living endowments" until a severe decline in applicants to sisterhoods commenced nationally in the early 1960s.[33]

The labor involved in running a college cheaply did not rest only on sister-faculty. In 1909, the School Sisters of Notre Dame purchased 275 acres of farmland and a "fine building" in Glen Arm, Maryland, about sixteen miles from Baltimore, to serve as a sanitorium for sisters as well as a truck farm, retreat, and vacation house. Villa Marie, popularly called Notch Cliff, played a critical role in supporting the college. From the 1870s, the Collegiate Institute and its successor college had relied heavily on campus gardens, poultry, and livestock for the food needs of students and sisters, with lay sisters providing much of the manual labor. "Have you a good vegetable and fruit harvest this year?" Caroline Friess inquired of Theophila Bauer in 1891. "What is the condition of the cattle? Is it profitable?"[34] Notch Cliff promised a more abundant and reliable supply of fresh milk, meat, eggs, and vegetables for the expanding college, lower schools, and convent.[35] "The sisters' farm," supervised by Sister Florentine Riley, significantly benefited the college financially in its early years. Until the late 1910s, the entire college, faculty as well as students, enjoyed an annual three-day excursion to Notch Cliff for picnics, games, shopping, and the singing of college songs.[36]

Revenue for the College of Notre Dame also came from the order's other projects. The Congregation of the School Sisters of Notre Dame was a large international organization of culturally diverse provinces. In this feature, it differed from the numerous diocesan-based sisterhoods that drew members from their local areas. While many large orders staffed social agencies, hospitals, and orphanages as well as schools, the School Sisters of Notre Dame specialized in education, staffing diocesan-owned parochial schools as well as a number of tuition academies for girls that it founded and owned. Tuition revenues from these academies helped finance new educational projects, among them the College of Notre Dame. Later, the order's preparatory schools around the country joined the alumnae association's 1930s scholarship campaign. Sisters conducting schools in Brooklyn, New York, raised funds for a four-year tuition, room, and board scholarship to Notre Dame for the student from one of their schools who scored highest in a competitive examination. Chatawa, Mississippi, sisters staffing Saint Mary of the Pines

School raised funds for a four-year tuition scholarship to Notre Dame for one of their graduates. Other schools followed suit.[37] Closer to home, the preparatory school on campus funded the Notre Dame Tuition Scholarship for its highest-ranking graduate.[38]

Neither a farm nor a few scholarships, however, could resolve the growing college's largest expense: the consistent need for new, expanded, and renovated buildings. Like other Catholic women's colleges, Notre Dame relied heavily on its founding order to finance major capital projects. Trustees, mostly sisters, financed major building construction by borrowing from local banks and by appealing to laity, especially alumnae of schools conducted by the order, to advance the cause. The policy of most orders was to refuse to consider funding a second capital project until they had fully repaid loans taken to finance earlier buildings.

College administrators viewed this strategy as much too conservative and slow. Their religious superiors, on the other hand, viewed "the American way" of constructing buildings while concurrently raising funds to pay for them as fiscally imprudent. At the College of Notre Dame, paying off the large debt incurred in the 1870s to acquire property and construct the Collegiate Institute building preoccupied leaders of the School Sisters of Notre Dame for decades. The Baltimore sisters turned to the worldwide order of the School Sisters of Notre Dame for help. At a general chapter in September 1885, the provincial superior, Mother Theophila Bauer, appealed to her fellow delegates for financial support for the Collegiate Institute, then struggling under the weight of construction debt.[39] She "plead[ed] so eloquently in favor of Notre Dame College before the members of the General Chapter in Munich that all the houses of the order united in giving aid to pay off the great debt that hindered and embarrassed the development of the school."[40] On March 21, 1892 (the year of Caroline Friess's death), the Baltimore sisters made the last payment of $5,000 to the Equitable Society. The property was now mortgage free, although the financial situation remained tenuous.

With the order's financial support, in mid-1895 Bauer moved quickly to add a four-story wing to the school's original building, effectively doubling the physical space available for academic use. Known as "the Annex," Theresa Hall accommodated the sisters' dining and community rooms and a chaplain's apartment on the first floor, a 250-seat chapel and two guest suites on the second floor, and private living quarters for the nuns on the third and fourth floors. The quarters on the fifth floor of the school building that had formerly housed the sisters became student housing.[41] The striking edifice led some disenchanted sisters to protest to the Munich generalate that the new building's scale and furnishings were too ornate for a college operated by nuns, a criticism reminiscent of that leveled against Sister Ildephonsa Wegman when the original Collegiate Institute building opened two decades earlier. Superior General Mother Mary Herman Joseph, on a visit in late 1897, summarily rebuffed complaints "that we lived in a very luxurious home, and had many superfluous surroundings."[42] By 1899, bills for the construction of Theresa Hall and operating the college totaled $500,000. "With the exception of a small amount," the sisters wrote to the *Catholic World*, "this was all contributed exclusively by the members of the order."[43]

Once final payment on the loan to construct Theresa Hall was made in 1905, the order authorized college president and local superior Florentine Riley to proceed with plans for Notre Dame's next building, the long-anticipated College Hall.[44] To finance this project, the order borrowed $150,000 from the Savings Bank of Baltimore, secured by a two-year mortgage on its Charles Street property; $60,000 from the Eutaw Savings Bank, secured by a five-year mortgage on property in Glen Arm and a second mortgage on the Charles Street property; and $7,500 from several other sources.[45]

In addition to buildings, finding funds for salaries and benefits, especially for lay faculty, would be a struggle throughout the college's history. Early on, especially, this was in part because mainstream foundation support was out of the question. In 1905, the steel baron Andrew Carnegie established a $10 million pension fund to assist retired college professors, but "sectarian" colleges were ineligible to participate. The press brushed aside protests of discrimination from leaders of Catholic colleges and seminaries, which in 1905 numbered 274 nationally.[46] "If Mr. Carnegie's gift does not pension Catholic teachers," commented the *Independent* in 1914, "then let them find some [Catholic financier like] Thomas F. Ryan who will make the desired benefaction. . . . Of all college teachers, the Catholics least need pensions, as the most of their teachers belong to religious orders and have no families and are provided for as long as they live. There is no reason to believe that it was from any hostility to religion that Mr. Carnegie limited his gift to the benefit of colleges not tied to a religious sect."[47]

As the college added more full-time lay faculty, the salary issue grew in importance. In 1950, accreditors criticized the salary scale of the College of Notre Dame as not "up to the average for many colleges of this type."[48] It was more in line with Maryland teachers' colleges than with liberal arts colleges. Professor Elizabeth Morrissy had taught at Notre Dame for thirty years and was the college's only full professor and its highest-paid faculty member. In 1950, her salary of $4,500 did not reach the $4,700 median salary for full professors at Goucher College.[49] The loyalty of lay faculty like Morrissy who remained at the college despite its low salary scale impressed accreditors.

By 1960, the salary scale had risen to $5,500–$6,000 for full professors; $5,000–$5,400 for associate professors; $4,500–$5,000 for assistant professors; and $4,000–$4,400 for instructors.[50] Again, accreditors called on the college to make raising faculty salaries a top priority. A faculty committee of three laypersons and one religious sister examined salary and promotion data at comparable institutions, and in March 1961 presented a proposed new salary scale. The trustees raised the full-time faculty salary scale by 7 percent for 1961–62 and by an additional 20 percent effective in September 1962.[51] Although these steps nudged the college's salary scale closer to those of other private colleges, President Margaret Mary O'Connell acknowledged that progress was slow.[52] In 1966–67, the top of Notre Dame's full-professor salary range was 16 percent below the minimum salary for that rank at nearby Goucher College.[53] At this time, the full-time faculty included sixteen full professors, thirteen associate professors, fourteen assistant professors, and twenty instructors. Part-time faculty numbered twenty-five lecturers and laboratory instructors. Dean Bridget Marie Engelmeyer attributed Notre Dame's poor showing relative to other women's colleges in AAUP salary reports in this decade to O'Connell's focus on construction: "More money should go into the academic program and less into housekeeping if we want to have the college approach what it was relatively."[54]

In 1971, the college board of trustees elected Sister Kathleen Feeley to the presidency.[55] Raising faculty salaries was among the new leader's top concerns, but the college's deteriorating financial situation slowed progress in this area. When, in 1975, she allotted $20,000 from the college's Leigh Pangborn Endowment Fund to aid faculty research projects, the faculty appreciated the modest step.[56] Another comparative study of faculty salaries, undertaken by the Rank, Tenure, and Salary Committee of the Faculty Senate in 1976, reported that across faculty ranks, Notre Dame's lay faculty still received "not only the lowest salaries in Maryland, but salaries which fall far below any kind of 'norm' for the state."[57] Acknowledging the institution's limited financial resources as well as its diminishing corps of sister-faculty and their contributed services, the Faculty Senate proposed "an increase of at least 15% for the academic year 1977–1978," rather than 25 percent, the minimum they deserved.[58]

A $5 million Second Spring Development Fund campaign commenced in 1978, with faculty salaries, facility improvements, and scholarships as its top priorities. Trustee Henry J. Knott immediately contributed a $2 million deferred gift for scholarship aid.[59] The scholarship fund also benefited significantly in 1981 when Knott established the Marion Burk Knott Scholarship Fund, since 45 percent of its income benefited students attending the College of Notre Dame, Loyola College, and Mount Saint Mary's College, Emmitsburg.[60] In 1981, the college awarded its first Knott Scholarships and the Second Spring Development Fund campaign reached its goal.[61] The year was also made memorable by the establishment of the first endowed faculty chair, funded by Esther Eberstadt Baldwin '15 and the National Endowment for the Humanities.[62] While this represented a major step, it also marked nearly a century of creative efforts by college administrators to establish a top-quality academic program on a shoestring budget.

Developing a Faculty for Catholic Women's Colleges

In the late nineteenth century, women's colleges seeking to be on a par with the best male institutions had to build faculties of comparable quality. "For the success of the experiments that the college is to try, and for which, to a considerable extent, it exists, the best teachers must be had," stressed Smith College English professor Mary Jordan. However, qualified women were still few in number and male professors were not much interested. "At present," Jordan wrote, "teaching women is not so attractive to men as teaching men, other things being equal."[63] In order to lure them to "segregated women's colleges" they had to receive higher salaries than those paid to female faculty members.[64] In 1887, for example, Mount Holyoke Seminary trustees, preparing to open Mount Holyoke College, concluded that its faculty would have to be entirely female, since "an endowment of $200,000 would not be sufficient for the employment of male professors."[65] Ten years later, a professor of music was the sole male on the faculty.[66]

A movement among women's institutions to add men to their faculties and presidencies gained momentum, and by the 1920s, higher-education authorities generally agreed that women's colleges with predominantly female faculties were probably academically deficient.[67] When William Allan Neilson became president of Smith College in 1917, one-third of the faculty was male. By the end of his term in 1939, that proportion had risen to one-half.[68] Prominent educators increasingly agreed that a women's college that lacked a significant number of male faculty was "too much of a convent."[69]

Women's colleges not only typically hired men at higher faculty ranks but also paid them more than equally qualified women. In the 1940s, Dean Virginia Gildersleeve of Barnard College reserved faculty openings at the higher ranks for men: "She knew that she would always have an ample pool of talented women to fill the lower ranks," notes the historian Rosalind

Rosenberg.[70] Forty years later, approximately two-thirds of the full professors at Mount Holyoke and Smith Colleges were men.[71] The practice of preferring men over women for faculty openings at higher ranks, and offering men higher salaries at all ranks, discouraged many women from undertaking professional careers in higher education.

By midcentury, some Catholic women's college administrators agreed that the very high proportion of women on their faculties placed the institutions at a competitive disadvantage. "The better the college for women, the healthier ballast of scholarly men it will invite to its faculty," maintained Madeleva Wolff, CSC, president of Saint Mary's College, Indiana.[72] A majority of the faculty in Catholic women's colleges, however, resided in the large convents that continued to be campus landmarks for almost a century. A religious community of celibate, professional female educators was ever before the eyes of students. The 1920 census reported that seventy-four sisters resided on the Notre Dame campus, a number that reached ninety-eight by 1931. At this time the campus convent housed faculty and administrators of the college, teachers and staff of the campus preparatory and elementary schools, and superiors, staff, and candidates of the religious order. Of fifty-four full-time faculty members at the College of Notre Dame in 1950, nearly two-thirds were nuns, a proportion slightly below the average for Catholic women's colleges nationally. A 1955 survey of 2,074 faculty members at sixty-seven of these institutions revealed that, on average, nuns made up 74 percent of faculties, and women also dominated lay faculties.[73] Notre Dame students took the skewed gender composition of the faculty for granted, although they agreed that men's "approach to education is vastly different from a nun's, *or even a woman's*."[74] Financial considerations hindered reform, and in 1987 nuns and laywomen (who also commanded much lower salaries than men) still accounted for about 75 percent of Notre Dame's full-time faculty.[75]

The Early Faculty

Catholic women's college leaders recognized from the start that hiring part-time lay faculty to supplement their small full-time faculty was only a stopgap solution to a critical problem. To be registered with the New York Regents in the late 1890s, colleges needed six or more full-time faculty members, enough courses in liberal arts and sciences to make up four years of college work, and a minimum admission requirement of a four-year high school course.[76] Preparing a sister for the faculty, though, was difficult because earning a PhD meant temporarily removing her from the order's workforce.

However, opportunities for women to earn advanced degrees at local universities were beginning to widen in the early 1900s. Johns Hopkins University admitted women to its graduate school in 1907, Catholic University followed in 1911, and Fordham University in 1916. The order's Baltimore superiors moved immediately to assign sisters to enroll in graduate programs at these institutions in preparation for joining the College of Notre Dame's faculty.

Hiring large complements of full-time lay faculty was always financially out of the question. Religious sisterhoods would educate sisters for college faculties and then contribute their services to the colleges. But until sufficient numbers of sisters held graduate degrees, colleges like Notre Dame had little choice but to employ relatively costly lay faculty. "Our classes are working up, so as to merit a degree," remarked the College of Notre Dame annalist in 1897. "This necessitates more teachers. As Mother [Superior] has no one to offer us, we have decided on engaging outside help."[77] Most of Notre Dame's first faculty were sisters who had taught in the recently closed Collegiate Institute. None as yet held bachelor's degrees. This was typical of early Catholic women's colleges. Among the sisters on Trinity College's pioneer faculty, for example, only one held a degree, an MD that she had earned before joining the order.[78]

The development of the early faculty at the College of Notre Dame benefited immensely from the exceptional intellectual and social leadership of its founder and first dean, Sister Meletia Foley. The longtime faculty member Rev. Edmund Shanahan remembered "the vigorous impress of her spirit, something of her dash and courage, not to forget her straightforwardness in preparing her charges for the life beyond the college,—all this was plainly discernible in the student body. . . . She was a human dynamo that gave the school its prestige and power."[79] She held firmly to her principles, yet possessed a democratic style that the faculty valued. Alumnae memories similarly portray a strong leader. As one put it, "When convinced she was right, she was absolutely fearless and seemed to love a daring sense of right in others."[80] Although students respected her, some found her intimidating. "Many feared Sister Meletia," observed an early graduate. "Many learned through contact with her the fine art of self-defense."[81] She was "an exacting task master," another recalled. "Gentleness was close to severity. She inspired the meek and leveled the proud."[82]

At Notre Dame, Foley moved immediately to engage faculty from Johns Hopkins and Catholic University to come to the college "regularly to instruct the Sisters who taught in the science and philosophy departments." She appointed men with graduate degrees to serve as department chairs.[83] These part-time professors supervised sister-teachers and advised them on courses of study and other college matters. As chair of the Philosophy Department, Edmund Shanahan found himself in the awkward position of supervising the dean herself, who offered a course related to his field. Similarly, Dr. J. J. Jenkins, from the University of Maryland School of Medicine, not only chaired the Chemistry Department but also supervised Sister Florentine Riley, a chemistry instructor. In 1897, Helena T. Goessmann, who held a PhM in history, literature, and ethics from Ohio University, chaired the History Department. She was among Notre Dame's first full-time lay faculty members.

Foley drew on Baltimore's rich cultural and academic resources to build the early faculty, as she had at the Collegiate Institute. She forged alliances wherever she could, persuading professors from Johns Hopkins University, the University of Maryland, and Catholic University to offer courses in various fields. Some, who were beginning their academic careers, remained only a brief time. After a year as professor of French at Notre Dame in 1905, Edward J. Fortier left to become an instructor at Yale.[84] These visiting faculty supplemented a small faculty of sisters at relatively low cost and helped build a vibrant campus community. Early college catalogs, publications, and advertisements emphasized the importance of these lay faculty. The 1899 college catalog, for example, stated that "the curriculum of the school is broadened by courses of lectures, given by specialists of national reputation." Similarly, a 1904 press release described the school's "able and progressive faculty—specialists in every department. Lecturers of national reputation."[85]

Its use of part-time professors from secular universities separated Notre Dame from other early twentieth-century Catholic women's colleges that relied heavily on local Catholic men's colleges for part-time instructors. In 1906, for example, the Trinity College faculty comprised nineteen Sisters of Notre Dame de Namur and seven Catholic University "professors," nearly all of them clergy.[86] For many years thereafter, Trinity relied on part-time faculty from Catholic University. "It was intended from the beginning," notes Carr E. Worland, "that the professors of Catholic University would teach selected courses at Trinity, which was the reason for the proximity of the two schools."[87] Notre Dame's part-time faculty, in contrast, included relatively few clergy. During its first half century, only eight Jesuits from nearby Loyola College were invited to teach at Notre Dame.[88] A succession of five resident chaplains, whose terms of service ranged from one to fifteen years, served the campus community in the first half of the twentieth century. However, with the exception of Rev. Lucian Johnston, who taught courses in religion and church history intermittently between 1899 and 1935, these men did not teach at the college.[89] Their duties included offering daily Mass for sisters and students in the college and the lower schools, presiding over religious ceremonies on the campus, and counseling students, faculty, and staff.

More typical of part-time faculty in the late 1890s was Johns Hopkins professor George Burbank Shattuck, whose "course of lectures on geology" carried credits toward the degree.[90] Ties to Johns Hopkins grew stronger after 1901 when the university moved its campus from downtown Baltimore to within easy walking distance of the College of Notre Dame. Soon the adjunct faculty from Johns Hopkins included men like the archaeologist and classicist David Moore Robinson, a perennial favorite of Notre Dame students who taught Greek from 1921 until 1935. A 1931 alumna remembered his "course in Greek literature [in translation] which everybody got into . . . who could possibly do it."[91] He delighted students by ignoring the college tradition of observing a moment of silence before beginning a class. "Dr. Robinson always invoked the Greek Muse when he began his classes," recalled Sister Maura Eichner. "He would say, 'Ida, Mother Ida, harken ere I die,' and move into some great Greek poem, which lifted us into Greek literature."[92] The fact that students could substitute Robinson's two-year elementary course in Greek for the college's required one-year course in a natural science ensured a consistently full enrollment.[93]

By assembling a staff of outside lecturers and instructors, Dean Foley developed a solid curriculum. It was "the best that the world has to offer in the line of education," according to Edmund Shanahan, and its diversity contributed to building a dynamic campus spirit. "Whichever way you turned," Shanahan recalled, "bounding life and enthusiasm met you, until everything and everybody seemed to be on the wing. Even the outside lecturers on art, literature, philosophy, and travel seemed to catch the genius of the place."[94] Part-time instructors, whether offering "regular classes throughout the year" or giving "special courses from time to time," were, as the college's 1910–11 catalog put it, all "university men specializing in the topics which made their professional reputation as teachers and investigators."[95] To attract the best part-time faculty, Foley readily accommodated their preferred teaching hours. As a result, the college's academic schedule ranged over all hours of the day, an early flexibility that, while relatively short lived, was to return in the 1970s with the introduction of continuing education, adult education, and weekend college programs.

From the beginning, the college also had part-time and full-time sister-faculty. Early faculty in the arts were especially proficient and appreciated by students. Marie de Ford Keller, for example, had studied at the Pennsylvania Academy of the Fine Arts before becoming a Catholic and entering the order. As Sister Maurelian, she taught art at the college from 1897 until 1906, when she resigned from the order. She later became a prominent artist, known for her fine oil portraits. Sister Casilda Benning, a gifted harpist, chaired the Music Department from 1895 until 1938. The music student Helen Burr-Brand '99 described her as "the Sun around whom I revolved, whose shadow I was." Burr-Brand, later a noted harpist and music educator in her own right, remembered Foley and Benning as fully "sympathetic with a professional career for women."[96]

The arts curriculum was important for the college's middle- and upper-middle-class female students, and the expansion of the university extension movement in the 1890s provided Foley with the financial assistance she needed to bring noted artists and scholars to the tiny college. The American Society for the Extension of University Teaching (ASEUT) began in 1890 with the backing of University of Pennsylvania provost William Pepper. Modeled on older English extension programs, especially the Oxford Extension Society (OES), and endorsed by leading American universities, it functioned in an advisory capacity for member institutions in devising curricula and attracting lecturers.[97] Among Notre Dame's early ASEUT lecturers was Dr. Frederick Henry Sykes, a Johns Hopkins University graduate, who

FIGURE 4.   Art studio, circa 1902. Photo from NDMA.

taught English literature between 1899 until 1902, when he became the first president of Connecticut College for Women.[98]

In 1907, a group of Boston public school teachers, eager to qualify as high school teachers, petitioned Harvard University for the opportunity to earn Harvard degrees through a university extension program. Women constituted two-thirds of the student body when the program commenced two years later.[99] Demand for similar opportunities spread, and a national movement to unite public and private university extension programs was soon underway. In 1915, delegates from twenty-four colleges in nineteen states attended the inaugural meeting of the National University Extension Association at the University of Wisconsin, Madison.[100]

In 1909–10, ASEUT and OES funded a series of five public lectures in the humanities at the College of Notre Dame. The British folk song artist and writer A. Foxton Ferguson and Princeton University English professor John Duncan Spaeth, a strong supporter of Dean Foley, were among the speakers. Spaeth was soon a frequent campus visitor. "Dr. Spaeth is an old friend of Notre Dame," commented the *Baltimore Sun* when the college honored him at commencement a decade later.[101] The prominent Protestant English novelist and poet John Cowper Powys, who also participated in the 1909–10 series, first came to the United States in 1904 under the Oxford Extension Public Lecture Program, and remained until 1934. He was a frequent visitor at Notre Dame, preferring to concentrate his lecture trips on "small colleges and the remoter State colleges." While "thrilled by lecturing to Nuns and Novices," Powys took a dim view of convents: "I would think it my duty to exert all the influence I had to stop a daughter of mine from becoming a nun."[102] He clearly liked Notre Dame students, though, and they considered Powys a good "friend and teacher." While his formal lectures on "the 'm-u-u-r-r-k-y' gloom of Coleridge and the 'mellow harmony' of Keats, and the 'aetherial wistfulness' of Shelley" were unforgettable, the students particularly recalled informal exchanges with him on his concept of "life-illusion," one's vision of oneself and one's world.[103]

Notre Dame's part-time lay instructors, and faculty from the Catholic University of America and Loyola College, regularly participated in the annual lecture series. In 1910, for example, chemistry instructor Rev. John Griffin offered several "experimental lectures" on electricity, light and color, and acoustics, along with seven lectures on world geography and history. Administrators worked to include nationally known speakers in a variety of fields. The 1910 program listed the celebrated photographer and naturalist Frederick Munson, a fellow of the Royal Geographical Society, who spoke on Navajo and Hopi reservation life in Arizona.[104] In 1904, Mrs. Charles W.

Billings (Mary B. White), an 1890 Collegiate Institute graduate, established the college's first endowed lecture series in memory of her father, Robert B. White.[105] Professor George Shattuck from Johns Hopkins University gave the inaugural Robert White Course of Lectures on geology and physical geography in 1905.[106]

Throughout her administration, Foley refused to distinguish between full-time and part-time faculty. The college did not adopt the conventional practice of listing regular full-time and part-time faculty on the faculty roster, with "visiting lecturers" listed separately, until 1918. On Notre Dame's first official faculty roster, in 1913, visiting lecturers were listed with regular full- and part-time faculty. In addition to John Cowper Powys and John Duncan Spaeth, they included German professor Hans Froelicher from Goucher College and Garrett Putnam Serviss, a national writer and lecturer on astronomy. The sole woman among that year's visiting lecturers was Julia Martinez, PhD, an 1876 alumna of the Collegiate Institute and a faculty member at the Normal School of Havana, who gained fame as "the Jane Addams of Cuba" for her work as an educator and campaigner for female suffrage.[107] Women presented concerts and dance performances at the college, but aside from Martinez, the ranks of visiting lecturers remained entirely male until 1920.[108]

Developing a Lay Faculty, 1920s–50s

Notre Dame relied on part-time faculty until the 1930s, when national accreditation standards for institutions of higher education restricted their employment. The practice, while not ideal, had allowed the small college to diversify its course offerings. The system proved efficient and effective in the short term until sisters with graduate degrees were available to assume departmental leadership. By this time, too, the college was taking tentative steps toward hiring lay female faculty on a full-time basis. Although always far fewer in number than sisters, these women proved to be exceptionally influential in the development of the college. Among the earliest lay faculty was Elizabeth Morrissy (1887–1981), who arrived in 1920 while still a Johns Hopkins University graduate student in economics. A 1908 Beloit College graduate, Morrissy had taught in an Iowa public high school for twelve years before enrolling at Johns Hopkins. Dr. John French, a professor of English and director of the university's appointments bureau, accompanied her to Notre Dame to meet President Philemon Doyle and Dean Mary Dillon. With his endorsement, they hired her immediately to teach in the History Department. She received campus housing, a teaching program that accommodated her course schedule at Johns Hopkins, and the services of the college chauffeur to drive her to and from her university classes. "If Notre Dame hadn't done all that, I couldn't have finished," she recalled. "I taught full-time when I got my master's and my doctor's [degrees]."[109]

Morrissy, Anne Kean of the Physical Education Department, and German instructor Zerline Stauf, then in her fifties, constituted the first group of full-time lay faculty.[110] Morrissy's campus housing benefit was common; faculties of early female colleges typically resided on campus, and some institutions, like Wellesley College, required that they do so. In 1898, the Wellesley trustee Alice Freeman Palmer backed a faculty appeal for "the elimination of the requirement that faculty live in college," and within a few years, most faculty had moved off campus.[111] Some colleges retained the policy longer, but by the 1910s, faculty resistance was widespread. "In the ideal college for girls that I would found," a Mount Holyoke professor commented in 1913, "every woman who taught should live in her own home, or at least in her private suite of apartments."[112] By the 1920s and 1930s, this policy had mostly faded as a requirement, but finances kept the small band of lay faculty at the College of Notre Dame living in campus apartments and rooms in College Hall.

According to an alumna of the 1930s, "those civilian teachers" were "very close, very close. They supported each other, and they were marvelous, marvelous friends. . . . Miss Morrissy would have been older, but the other ones were probably only in their thirties."[113] When they could afford to do so in the 1940s, they moved off campus, settling in the Homewood area near Johns Hopkins University, where they formed their own small community. "Three of the teachers lived with me," remembered Morrissy, "and the rest of the lay faculty were there [at her home] most of the time."[114] As "dean" of the lay faculty, Morrissy was a powerful advocate, always looking out for their welfare.

The college's location near universities in Baltimore and Washington made it easy to attract a cadre of full-time lay faculty in the 1940s and 1950s. Most were young, unmarried women who were finishing work for their doctorates and were willing to accept the low salaries offered by Notre Dame. These women brought their own vitality and diversity to the faculty and the campus. Their time at the college tended to be relatively brief, since it continued only until sisters had earned graduate degrees in their fields and returned to join the faculty. But a few stayed permanently. The Jewish émigré Regina Soria (LittD, University of Rome) joined the Foreign Languages Department in 1942, and Lavinia Wenger, a Moravian, who was completing work for an EdD at Johns Hopkins, arrived the following year to teach education. Both remained at the college for their professional careers.

"A new spirit was abroad among the Catholic intellectuals. At Notre Dame, it manifested itself in various ways," Soria observed. "The curriculum was completely revised, giving strength to English, modern languages, and art, besides, of course, the already strong science department." The nuns' liberal educational philosophy surprised Wenger. "They were cloistered sisters then, we had a cloister up here. I wonder[ed] how they could be so generous towards the demands of the world, but they really were."[115]

Sister-Faculty: SSNDs as College Professors

A problem that had nearly derailed the college's accreditation by the Association of Colleges and Secondary Schools of the Middle States and Maryland (MSA) in the 1920s was the education of its faculty. While part-time instructors were highly qualified, few of Notre Dame's regular full-time faculty held PhDs. In 1925, the MSA's Commission on Institutions of Higher Education acknowledged the college's improvement in this area, but called on it to do more: "Your Faculty are so generally increasing their scholarship by taking graduate courses at the Johns Hopkins University and elsewhere. . . . If in the future other members of your Faculty could earn the Doctor's degree at institutions such as the Johns Hopkins University the confidence of the Commission would be still further strengthened."[116]

With lay faculty representing a significant ongoing expense, the only feasible way to add more faculty with doctorates from leading institutions was to send sisters to earn graduate degrees. While most young sisters prepared for careers in parochial schools in the order's normal school, each year several were assigned to study full time for bachelor's degrees in other fields. Seven nuns enrolled in the college in 1932, two in 1933, and three in 1934; upon graduation they proceeded to further study for advanced degrees. Meanwhile, the college employed lay faculty as stopgaps. Elizabeth Morrissy described the strategy: "You hired a lay teacher until you had a sister ready to fill your place. That was why a lay teacher had no tenure in those days, because all Catholic schools used sisters almost entirely."[117]

In the 1930s and 1940s, adding sisters to the faculty and administration was a straightforward procedure. President Frances Smith and the dean reviewed the current and projected needs of the college in various academic departments and administrative offices for the board of directors, who were members of the order. The board then determined which sister-faculty to assign to full-time graduate study and approved the lay faculty hired to replace them.[118] In 1949, for example, Smith informed the board that the college needed faculty for the Biology, Mathematics, English, Education, and Music

Departments. She looked far ahead in making her recommendations, calling on the board to assign "two young Sisters, desirable for future college use, to study for A.B. and assist with corridor duty, second and third floors." Once they had the bachelor's degree in hand, they could enroll in graduate programs and, in time, return to join the Notre Dame faculty. She also proposed that the board give her an assistant, "a young Sister of worth and promise who could study and prepare for the Office [of president]."[119]

Most young sisters typically earned their bachelor's degrees on a part-time basis in colleges conducted by their orders, a relatively inexpensive arrangement. Preparing sisters for college faculties was more challenging. These sister-students often faced immense hurdles. For financial reasons, some superiors required that they teach full time in the college while they took graduate courses on a part-time basis at a local university. The arrangement had obvious drawbacks. Not only did it limit sisters' access to the best graduate programs in specific fields, but it also greatly slowed their progress in earning advanced degrees. In 1921, for example, the Notre Dame faculty members Sisters Denise Dooley and Cordia Karl enrolled in PhD programs in chemistry and mathematics, respectively, at Johns Hopkins. "We had no time off from teaching," observed Dooley, who did not receive her PhD until 1934.[120] At other times religious superiors, despite the protests of college administrators, abruptly withdrew sisters from graduate programs. In 1932, for instance, the Notre Dame annalist reported that "quite unexpectedly to us," the order had reassigned Sister Eugene Coleman, then studying for her PhD in English at Johns Hopkins and teaching part time at Notre Dame, to be "superior and principal of the high school at Prairie-du-Chien," Wisconsin.[121]

Another question was that of which institutions were acceptable for educating women religious. At the turn of the century, several communities needing college faculty enrolled a few sisters in secular universities. These orders invariably selected fully professed sisters, not young candidates or postulants, for these important assignments. Even so, this was an unusual step, since it required an accommodating bishop. The prevailing episcopal mindset was that as sisters acquired secular knowledge in secular universities, they lost much in the religious vein. In 1919, a well-known Catholic University professor argued that sisters' religious spirit could not withstand "a prolonged sojourn in the chill naturalism and materialistic atmosphere of our secular universities."[122] A 1917 revision of the Code of Canon Law regulating female religious communities significantly tightened the traditional cloister regulations that restricted sisters' mobility and public activities. These rules further hampered the freedom of sisters and slowed the development of qualified faculties for women's colleges.

As professional standards for faculty rose steadily, religious superiors attempted to circumvent the cloister rules and episcopal edicts that hampered them, but not their male counterparts, in educating their members. Probably the most creative approach was that taken in the early twentieth century by a Michigan community, the Servants of the Immaculate Heart of Mary. Between 1906 and 1932, superiors instructed some of the young women applying for admission to this order, who as yet had no canonical status, to enroll at the University of Michigan. Once these "postulants" held undergraduate and, occasionally, graduate degrees, they began their formal novitiate training in preparation for full membership in the order.[123] But few communities were able to follow this model. Most, like the Religious of the Sacred Heart, a group that by 1930 was conducting eight colleges across the country, struggled mightily to honor episcopal directives on sisters' education that varied markedly from diocese to diocese.[124] At this time, according to an American Council on Education report, only two Catholic institutions were qualified to award doctoral degrees: Catholic University, in five fields, and the University of Notre Dame, in one field.[125] In 1935–36, nuns accounted for 42 percent of the full-time enrollment in the Catholic University Graduate School of Arts and Sciences.[126]

School Sisters of Notre Dame did enroll in graduate programs in secular as well as Catholic universities. The proximity to the college of several excellent secular universities proved beneficial; conservative clerics could hardly object to sisters studying for advanced degrees at Johns Hopkins or the University of Maryland, since they continued to reside in their order's convents at or near the College of Notre Dame. They were in no more spiritual danger than sisters studying at Catholic University. In the summer of 1930, nine School Sisters of Notre Dame were pursuing PhDs: four at Johns Hopkins, two at Catholic University, and three at Fordham University. By 1936, following the same strategy, twelve were also attending the Chicago Art Institute and Western Reserve University. To deflect episcopal criticism, superiors continued to limit the public appearances of nuns, even for events that related directly to their professional lives. School Sisters of Notre Dame did not attend their own commencements, whether at secular or Catholic universities. In 1937, the College of Notre Dame faculty members Mary Louis Whalen (MA, chemistry) and Cordia Karl (MA, mathematics) received their degrees from Johns Hopkins *in absentia*. Similarly, Sister Theresine Staab received her master's degree in music *in absentia* from Catholic University in 1940.[127]

Restrictions on sisters' professional activities were an increasing problem as they sought acceptance by the mainstream educational world. Higher-education leaders in the 1930s increasingly criticized the faculty "inbreeding" that marked many US colleges. The difference between Catholic and secular colleges in this regard was substantial. A 1935 study of nearly seventeen thousand faculty members at two hundred public and private institutions found that, on average, 34 percent had received part or all of their training at the institution where they were teaching. The median was about 25 percent. Colleges sponsored by the Catholic Church, meanwhile, reported 49 percent, a higher figure than that of other religious denominations sponsoring at least five colleges. "If inbreeding exceeds 50 percent," concluded the authors, "administrators should endeavor to reduce this figure."[128]

At Catholic women's institutions, sister-faculty typically held bachelor's degrees from the colleges where they taught and earned graduate degrees at a small number of Catholic universities. To avoid the perennial charge of inbreeding, colleges endeavored to assemble a lay faculty, full and part time, that held undergraduate and graduate degrees from a range of higher-education institutions. To ensure appropriate treatment of Catholic social principles, they generally favored faculty with degrees from Catholic universities for the religion, philosophy, and sociology departments. They also advised graduates seeking to earn graduate degrees in these fields to apply to Catholic universities. A few universities supported this effort. In 1921, for example, and continuing for two decades, Loyola College in Chicago offered two scholarships annually for its MSW degree program to Notre Dame alumnae.[129] But by the 1950s, fewer bishops were impeding the enrollment of sisters in secular universities, and nuns sought graduate degrees from a wide range of institutions. By 1959, Notre Dame's fifty-seven faculty members held advanced degrees from twenty universities.[130]

While pressures from church officials were daunting, so too were traditional rules of life observed by female orders. The movement to relax cloister rules was a slow process. For example, the regulation that a School Sister of Notre Dame must be accompanied by another sister when she left convent grounds could present an insurmountable hurdle for a sister seeking to study at a secular university distant from one of the order's convents. In 1938, for example, as Sister Dorothea Marengo prepared to begin her second year of study at the Art Institute of Chicago, her religious superiors transferred her to Catholic University, as "there was no companion in the West to attend the Art Institute with her."[131] Such "companion rules" persisted into the 1960s in many women's communities. Not only were they difficult for individual sister-students, but they also seriously handicapped the efforts of college presidents and deans seeking to build qualified faculties with advanced degrees from universities offering the best programs in their fields.

Cloister regulations had always hampered sisters' mobility in professional circles. And the expectation that nuns be retiring and self-effacing precluded any public recognition of their personal professional achievements.[132] On college campuses, the professional and scholarly attainments of lay faculty were publicly announced and celebrated while, for many years, those of sister-faculty were not. American nuns rarely played active roles in mainstream forums in their professional fields in the 1920s. When Mary McGrath, IHM, professor of psychology at Saint Mary's College (Monroe, Michigan), presented a paper on "research findings in the moral development of children" at the 1924 meeting of the American Association for the Advancement of Science, the extraordinary occurrence received wide coverage in the Catholic press. As usual, one report observed, "she was the only religious on the program."[133] Until the 1940s, the cloister issue greatly hampered routine participation by nuns on equal terms with their mainstream faculty peers in national scholarly societies and higher-education associations.

Convent rules adversely affected individual sisters as well as the colleges, as the experience of Sister Cordia Karl attests. She was one of Hunter College's highest-ranking graduates in 1916. In 1921, when the Nu chapter of Phi Beta Kappa was established at Hunter, the college elected Karl retroactively to membership. Since by this time she was a novice in the School Sisters of Notre Dame, she was instructed to decline the honor. Karl went on to earn her PhD in mathematics at Johns Hopkins University and join the faculty at Notre Dame. In April 1948, the Hunter College chapter of Phi Beta Kappa "re-affirmed" her 1921 election. This time, when Karl received her Phi Beta Kappa key at Hunter's public induction ceremony, the *New York Times* reported on the exceptional honor.[134]

Collaboration, Dynamism, and Change, 1940s–50s

By the 1940s, the College of Notre Dame was becoming a dynamic institution. For faculty and students at midcentury, Dean Bridget Marie Engelmeyer (1905–2001) embodied the institution's highest intellectual values and expectations. A Baltimore native, she attended Saint Catherine's Normal Institute and the College of Notre Dame (BA, 1926), and entered the SSNDs in 1937. After earning an MA in English from Catholic University in 1941, she joined the English faculty, serving also as college registrar. In 1947, she became dean of the college.[135] As dean from 1947 until 1971, she held ultimate authority over the faculty and oversaw all areas of student life, extracurricular as well as academic.[136] As Engelmeyer frequently reminded the college community, the dean at Notre Dame was "not the Academic Dean, she [was] the Dean of

FIGURE 5. Dean Bridget Marie Engelmeyer, SSND, 1940s. Photo from NDMA.

the College."[137] She visited classes regularly, recalled a young faculty member from the 1950s, who said, "She took that as a . . . responsibility to monitor teaching that way." Similarly, at the end of every term, she interviewed each student personally to discuss her progress, a practice "that certainly helped the intellectual level." Students and faculty agreed that under Engelmeyer's leadership, "the intellectual life was stimulating. . . . We felt that Notre Dame cared about things of the intellect."[138]

The campus's vibrancy during the 1940s and 1950s owed much to its history under earlier administrations. During the 1920s and 1930s, Dean Mary Dillon had continued to bring national and international scholars and religious leaders to the campus. Social theorists and religious and political reformers, rare among earlier lecturers, now became prominent. Maud Wood Park, president of the International League of Women Voters, spoke in 1925 on "the enrichment of life by the power to vote," and Rev. John A. Ryan, theologian and social reformer, lectured the following year on "the Catholic Church and the social question."[139] At the same time, Notre Dame faculty began to seek ways to share the college's scholarly and cultural resources with the wider community. In 1924 the college hosted the inaugural meetings of the Catholic Drama Guild of America. By the 1930s, sister-administrators regularly attended meetings of national educational associations, and by the 1940s, sister-faculty were actively participating in professional societies and cultural conferences and enjoying greater autonomy in their personal career decisions.[140] Baltimore's Enoch Pratt Library's 1944 public lecture series featured College of Notre Dame English professor Sister Angeline Hughes, who spoke on "Irish poetry." Sister Dominic Ramacciotti, dean of the college since 1941, resigned in 1947 to join the graduate faculty at Catholic University.[141] In December 1949, the Demotte Galleries in New York City, the site of Pablo Picasso's first show in the United States in 1931, opened a monthlong exhibition of the paintings of Notre Dame art professor Sister Noreen Gormley.[142]

The college's art faculty and curriculum broadened in the 1930s and 1940s under the guidance of Gormley and the Baltimore portraitist and muralist R. McGill Mackall (1889–1982). The longtime head of the Fine Arts Department at the Maryland Institute College of Art, Mackall was judged to be among Baltimore's "most renowned artists during the first half of the 20th century."[143] He and Charles R. Rogers, assistant director of the Baltimore Museum of Art, were powerful supporters of Gormley's interest in developing a first-rate college art program. Gormley also hoped to find a way to enrich the quality of art instruction in local Catholic schools. Soon after the founding of the Catholic Art Association in 1937 by Esther Newport, SP, an art professor at Saint Mary-of-the-Woods College (Indiana), and the artist Graham Carey, Gormley established the Catholic College Art Association of the East, to "include all our Catholic schools in a general program for Art Education, with the Catholic philosophy behind it, the Christian Art as an ideal—and emphasis on the Liturgical Arts."[144]

Gormley's interest and her partnership with local arts professionals kept the college at a high artistic level throughout her tenure. Regina Soria, who had just joined the faculty, recalled her surprise: "We had [an] exhibition of [the French modernist Georges] Rouault. We had [the Mexican modernist] Rufino Tamayo come every week from New York, and André Girard." Girard, Rouault's student, a Resistance member who escaped from France during World War II, had a prolific career in the United States as a painter and liturgical artist. He taught at intervals at Notre Dame between 1948 and 1952, and returned to campus in 1960 to give the eulogy at Gormley's funeral.[145]

The 1940s saw a steady stream of European intellectuals and artists like Girard who, exiled from Europe by World War II, settled in the eastern United States either temporarily or permanently. Among them was Rev. Marie-Alain Couturier, OP, a respected artist, writer, and authority on modern sacred art and religious architecture in the 1940s and 1950s and an associate of Georges Braque, Henri Matisse, Pablo Picasso, Fernand Leger, Georges Rouault, and Le Corbusier. Eager to introduce Notre Dame students to leading contemporary artists, Gormley invited Couturier to teach at the college. He responded enthusiastically, offering classes in Christian art on Saturdays in the fall of 1941. He continued to lecture, stage exhibits, and paint regularly at Notre Dame until his return to France in 1945. Until about 1950, he offered courses on his occasional visits to the college.[146]

Couturier's presence at the College of Notre Dame, although concentrated in the 1940s, had a dynamic and lasting influence. During his periods in residence, he worked closely with faculty, instructed students, and occasionally exhibited their works. Free to come at will and to arrange his own teaching and studio schedules, he invited noted artists and writers to the campus. Typical was the novelist Julien Green, who considered Couturier his spiritual adviser. French-born of American parentage, Green lived in Baltimore during the war years. In 1942, Couturier arranged for him to give a series of spring and summer lectures on the poet and essayist Charles Peguy. While attendance at these formal events was small (only "Father C," the nuns, and some students appeared for the March 20 lecture), Green enjoyed his time on campus for the chance it afforded him to visit the campus convent, where he engaged the sister-faculty in debates on current church topics, among them "the abandonment of the monastic habit and the de-romanizing of the Church in America."[147]

As important as such visitors were to campus intellectual life, it was the full-time faculty that were the students' key role models. According to a student leader of the late 1940s, "I don't think we were nearly aware of the powerful influence [the sisters] had on us as women who were capable, active, assumed tremendous responsibility. . . . [It] was probably sensed by us more than anything else." Students also looked up to the female lay faculty. The same student described Elizabeth Morrissy, chair of the Economics Department, as "very active in community and civic affairs. She really did a lot to change the world she lived in, and . . . I felt I would like to live like that."[148] The curriculum these women and their male collaborators developed aimed to foster such ambitions and facilitate their achievement.

By the end of the 1940s, the College of Notre Dame had achieved substantial goals. It had established a dedicated and well-qualified faculty despite episcopal restrictions and financial challenges, raised funds for scholarships and several substantial buildings, and developed a rigorous curriculum. In doing all this, it had benefited from the talents and drive of several exceptional early administrators, as well as from the collective support of the School Sisters of Notre Dame both locally and worldwide. In the second half of the twentieth century, the college continued to benefit from the willingness of its faculty and administration to cope creatively with fewer resources than comparable colleges. As the College of Notre Dame developed throughout the twentieth century, it dealt with other critical challenges, arising from diverse constituencies within (and sometimes barred from) its community. Its struggles and successes in dealing with difference are the subject of the next chapter.

CHAPTER 3

Divided or Diverse?

Questions of Class, Race, and Religious Life

Entrenched social and religious values shaped the movement of Catholic women's colleges toward becoming more democratic and racially diverse institutions. Over the course of the twentieth century, the College of Notre Dame, like many of its peers, faced challenges that affected its social and academic progress. How did it respond in the critical areas of race and social class? At its foundation in 1895, Notre Dame admitted only white students and favored financially comfortable students who, with the occasional exception, resided on campus; many of these young women had previously attended SSND academies, in Baltimore and around the country. Diversity on both fronts came slowly, for many reasons ranging from faculty, student, and parent prejudice to lack of episcopal interest to financial concerns. But the great postwar transformation of US higher education, ultimately including both racial integration and the expansion of access to students from poorer families (often at the same time), changed the College of Notre Dame as well. During the same postwar period, sister-administrators and faculty were changing their relationship with their lay peers, a challenging shift for all parties involved as lay faculty sought more democratic forms of faculty governance and sister-faculty in turn began to reconsider their own financial and professional relationship to the college.

Class at the College of Notre Dame

The reluctance of Notre Dame administrators and faculty, most of them nuns, to address class tensions within the college community, as well as the institution's restrictive racial policy, reflected, in part, two historic features of many religious congregations of women in the United States. Many maintained a two-tiered membership structure based on social class, a feature more common in groups governed by European motherhouses, and virtually all refused to admit African American women to membership. These attributes influenced the progress (or lack thereof) in achieving class and racial diversity in colleges they founded.

Class in Women's Religious Orders

Customs and internal policies of founding religious communities deeply affected the social culture and democratic spirit of institutions they conducted. Many, like the School Sisters of Notre Dame, had European roots, and most of these had a two-tiered membership structure.[1] "Choir" sisters typically entered with dowries and carried out the orders' public ministries in schools, hospitals, and social institutions. "Lay" sisters entered without dowries and performed manual labor and diverse nonprofessional services in convents, schools, and other institutions conducted by the order. Lay and choir sisters usually differed in religious dress.

In the Congregation of the School Sisters of Notre Dame, lay sisters were called "house sisters." Their white veils contrasted with the black veils worn by choir sisters, called "school sisters." House sisters enjoyed "neither active nor passive vote," whereas school sisters could vote in elections for superiors and stand for election to community offices.[2] As early as the 1870s, few young women wanted to join the order as house sisters. The decline in applicants was especially alarming in the democratic United States. "We are trying to get [German] girls from our orphanages to serve in that capacity," Mother Theresa Gerhardinger informed a Baltimore priest. Of sixty-four American candidates in 1879, only three were willing to apply as lay sisters.[3]

While the order did not require a dowry for admission, it determined the status of applicants as school or house sisters by their social and educational backgrounds. In 1889 the chronicler for the Baltimore province reported that "the [forty] postulants were required to take an examination. The result was to decide their status as teachers, or if not qualified as such, to become house sisters."[4] Since house sisters wore white veils to distinguish them from black-veiled teaching sisters, local citizens, including some clergy, disparaged them as second-class nuns who were "neither in nor out of the convent."[5] To avoid such remarks, Mother Gerhardinger allowed them to wear black veils when they appeared in public but insisted that "indoors, the sisters must wear their white veils."[6] In 1890, house sisters gained permission to wear the black veil "by way of exception," but, beyond that concession, their subordinate status relative to the teaching sisters continued.[7]

By the early twentieth century, many sisterhoods in the United States had eliminated such internal hierarchies. In 1917, a revision of the Code of Canon Law governing women religious required that all orders have a single membership class, regardless of the type of work done by individual sisters. But although the Congregation of the School Sisters of Notre Dame removed the term "house sister" from the 1924 edition of its constitutions, sisters continued to use it informally. The convent annalist in the mid-1930s, for example, recorded that "Mother Philemon brought us a new house sister."[8] And the SSNDs worldwide did not make the abolishment of the two-class structure fully official until the congregation's general chapter in 1950. Other international groups took even longer to move to single membership status. The Society of the Sacred Heart of Jesus, for example, did not absorb its coadjutrix (lay) sisters until 1964.[9] The two-tiered membership structure that characterized the School Sisters of Notre Dame thus marked most orders of women that founded and conducted colleges. The tensions that accompanied it affected, in varying degrees, the progress of the institutions they founded. Notre Dame's experience was not unique.

Students and Social Class

Collegiate Institute catalogs from 1873 included a description of an unusual category of student. In addition to regular students, the institution admitted "parlor boarders," special students who took courses at will for personal enrichment and enjoyed superior living quarters. They favored languages and the arts and were not interested in completing the program of study required for a "degree." By completing a sequence of courses in one field, they qualified for a "certificate of honor." These special students typically enjoyed private rooms and their own dining room, and paid tuition, room, and board charges that were 66 percent higher than those charged regular students.[10] In 1876, tuition, room, and board charges for regular students were $250 per year, increasing to $275 by 1902, while parlor boarders paid $300 and $450, respectively.[11] Their presence at the school was always controversial. Faculty objected that their admission lowered the school's academic reputation and that they were not a positive influence on younger, full-time students. They generated badly needed revenue, however, so they remained, despite faculty protest, until the World War I era.[12]

"Special students" at the Collegiate Institute, and later at the College of Notre Dame, also reflected the creative flux of a higher-education system that had not yet settled into its contemporary outlines. Nineteenth-century women's colleges routinely admitted atypical students, usually older than traditional students, who did not seek degrees but otherwise qualified for admission. "Under exceptional circumstances," the Woman's College of Baltimore accepted students "who desire to study without reference to obtaining a degree." In 1877–78, Wellesley introduced a "teacher specials" program, a popular service that allowed schoolteachers to register for courses in any field without obligation. When Radcliffe College received its charter in 1894, it enrolled 136 special students, "mature women who are at work in special lines." Special students at Mount Holyoke College in this era included graduates of other colleges seeking "special lines" of study, school-teachers who were at least twenty-one years of age and had taught school for a year or more, and music students who agreed to elect some courses in other fields. "When desired," special students received certificates of work satisfactorily completed.[13]

The discussion of special students highlights another clear class distinction on campus: between those who boarded (at the typical or the parlor level) and those who instead commuted as "day students." The Collegiate Institute remained a "select" boarding school in the late nineteenth century, although there were always a few day students. The college's sequestered location reinforced this near requirement during the early decades. While by the 1890s downtown Baltimore had electrified streetcars, public transportation in the city's outskirts was minimal. In 1922, according to a prospective student, "there was no transportation—it was a road, there wasn't even any bus up there at that time."[14] Dean Meletia Foley had aimed to build a residential college, a Catholic equivalent of the Seven Sisters. For financial reasons, however, Notre Dame had always welcomed some applicants on a day basis. An 1896 circular described the new college and the preparatory school as "A Model School for City Students," where day students could enjoy a "substantial dinner" for $1.50 per week. However, Rev. John Griffin recalled that in 1900 the campus was "all boarding school, with perhaps eight or ten day students in the entire school from the baby grade to senior year in college."[15]

During her tenure as dean of the college (1895–1917), Foley devoted special attention to attracting boarding students. Daughters of financially comfortable Baltimore families boarded at the college. She wanted these students to have a similar living style and social experience as those enjoyed by their peers in elite secular women's colleges.[16] College Hall, completed in 1910, reserved "a spacious suite of apartments" where students would receive proper training in the social graces.[17] But enrollment continued to be chronically low relative to other Catholic women's colleges, and Dean Mary Immaculata Dillon (1923–31) did not share her predecessor's commitment to the elite residential college model. During the 1920s, public transportation was improving, and the number of applicants wishing to enroll on a nonresident basis rose. Dillon saw this group as a way to boost both enrollment and endowment, areas of special interest to higher-education accrediting agencies. For the first time, the college actively recruited day students. In 1920, resident students made up 88 percent of the college's full-time enrollment; by 1929 they accounted for only half of its full-time enrollment of 156.[18]

The economic distress of the Great Depression in the 1930s caused boarding enrollments to decline significantly at all women's colleges. In 1934, for example, boarding students accounted for only 45 percent of Pembroke College's enrollment.[19] At the College of Notre Dame, likewise, fewer potential students could afford to board, and the college could offer little scholarship aid. Admitting more day students was the obvious solution to the enrollment crisis, and the college actively advertised for them, offering "special rates" for those in need of extra assistance. In 1937, day students made up two-thirds of Notre Dame's enrollment.[20] The Depression had quickly turned the boarders into a minority, a situation that continued to obtain after its end. Although the college's total enrollment doubled during the 1940s, boarding students accounted for only one-third of the enrollment in 1948. Boarders became more numerous in the 1950s and 1960s, but day students continued to outnumber them. This imbalance distinguished most Catholic women's colleges, especially those in urban locations where many students remained at home while attending classes.

Class Distinctions and Social Life

In the college's early years, campus social activities included everyone. The entire college, including administrators and faculty, took weekend boat trips to Norfolk, Virginia, and Virginia Beach, "returning Monday morning in time for classes."[21] Administrators and faculty applauded the college's unique "community spirit," as evidenced in near-total student participation in religious, sports, and musical events. But as day students applied in growing numbers, divisions appeared in some areas of campus life. Many colleges began to struggle with the question of sororities and exclusive social clubs, reflecting growing tensions between elitism and democracy, and the College of Notre Dame was no exception. Dean Foley had aimed to provide social opportunities comparable to those enjoyed by students at other women's colleges. To this end, she encouraged students to establish an intramural sorority. By 1908, Kappa Rho Sigma was flourishing; a student editor, garbling a line from Alexander Pope, described the typical sorority meeting as a "flow of reason and feast of soul."[22] In fact, members spent most of their time socializing, dining, and playing card and popular parlor games like thought transference. The only extant KRS photograph, taken about 1916, shows twenty-two members. The fact that none is a native of Maryland indicates the sorority's resident-only membership policy.[23]

Women's college administrators were increasingly concerned that sororities were dividing their student bodies. In 1912, the Women's College in Brown University had disbanded these organizations, despite student protest that Greek societies in the men's college continued unchallenged. Catholic women's colleges typically opposed sororities, arguing that they elevated their members over other students. As Tracy Mitrano puts it, "The exclusive nature of social bonding in sororities contradicted the inclusive nature of the religious experience as it was defined in Catholic culture."[24] Beyond this, both secular and church-related institutions were concerned that as secret societies, both sororities and fraternities enjoyed undesirable independence from college authorities. Since the early twentieth century, Harvard College had banned fraternities and refused to recognize chapters of national Greek societies, explaining that "we want student groups . . . to operate under the authority of Harvard College and the dean's office, rather than some other authority."[25]

Although KRS inducted twelve new members in early 1917, Foley's death that year signaled the sorority's demise.[26] Faculty and administrators who had never shared her liking for the group argued that a recent move by KRS to affiliate with Kappa Pi Epsilon, a social sorority founded in 1895 at the University of Arkansas, threatened the college's authority. In November 1917, they disbanded the sorority on the grounds that it was socially exclusive, and the college catalog stated that the institution did not permit "sororities with secret initiations."[27]

Following the discontinuance of the sorority, administrators encouraged Kymry, a campus social club founded in 1913, to become "the successor to the KRS Fraternity."[28] Kymry's stated mission was "to form a more perfect union in thought and sentiment, to further the spirit of comradeship, and to promote loyalty and good cheer among the students of NDC."[29] However, using its "power to exclude," Kymry admitted only resident students to membership. Thus it enjoyed all the attributes of a traditional sorority, with the exception of secretiveness. Administrators raised no objection to this discriminating clause. Now, as the only social club on campus, Kymry flourished. Given the college's small size, the club's total registration of 175 over the 1916–26 decade suggests a robust organization.

Even as the proportion of day students at Notre Dame rose sharply in the 1920s and 1930s, campus social activities continued to revolve around resident students. In the interwar era, day students were sensitive to social distinctions on campus, especially to being excluded from membership in Kymry. A 1928 graduate recalled that it was "supposedly the social club, but practically all the activities had to do with the girls on the campus."[30] Day students tried to minimize their segregation. "They had a little Kymry Club or something with a club for boarders, and it didn't bother us any," recalled a 1940 graduate, perhaps a little unconvincingly. "We didn't care."[31] Kymry's restricted membership policy persisted into the 1950s. According to the 1950 yearbook, it was "the social club of the resident students at Notre Dame [and] its goal is the promotion of loyalty and good cheer among boarders." College catalogs in this decade also alluded to Kymry as the "resident student social organization."[32]

In academic matters and departmental clubs, students were treated equally. In campus social activities, however, they were not. The faculty "knew everybody in the school," according to history professor Sr. Virgina Geiger, but they enjoyed less informal rapport with day students.[33] "The boarders, the resident students, had a better relationship with the sisters," recalled a day student of the 1940s. "They were living there, and I think that made a difference."[34] Since the Kymry Club sponsored elaborate holiday celebrations, social distinctions between day students and boarders could become painfully apparent at these times. An attendee at a formal Christmas party in the 1920s recalled that students wore evening dresses. "All the sisters came, and all the girls came. . . . There was a great . . . friendly relationship between the students and the sisters."[35] In the 1940s, Dean Bridget Marie Engelmeyer noted in her diary that day students played a decidedly subordinate role in this annual event: "Christmas Dinner was for college boarders. Some day students served."[36] A few years later, again without comment, she recorded that only "resident students & lay faculty" attended Kymry's formal-dress Christmas supper.[37] A senior remembered that occasion as "a really elegant candlelight dinner, served by day-hops."[38] Such distinctions persisted into the 1950s. In December 1951, the college annalist wrote that "Sister Superior

M. Vitalia entertained the college lay faculty and the resident students tonight with a Christmas dinner." The Kymry Christmas party followed the dinner. Day students were not part of this "real family occasion."[39]

The Kymry Club's insensitivity extended beyond its exclusionary membership policy. Occasional entertainments provided by the club for the entire college community revealed a considerable lack of social awareness. According to a description of a 1938 Valentine's Day party in the campus newspaper, *Columns*, captioned "Boarders Frolic at Poverty Party," club members decorated the hall as "a scene of utter desolation. . . . Each member came dressed in old clothes. . . . For the refreshments a bread line was formed." Those wearing the most "impoverished" outfits won prizes. Faculty and administrators in the audience raised no objections to the show. It was "one of the most unusual novelty parties ever held at Notre Dame," observed a faculty member. No doubt.[40]

With the onset of World War II, interest in campus social clubs fell off as day and resident students became active in war efforts. In 1942, as *Columns* reported, Notre Dame became Maryland's first college "to have a student defense unit and to receive the first Volunteer First Aid Detachment charter granted by the American Red Cross."[41] By the late 1940s, distinctions between day and boarding students had considerably abated. Student government, the athletic association, and departmental clubs offered broader opportunities for all students to participate on equal terms. But while longstanding divisions between day and boarding students had faded, they had not disappeared. Concerned administrators agreed that "dayhops and residents need to be more closely united."[42] Thus President Margaret Mary O'Connell welcomed a 1959 student proposal that the Resident Student Association merge with the all-college Student Association. The Kymry Club retained its exclusionary membership policy until this occurred in 1964.[43] Despite the merger, day students in the 1960s continued to believe that resident students ranked above them in campus social life. "Dayhops have no real part in the life here" was a common observation.[44] And two decades later, 44 percent of respondents to a student satisfaction survey still reported dissatisfaction with relations between day and resident students.[45]

The development of college-wide clubs had compensated somewhat for the social divisiveness of the Kymry Club. Notre Dame's oldest student club was the Athletic Association. It admitted preparatory school as well as college students until 1916, when a separate college athletics association, supervised by the Physical Education Department, commenced. Because membership was mandatory, it was the largest extracurricular organization on campus, embracing both resident and day students. It sponsored two annual events:

Field Day, a program long popular in women's colleges, and Sing Song, an entertainment program unique to Notre Dame.[46]

In 1895, Vassar College became the first women's institution to hold a Field Day, and the event was soon "wildly popular" at its sister colleges. Typically, the college's Athletic Department sponsored campus-wide competitions that concluded in an "elaborate meal." According to a 1904 press report, the athletic performance levels exhibited at Notre Dame's early Field Days matched those of its better-known mainstream counterparts: "Yesterday was field day at Notre Dame of Maryland. Although a convent school, Notre Dame is fully abreast of other female institutions in matters pertaining to physical development and holds, it is said, the record among women's colleges for ball throwing."[47] By the 1910s, the day featured hotly contested competitions in every campus sport. "Various kinds of drills, races, long distance throws and folk dancing" marked the day in the 1920s.[48] In its early years, preparatory school students as well as college students competed, but by 1935, Field Day was strictly a college event.[49] The college had introduced the "all year sport" of horseback riding by the 1910s, and in the 1920s, several benevolent organizations held their equestrian exhibitions on the campus. By the late 1930s, Field Day included a "horse show," and a decade later a riding competition.[50] In addition to horseback riding, Field Day competitions by this time included baseball, archery, golf, swimming, and gymnastics. The entire college community attended Field Day banquets, where Athletic Association leaders announced new officers and distributed the day's prizes. The class scoring highest in the day's events received a trophy. Following the all-college dinner, students entertained with singing, dancing, and comic skits.[51] Interest in Field Day fell off sharply in the 1960s, and by the 1970s the event had disappeared.[52]

Singing clubs and musical competitions were ubiquitous on early twentieth-century college campuses. Notre Dame's 1913 Commencement Week program featured "the singing on the steps," an event popular at women's colleges.[53] Unique to Notre Dame, however, was Sing Song, an annual interclass musical variety show and competition. It had evolved from Stunt Night, a far less ambitious entertainment dating from the college's first years. Sing Song debuted on March 3–7, 1927, the first event held in the new LeClerc gymnasium. With the support of Anne Kean, chair of the Physical Education Department and Athletic Association adviser, it soon developed into an extravagant show that played to standing-room-only crowds. The four college classes competed in music, theme, and stage setting. Each class presented "a marching song, a school song, a song for their sister year, and a 'hit' song which was original and explained their costumes."[54] Professionals from the Peabody Conservatory of Music and the Federated Music Clubs of Baltimore, as well as the drama critic from the *Baltimore Sun*, who volunteered as early Sing Song judges, agreed that the programs were of high quality.[55]

Administrators and faculty concerned about discord between resident and day students saw an all-college event like Sing Song as a way to unify the student body and revive community spirit. They called on all students, resident and day, to participate in the event in some capacity each year, either as a performer or member of the production crew. "Everybody had to be in Sing Song—it was compulsory," a faculty member later recalled.[56] The entire student body, as well as all faculty, administrators, and staff, attended the shows, as did parents of students, alumnae, and Baltimore citizens. But from its inception, a sizable number of students considered the obligatory nature of Sing Song to outweigh its potential unifying benefits. In 1937, one annoyed performer queried, "Has any student who sang on that program benefited in any way whatsoever by it? I say, 'No!'"[57] Others objected to lengthy rehearsals: "The practices morning, noon, and night have made us see a close relationship between Sing Song and Sing Sing."[58] But the majority of students defended Sing Song as "the one thing which united us as a class."[59] When President Frances Smith announced that she had canceled the 1943 Sing Song performance as inappropriate in a time of war, student outrage was so intense that she hastily backtracked.[60] Whatever the circumstances, she promised, the 1944 show would go on.[61] Even after student participation in Sing Song became optional in 1945, most students continued to join in the show. A 1954 graduate credited Sing Song with unifying the campus: "Every kind of talent is brought out. . . . The necessity of working together is proved with a vengeance. For everybody it is a super-charging of class spirit that overflows the whole school. It is the time of the year when the school is more tightly knit and integrated than at any other time."[62]

Bridget Marie Engelmeyer considered the 1950s to be Sing Song's golden age (see figure 6). She felt that it still "engag[ed] the student creatively and, in general, intellectually."[63] But Sing Song was already in trouble. Copyright concerns had ended the long-standing student practice of setting their verses to popular musical scores, a serious blow to the quality of Sing Song music.[64] In 1956, for the first time, a performance was not sold out, and within a decade Sing Song was playing "to an uncrowded LeClerc Hall."[65] When the 1970 Sing Song attacked the college's social code, administrators and faculty were dismayed. "The spirit evidenced both in costumes and in words was disconcerting and depressing," commented the annalist, "because it appeared to convey sneers at many of the college's cherished traditions. . . . This year's

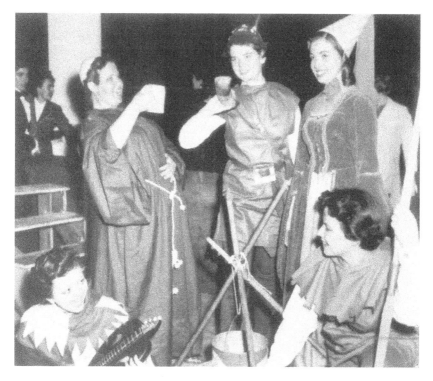

FIGURE 6.   Sing Song dress rehearsal for "Ye Merrie Lads of Sherwood," 1958. Photo from NDMA.

performance, I think, has convinced many of the faculty, reluctantly, that Sing Song should end."[66] While a late 1980s catalog described Sing Song in glowing terms as "a guaranteed sell-out that brings alumnae back to campus each spring," in fact it was barely alive.[67] "It came to the point where you had a fifth of the class participating," recalled a faculty member, and in 1987 the entire junior class opted out.[68] To the relief of administrators and faculty, 1988 marked Sing Song's sixtieth and final performance.[69] "It wasn't a real Sing Song," remembered a long-term faculty member, "and the competition was very weak."[70]

Race at the College of Notre Dame

As with the two-tier class structure, women's religious orders in the United States were also deeply marked by racial distinctions.[71] Until the 1960s, no women's order could be considered "integrated." All-white religious orders received regular applications from black women, many of whom had attended their schools but were encouraged instead to join the small number of all-black sisterhoods.[72] Even the Sisters of the Blessed Sacrament, founded in 1891 by the Philadelphia heiress Katharine Drexel to educate blacks and Native Americans, admitted only white women until the 1950s (when they began to admit a small number of African American and Native American applicants). Drexel explained that in the segregated South, where her order would open and staff schools for blacks, state laws made it impossible to have racially integrated convents. Nor did she wish her order to compete for members with the nation's two small black sisterhoods, based in New Orleans and Baltimore.[73]

Nineteenth-century women's colleges generally had minimal interest in promoting racial integration. Wellesley College awarded its first degree to an African American woman in 1887, Radcliffe College in 1898, Mount Holyoke College in 1898, and Smith College in 1900; the others among the Seven Sisters followed more slowly, with Barnard College in 1928, Bryn Mawr College in 1931, and Vassar College only in 1940.[74] But unwritten racial quotas kept the number of black students very low. Overall, until the civil rights movement of the 1960s, progress toward racial integration on most US college campuses was very slow.

Catholic colleges, founded and staffed by religious orders that admitted only whites, followed this typical pattern. Of the Catholic colleges that admitted African Americans before 1925, none was a women's institution. This discriminatory policy deeply offended African American Catholics. "Apropos our Catholic sisters multiplying 'colleges for the daughters of the wealthier classes,'" wrote a journalist in the 1930s, "it might be remarked that non-Catholics do likewise, but are not usually so stupid as to exclude colored girls."[75] But during Notre Dame's first quarter century, administrators and faculty rarely discussed the racial question. The Collegiate Institute had admitted wealthy students from Caribbean countries during the 1870s and 1880s, but black students were a different matter altogether. The School Sisters of Notre Dame had been educating black children in parochial schools across the country since the 1850s, and in Maryland they had staffed racially segregated schools in Bryantown since 1913 and in Ellicott City since 1923.[76] But the black Catholic population was relatively small, and few families could afford to send their daughters to college. Campus racial attitudes were characteristically southern, revealing the concern that altering the racial texture of the student body would change the college in inauspicious ways. In 1899, Helene Goessmann, head of the History Department, lost her position after commenting in a lecture on the Civil War that she felt no racial prejudice and socialized freely with African Americans. "That was too much for the Southern girls," related a 1901 alumna.[77]

In the 1920s, the college did take a modest step toward racial integration in response to a request from a local black sisterhood. The Oblate Sisters of Providence had staffed Catholic schools for black children in Baltimore since the 1860s, but most of the sisters had little formal education. As state teacher accreditation standards rose in the 1920s, they faced a seemingly insurmountable problem, as Maryland normal schools refused to admit them. They turned to the College of Notre Dame, which assigned faculty to offer college extension courses at the Oblate motherhouse on Chase Street.[78] By 1933, Oblates were commuting to the Notre Dame campus, where they joined white sisters in summer school classes. The college's regular full-time lay students were not in residence during the summer, and neither they nor their parents were aware of the arrangement. This initiative made Notre Dame the first college in the Baltimore area to admit blacks to on-campus programs. During the academic year, however, to avoid the certain opposition of undergraduates and their parents, Oblate Sisters had to take their extension courses in their own convents. Nonetheless, the ice was broken, and by the late 1940s, Oblate Sisters were attending extension classes on the Notre Dame campus "as day students during the week."[79]

Meanwhile, Manhattanville College of the Sacred Heart in New York had become the first Catholic women's college to publicly address the issue of undergraduate racial exclusion. Its president, Grace Dammann, RSCJ, had invited George Hunton, a leader in the Catholic interracial movement, to address the college community on racism as a moral question. Inspired by his speech, Manhattanville students composed a set of resolutions and published them in pamphlet form. *All Men Are Equal* generated intense interest on Catholic college campuses nationwide.[80] In 1938, when Manhattanville announced its intention to admit its first black student, alumnae mobilized in protest. Dammann responded with "Principles versus Prejudices: A Talk Given to the Alumnae on Class Day, May 31st, 1938."[81] Her eloquent affirmation of the moral imperative of racial integration, widely circulated among leaders of Catholic women's colleges, was a national call to action, and by the early 1940s, twenty-one Catholic women's institutions were admitting at least a few black students.[82]

Reform leaders and organizations pressed the College of Notre Dame for action. In a hard-hitting 1942 address to the School Sisters of Notre Dame, the social activist Catherine de Hueck, a leader in the Catholic interracial movement and founder of Harlem's Friendship House, unsettled her audience by blaming Notre Dame's segregationist policy on racial prejudice within the religious order itself. "That we have no black members in our community was especially attacked," Engelmeyer's notes on the talk recorded. Since as yet no sisterhood in the United States was racially inte-grated, the nuns attributed de Hueck's comments to "zeal [that] descended to discourtesy."[83] But change was coming—spurred here as elsewhere in the United States by the obvious contrast between the fight against "racism" in Nazi Germany and typical segregationist practices at home. In the mid-1940s, sociology professor Sister Maria Mercedes Hartmann, a leader of the Foundation of Catholics for Human Brotherhood (established in New York to fight racial as well as religious bigotry), mobilized her faculty colleagues, religious and lay, to call on the board of trustees to admit black students immediately.[84]

While the faculty began to press for racial integration, the student body remained divided. In the mid-1940s, Children of Mary Sodality members debated the question. Maryland was a southern state, and that fact settled the matter for some. "The South must necessarily be dealt with differently from the North," the sodality minutes concluded; "in the South, colored colleges should be separate from the white colleges."[85] Alumnae, parents of students, and Catholic parishioners in large numbers shared that view. Confronted with significant opposition, President Smith and the trustees considered it foolhardy for Notre Dame to act without the permission of the archbishop of Baltimore, Michael Curley (1921–47), who opposed racial integration. As a result, the College of Notre Dame continued to admit only white students.[86]

The students were not wrong to regard the region as "southern" and deeply segregated. Even as Baltimore's commerce and industry developed in the decades after the Civil War, racial division in Maryland intensified. By 1940, 75 percent of the state's black citizens lived in Baltimore and nearby counties, over half within the city itself.[87] Many white Marylanders voted for George Wallace's segregationist campaigns during the 1960s; Wallace won Howard County, bordering Baltimore, in the 1964 Democratic primary. Reflecting this history, the color line was firm at local colleges and universi-ties as well as at lower schools, public and private.[88]

Archbishop Curley concurred. Baltimore was very much a southern city, he remarked in 1932, and "whatever we may think about it, the fact is that the color line is drawn everywhere."[89] Sometimes he drew it himself. The Catholic University of America in Washington, DC, located within the Archdiocese of Baltimore at the time, had no racial barriers until 1920, when its board of trustees, noting the "local race problem" and fearing that black students might "dominate the institution completely," voted to exclude them. Rev. Thomas Shahan, president of the university, and Rev. Edward Dyer, president of Saint Mary's Seminary, easily convinced Curley that this step was essential for the institution to succeed.[90] Despite outrage among local black Catholics, the discriminatory policy continued until 1936.[91] In the 1940s, an aging Curley predicted a rise in racial violence as Communism spread within the black community.[92] He also disapproved of black priests and approved racial segregation during church services and in lay church organizations. Black parishioners, unsurprisingly, did not regard him highly.[93]

At Notre Dame, Frances Smith's reluctance to act without prior approbation from the local bishop was typical of leaders of women's colleges. Once they had episcopal permission, they moved quickly. Trinity College, for example, admitted its first black students in 1948, following the appointment of Patrick O'Boyle, a social progressive, as the first resident archbishop of Washington, DC.[94] Leaders of Catholic men's colleges were typically more independent of local bishops than their female counterparts. Jesuits at Saint Louis University, for example, admitted black students for the first time in 1944 despite Cardinal John Glennon's vehement resistance to the racial integration of parish schools.[95] Following Glennon's death two years later, the Sisters of Loretto at local Webster College raised the question with his liberal successor, Archbishop Joseph Ritter. "Admit any qualified Catholic student, irrespective of color," Ritter told them.[96] Frances Smith and the Notre Dame trustees, on the other hand, were unable to gain episcopal authorization for such a step.

In the 1940s, the racial segregation issue increasingly preoccupied Maryland college and university leaders. Following the 1936 Maryland Court of Appeals decision in *University v. Murray*, the University of Maryland Law School accepted black applicants.[97] However, the university's main College Park campus remained segregated for another fifteen years. Although a black student had enrolled in the Johns Hopkins University graduate school in 1887, he withdrew within two years, and nearly six decades passed before the university registered its first full-time black undergraduate. The Jesuits' Loyola College, adjacent to Notre Dame, had admitted a few black students to graduate and part-time evening programs, but its first black undergraduate did not arrive until 1950. The two local women's colleges, Notre Dame and Goucher, enrolled black students for the first time in 1951 and 1959, respectively.[98]

Notre Dame's transition was eased by Archbishop's Curley's death in 1947. Hoping to have firm data in hand before approaching his successor, Archbishop Francis Keough, about admitting black students to the College of Notre Dame, Smith decided to poll campus constituencies. At a February 1948 assembly of the student body, she read a letter from a Massachusetts-based organization, Catholic Scholarships for Negroes, offering a boarding scholarship for a black student admitted to Notre Dame. Students were to "pray and reflect" on whether the college should accept the offer; the following week they would be asked to sign ballots and vote "Yes," "No," or "Not just yet" on the question. Of 336 votes cast, 179 voted to admit blacks, 86 voted no, and 71 voted "not yet."[99] Smith followed the same process in her meeting with alumnae, parents, and guardians on "the burning question." To the proposal that Notre Dame become a racially integrated college, one faculty member recalled, these groups responded with "a resounding 'No.' . . . People promised to take their daughters out of the college and alumnae promised not to support the college."[100]

Smith was disappointed. However, polling was a risky strategy on an issue that was very controversial in Maryland. Trustees of the elite Bryn Mawr School for girls, located near Notre Dame, had a similar experience when they polled alumnae and parents of students on the question. By a two-to-one margin, respondents had opposed any change in school policy; as a result, the school remained racially segregated until 1963, even as other schools began cautiously integrating.[101] Following the 1954 Supreme Court decision in *Brown v. Board of Education*, the process of desegregating Maryland public schools commenced. Catholic schools in a few southern Maryland counties admitted black children in primary grades, but these institutions were situated in the Archdiocese of Washington. Maryland schools within the Archdiocese of Baltimore remained segregated until 1961, when Archbishop Lawrence Shehan ordered their integration.[102]

In 1948, however, with nearly half the Notre Dame student body against the immediate admission of black students, and alumnae and parents overwhelmingly opposed to the idea, Smith lacked the support she needed to gain the new archbishop's backing. As other Maryland colleges, including Loyola, began to admit some black undergraduates, Smith's only public explanation for keeping Notre Dame segregated—"the time is not right"—incensed social reformers across the country. Protests poured in, first from Caroline Jenkins Putnam, a member of a prominent Maryland family and president of Catholic Scholarships for Negroes. Putnam had the endorsement and powerful support of Archbishop Richard J. Cushing of Boston. Within weeks of Smith's polls, Putnam reiterated her offer of full tuition, room, board, and fees for a black student to attend Notre Dame. Advisory board member Roy Deferrari, who was serving on the board of Catholic Scholarships for Negroes, pressed Smith to accept the offer. However, she explained diplomatically to Putnam, "the situation here is so complex that no decision has yet been reached."[103]

The Baltimore Urban League and the Oblate Sisters of Providence, who by this point had attended the college as special students for two decades, also took up the cause. Sister Liberata Dedeaux, OSP, on behalf of a local girls' boarding school, Saint Frances Academy, asked Smith to "accept colored girls as students in September."[104] Smith contacted Archbishop Keough: "May we ask your advice in regard to the enclosed letter? . . . This racial question is a problem of such serious proportions that we need your counsel and guidance."[105] When Keough did not reply, Smith informed Sister Dedeaux that "the Board has not yet decided what is to be done regarding this question, so I cannot act."[106]

Attacks on the college's all-white policy from Catholic social activists intensified. How, asked critics, could the nation's first Catholic women's college justify its discriminatory stand? The civil rights leader Rev. Arthur C. Winters demanded to know how it could possibly be "imprudent or inopportune for a Catholic school to take a Christian stand in the matter."[107] Smith's replies to such queries reflected the college's financial concerns and the need for women's orders to have episcopal approbation for such a major step. "Attacks from parents & others" also precluded change, Dean Engelmeyer wrote.[108] Smith regretted that Notre Dame was racially segregated, she told Rev. Clarence J. Howard, editor of *Saint Augustine's Messenger*, in March of 1950, but "as yet, I have not been able to secure the necessary permission."[109] That year's Sing Song performance, meanwhile, featured students who "dressed as chocolate angels and sang Negro spirituals in a colorful 'darky heaven.'"[110]

By this time, Catholic Scholarships for Negroes was supporting fifty-one students at thirty Catholic colleges and universities, among them thirteen women's colleges.[111] Hoping to elicit a positive response from Sister Margaret Mary O'Connell, Frances Smith's successor as president of Notre Dame, the organization once again offered a full scholarship and "incidental expenses" for a black student to attend.[112] The new president, bolder than Smith, immediately accepted the award, and in September 1951 two black day students enrolled: a Saint Frances Academy graduate and a transfer student from Morgan State College.[113]

Campus community spirit was notably cooler in 1955 when Sylvia Browne, the college's first black resident student, was admitted. To deter controversy, administrators assigned her to a private room in the apartment of the lay resident director rather than to a dormitory room with a white student roommate.[114] Despite this inauspicious start, Browne, a music major, was a popular student. Although not a Catholic, she was generous with her

FIGURE 7. A 1959 yearbook photo highlighted African American and Latina students, with the caption, "Dolores Thompson waits to perform the next operation on the frog whose heartbeat Awilda Maldonado is measuring. Barbara Helfrick watches carefully. Ann Kennedy, oblivious to distractions, concentrates on her own senior problem." Photo from *Arras*, 1959, NDMA.

talents at chapel services and other campus events. In 1959, her required senior voice recital attracted an audience of four hundred from the campus community, the Catholic Interracial Council of Baltimore, and many Baltimoreans.[115]

The number of black students remained small for the next decade. Only two, both day students, graduated in 1962.[116] A racially integrated faculty developed still more slowly. In 1961, Regina Goff, a member of the Morgan State College faculty, taught in the Human Relations Institute, a summer program funded by the National Conference of Christians and Jews. She was the first African American to teach at Notre Dame, "though we are not emphasizing the fact," wrote the annalist.[117] It was another five years before the sociologist Abraham Davis became "the first Negro to have a full-time position on our faculty."[118] Nonetheless, the arrival of these early African American students and faculty proved to be a breakthrough in Notre Dame's evolution into a democratic college. By the end of the decade, Catholic women's colleges in urban centers were actively recruiting African American students. Their overtures were met with an overwhelming response. When, in 1967, Detroit's Marygrove College offered one scholarship to each city high school in Detroit and Philadelphia, it received a flood of applications. Within a year, African Americans accounted for one-quarter of its freshman class.[119]

At the College of Notre Dame, the increase in minority students was less dramatic until the 1970s. *Columns* still seemed slightly bemused by the prointegration "beliefs of Sister Maria Mercedes," interviewed at the time of the March on Washington.[120] The college also did not experience the kinds of sustained protests that took place on other campuses in the late 1960s, perhaps because it still had relatively few black students.[121] The Student Nonviolent Coordinating Committee's Julian Bond, at the time a state legislator in Georgia, did speak on campus about the Black Power movement in November 1968, and the next year students were offered a course on the sociology of Black Power through a consortium with two other local Catholic colleges.[122] Following the 1968 assassination of Dr. Martin Luther King Jr., faculty members and student leaders initiated Campus Action for Racial Equality (CARE) to advance racial integration in all areas of college life.[123]

In 1974, undergraduate students of color accounted for approximately 4 percent of total enrollment, a proportion that reached 11 percent a decade later.[124] In 1988, Cynthia Edmunds became the first African American to be elected president of the student government.[125] During the 1980s, a Black Student Association became active; 1989 saw the launch of both a BSA newsletter, *Hopes and Dreams*, and a mentoring program connecting black students with professional black women in Baltimore. In announcing this mentoring program, Dean of Students Mary Funke noted that there were far more resident black students than had been the case fifteen years earlier, when most had commuted.[126] The BSA's regular events during the early 1990s, including an African dance and other events in honor of Black History Month, testified to a critical mass of black students on campus.[127] By 2018, students of color (including Hispanic, Asian, and biracial students) represented 55 percent of undergraduate and 34 percent of graduate students; 29 percent of undergraduates were African American.

Lay and Religious: Tension and Cooperation

While all US colleges faced issues related to class and racial diversity (or the lack thereof) on campus, Catholic colleges founded and staffed by religious orders had another realm of diversity to navigate. In founding the College of Notre Dame, the School Sisters of Notre Dame had entered a new and secular realm. Conflicts between cloister values and professionalism appeared early. In the college, lay and sister faculty collaborated in all academic affairs. However, the nuns' cloister rules severely impeded social interaction between the two groups for decades. Convent regulations created divisions in campus activities. In 1948, for example, only lay faculty were invited to a dinner hosted by President Frances Smith to honor Sister Cordia Karl upon her induction into Phi Beta Kappa and Professor Elizabeth Morrissy on her appointment to the Baltimore Board of School Commissioners.[128] In 1953, President Margaret Mary O'Connell honored Professor Anne Kean's twenty-five years of faculty service by inviting "all the laywomen of the faculty" to a banquet. She called on sister-faculty to serve the dinner.[129]

The entire faculty, religious and lay, regretted the inability to share meals. "That was a great deprivation that nuns could not eat with us for a long time. We felt very much for them," recalled Professor Regina Soria. "It would have been so much better if we could have been closer than we were."[130] Lay faculty, too, felt isolated. According to Professor Anne Cullen, "It was . . . harder to get to know the sisters at that time. . . . There was considerable professional contact, but at social occasions, lay faculties pretty much were on their own. . . . [The sisters] were not able to be there with us when we ate."[131]

Occasionally, those excluded from social events were lay faculty. In 1961, for example, only sister-faculty received invitations to a gala reception in honor of the graduating class. The noticeable absence of the lay faculty "cast a slight chill on the atmosphere," observed the college annalist.[132] By this time, however, lay-religious distinctions were fading, even in advance of the reforms of religious life that followed Vatican II. At commencement exercises that year, sister-faculty sat with their lay colleagues on the stage for the first time.[133] The following year, dining restrictions on the sisters ended, to the cheers of the entire faculty. The annalist recorded that the Faculty Seminar Day luncheon that year was "made the more exciting by the participation of the Sisters with the lay folk."[134]

Social interaction was not the only area where the lay-religious distinction played an important role, however. The sisters' numerical dominance on the faculty and the order's legal control of the college limited opportunities for lay faculty to participate in college governance. In the 1930s and early 1940s, religious superiors routinely convened meetings of sister-administrators and sister-faculty to address college policies and problems, with lay faculty not invited. Formal meetings of the full faculty, lay and religious, did not get underway until the 1940s. These early gatherings consisted mainly of policy directives from administrators and progress reports on college projects.[135] Faculty meetings well into the 1960s, according to one sister-administrator, continued to serve chiefly as "a way for the administration to communicate

its policies to the faculty."[136] The faculty's role was to implement these policies. A 1968 faculty meeting illustrates this sequence. A faculty "summer
study committee," charged with drafting a revision of the curriculum committee, presented its report, and proposed that the college establish "an
academic council with jurisdictional powers." When acting president Elissa
McGuire refused to acknowledge "the competence of a faculty committee"
to make such a proposal, the faculty rejected the report of its own summer
study committee.[137]

In the late 1940s, Mother M. Myles Carton, newly elected Baltimore provincial superior and chair of the college's board of directors, briefly institu-
tionalized the lay faculty's second-class position in the area of governance.
She considered the college to be in crisis, as student religious observance on
campus was declining along with, in her opinion, the institution's Catholic
identity. "At present religion does not seem to carry over into the daily lives
of students," she complained. "The courses are too apologetic, not sufficiently practical."[138] She also felt that conflict among sisters on the faculty
was growing, and that the order was in danger of losing its control over the
college. In the fall of 1947 Mother Carton established an Advisory Council,
naming herself as its chair. She appointed ten sister-faculty as regular council members and stated explicitly that "no member of the Lay Faculty may
serve on the Advisory Council."[139] The college president and academic dean
were members *ex officio*.[140] As chair, Carton drew up agendas for the council's
monthly meetings, with its decisions to be "conveyed to the entire college
staff at the general faculty meeting." The council would serve to "keep fin-
ger [sic] on the pulse of the school . . . [and] keep ear to ground to keep the
College vital, healthy, and right."[141]

But members of the Advisory Council did not share Carton's academic
priorities, and meetings were typically tense. At an October 1948 meeting,
for example, Frances Smith requested assistance from committee members
in completing the college's application process for affiliation with the Association of American Universities. Mother Carton, according to the meeting
minutes, promptly "reminded the Council that if the college was fulfilling
its purpose of Catholic education and living up to its philosophy then refusal
of this secular affiliation should not discourage us."[142] Carton, who found
Advisory Council meetings increasingly unsatisfactory, confided to Dean
Engelmeyer that the college "continues to be a source of deep concern and
anxiety for me."[143] In the summer of 1951, the council held its final meeting. But in formation, membership, and focus, Mother Carton's short-lived
Advisory Council graphically impressed on both lay and sister faculty their
marginal status in college decision-making.[144]

From the college's founding, the number of sisters on the faculty and in administrative offices greatly exceeded that of laity. That picture changed quickly in the 1960s, as did faculty perspectives on governance, curriculum, and student life. As long as the faculty was predominantly religious, noted one sister faculty member, "our goals, our viewpoints, were very much the same." But as the proportion of lay faculty members rose, so did diversity in faculty opinion.[145] Notre Dame's first organized faculty forum was a chapter of the American Association of University Professors (AAUP), established in October 1964. It was to play a critical role in advancing faculty rights and defining faculty roles in college governance. Under the leadership of Art Department chair Ruth Nagle Watkins, the chapter soon enrolled a majority of the faculty, both lay and religious.[146] In 1967, the chapter elected a ten-member Faculty Senate to serve as "a clearing house for the views of the faculty and be a two-way bridge of advice to and communication with the administration."[147] Faculty elected colleagues who would represent them vigorously. Professor Anne Cullen, a member of the Modern Language Department faculty since 1959, became the Faculty Senate's first chair. "When you think of what Notre Dame was like," remarked a sister who joined the faculty in the 1960s, the Senate was a bold step. "We were a college run by religious sisters, and it was very authoritarian."[148]

Prior to its 1970 accreditation visit, the Association of Colleges and Secondary Schools of the Middle States and Maryland (MSA) asked Notre Dame's trustees how they "maintain[ed] an accurate and comprehensive knowledge of faculty and student thinking." Up to this point, the trustees had relied almost entirely on reports from college administrators. Now they formed a Trustee Committee on Student Affairs that would "serve at the President's request."[149] They also created a Faculty Affairs Committee of trustees to meet with the Faculty Senate at least three times a year.[150] At their first meeting with George Constable and Henry Knott from the Faculty Affairs Committee in 1970, representatives from the Faculty Senate asked that the chair of the board of trustees be informed of the Senate's unanimous resolution that an elected faculty member join the board of trustees, preferably as a voting member.[151]

Professor Ruth Nagle Watkins, who chaired the AAUP chapter as well as the Faculty Senate at this time, recalled the consternation that followed. Sister-administrators feared that should the resolution be approved, the faculty might decide to elect a layperson as their representative. "We thought we were moving with the times," observed Watkins of the faculty's proposal, "but it was too advanced at that time, without a doubt."[152] The board of trustees took up the Faculty Senate proposal the following year. Acting

president Elissa McGuire strongly opposed it. Quoting a "verbal recommendation" of the MSA evaluating team that the president of the college should
be the only faculty member on its board of trustees, she called on Engelmeyer and board secretary Sister Paula Manning, both faculty members, to
resign. The trustees spurned McGuire's proposition.[153] They also rejected
the Faculty Senate's resolution on the grounds that the board's bylaws
required that trustees be elected by the board. In addition, they believed
that the presence of an elected faculty member might divert the board from
its long-range planning duties or, by creating conflicts of interest, weaken
the president's authority.

While disappointed, the Faculty Senate continued to argue that "the
present system of communication" between the faculty and trustees was
not working. After surveying eighteen colleges, the Senate noted that seven
of these institutions, including five Catholic women's colleges, already had
some faculty representation on their governing boards, three as voting members, four as observers. The Senate saw no merit in the trustees' concern that
a faculty representative might "by-pass the President" or pose a conflict of
interest for the board. In September 1972, the Senate again proposed that
an elected faculty member join Notre Dame's board of trustees as a voting member, adding that if the trustees found this resolution unacceptable,
the Senate was amenable to "the election of a faculty member as a voiced
observer."[154] This time, the faculty campaign met with conspicuous success.
By a wide majority, the trustees resolved "that an elected faculty representative be invited to be present at Board meetings as a voiced observer, according to the norms of parliamentary procedure."[155] The faculty representative
would not attend executive sessions dealing with sensitive matters. A jubilant
Notre Dame faculty elected Ruth Nagle Watkins as its first representative.
By the mid-1980s, the elected faculty representative was a member of the
board's standing committee on academic affairs.[156]

Tenure, salary, and promotion were other areas where treatment of sister-
faculty and lay faculty sometimes diverged. In 1950, Notre Dame had forty-
one full-time faculty at the assistant professor rank or higher; 63 percent
were sisters. Ten full professors, nine of them sisters, were considered to
be tenured. Faculty at lower ranks received renewable two-year contracts.
After a yearlong study of issues related to faculty rank, tenure, and salaries, a
five-member faculty committee in 1966 recommended that faculty members
be eligible to apply for tenure after seven years of full-time teaching, five of
them at Notre Dame. Tenure would continue to age sixty-five; it could be
revoked only for grave reasons. The faculty committee also proposed the
establishment of a permanent committee on tenure, promotion, and salary

issues that, as a subcommittee of the Faculty Senate, would recommend to the president lay faculty qualifying for promotions. The report left unaddressed the matter of tenure for sisters, who formed the majority of faculty. In 1967 trustees asked whether sister-faculty could apply for tenure; the order's representative replied, "Theoretically yes."[157] As it turned out, by the time the college finally resolved its tenure policy, the percentage of sister-faculty was in steep decline.

While lay faculty often felt they had little control over the college and sought to improve their involvement in governance, sister-faculty in turn began to seek benefits that at first were available only to their lay colleagues. Although, over the second half of the twentieth century, colleges like Notre Dame gradually increased salaries and fringe benefits paid to their lay faculty members, there was no corresponding change in reimbursements made to religious orders for the services of sister-faculty and staff. When President Kathleen Feeley took office in 1971, the college provided campus housing for sisters and paid the order a small annual stipend for each sister it employed. The accrediting team of the MSA called on the college to extend to sister-faculty the fringe benefits it provided lay faculty. In response, the 1972–73 operating budget included a $6,000 fund for sisters' medical expenses, and the board of trustees approved sisters' membership in the college's Blue Cross/Blue Shield plan. To offset these costs, tuition for 1973–74 would rise to $1,600.[158]

In this decade, sister-faculty also began to press for the professional benefits enjoyed by their lay colleagues. Professor Maura Eichner of the English Department was the first to test the policy of reserving sabbaticals for lay faculty when she applied for a semester's sabbatical leave. At the February 1974 meeting of the board of trustees, Feeley proposed that a sister-faculty member be eligible for sabbatical benefits equal to "the [lay-equivalent] semester salary which is 'on the books' for her."[159] She suggested using endowment income for this purpose. Sister Bridget Marie Engelmeyer objected. "Abolishing the distinction between financial arrangements for lay and religious faculty—regarding tenure and pensions as well as sabbaticals" was perilous, she said. "Carried to its logical conclusion the trend would mark the end of contributed services [of sisters] as endowment."[160] A majority of trustees, however, approved the president's plan.

The 1976 report of the Rank, Tenure, and Salary Committee of the Faculty Senate was entitled *Up by Our Boot Straps: A Report on the State of Faculty Salaries at the College of Notre Dame of Maryland*.[161] Like the 1960s faculty study, it pertained only to lay faculty salaries. The trustees now turned to the question of the salaries of the majority of the faculty: the sisters. At this time, the School Sisters of Notre Dame order was receiving from the college a $2,375 annual stipend for each sister employed as a faculty or staff member to cover her living expenses. The trustees recommended an increase in the stipend to $3,000 for 1977–78 and called for an investigation of inequities in faculty salaries.[162] The 1978–79 college budget set the total value of contributed services of forty-five sisters at $518,338, based on their lay-equivalent salaries. (The lay-equivalent value of a sister's contributed services corresponded to the salary currently being paid to a lay faculty member of the same rank and years of service.) By 1979, the college was paying the order a yearly stipend of $4,264, plus a retirement benefit of $117, for each sister employed at the college.[163] The annual stipend stood at $9,200 in 1986, and the retirement benefit at $800.[164] These payments were comparable to those provided by many other Catholic women's colleges across the country at this time. Mount Saint Mary's College in Los Angeles, for example, was paying each sister on its faculty and staff $8,000 annually.[165]

Progress continued steadily at Notre Dame of Maryland, and by 1991 the order was receiving 80 percent of the lay-equivalent salary for each member of the sister-faculty. On principle, Feeley opposed paying the full 100 percent. For nearly a century, the sisters' contributed services had publicly witnessed to the religious order's "ownership" of the college. She did not want to lose this crucial testimony. "Whether those [contributed] services should be 20% of the professional salary, 25%, or 15% is a subject for discussion," she wrote. "The percentage must be significant enough to make a difference."[166] Despite shrinking membership, the religious order also continued to support the college generously in loans and gifts. Loans often became gifts, as, for example, when the president announced in 1987 that "the loan of $200,000 by the Generalate of the School Sisters of Notre Dame to the college last year has become a gift."[167] Noting that, at this time, the total annual contributed services of thirty-eight sister administrators, faculty, and staff to the college was approximately $500,000, she estimated that "an endowment of $7 million would be needed to produce this sum."[168] The inexorable decline in the order's membership, however, directly affected its benevolence. The sisters' contributed services to the college by the mid-1990s was only $141,039, a steep decline from the value of those services less than a decade earlier.[169]

Times do change. By 2017, a college that for many decades resisted the introduction of class and racial diversity was looking back into its history for evidence that, as the title of an article on the college's website put it, "Diversity Is Foundational."[170] White students made up roughly 38 percent of the undergraduate student body in fall 2018. Since only 68 percent of full-time students lived on campus, the "day student"—now rechristened a "commuter"—is alive and well.[171] As many of these students join in recent trends seeking professional education, conversations about the place of the liberal arts in the curriculum are ongoing. As the next chapter will make clear, the tension between the faculty's desire for a liberal arts curriculum and the general demand for professional courses and programs has been a constant in the College of Notre Dame's history, as it has been for nearly all US institutions of higher education.

CHAPTER 4

Educating Catholic Women

The Liberal and Practical Arts at the
College of Notre Dame

As higher education for women expanded rapidly in the late nineteenth and early twentieth centuries, and then again from the postwar era to the early twenty-first century, the question of its purpose was constantly raised, and frequently answered, by colleges' curricular decisions. What did women need to know by the time they graduated from college? How were they to be formed for their future lives? The College of Notre Dame, like other women's colleges, Catholic and otherwise, navigated between its aspirations for mainstream educational approbation (measured by accreditation, awards, and students admitted to graduate school) and pressures from students, parents, and church and civic leaders for a practical curriculum preparing students for specific careers as homemakers, educators, social workers, and more.

While men's colleges faced similar questions about the relationship of liberal arts and vocational training, the fact of their institutional existence seldom came under attack. Not so with women's colleges, commonly and correctly associated with radical ongoing shifts in the social, political, and economic place of its female students and graduates. James Cardinal Gibbons, who approved Notre Dame of Maryland's foundation, held liberal views on social issues, especially the rights of labor. In the matter of women's rights, however, he took a reactionary position. "The women of this and other countries confuse 'equal rights' with 'similar rights,'" he pronounced.

"The noblest work given to woman is to take care of her children."[1] He instructed Catholic women not to join the suffrage movement; their place was in the home. Baltimore clergy dependably backed him up. In 1911, Rev. Lucian Johnston blamed the "unchristian, unmoral element" in women's movements for the increasing unwillingness of women to view domesticity and motherhood as their chief sphere of influence.[2]

One way to square these views with the reality of higher education for women was to insist that it was primarily preparation for mothering a family. Gender-specific messages to female collegians from bishops and clergy continued for decades. A 1933 baccalaureate sermon at the College of Notre Dame reflects a prevailing perspective on the potential of educated women and the purpose of women's colleges. After informing the graduates that "we know full well that, both as a group and as individuals, you will not startle the world or the country or the city," President Henri Wiesel, SJ, of Loyola College suggested that they "learn the humble arts of cooking and sewing and mending . . . [and] assume the responsibilities of child-bearing and child-rearing."[3]

The 1940s saw little change. Hunter Ross Guthrie, SJ, a professor of philosophy at Georgetown University and the College of Notre Dame's 1940 commencement speaker, spoke at length on "what precise good . . . women can do in the world today." He concluded that it was their unique role to restore to world culture a sense of reverence, a greater appreciation of the family unit, and a true assessment of suffering, crucial elements that the feminist movement had severely weakened. Guthrie's speech so impressed Baltimore's archbishop, Michael Curley, that he called for its publication and national distribution.[4] At the 1944 freshman cap-and-gown ceremony, thirty-year-old Walter Burghardt, SJ, who was to become a noted theologian and preacher, emphasized that "man can be forgiven for being selfish, but not woman. . . . God willed thus when he made woman to be a help to man." The purpose of the higher education of Christian women, he said, was to prepare them for "the gift of giving and the life of giving."[5]

These harangues, however, could not compete with the messages students were receiving on a daily basis from the faculty and administrators at Catholic women's colleges. In classes, assemblies, official communications, and informal campus interactions where they did not attract the critiques of churchmen, sister-faculty and their lay counterparts encouraged young women to prepare to assume leadership roles in the professions, social service, and political life on equal terms with men; this was their responsibility as educated women. A supplement to the College of Notre Dame's 1933 yearbook not only reprinted Henri Wiesel's unenlightened address but also featured a spirited letter to "My Dear Young Friends" from the order's thirty-six-year-old leader, Mother General Mary Almeda Schricker. Herself a graduate of the University of Munich, Schricker encouraged Notre Dame students "to travel along the narrow road with the few chosen ones who have written upon their banner, 'Self-discipline, Fidelity to Duty, Morality, Religion.'"[6] She said nothing about the duties of motherhood or woman's place in the home. Later college leaders and faculty seized every opportunity to reaffirm that message. An excerpt from the 1968 Christmas letter from the college dean to the student body memorably captures its essence. "Dear Notre Dame Students," wrote Dean Bridget Marie Engelmeyer, "I thought I would give you wishes from the liturgy for Christmas Eve. It tells us something about action, freedom, and the future. . . . 'Loose the bonds from your neck, O captive daughter.' Untie your false freedoms—those that free you only to choose your chains that somehow look like a garland."[7]

Over more than a century, the curriculum at the College of Notre Dame changed multiple times to meet the competing demands of its various stakeholders, often either in tune with or deliberately modeled against developments both at elite Protestant and secular women's colleges and at its sister Catholic institutions. Working-class values underlay an enduring view among ordinary American Catholics that the purpose of a women's college was to prepare students to support themselves between graduation and marriage. In seeking colleges for their daughters, parents tended to favor those offering career-related programs such as education, nursing, and home economics. A majority of Catholic women's institutions readily accommodated this demand. As a result, a college like Notre Dame of Maryland, intent on following the strictly liberal arts curriculum of the Seven Sister colleges, was inevitably smaller than institutions with career-oriented curricula. Over time, however, the college often modified its curriculum to center the liberal arts and provide the kind of professional education needed by three groups of students: in the first half of the twentieth century, young nuns slated to teach in parochial schools as well as upper-class lay students, and, from the 1970s to the present, working- and middle-class Baltimoreans. The costs and benefits of the college's ongoing commitment to the liberal arts lie at the center of its story.

A Liberal Arts Education for Women

The commitment to a serious academic, artistic, and social education for women dated to the college's foundation. The first dean, Sister Meletia Foley, summarily rejected the European-style, seminary-based curriculum of US

Catholic men's institutions in favor of that offered in leading mainstream women's colleges. The institution, she said, was to be "on an equal plane of efficiency with the best Catholic Colleges for men, and inferior to none of the existing Colleges for women."[8] There was, however, considerable variety in the requirements for degrees awarded by Seven Sister colleges in the 1890s. "Vassar gives its degree without Greek; Smith offers three degrees—in arts, in science, and in letters; Bryn Mawr adopts the group system; and Wellesley offers two courses [degrees]," recorded one journalist in 1892.[9] Mount Holyoke offered three degrees: bachelor of arts, bachelor of science, and bachelor of literature. The bachelor of literature degree focused more on modern languages and literature than the BA and less on science and mathematics than the BS. The college introduced it to protect "the integrity of the traditional classical course."[10] There was no consensus about the value of the BS degree; Mount Holyoke abandoned it after four years, Barnard after twelve, and Wellesley after fifteen, although Radcliffe offered it until 1946.[11]

In 1895, the College of Notre Dame, following the Mount Holyoke model, offered BA, BS, and BLitt degrees. For the BA degree, students completed the "regular" or classical course of four years of Latin, mathematics, science, and English, and a course in civics and economics. For the BS degree, they fulfilled a four-year sequence in science and mathematics. Those opting for the "literary" course, culminating in the BLitt degree, were not required to take mathematics, and the science obligation (a second-year course in natural science) was minimal. The curriculum planned for the newly founded Trinity College in 1900 adopted the same degree programs.[12] Within three years, however, Notre Dame dropped the "scientific" course and the BS degree.[13] After 1902, the science curriculum was folded into the general BA degree.[14]

General education requirements included English, chemistry, hygiene, modern language, Latin, religion, and philosophy.[15] Like mainstream women's colleges at the turn of the century, Notre Dame required Latin for admission, but was less demanding in modern language preparation. Mount Holyoke College applicants were expected to have studied Latin as well as two other languages, whereas Notre Dame required two foreign languages, "one Latin, the other German, French, or Spanish."[16] Until the 1960s, the college expected students admitted with a deficiency in Latin to select that language to fulfill their general education foreign-language requirement. A typical Notre Dame student in the class of 1899 earned a total of thirty-six semester hours' credit over the two semesters of her junior year: English (ten hours); Latin (six hours); French (six hours); mathematics (six hours); modern history (four hours); astronomy (two hours); and geology (two hours). In her senior year, in addition to English, Latin, and mathematics, she took philosophy (four hours) and political science (four hours). In both her junior and senior years, she completed required courses in religion and physical education and electives in music.[17] Students fulfilled philosophy requirements in weekly classes of two hours, with freshmen studying logic; sophomores, psychology; juniors, cosmic philosophy; and seniors, ethics.

Like other turn-of-the-century small women's colleges, Notre Dame's four-year course of study allowed few electives. Freshmen and sophomores could elect one course annually in French, German, or history; juniors could choose among courses in civil government and political economy; and seniors were able to substitute French or German for Latin.[18] Some southern women's institutions in this era were even more confining. At Wesleyan Female College in Macon, Georgia, according to one historian, "course requirements were so rigid as to compel students to take the same subjects together throughout their entire college lives."[19] To the north, students in the Seven Sister colleges had somewhat more discretion over their courses of study. At Mount Holyoke, notes another historian, "required work [in 1899] amounted to about half of the whole and occupied most of the first two years. About twenty hours were credited to 'free electives' amounting to five or six courses, mostly in the senior year."[20] With the exception of Bryn Mawr, which by 1902 did not have a Christian doctrine requirement, these institutions also expected students to take a course in Bible history, literature, or interpretation.[21]

Notre Dame's first general curriculum emphasized the applied sciences, especially chemistry.[22] By 1902, the college had added a new basement laboratory, "as the students [had] increased in the chemistry department."[23] This focus was attributable almost entirely to the efforts of Rev. John J. Griffin, who, from his days as a graduate student in chemistry at Johns Hopkins in the 1890s until his death in 1921, was a part-time faculty member at Notre Dame, first at the Collegiate Institute and then at the college. After earning his PhD in 1895, he joined the full-time faculty at Catholic University, but his loyalty to Notre Dame did not diminish. "I am going to do all in my power to build up the Science Department," he told his colleague Rev. Edmund T. Shanahan, "because that will make for accuracy and prove a fine moralizing discipline."[24] Inspired by Griffin's enthusiasm for the new women's college, Shanahan also joined its faculty as part-time professor of philosophy, a position he held until 1917.

Like other liberal arts colleges, Notre Dame slowly made the transition from a general curriculum for all four years to a hybrid model incorporating liberal arts "general education" and the newer university model emphasizing close study of a single discipline. "Before 1910 or 1920,"

Bridget Engelmeyer recalled, "there were three programs, corresponding to majors: English, Science, Modern Language. All had requirements in English, chemistry, religion, philosophy, hygiene, and modern language. The English program required Latin; the science program required mathematics, physics, astronomy, geology in addition to chemistry which was the basic study; the language program required both French and German. There were electives varying from 8 to 12 hours and these were chosen from offerings in any of the majors."[25] Programs in English, modern languages, and science served as proxies for student majors until about 1915, when, according to Margaret Mary O'Connell, "major and minor fields of study were designated for upper-classmen, while freshmen continued to follow prescribed courses."[26]

The science curriculum became a notable strength over the first half of the twentieth century. When College Hall opened in 1910, it incorporated a chemistry laboratory with Father Griffin in charge. "Chemistry," recalled one sister, "was the only science we had then in the college and everybody had to take it."[27] Other science offerings and faculty were still sparse in the 1930s. A chemistry major from that decade reported that she had spent the majority of her time "in the chemistry lab, and worked under Sister Denise."[28] Sister Alma McNicholas, who joined the Biology Department faculty in 1937 as its only full-time member, faced a "skeletal situation, both in physical plant, in materials, in faculty." She and a part-time instructor shared "one room where we had all classes."[29] In 1938, 40 percent of the senior class majored in mathematics, physical sciences, or biological sciences, a trend that continued into the 1940s, when approximately one-third of each graduating class majored in a science field.[30] At Vassar College, on average, 17 percent of seniors in the years 1931–34 majored in a science, a proportion that rose to 26 percent for the years 1943–45.[31]

At Notre Dame the dominance of science among the majors chosen by students was a striking feature in the 1940s and 1950s. The average percentage of bachelor's degrees awarded in the natural sciences by US colleges and universities in the years 1946–50 was nearly 11 percent. By contrast, from 1949 to 1958, about one-third of each senior class at the College of Notre Dame majored in biology, chemistry, or mathematics. In this feature, Notre Dame resembled elite mainstream women's colleges more than Catholic women's institutions, where, in 1955, on average, only 17 percent of students opted to major in mathematics, chemistry, biology, or physics.[32] Science students worked with faculty on their research projects, and spent considerable time in laboratories. A biology major described her program in the early 1950s: "I had Sister Alma [McNicholas] every semester of every year that

I was a student here. . . . As science majors with two or three labs a week always, we were really in class from 8:30 to 4:30."[33]

A notable feature distinguishing Catholic women's institutions was the place and expression of religion in collegiate life. Founding orders saw the provision of a liberal arts education under church auspices as a way to advance women not only intellectually but also socially and spiritually. Religion was integral to institutional identities. Colleges may have varied in their curricular offerings, but all emphasized Catholic moral teachings as a way to support their primary intellectual purpose. According to its 1912–13 catalog, the College of Notre Dame, by offering the student a fine liberal arts education, developed in her "the highest ideals by which to measure her own life; the broadest view by which to value kindly all life; and the deepest sympathy by which to view her life and all life with reverence; hence to give the young woman not only ideals by power—mental, physical, and social—and so to lead her to find power spiritual."[34]

Clergy from Catholic University in Washington and from nearby Loyola College taught courses in religion and philosophy until midcentury, when Catholic theological schools began to admit women.[35] During Notre Dame's first half century, eighteen of the twenty-two priests listed as faculty taught only religion or philosophy. Their turnover was very high, with nearly three-quarters departing after only a year or two. Women first taught philosophy in 1943, religion a decade later. In 1910, religion courses included Christian doctrine, ecclesiastical history, and sacred history.[36] Traditional Bible studies and hagiology (now more commonly known as hagiography) courses offered by sister-faculty since the founding of the college were not considered "real" religion courses. Dean Meletia Foley's hagiology course, for example, gave more attention to the cultural influences of religion than to church doctrine. As a 1917 alumna reminisced, "When I told her I was not sure I wanted to study Hagiology (her particular subject) as I was not a Catholic, she said, 'Are you going to be . . . [visiting] galleries?' I learned it was convenient to know the Saints and recognize them in the great paintings here and abroad."[37]

For decades, religion courses did not carry credits toward the bachelor's degree. By the 1930s, while "required subjects for the degree" included four years of religion courses in Christian doctrine and church history,[38] these courses were over and above the 120-point credit requirement set by Maryland accrediting agencies for a bachelor's degree.[39] However, Notre Dame did not offer majors in religion and philosophy. This was not unusual among mainstream colleges. Harvard, for example, did not offer an undergraduate concentration in the study of religion until 1974. Catholic women's colleges began to move in this direction in the 1940s. Saint Mary's College (Indiana) introduced a graduate-level program in theology in 1943, and undergraduates were soon majoring and minoring in the field. President Madeleva Wolff, CSC, considered religion to be the college's "strongest and pivotal department."[40] In the 1940s, sister-faculty at the College of Notre Dame introduced a few innovative courses in "applied religion," focusing on such topics as the life of Christ, the liturgy, "life problems of the average Catholic," and Christian principles for non-Catholic students.[41] Nonetheless, until the 1960s religion and philosophy courses, like those at other Catholic colleges, concentrated firmly on the *Summa Theologica* of Saint Thomas Aquinas.[42] "We never really studied the other philosophers," recalled the 1937 alumna (and later faculty member) Virgina Geiger, SSND, "except to find out really what was the matter with them."[43]

"Practical Work" and Vocational Training

As the liberal arts curriculum developed, there were constant questions about whether and how to add what College of Notre Dame catalogs of the 1910s called "practical work" courses that were "purely elective and [did] not count toward the A.B. degree," including religion, art, music, business, and domestic science.[44] These disparate subjects, while banished from the regular curriculum, were nonetheless regarded as necessary to a college education for several reasons. Religion, for example, while required for all students, was not recognized by Maryland state accreditors as a subject worthy of college credit. Hence, it could not be part of the official curriculum leading to the degree.

Physical Education

From their inception, eastern women's colleges emphasized physical education. In the 1860s, wrote Mary F. Eastman, Matthew Vassar "provided a gymnasium and provided for out of door sports. He instituted a professorship of physiology and hygiene, and made its incumbent 'resident physician' and supervisor of sanitary arrangements."[45] The subject was among Rev. John Franklin Goucher's top priorities when he became president of the Woman's College of Baltimore in 1890. He established a faculty position in physiology and bacteriology and introduced a four-year physical education requirement. The college's innovative curriculum, as well as its state-of-the-art gymnasium and swimming pool, was attracting national attention.[46]

Stirred by Goucher's progress, Meletia Foley took steps to improve Notre Dame's limited facilities and curriculum, and by 1896 the *Baltimore American* was praising its "well-appointed" gymnasium, where a qualified teacher gave daily instruction in physical culture.[47] "Three good tennis courts" were in place in 1906, and plans were underway for improved baseball and croquet playing fields. Most women's colleges had always offered gymnastics and calisthenics classes, and by the mid-1890s team sports, especially basketball, baseball, and field hockey, were becoming extremely popular. Critics argued that these "men's sports" encouraged competitiveness and aggression, features prejudicial to the nation's future mothers. The 1901 Radcliffe commencement speaker, Professor Charles Eliot Norton, warned his audience against field hockey and similar competitive sports: "But there is one form of vulgarity to which you young women are in these days especially susceptible and exposed. . . . You are tempted to rival your brothers in sports fit for men alone."[48] Notre Dame students heard the same message. When a Baltimore journalist detailed his repugnance at the sight of the students playing baseball, and condemned the college for allowing it, Rev. Lucian Johnston countered that there was no resemblance between the way women and men played baseball, and reassured the reporter that there was little danger that "the Sisters of Notre Dame are become inoculated with dangerous 'modernism.'"[49]

The College of Notre Dame's emphasis on outdoor physical education activities suggests a somewhat limited indoor program. Early students played tennis, basketball, and croquet, and in season rowed or skated on the campus lake. But winter offerings amounted to little more than marching around the campus. By 1910, a temporary gymnasium had appeared, and students enjoyed bowling alleys with "two runs [and] . . . the standard outfits of ten pins and duck pins" in the basement of the new College Hall.[50] Initially the absence of indoor facilities was not a major drawback since college women generally preferred outdoor sports to indoor gymnastics. "All the girls' colleges have splendid gymnasiums, . . . [but] they are not popular," wrote a *Cosmopolitan* reporter.[51]

Dean Foley and physical education instructor Lucille Johnston agreed that the complete separation of college and academy students was crucial. However, as lack of funds made this goal unrealistic, they encouraged students to form a college Athletic Association, "entirely separate from that of the Academy," and tried to appease them by improving outdoor sports facilities.[52] Few eastern colleges yet had golf courses of any size. Vassar had constructed a nine-hole course in 1896, but for three decades used the land for other purposes. Wellesley and Yale had nine-hole courses by 1917.[53] Following a campus chestnut tree blight in 1916, Foley hired a Baltimore Country Club professional to design a four-hole golf course. By the following March, to loud cheers from the Athletic Association, the course was being laid out on land bordered by Charles Street and Homeland Avenue. But when Foley died two months later, college officials dashed the students' hopes by calling a permanent halt to the ambitious golf course project.

Notre Dame's outdoor basketball teams competed in the 1920s and 1930s with local institutions, among them the Lutheran-affiliated Maryland College for Women, the Methodist-affiliated Western Maryland College, the College of William & Mary, and Goucher College.[54] According to an alumna of the era, for these intercollegiate competitions "the whole college went to the games in buses."[55] Outdoor campus facilities at this time consisted of "six tennis courts, a hockey field and volley ball court, archery targets, jumping pit, and track."[56] In 1925, the Association of Colleges and Secondary Schools of the Middle States and Maryland (MSA) recommended that the college construct a proper gymnasium.[57]

With the debt incurred to construct College Hall in 1910 finally paid off in 1926, the trustees readily approved the college's next capital project, a gymnasium and auditorium building. Following traditional practice, they borrowed $450,000 and engaged Henry A. Knott as contractor. A first-class gymnasium, named in honor of Alix LeClerc, a founder of the Congregation of Notre Dame, opened on February 16, 1927. Students celebrated by "testing their strength by climbing about on the apparatus and swinging from bar to bar."[58] It was the largest physical education facility in Maryland, boasting a large swimming pool, basketball and dodgeball courts, and an indoor baseball field. Its auditorium seated over one thousand, with excellent acoustics for dramatics, a balcony for moving pictures, music rooms, a dance studio, and bowling alleys.

In the 1930s and 1940s, the physical education requirement was three hours weekly for freshmen and sophomores, and two hours weekly for juniors and seniors; all students had to pass an annual swimming test. Given that 85 percent of higher-education institutions in the mid-1940s demanded only two years of physical education, these were relatively serious requirements. By 1960, the college offered a two-credit elective course for students aiming to work as athletics instructors or coaches in public schools.[59]

Career Training

Other "practical work" subjects, beyond religion and physical education, were more fraught. Turn-of-the-century mainstream women's colleges offered many courses in art and music but resisted awarding academic credit for them. Because men's colleges did not emphasize the arts, administrators of

FIGURE 8.   Archery students, 1930s. Photo from NDMA.

female colleges worried that if courses in so-called ornamental studies were offered for academic credit, critics would view their institutions as glorified finishing schools. Founders of early Catholic women's colleges agreed. Yet these fields were areas of strength, and highly popular with both students and parents. In 1912–13, the College of Notre Dame's Art Department claimed to "offer to all students, whether possessed of natural artistic talent or not, a broad introduction into the field of fine arts." Music and art faculty alike encouraged students to pursue electives in these fields and to consider careers in them.[60] By 1915, elective courses in art and music were carrying credit toward the bachelor's degree. The college introduced an art major in 1937.

Domestic science was another area that carried significant cultural freight, as it raised the still-troublesome question of the purpose of women's education. By the early twentieth century, men's colleges had begun to add "utilitarian subjects" to their curricula, and public coeducational institutions were developing a range of gender-specific vocational programs.[61] Educational leaders and the popular press alike pressed the nation's women's colleges to follow suit. Every female student should complete a course in "the science of house- and husband-keeping," *Cosmopolitan* argued in 1901. "While mathematics will be a very good thing for giving balance to her mind and poise to her conceptions generally, she can't feed them to the baby; and she can't talk Greek to the cook."[62] G. Stanley Hall, a psychologist and the president of Clark University, reiterated that message in 1909, advising parents that since their daughters were likely to marry, they should attend schools with "well-developed departments in domestic science, music and art."[63] A Scripps College Special Committee on Vocational Training, notes historian Helen Lefkowitz Horowitz, "argued that the first two years of required courses should address women's distinctive attributes while the final two years should center on prevocational training. Public health, child training, social research, business, and art" were more suitable fields of study for women, most of whom would become child-rearers, than a strictly liberal arts curriculum.[64] Vassar's president, Henry Noble McCracken, upon adding a euthenics division to the school's curriculum in the 1920s, declared that "women must be trained for their careers of home-making." As a result, he continued, "Under the new regime a student can major in euthenics just as she might in English or History. . . . We are interested in teaching women to make the family and the home a worthwhile place to stay."[65]

Although Vassar's euthenics program was short lived, vocationally oriented curricula grew in popularity in the 1930s, and calls from prominent male educators for women's colleges to introduce home economics programs escalated in the 1940s as postwar pressure mounted for women to leave the workforce.[66] According to a 1947 study of graduates of accredited colleges by Ernest Havemann and Patricia Salter West, 31 percent of female college graduates had never married. This contrasted with a 13 percent rate for all adult American women. The rate for Catholic women was much higher, at 48 percent. "When our statistics are controlled for all possible extraneous factors, the findings are still the same," the authors observed. "Age for age, family for family, college for college, and course for course, the Catholic girls are still overwhelmingly the most likely to remain spinsters . . . whether they go to Catholic colleges or non-sectarian schools. Our statistics give no clue as to the reason."[67] Since a majority of Catholic women college graduates attended coeducational institutions, the explanation does not lie with the heavily female faculties of the Catholic women's colleges. Nonetheless, these colleges in the 1940s and 1950s experienced growing pressure from church authorities to adopt gender-differentiated curricula. In a major

1945 address to members of Catholic Women's Associations, Pope Pius XII extolled "schools of domestic economy, whose object is to make the child and girl of today the woman and mother of tomorrow."[68]

Most Catholic women's colleges immediately responded to demands from church and public officials for career-related programs in education, nursing, and home economics. From its establishment in 1906, according to Mary B. Syron, the College of New Rochelle had a "fairly well developed" Department of Domestic Economy that offered "a general course, elementary cooking, fancy and invalid cooking, general sewing and laundry work." By 1918 it also offered a BS degree (in secretarial studies) and a BM degree (in music).[69] In the 1910s, Trinity College students could follow a sequence of noncredit courses in domestic science.[70] Saint Mary's College in Indiana organized its domestic arts courses into a three-year program at this time, and conferred its first degrees in the field in 1917. With the passage of the Smith-Levering Act (1914), funding agricultural extension courses, and the Smith-Hughes Act (1917), promoting home economics teacher-training programs at land-grant colleges, home economics and a variety of other career-oriented programs appeared in most Catholic women's institutions. More than 40 percent of the graduates of the College of Saint Scholastica in Duluth, Minnesota, from its foundation in 1926 until 1941, earned BS degrees.[71] At this time, the college was offering programs in medical technology, library science, home economics, nursing, journalism, commercial education, secretarial training, medical records, speech, and education. Such practical curricula promised to prepare students for reliable employment before marriage.

In the 1920s, in contrast, Notre Dame continued to award only the BA degree; students could concentrate in biology, chemistry, English, French, German, or history, and by 1935, mathematics and Latin. Core requirements for all students included English, history, Latin, a modern language, philosophy, and a science, and for Catholic students, religion.[72] Students seeking a full course in studio work each year had to spend an additional year at the college to earn their bachelor's degrees.[73] A 1910 statement explains the sisters' perspective: "It is the endeavor of Notre Dame of Maryland to impart a training which affects the life of woman in all her aspects, sending her forth into the world with the ability to see, feel and act for her own life and for others, in the fullness of distinctively feminine power that is not an imitation of masculine force. This is accomplished by a suitable curriculum, of which letters, history, mathematics, science and philosophy are the fundamentals."[74] Notably missing from this suitable feminine curriculum was a domestic arts program. Because the College of Notre Dame proscribed vocational subjects, Catholic families viewed it as a "bluestocking" sort of institution. They preferred colleges with broader curricular options. As a result, in 1936, while New Rochelle College, then the largest of the Catholic women's colleges, graduated 142, Notre Dame graduated only 22.[75]

Notre Dame offered fewer fields of concentration in the 1920s than secular women's institutions, but its curriculum, like theirs, focused on the liberal arts. Music and art remained noncredit subjects. As national demand for music and art teachers in public elementary and high schools was increasing, however, administrators and faculty of women's colleges began cautiously to revise their policies. In 1919 Vassar allowed "advanced practical work" in speech, music, and art to count for 8 of the 120 credit hours required for the degree, "a proportion assuredly small enough to preclude the charge of our becoming a school of music, art, or dramatics."[76] Smith College administrators had also begun to discuss "pre-vocational majors" to accommodate students aiming to pursue careers in medicine and public health. By 1930, the college was offering majors in landscape architecture and dramatic arts.[77] Both colleges awarded the same number of credits for studio hours in art as for laboratory hours in the sciences.[78]

Sister Frances Smith, who took office as president of Notre Dame in 1935, followed these mainstream initiatives. Catholic Church leaders viewed social work as an appropriate profession for women, and "a country-wide movement of Catholicity in this direction" was already well underway in 1916 when Notre Dame offered its first sociology course, with fieldwork.[79] Smith moved quickly to expand a program in social work, promising skeptics that it would "encourage Catholic social workers to restore charity to the place in Christian economy that our Blessed Saviour destined for it."[80]

In the 1930s, Notre Dame had long since expunged from its curriculum the few electives in business and domestic science it had offered in its initial years, and Smith's effort to restore the BS degree, defunct since 1903, to prepare science majors for employment in industry and science, did not survive the Depression decade.[81] In fact, by this time, Notre Dame's only "professional" offering dating from its 1895 foundation was a minor in the field of education. Now, as demand for public school teachers, especially in home economics, music, and art, rose during the 1930s, the field of education became the key "practical work" component in the college's liberal arts curriculum.

The development of Notre Dame's education program paralleled that of elite eastern women's colleges. Mount Holyoke College had introduced a Pedagogy Department in 1899 to meet the rising demand for public high school teachers.[82] Such programs were popular among students, but the rising concentration of alumnae in schoolteaching almost immediately met with sharp press criticism. The journalist Frances Abbott, for example, remarked that "in the whole roll of Vassar alumnae over seventy-five percent are engaged in matrimony or teaching—two time-honored professions which certainly could be followed by women who had never received the degree of A.B." Over three-quarters of Radcliffe's 1900 graduating class opted for teaching positions, and Abbott estimated that at this time, "probably two-thirds of every class at Vassar, immediately upon graduation, experiment more or less with pupils."[83] A US Bureau of Education survey of five of the Seven Sister colleges confirmed that between 31 and 74 percent of their 1912 graduates became teachers.[84]

Mary Van Kleeck's 1918 study of the marital and occupational status of 16,700 college women reported that 70 percent had been in the labor force, with two-thirds working as teachers.[85] This state of affairs reflected the fact that schoolteaching was the most accessible career open to early twentieth-century female college graduates. Even elite women's colleges that prided themselves on their strict liberal arts curriculum justified education programs, as well as studio programs in music and art, that would prepare students for professional careers in these fields. As Smith College president William Allan Neilson observed in 1918, "In one respect we have long been vocational: we have prepared large numbers for the vocation of teaching. We have few courses explicitly announced as for teachers; but the vocational element has pervaded our curriculum and determined the choice of studies far more than is indicated by these special courses."[86] In their direct link to postcollege employment opportunities, the education programs at women's institutions resembled the expanding commerce and engineering programs at men's colleges.

From its 1895 founding, the College of Notre Dame had offered a single noncredit "teachers' course" to prepare students for careers in public high school teaching. Concern over the quality of teacher training in Maryland was rising in this era. There was general agreement among educators that the Maryland State Normal School was inferior to normal schools in New England, New York, Georgia, and California, as its curriculum did not reach the four-year high school level and it admitted some students directly from the sixth and seventh grades.[87] In 1910, Goucher College and Johns Hopkins University joined forces to offer what the *Baltimore Sun* described as a "special college course for teachers . . . conducted independently of the regular collegiate instruction of the institutions." Classes met on weekdays in the late afternoon and on Saturday mornings during the school year, and both institutions offered credit toward the BA degree for satisfactory completion of course work.[88]

In 1915, Notre Dame's Department of Education offered courses in educational psychology and the history of education. By 1922, it had added courses in teaching methods and secondary school management, as well as a practice-teaching requirement at the high school level. Following a 1923 MSA inspection visit, the Maryland State Board of Education confirmed that Notre Dame students "who have completed the required courses in education" would receive state teachers' certificates, qualifying them to teach in public high schools.[89] All members of the class of 1926 qualified for certificates from the Maryland or Pennsylvania State Board of Education.[90]

Students at women's colleges in the 1930s were, of necessity, more career focused than their predecessors.[91] In a depression economy, public school teaching promised dependable employment. Colleges, public and private, responded quickly. In 1934, the Maryland State Normal School in Towson developed into a four-year teachers' college offering a BS degree.[92] Among Catholic institutions, demand for programs in education also surged. Between 1933 and 1938, three-fifths of the graduates of Saint Benedict's College (Minnesota) became teachers, and this percentage was not unusual.[93] The College of Notre Dame introduced majors in art, music, and speech, fields in high demand among teaching positions in public high schools. In 1936, Frances Jackman Civis, supervisor of music in the Baltimore public schools, joined the faculty and, with music instructor Sister Theresine Staab, developed a major in public school music, with specializations in elementary- as well as high-school-level music.[94]

The sharp rise in births following World War II resulted in a critical teacher shortage in public elementary schools. As the population of children entering these schools escalated, education departments at women's colleges expanded to meet the new demand for lower schoolteachers. In 1948, half the respondents to an American Association of University Women national survey of female college graduates were engaged in schoolteaching.[95] Even as employment opportunities in other fields widened in the 1950s, graduates of Catholic women's colleges, more than their peers from similar institutions, continued to favor the teaching profession. Forty percent of Notre Dame graduates in this decade reported teaching as their employment, a proportion that continued in the 1960s.[96] College administrators and faculty defended this concentration, arguing that the education of "a dedicated corps of young women" for teaching careers was fully in keeping with the college's liberal arts tradition.[97] They justified adding courses in education to the traditional liberal arts curriculum in religious as well as populist terms: "Because the community which conducts the college is a religious order of the Catholic Church devoted especially to teaching," said President Margaret Mary O'Connell, "the college—although not thereby committed—has a special dedication to the training of teachers." At the same time, she added, "the college considers the teaching profession one of vital importance in a democratic society. . . . It desires to make this field of service available to its best students."[98]

Parochial Schools and Teacher Education

Catholic female colleges like Notre Dame had a long-standing and distinctive interest in the field of elementary education. At their 1884 meeting at the Third Baltimore Council, the church hierarchy called on every parish to build an elementary school. While this goal was never achieved, the number of parochial schools increased dramatically. Bishops took it for granted that teaching sisterhoods would provide faculties for these institutions. State teacher certification was becoming a matter of urgent concern for Catholic schools nationally, and young sisters had to be educated for parochial school classrooms. Since Catholic men's colleges would not admit women, and bishops, for the most part, opposed sisters' attendance at public institutions, the burden rested on the women's colleges. Orders that sent sisters to study at state colleges met with resistance from some of these institutions as well. In the early 1920s, for example, Benedictine sisters seeking teacher certification in Minnesota enrolled in the state normal school in Duluth, since the College of Saint Scholastica, a Duluth institution conducted by their order, did not have an education department. When Minnesota's attorney general decreed that it violated state law for practice teachers in public normal schools to wear religious dress, the sisters commuted to the teacher's college in Superior, Wisconsin, a state that did not prohibit the wearing of the religious habit.

Catholic women's colleges quickly became central agents across the country for the professional advancement of teaching nuns. By 1934, Saint Scholastica had added an education department, and the state of Minnesota permitted sister-students at the state college in Duluth to earn practice-teaching credits in local parochial schools under its direction.[99] For the most part, Catholic women's colleges fulfilled this commission nearly single-handedly. Neither hierarchy nor laity contributed financially to the education of parochial schoolteachers, although several noted bishops provided indispensable moral support for the cause. As early as 1890, for example, Bishop John Lancaster Spalding of Peoria, Illinois, pushed for the education of sisters to the normal school level. And in 1911, Rev. Thomas Shields, a professor of education at Catholic University, was the force behind the establishment of a Catholic Sisters' College there.[100]

Local bishops and pastors' intense pressure on sisterhoods for school-teachers dictated that young nuns be educated on a part-time basis via extension and summer programs. They fulfilled minimum state certification standards in this way, although achieving bachelor's degrees could take a decade or more. Most sister-teachers entering parochial school classrooms were inadequately prepared relative to their public school counterparts. This situation explains why Catholic women's colleges were more willing than other female institutions to introduce summer schools. Harvard University had opened its summer school in 1871 and an extension school in 1910. Between 1909 and 1911, Johns Hopkins University introduced its College Courses for Teachers, a part-time degree program that allowed employed teachers to take professional and liberal arts courses part time during the school year and in summer sessions.[101] By 1908, the Education Department of the four-year-old College of Saint Angela (New Rochelle, New York) had opened extension branches in Manhattan, Albany, and Brooklyn.[102] Elite women's colleges, however, resisted the concept of extension courses until late in the twentieth century. Vassar's 1949 program of extension courses for local citizens lasted only three semesters.[103] In contrast, educating employed adults had been integral to the mission of Catholic women's colleges from their inceptions. In this group, the College of Notre Dame was a pioneer in offering a part-time program for sister-teachers. Over one hundred students enrolled in its first four-week summer school in 1897; they included members of other local orders as well as School Sisters of Notre Dame, all eager to "avail themselves of the opportunity for advanced study."[104] Dr. J. G. Wells taught elocution; Rev. C. Warren Currier, psychology; and Dr. Richard Malcolm Johnston, English literature. Sisters from the college faculty taught mathematics, English grammar, geography, and psychology. Daily assemblies addressed pedagogical techniques.[105]

Following their novitiate training, a majority of the School Sisters of Notre Dame taught full time in local parochial schools and enrolled in the college's summer sessions to prepare to qualify for state teaching certification. Notre Dame's 1922 summer school, directed by Professor Elizabeth Morrissy and staffed by thirteen sister-faculty, registered eighty-three sisters and twenty-five candidates in the order. Since the religious order did not yet require applicants for admission to its ranks to hold a high school diploma, many students enrolled in the "high school summer course," a program in English, history, mathematics, foreign language, and science.[106] Of seventy-eight sisters in the 1925 summer school, only 46 percent were taking "college work."[107] At the behest of local bishops, a few Jesuit men's colleges advanced the cause by offering summer and extension programs so that nuns teaching in church schools could earn credits toward state teaching certification. In 1919, Fordham University added a six-week summer course "for the various teaching communities."[108]

By 1929, the School Sisters of Notre Dame admitted only applicants with high school diplomas, and most of the seventy-three summer school students that year were taking post-high-school-level courses.[109] The college's extension program gradually included not only the summer school but also Saturday morning and Monday afternoon courses held during the academic year. By 1934, the Notre Dame Teacher Training School, located at the order's motherhouse, had opened. Accredited by the Maryland State Department of Education in 1936, it prepared young sisters to qualify for state teaching certificates in elementary education after two full years and one summer of study.[110] The summer session remained popular. Enrollment in 1959 was 546, the largest in its history.[111]

Notre Dame faced opposition from public school authorities over the question of whether its education students could fulfill their practice-teaching requirements in local public schools. Until the 1930s, students fulfilled practice-teaching requirements for high school certification in just two girls' high schools: one located on campus, the other in downtown Baltimore.[112] Notre Dame's Education Department faculty had to observe practice teaching under conditions that did not meet minimum state standards.[113] Unlike students from other local colleges, however, who fulfilled their practice-teaching requirements in public high schools, Notre Dame students were denied this option because public school authorities feared public outcry should nuns in religious habits enter public school classrooms to observe practice teaching by their students. College administrators resolved the impasse by assigning only lay faculty to oversee practice teaching by Notre Dame students in the public high schools.[114] After the college added a program in elementary education in the next decade, lay faculty supervised practice teaching by lay students in public schools, and both lay and religious faculty supervised sister-students' practice teaching in local parochial schools. Many members of the Notre Dame faculty felt that sister-students, like their lay peers, should be able to practice teach in local public as well as parochial schools.[115] At this time, however, New Mexico's practice of employing nuns in religious habits as public school teachers had become a contentious topic of national debate, with a court challenge on constitutional grounds underway. So practice teaching by Notre Dame's sister-students remained confined to parochial schools.[116]

By the mid-twentieth century, the competitive spirit that traditionally marked relations among Catholic sisterhoods had begun to dissolve in the face of a common predicament. National and state requirements for the professional preparation of teachers, nurses, and social workers were rising rapidly, and young sisters needed proper training before embarking on professional careers. In her 1941 doctoral dissertation, Sister Bertrande Meyers, SC, called for major reform in the education of nuns. The initial response was negligible.[117] However, at the 1949 meeting of the National Catholic Educational Association, the issue came to center stage. Sister Madeleva Wolff, CSC, president of Saint Mary's College in Indiana, gave a stirring lecture titled "The Education of Sister Lucy." She galvanized her audience. Her message, which attracted intense national interest among Catholics, especially religious sisterhoods, became a catalyst for the Sister Formation Conference, which held its first national congress in August 1952.[118]

The Sister Formation Movement called for and facilitated the proper professional education of young sisters before they undertook full-time careers in church schools, hospitals, and social agencies. The idea met with considerable opposition from lay educators as well as ecclesiastics, who were concerned that it would delay the number of teachers available for expanding parochial schools. Foremost among lay critics was Roy J. Deferrari, a member of the College of Notre Dame's advisory board. In his judgment, traditional motherhouse training programs and part-time summer programs were adequate preparation for elementary school teachers.[119] That position mobilized sisterhoods across the country. At the College of Notre Dame, English professor Sister Maura Eichner answered Deferrari's position. For her, the Sister Formation Movement, with its "broad intellectual as well as spiritual and professional training," brought her hope for lasting reform: "We look forward," she said, "to the promise of the young religious."[120] Superiors of sisterhoods across the country united to ensure that their young sisters held college degrees before they began their professional work as teachers, nurses, and social workers in church institutions.

The College of Notre Dame's Education Department had prepared lay and sister students for certification as high school teachers since 1895. Although the State of Maryland had accredited the department in 1921–22, students could not major in the field until 1954. At that time, Provincial Superior Vitalia Arnold, chair of the college's board of trustees, proposed that Notre Dame apply for state certification for an elementary education program.[121] This would allow junior sisters, most of whom were preparing to teach in elementary schools, to complete a specialized course in education in the order's Teacher Training Institute, located close to the college campus, and, at the same time, earn a liberal arts degree from Notre Dame.[122] Dean Bridget Marie Engelmeyer and several faculty members objected unsuccessfully that prominent eastern women's colleges were at this time reducing their education programs. Arnold's plan, they argued, would weaken the college's reputation among liberal arts institutions.[123]

In 1957, Engelmeyer later recalled, the board of trustees "accepted the [Teacher Training] Institute as the Bellona Avenue Campus of the College of Notre Dame of Maryland, expanded its faculty and curriculum, and gave its graduates the bachelor of arts degree."[124] Henceforth, sisters and candidates in the order who met the college's entrance requirements would matriculate at Notre Dame. By 1958, the new elementary education program was in place. Since cloister rules still restricted candidates, novices, and junior sisters from attending classes with lay students, the college faculty repeated their lectures at the Bellona Avenue campus.[125] Sister Delia Dowling, later professor of mathematics and dean of the college, had a typical educational itinerary for a young sister in this era. After graduating from high school, she entered the School Sisters of Notre Dame in 1963 and, as a novice, resided at the Bellona Avenue campus. There she completed two years of general studies courses taught by Notre Dame faculty. After making her religious profession, she became a day student on Notre Dame's main campus, taking classes with lay students and graduating in 1967.[126] At this time, applications to the order were falling off sharply, cloister rules were disappearing, and by 1970 the Bellona Avenue campus had all but closed. The catalog for that year stated simply that "the college provides some courses for students who are SSND."[127]

Seeking Mainstream Recognition

Curriculum decisions—what to require, what to offer, which departments to staff and fund—were always of intense import as Catholic women's institutions sought to gain recognition within church and mainstream higher-education circles. When the Association of Catholic Colleges was founded in 1899, under the direction of the rector of Catholic University, the College of Notre Dame immediately applied for membership.[128] In 1920, the Maryland State Board of Education placed the college on its list of standardized institutions.[129] Two years later, the New York State Board of Regents of the University of New York formally registered the College of Notre Dame of Maryland's bachelor of arts program.[130] To qualify for inclusion on the "fully approved list" of the MSA, an institution had to enroll at least one hundred students. Notre Dame met this requirement only in 1925.[131] The college gained membership in the American Council on Education in 1926 and in the Association of American Colleges in 1927.[132]

While Catholics at this time were making strides in social and economic integration into the American mainstream, in a number of ways they remained religious "outsiders." Well into the twentieth century, the College of Notre Dame remained unfamiliar to most Baltimore Protestants, and stereotypes of nuns, endemic in American culture, lingered. George Constable, a Princeton graduate and convert to Catholicism who later became the college's legal adviser, recalled his first impression of the institution in the 1930s: "To a non-Catholic [it was] an unknown quantity sitting up here on the hill, not reaching out to the community. . . . It was a forbidding place to a non-Catholic driving by, not knowing anything about it."[133] Sister Frances Smith, who became president of the college in 1935, set out to change that image. Among her primary objectives was to see Notre Dame included on the "approved list of colleges" published by the Association of American Universities (AAU), a major national higher-education organization.[134]

Founded in 1900 by fourteen PhD-granting universities, the AAU for many years maintained an "Approved List of Colleges and Universities" whose graduates qualified for admission to the graduate programs of AAU member institutions. Inclusion on the AAU list represented national recognition of an institution's quality. It was also a precondition for institutional membership in other prestigious educational associations and honor societies, among them Phi Beta Kappa and the American Association of University Women. In the 1930s, approval by the AAU was the top qualification set by Phi Beta Kappa's committee on qualifications.[135] In 1917, several Catholic women's colleges appeared for the first time on the AAU list: the College of Saint Catherine (Saint Paul, Minnesota), the College of Saint Elizabeth (Morristown, New Jersey), and Trinity College (Washington, DC).

Dr. Adam Leroy Jones, a representative of the AAU Committee on Classification of Colleges in the late 1920s, discouraged Notre Dame administrators from applying for inclusion on its approved list. He had, he said, "some doubts as to whether the time is yet ripe for the College of Notre Dame to apply."[136] In February 1932, however, the AAU accepted a preliminary application from Notre Dame president Sister Ethelbert Roche.[137] Ryland Newman Dempster, registrar at Johns Hopkins University, completed an on-site inspection in October. At its November 15, 1932, meeting, the AAU committee took final "adverse action" on Notre Dame's application. "A point . . . which the Committee found to be crucial," Jones told Roche, "was in the records of graduates of the college in 'leading graduate, professional and research institutions.' The amount of such evidence . . . was so small that it was quite impossible for the committee to make a favorable recommendation." Jones rejected Roche's defense that the college's enrollment was small and that many alumnae married soon after graduation: "On the reasoning of the Association a college which is doing really first rate work will stimulate a fair percentage of students to go on for more advanced study."[138]

Sister Frances Smith, who succeeded Roche as president of Notre Dame in 1935, believed that since Notre Dame qualified for the AAU approved list "in every particular, except this of graduate study," its chances for approval were good. In 1939 and again in 1942, however, preliminary applications did not lead to success, both times on the grounds that few students went on to graduate study.[139] Roy Deferrari offered to help prepare a new application. As secretary-general at Catholic University, during the 1930s and 1940s Deferrari enjoyed a national reputation for providing expert counsel on academic matters to sister-administrators of Catholic women's colleges. Constrained by episcopal oversight and cloister regulations, the sisters appreciated his assistance. At Notre Dame, he became Frances Smith's trusted intermediary with the AAU. But reliance on external advisers like Deferrari was a risky strategy. In Catholic circles, many continued to hold very conservative views on women's education. Notre Dame's lengthy and ultimately unsuccessful campaign for AAU recognition revealed some of these dangers.

Like many male academics of his generation, Deferrari did not believe that women and men should have identical educations: "The qualities of womanhood are such that women can on the whole best attain the desired ends of a liberal education by concentrating on subjects ordinarily not so popular with men, and sometimes by receiving a type of instruction rather different from that applied to men."[140] In a lecture at Notre Dame in 1945, he spelled out exactly what that instruction ought to be: "The most important and most obvious contribution [of the Catholic women's college] . . . is the training of women to become home-makers."[141] In advising Smith, Deferrari consistently minimized AAU criticism of Notre Dame's deficiencies in producing alumnae with advanced degrees. As he saw it, the college was unable to gain AAU approval because of its low enrollment. If Notre Dame wanted to reach the average size of the Catholic women's colleges on the AAU list, it should abandon its commitment to a strictly classical curriculum and introduce professional majors.

Despite Deferrari's conviction that low enrollment was the college's foremost problem, AAU secretary Frank Bowles's comments on Notre Dame's unsuccessful 1942 preliminary application focused on the need for the college to send more students to graduate study.[142] When a 1946 application was again rejected,[143] Smith, trustees, and faculty, who had anticipated that the college would finally join the fifteen Catholic women's colleges on the association's list of approved institutions, were perplexed and disheartened.[144]

Deferrari showed no interest in pursuing the AAU's suggestion that the college submit a "new preliminary application" for consideration at its fall 1948 meeting.[145] Nonetheless, Smith swiftly prepared a new preliminary application, taking pains to provide an extra copy of the graduate school enrollment data incorporated in it.[146] Before the scheduled 1948 committee meeting took place, however, the AAU voted to terminate its accrediting function permanently.

Notre Dame's long campaign for AAU recognition was over.[147] But despite failing in its ostensible goal, the quest itself had produced some vital reforms in the areas of faculty qualifications, curriculum, and the rate of alumnae earning graduate degrees. A March 1959 faculty survey of a total of 653 graduates in the decade 1949–58 regarding graduate study yielded a response rate of 84 percent. Among the respondents, 61 percent were married, and 8 percent were nuns; 8 percent held graduate degrees, and 6 percent were currently enrolled in graduate programs. Some alumnae commented that the college ought to have done more to prepare students socially for postcollege life, whether in graduate schools or in first jobs. "The great problem [for the Notre Dame graduate] is a certain naiveté and consequent insulation or isolation in the face of less intellectual, more worldly fellows," one alumna wrote, adding that a graduate of Notre Dame does "not show well against her Vassar and Holyoke sisters (at least at first)." But the faculty also polled the universities where Notre Dame students had completed or were currently enrolled in graduate programs, regarding their academic performance relative to students from other colleges. Forty-two universities reported on a total of 155 students. They considered 10 percent to be superior, 43 percent above average, 44 percent average, and 3 percent unsatisfactory.[148]

As the AAU battle in the 1930s and 1940s played out behind the scenes, Notre Dame leaders became acutely aware of the need to gain mainstream recognition of the college's academic quality, beginning with encouraging its graduates to go on for further study but expanding to other areas as well. In the 1950s, Notre Dame leaders and faculty helped students to apply for graduate fellowships and awards. Between 1950 and 1954, three students won Fulbright Scholarships for graduate study.[149] "Unsolicited publicity of a very helpful nature" followed a 1953 *Mademoiselle* article reporting that Notre Dame ranked fourteenth in a national survey of fifty-three women's colleges that had averaged at least 5.6 scholars per 1,000 graduates annually since 1946.[150] For the first time, too, the college sought visibility and public recognition for the professional achievements of its sister-faculty as well as its lay faculty. Whereas tradition had long dictated that sisters receive their graduate degrees in absentia, five sisters attended their 1944 commencement

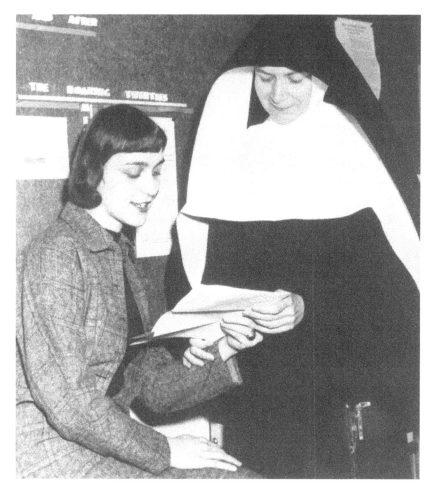

FIGURE 9.   Dolores Warwick '58 and Maura Eichner, SSND. Photo from NDMA.

ceremonies at Catholic University and publicly accepted their diplomas.[151] When English professor Sister Maura Eichner's book of poems took second place in the national 1951 Poetry Awards contest, the entire campus celebrated.[152]

Notre Dame faculty also began to encourage students to enter national writing competitions, a common practice at mainstream colleges and increasingly at Catholic colleges as well. Winners of national contests brought desirable publicity to their schools. In 1946, a sonnet submitted by a junior at the College of Notre Dame took first place in the annual contest of the American Classical League.[153] Eichner earned national recognition not only for her own prize-winning poetry but also for her success as a teacher of writing.[154] In the 1950s, her students gained recognition in writing competitions for college students. In 1953, a Notre Dame junior took first place in the national poetry contest sponsored by the *Atlantic Monthly*.[155] A senior won first prize in the 1955 poetry contest as well as several other prizes in the same contest.[156] In the 1957 poetry competition, a junior won first prize. Of 464 entries in the magazine's 1958 poetry contest, Notre Dame students accounted for nine of the top twenty entries.[157] They continued to rank high among *Atlantic Monthly* poetry contest winners in the 1960s, taking first and fourth prizes in 1968, first and second prizes in 1969, and first and third prizes in 1970.[158] Eichner once explained why she preferred the *Atlantic* contests over other competitions: "The application blank . . . did not give the name of the college you attended. . . . The judges reading our students' work did not know whether they came from Barnard or . . . from Radcliffe, or a small women's College in Maryland. We did better that way."[159] Notre Dame's successes in these contests significantly raised its visibility.

In 1948, when the Association of American Universities discontinued its practice of reviewing colleges, the College of Notre Dame had not yet achieved its goal of inclusion on the association's approved list. Yet its lengthy and painful struggle to meet AAU standards in admissions, faculty quality, curriculum, endowment, and the rate of alumnae earning graduate degrees proved to be a watershed in its movement to participate on equal terms within mainstream higher-education circles. At the same time, by midcentury the small college was conspicuous among Catholic women's institutions for its excellent science and mathematics programs and the disproportionate success of its students in national college writing competitions. As the higher-education landscape changed dramatically in the postwar decades, Notre Dame was well prepared not only to maintain a strong liberal arts curriculum for traditional undergraduates but also to shift toward a new population of adult students in Baltimore.

The Late Twentieth Century

During the College of Notre Dame's first half century, decisions about its curriculum responded to contingencies, including the faculty's desire for a prestigious liberal arts curriculum, students' sometimes competing desire for 'practical' education, bishops' demands for schoolteachers, accreditors' requirements, and more. The second half of the twentieth century featured similar curricular responses to changing circumstances.

Patriotic demands, for example, led college administrators and faculties to re-confront the question of "practical" education during World War II.

Federal and state government agencies and the American Council on Education called on colleges and universities to offer "accelerated courses" in technical fields to meet the needs of the crisis.[160] Notre Dame's faculty, noting that "educational authorities do not consider a general program of acceleration in women's colleges either necessary or desirable,"[161] only reluctantly conceded to national pressure to modify requirements for the degree. They followed elite women's colleges in responding rather grudgingly; in July 1948, when Vassar awarded degrees to the final group of students in its three-year wartime accelerated plan, it took pains to keep the ceremony entirely separate from the May graduation of those who had completed "a normal four-year program."[162] Noting the need for medical technicians, Notre Dame did allow high-ranking science and mathematics majors to accelerate. In 1943 the American Medical Association authorized Saint Joseph's Hospital and Notre Dame's Biology Department "to conduct a training school for laboratory technicians." After completing the program, students could "take the examination of the American Society of Clinical Pathologists for registry as medical technicians."[163] Once the war ended, Notre Dame, following leading secular women's colleges, returned to its traditional four-year degree program and strict liberal arts curriculum.

The question of professional education was also ever present. President Margaret Mary O'Connell exaggerated when she declared that until 1950 "the vocational motive . . . [was] not reckoned with at all."[164] But in 1943, faculty and administrators had again rejected the idea of introducing home economics and other professional programs. Chemistry professor Sister Mary Agnes Klug summed up the majority view: "[We] decided it was better to be a small college. You cannot do everything well, and if you start spreading yourself too thin, it is not very good. So if you hold to doing the one thing that we do, which is to give the B.A. degree and do a good job with it, it would be better than trying too many things."[165]

The 1950 inspection report of the Association of Colleges and Secondary Schools of the Middle States and Maryland noted that, unlike most of its peer institutions, Notre Dame remained committed to the liberal arts: "The only degree granted is the Bachelor of Arts and this represents very well the nature of the training given. Very little indeed of an applied, or semi-professional, or vocational nature has been permitted to enter the regular program." Except for religion, where "the lecture method seemed to be employed exclusively, with a corresponding relaxation of attention on the part of the students," the report found that "stimulating discussion and original thinking marked all classes."[166]

In 1950, President Sarah Blanding of Vassar College publicly opposed the introduction of vocational programs for women, such as home economics and family management.[167] Few leaders of Catholic women's colleges agreed with her stance. Notre Dame, however, was an exception. By this time, its emphasis on the liberal arts and sciences distinguished it from most of these institutions. According to a national survey of major fields chosen by sophomores and seniors at Catholic women's colleges in the mid-1950s, 38 percent of respondents selected a professional major, with education, at 18 percent, by far the most popular choice. No other single professional field accounted for more than 5 percent. Among the liberal arts and sciences, 17 percent of respondents enrolled in one of the physical sciences, 15 percent in English or a foreign language, 12 percent in history or a social science. Music and art majors represented 5 percent.[168] Schoolteaching, with its direct connection to the liberal arts, continued to dominate the chosen professions of Catholic women's college alumnae in the 1950s. While Notre Dame graduates during the decade 1949–58 found employment in a widening range of occupations, 40 percent reported that they engaged in schoolteaching.[169] This high rate continued into the next decade: "Of the 1964 graduating class of 142 girls," noted Margaret Mary O'Connell, "58 [41 percent] went into teaching."[170]

There remained a direct correlation between the college's liberal arts curriculum and its perennially small enrollment. As a sister-administrator noted in 1973, competing Catholic women's colleges had "at least eight B.S. programs . . . physical therapy and business . . . home economics, which we have never had."[171] Taught properly, some faculty argued, popular professional programs need not violate Notre Dame's commitment to the liberal arts. "Anything can be taught as a liberal art as long as the main thrust is the strengthening of the intellectual powers and the widening of cultural horizons," Dean Engelmeyer told alumnae at about the same time. "So taught, subjects preparing for a gainful occupation are validly within the liberal arts."[172]

These comments were made against the backdrop of a serious enrollment crisis that came close to forcing the college to merge with nearby and newly coeducational Loyola College (described in the conclusion). President Kathleen Feeley's priority was to attract more students. She expanded Notre Dame's traditional mission by considering a new applicant pool: high school graduates who were employed full time, a demographic group unlikely to interest other prestigious local colleges.

Notre Dame had had limited and generally unsuccessful prior experience with adult education, aside from its long-running extension programs for religious sisters seeking to qualify as parochial school teachers. An evening program in Italian, introduced in the 1940s, had failed, as had a noncredit adult education program. "The adult education has not been successful," President Frances Smith reported to the advisory board in 1950. "We conclude that Baltimore is very little interested in Adult Education in the strict sense of the word. Generally, credit is wanted for whatever course is taken."[173] Two decades later, however, Notre Dame returned to the adult-education idea to attract a new kind of student. In 1972, Feeley designed a Continuing Education Program for women who were at least twenty-five years of age and not in the labor force, "who wish to continue their education in search of a degree, to enlarge their 'world view,' or to prepare for volunteer or paid employment." They would take classes with the regular college students.[174] She also commissioned academic dean Sister Mary Oliver Hudon to design an "innovative program at the graduate level." When a proposal for such a program in management and human services garnered little faculty support, Feeley turned her attention to developing a program for employed adults of both sexes that she envisioned as an alternative to a night school for this population.[175] She was confident that they would welcome the opportunity.

Notre Dame's Weekend College, introduced in the 1970s, while rooted in the venerable extension school movement, seemed a radical concept in US higher-education circles at the time. The college offered adult women and men employed full time an opportunity to earn bachelor's degrees from a private college on a part-time basis. Faculty at elite women's colleges had generally opposed such initiatives. Barnard College president Rosemary Park (1962–67) recalled that she "thought that Barnard was a good place to hold weekend classes for women. . . . The husbands were home over the weekend; they could take care of the children for several hours and the women could come to Barnard Saturday morning. With an occasional week or so in the summer, a good deal of college credit could be earned. I tried this out on the Barnard faculty and there was absolutely no support."[176]

Other institutions also tested the weekend-college concept. In 1963, with the support of a Ford Foundation grant, Goddard College, a coeducational institution in Plainfield, Vermont, offered an Adult Degree Program that allowed employed adults to complete requirements for the college degree on a part-time basis. It was, according to a later Goddard catalog, "the prototype of the current intensive low-residency model . . . [and] the first program of its kind in the country."[177] In the 1970s, Yale College admitted a few nondegree special students who took courses on a part-time basis. A Degree Special Students Program followed in 1981, but enrollments remained small.[178]

Of course, while still uncommon in US higher education in the early 1970s, the education of adults on a part-time basis had had a long history at Catholic women's colleges, which had educated young sisters in this way for decades. Among Catholic women's colleges, in 1974 Chicago's Mundelein College became the first to develop a Weekend College for employed lay adults. At the College of Notre Dame, Feeley saw in the Goddard and Mundelein models a means to preserve the college's mission to women's higher education. With limited prior consultation with faculty, Feeley proposed to the board of trustees that the college introduce a Weekend College as soon as possible. When faculty protested "the precipitate development of the Week-End College without due recognition of faculty committee action," administrators insisted that the institution's alarming financial and enrollment situations required immediate action.[179] In the fall of 1975, the Weekend College registered its inaugural class of eighty-one students (sixty women and twenty-one men). Their median age was thirty-two; 15 percent were African Americans.[180] The new program was the first of its type in Maryland.[181]

In developing the Weekend College in the 1970s, Notre Dame built on its traditional commitment to educating employed women. Young sisters had been earning bachelor's degrees on a part-time basis at Notre Dame for three-quarters of a century, so faculty took the Weekend College's innovative calendar in stride. However, they had strong reservations about its potential effects on the liberal arts curriculum. There was a critical difference between the young nuns who had formed the college's contingent of part-time students until the 1960s and the Weekend College's part-time students. Whereas sister-students traditionally majored only in the liberal arts and education, the new Weekend College students, employed in a wide range of fields, looked for career-oriented courses. The Weekend College, as a result, would offer majors in business and communications as well as in the liberal arts.

For over sixty years, administrators, trustees, and faculty at Notre Dame had periodically considered adding professional programs. Each time, by a wide margin, they had opposed the move, with the sole concession being the introduction of a major in education in 1954. While other Catholic women's colleges had been offering professional programs for decades and were open to adding more, Notre Dame in the mid-1960s remained dedicated to its original mission. As President Margaret Mary O'Connell wrote in her 1964–65 annual report, "We have nothing to attract students but our dedication to learning and to the liberal arts tradition: no programs in nursing, secretarial, business, medical technology, etc., as do many other colleges; and we are not interested in dissipating our energies on trying to support such a multipurpose program."[182] She did not take into account how the popularity of the education major, introduced ten years before, had affected enrollment in other fields of concentration. By 1966, nearly 20 percent of the graduating class majored in elementary education, a figure equal to that of majors in science and mathematics combined.[183]

To provide career-oriented programs for employed adult students in the Weekend College, the college had to diverge from its traditional liberal arts focus. In September 1975, the *Baltimore Sun* reported that this exciting new program was already causing "some faculty members [to] worry about academic quality."[184] Supporters of the Weekend College argued that it posed no threat to Notre Dame's integrity as a liberal arts institution. Not only were general education requirements for Weekend College and day college students identical, but except for the human services program, so were the majors offered.[185] Full-time as well as part-time faculty taught in the day college, the Weekend College, the continuing education program, and the graduate program, "wherever they were needed."[186] Students in professional fields would be required to complete general education courses in the liberal arts and encouraged to elect more. At the same time, traditional liberal arts majors would enjoy wider opportunities to explore diverse career interests by choosing electives in professional fields.

In fact, the 1970s saw a revolutionary shift in the college's curriculum. While in the middle of the decade the college offered only three interdisciplinary concentrations (creative communication arts, social science, and urban studies),[187] by the end of the decade Weekend College students seeking a BA or BS degree could choose among six areas of concentration: business, communication arts, computer information systems, human services, liberal arts, and religious studies.[188] In addition, a cooperative Weekend College program, developed with local Saint Joseph's Hospital, offered a BS in nursing for registered nurses.[189] The Communications and English Departments had merged by 1979.[190]

At its 1980 visit to Notre Dame, the Middle States Association Evaluating Team expressed concern about the curricular direction of the college. While evaluators praised the high quality of the liberal arts program, they offered "one overall piece of advice. . . . Don't try to do everything; curb programs."[191] Despite this admonition, the 1980s were to see more new programs introduced via the Weekend College, among them a master of arts in human resources and a postbaccalaureate certificate in mathematics education.

The Weekend College's enrollment rose so swiftly that by 1983, full-time undergraduates constituted only one-third of the college's total enrollment of 1,764. At the same time, enrollment in liberal arts fields of study was declining. The largest departments were now economics/business management, communications, biology, and education. In contrast, history / political science comprised 6.6 percent of declared majors, and English and foreign language departments together accounted for 6.3 percent. In 1985, nearly half (47 percent) of undergraduate students were opting for professionally oriented majors; only about 6 percent majored in the sciences, English, and foreign languages combined.[192] These trends led a worried Faculty Senate to set as a top priority for 1985 "the vitality of the day division, i.e., the regular college, as distinct from the adult divisions."[193]

A 1985 *U.S. News & World Report* national survey of college presidents on the best US colleges strengthened growing faculty apprehension that career-oriented programs, introduced via the Weekend College, were diluting Notre Dame's traditional status as a liberal arts college. The survey singled out the College of Notre Dame of Maryland for its emphasis on career preparation and ranked it "among the ten highest colleges having fewer than 50% of its students in liberal education," noting particularly that 25 percent of its degrees went to majors in the health professions.[194] "We are receiving congratulations for being in the top ten," wrote the college annalist grimly, "but it is obvious that most people do not know what top ten."[195] President Feeley, however, whose controversial expansion of professional programs had probably saved the college, was, on balance, pleased with the results. "To the timeless value of the liberal arts," she wrote, "Notre Dame has connected timely innovations which mark its education as current and relevant."[196]

Catholic women's colleges still reflect the tension between a commitment to the liberal arts and a desire both to maintain financial stability and adequately serve the local community. In the early twenty-first century, some have enormously expanded their professional education programs, including offering online degrees. Some have virtually eliminated liberal arts majors, with those subjects relegated to a few general education requirements. Others, like the College of Notre Dame, have continued to try to balance the two. In 2018, Notre Dame enrolled 805 undergraduate and 1,263 professional / graduate women, along with approximately 300 men (mostly graduate students). Its most popular majors, including nursing and business, reflect trends in other sectors of higher education. But at the same time, it continues to offer a general liberal arts curriculum to a very wide range of traditional and adult students alike, and to maintain its identity as a place that balances both scholarship and practical education.

CHAPTER 5

Sectarian or Free?

Catholic Identity on Trial in the 1960s and 1970s

As the identifying feature of founding religious orders, Catholic belief and practice was an integral force in the culture and evolution of Catholic women's colleges. In the late nineteenth century, the Roman Catholic Church, with its heavily immigrant and working-class membership and unpopular religious teachings, faced a relatively inhospitable social environment. Although American Catholics were making rapid strides in economic mobility, a strong separatist mentality continued to affect their social interaction with the Protestant majority. Religious sisters had always welcomed Protestant girls in their boarding academies and worked hard to develop congenial relations with mainstream citizens of all faiths. Their approaches to women's higher education responded to mainstream stimuli, even as they were corollaries of a Catholic educational philosophy. But a Catholic spirit was felt everywhere on campuses, expressed most notably in formal worship services and college rituals as well as the requirement that students take religion courses.

Moreover, religious orders, both male and female, as the principal benefactors of church-related colleges, wielded extensive power in their governance. Unlike many Protestant churches that supported affiliated colleges, Catholic dioceses expected religious orders that established colleges to finance them internally. Since 1895, the School Sisters of Notre Dame had provided property for the College of Notre Dame, erected buildings, and paid the salaries of lay faculty and staff. Members of the order contributed lifetime service as faculty and administrators. Major lay donors were few, tuition revenues small, and financial support from the archdiocese minimal. As a result of both legal and financial structures, the order's control over the college and its administration was nearly complete for decades.

The weakening of legal ties between religious orders and their colleges, on the one hand, and of the daily formal expression of Catholic identity, on the other, is often attributed to the liberalizing results of the Second Vatican Council (1962–65). But this chapter argues that these changes were in large part the result of major legal cases in the 1960s and 1970s that established whether and how church-affiliated institutions of higher education could access federal and state funds for construction, salaries, scholarships, and other critical needs. Long-standing religious tensions in American society came to the fore in the 1960s and 1970s when the College of Notre Dame, as well as other colleges sponsored by denominational bodies, received state and federal funding to advance their educational missions. Extended legal contests forced the college for the first time to defend its religious affiliation in a mainstream forum. With mixed success, Notre Dame's trustees, administrators, and faculty testified before a divided legal system that the college's intellectual mission and its identity as a Catholic college were not in conflict. The *Horace Mann* and *Roemer* cases proved to be turning points for colleges like Notre Dame. In their wake, small women's colleges became more ecumenical in their modes of religious expression, more inclusive of laity in all areas of campus life, and better prepared to meet future challenges from the church community and the wider society.

This outcome was the result of a series of events rife with ironies. During the 1950s and 1960s, the College of Notre Dame came to apply for federal and state funding primarily because it could not find adequate funding from Catholic sources to finance dormitory, lab, and classroom construction. Partly as a result, its understanding of what "Catholic identity" meant in practice changed between its foundation and the early 1970s. Student religious practice and college governance alike reflected larger cultural trends in higher education across the decades, but events were also driven by the personalities of specific archbishops, religious superiors, and college presidents, among others. In the 1940s, eager to grow but severely constrained financially, college leaders sought episcopal permission for a fundraising campaign within the Archdiocese of Baltimore. When Archbishop Michael Curley denied the request, his exercise of control over the sisters and their college proved a defining moment in a way he could not have anticipated, setting off a chain of events that resulted in the legal severance of the college from its founding religious order and in its increased reliance on government funding instead of private philanthropy. When the college subsequently received a grant from the State of Maryland, it became a lightning rod for widespread public protest. As a defendant in two major court cases centering on the principle of separation of church and state,[1] the college had to defend both its academic integrity and its Catholic identity before a skeptical American public. These legal battles had important consequences for all church-related institutions of higher education. They shaped the direction not only of the College of Notre Dame but of its sister institutions across the country, as their traditional understanding of their public mission and intellectual goals changed rapidly and radically.

Fundraising and Growth in the Twentieth Century

As chapter 2 recounted, financing for Catholic women's colleges was always a major concern. Little support was available from bishops, so Catholic female colleges relied heavily for support on their founding orders and, to a lesser extent, on alumnae and a few benevolent laity. In contrast, church boards and religious benefactors often assisted Protestant-affiliated women's colleges in significant ways. A college's fiscal situation mattered deeply not only for keeping the lights on and paying regular bills, but also because a strong endowment enabled an institution to improve its academic offerings. By the 1890s, the Regents of the University of the State of New York were already suggesting the adoption of a minimum endowment standard of $500,000 for institutions of higher education seeking accreditation.[2] The Baltimore sisters realized the crucial role that endowment would soon play in accreditation decisions, but the College of Notre Dame as yet had virtually no cash endowment. Dean Meletia Foley and her colleagues moved quickly to ensure that the college met standards for inclusion on the New York Regents' list of approved colleges. They reached that goal in 1902 when the University of the State of New York approved Notre Dame's bachelor's degree as "appropriate preparation for advanced study."[3]

But building an adequate endowment remained a serious concern for the college. According to the Carnegie Foundation for the Advancement of Teaching, an approved college in 1906 held a minimum "productive endowment" of $200,000, including only "funds invested in securities and realty from which permanent and dependable income may be secured available for the uses of the institution."[4] The "permanent endowment" Notre Dame claimed, representing the contributed services of sister-faculty, had grown to an estimated $875,000 by 1930.[5] However, building a "productive endowment" that would finance major expenditures and building projects was a slow process.[6] Sister Frances Smith, inaugurated as president of the college in 1935, made the endowment a primary goal. To advance that end, she proposed that the college's board of directors, all of whom were religious sisters, set up an advisory board of prominent lay Catholics to assist the college, especially in the area of fundraising.[7]

As chair of the board of directors, Provincial Superior Philemon Doyle spoke for many members of the order when she questioned whether appointing lay members to the proposed advisory board would pose a threat to the order's control over the college. George Constable, Notre Dame's longtime lawyer, explained the sisters' concerns: "The whole college then was dominantly the sisters. . . . There was great fear [among] the sisters who had built up and run [the college and] were responsible for the organization. They didn't want to lose control. If they brought lay people in, then they might easily lose control. . . . Also, there was a vague background fear that the archbishop might become too dominant—not any particular archbishop, but they didn't want the diocese, so to speak, to be running the college, directly or indirectly. That was a sort of latent issue."[8] Leaders of other Catholic women's colleges in the 1930s and 1940s shared this wariness of "outsiders."

Archbishop Curley suggested the formation of a "preliminary committee" to plan the new advisory board. Its eight members included Curley; Doyle; Smith; Sister Alba Mattingly, superior of the campus religious community; Monsignor Harry Quinn, rector of the cathedral; Rev. John Barrett, superintendent of archdiocesan schools; Roy Deferrari, dean of the graduate school at Catholic University; and Margaret Meade, president of the Notre Dame Alumnae Association.[9] At the preliminary committee's first meeting, Mother Doyle nominated Elizabeth Morrissy, a lay faculty member trusted by the sisters, for a seat on the advisory board. Other committee members disagreed, arguing that lay members of the board should be prominent professional, business, and philanthropic leaders drawn from the greater Baltimore community. After all, the annalist noted, "the college is not sufficiently known even in our vicinity."[10]

By the fall of 1936, a twelve-member advisory board was in place. Two priests and four laymen constituted the regular membership, while the archbishop, four sisters, and a laywoman were members *ex officio*. In addition to the eight preliminary committee members, membership included H. Winship Wheatley, president of the Bar Association of the District of Columbia; Francis Litz, PhD, teacher of English in the Baltimore public school system; the alumna Marie Hebner, governor of the Maryland chapter of the International Federation of Catholic Alumni; and Sister Denise Dooley, dean of the college.[11] At the board's first meeting, Archbishop Curley, conscious of Mother Doyle's continued uneasiness, made it clear that lay members were to play a purely consultative role. The college was "the absolute and exclusive property of the School Sisters of Notre Dame," he emphasized, and "no organization of any kind whatsoever may be formed to interfere, even in the slightest degree, with the ownership of Notre Dame . . . [or] with the discipline, regulation and conduct of said College, except in so far as the [religious order] may accept advice or counsel."[12]

The board at once formed committees on scholarships and fellowships, library development, and expansion and publicity. Smith announced her plans for a $200,000 campaign to build a productive endowment. "Accrediting agencies," she noted, "have recognized the principle of 'Living Endowment' of Catholic colleges, at least in a half-hearted way—living endowment signifying monetary evaluations for contributed services of religious men and women in the cause of education," but these services did not provide funds to finance building construction, purchase equipment, or even cover operating costs. "Because the College of Notre Dame wants to be in the front rank of education today," she said, "and because accrediting agencies are considering the financial as well as the scholarship end, the college has started an Endowment Fund."[13] Mother Doyle, as chair of the board of directors, made a symbolic first gift of $1,000. Contributions, however, were slow to appear. In 1943 the productive endowment fund totaled only $27,230, mainly in the form of government securities and a mortgage on Camp Notre Dame in New Hampshire, contributed by the order.[14]

Smith and the advisory board recognized the need to professionalize their fundraising methods. In 1944, with the college's half-century mark approaching the following year, they decided to engage a professional fundraising firm to conduct a "Dream Drive." Archbishop Curley, whose approval they needed in order to proceed, did not favor this tactic. He instructed Smith to commission James E. Almond, president of a Chicago development firm, to conduct a feasibility study. Almond promptly pronounced it a bad idea. "The College of Notre Dame of Maryland has been so ably conducted," he informed Smith unctuously,

> that even your best friends simply cannot visualize any institutional needs which you have not already provided. The immediate reaction to practically every Baltimore approach we made was—"Notre Dame is such an ably conducted institution that additions to its structure would be merely carrying coals to Newcastle." Those more closely in touch with your expansion ambitions declared without hesitation that Baltimore had several other fund-raising problems which were much more immediate and acute than yours. . . . There was a belief that you could

expect a greater measure of financial support for your ambitious plans if you would wait a little longer, until the more pressing needs of local voluntary philanthropy had been met. . . . You would be very unwise to consider a Notre Dame fundraising campaign at the moment.[15]

A gratified Curley confided to Almond that "people here are not interested in Colleges or College education. . . . If young ladies want it, well then they get it and pay for it."[16]

Archbishop Curley had effectively thwarted the "Dream Drive," and other private fundraising efforts remained discouraging. An Alumnae Association appeal to endow a Golden Jubilee Alumnae Graduate Scholarship netted only $20,000 over two years. Students raised $6,000 for the building fund by May of 1945, and Parents and Friends of Notre Dame of Maryland, founded in 1940, contributed $2,644 in 1946. Smith's rigorous schedule of speeches before private gatherings on behalf of the endowment produced discouraging results.[17] Finally, in 1947, in response to significant and persistent pressure from powerful laymen on the advisory board, Curley approved the college's request to conduct a Golden Jubilee Fund Drive.[18] Promotional literature acknowledged the significance of the sisters' contributed services, but underscored that without financial assets, the college could not grow. Only a large productive endowment would provide essential income for facilities, construction, scholarships, lay faculty salaries, and graduate school tuitions for sister-faculty.[19] Led by Trinity College professor Mildred Buzek Otenesak '36, the Alumnae Association rallied to the cause. Proceeds from the Alumnae Glee Club's first public concert in LeClerc Hall before an audience of eight hundred went to the endowment fund.[20] Within two years, the fund reached nearly $175,000. While gratified, Smith pointed out that this was "still far from our goal of $200,000 and very far from what is considered an adequate endowment for a college of our size, $8 million, if we are to equal public institutions enjoying Federal Aid. They average $500 per student, while privately controlled institutions of higher learning average $70 per student. This presents a challenge."[21]

Searching for Federal Funding

Episcopal restrictions on fundraising drives increased the College of Notre Dame's incentive to seek out alternate foundation and public funding instead. In 1955, the Ford Foundation offered endowment grants for faculty salaries to accredited four-year private colleges.[22] Notre Dame received $122,800, based on its 1954–55 full-time lay faculty payroll.[23] The grant "seemed like a fortune when we first heard of it," recalled President Margaret Mary O'Connell, who raised full-time faculty salaries by $200 for the 1956–57 year.[24] At this time, the college departed from its traditionally conservative policy of investing only in government securities and established three portfolios of stocks and bonds, both corporate and government: an endowment fund, a scholarship fund, and the Ford Foundation fund.[25]

The college also joined the State Association of Independent Colleges of Maryland, founded in 1953 and affiliated with the Commission on Colleges and Industry of the Association of American Colleges.[26] In 1955 the organization raised $32,000, distributing 60 percent equally among member institutions, and 40 percent in proportion to their enrollments.[27] Two years later, when the State of Maryland for the first time awarded grants to students at private colleges, College of Notre Dame students were among the beneficiaries.[28] At about the same time, the federal government became a potential source of funds. Until World War II, the only federal legislation to benefit higher-education institutions was the Morrill Act of 1862, which supported public land-grant colleges. Now several new federal programs emerged. The Serviceman's Readjustment Act of 1944 (the GI Bill of Rights) assisted veterans enrolled in public, private, and church-affiliated colleges and universities. With the passage of the National Defense Education Act of 1958, students qualified for financial assistance through the National Defense Student Loan Program. The Higher Education Facilities Act of 1963 awarded grants and loans to construct and rehabilitate academic facilities at public and private colleges and universities. But some funds would become available to the College of Notre Dame only through a major change in its governance structure and its relationship with its founding order.

Reforming Governance

The College of Notre Dame's initial governance structure resembled that of most Catholic colleges of the day. The Congregation of the School Sisters of Notre Dame was a Maryland corporation formed under the Acts of the General Assembly of Maryland in 1864, Chapter 357, in the city of Baltimore. The corporation operated under a charter that covered the order's various educational institutions in the state, including the College of Notre Dame, established in 1895.[29] But by the mid-twentieth century, more complex circumstances meant that having a single corporation cover the college, the preparatory school, and the order's eastern province had resulted in "quite a mess," as George Constable recalled. The 1950 MSA report sharply criticized the intermingling of college financial records with those of the preparatory school and the order, as well as the fact that the college treasurer was also the treasurer of the religious community: "There are no separate books kept for the College. The accounting is an amalgamation of community, Preparatory School and College accounts. Account books [are] kept at the motherhouse, off campus."[30] The board of directors quickly revised the budgeting and accounting procedures and separated college finances from those of the order. Governance challenges were more intractable.[31] "The provincial superior . . . felt she could . . . step into the college and direct things, and I guess rightly so," Constable noted. "Then there was the superior of the [campus convent] community, who also played a role. And then there was the [college] president. . . . It was very difficult for her because of those pressures from different sources and the uncertainty of her own power to lead."[32]

The mingling of preparatory school, college, and order accounts was a long-standing issue, though it had begun naturally enough. In the early twentieth century, college educators took for granted the presence of affiliated high schools on their campuses. In 1897, Johns Hopkins University president Daniel Coit Gilman endorsed the establishment of a country school for boys on campus. The University of Notre Dame in Indiana, meanwhile, shared its campus with a preparatory school for boys over thirteen as well as a "primary school" for younger boys.[33] Likewise, the founders of many early women's colleges situated them on the campuses of established girls' preparatory schools. This strategy afforded a degree of financial security for fledgling colleges and provided a pool of students qualified to undertake college work, since many female public high school graduates could not meet college admissions standards.[34] The Methodist-affiliated Girls' Latin School of Baltimore opened in 1890 on the campus of the Woman's College of Baltimore "for the specific purpose of preparing girls for college, especially for the Woman's College of Baltimore."[35] Vassar, Smith, and Wellesley Colleges, as well as the Woman's College, honored certificates awarded by the Girls' Latin School of Baltimore. From its inception, the College of Notre Dame presented certificates of admission to graduates of its own campus preparatory school.[36]

By 1890, however, preparatory departments on elite campuses were becoming controversial. Colleges were closing their campus preparatory schools or moving them to separate campuses. Bryn Mawr and Smith Colleges never introduced preparatory departments, and by 1893, no Seven Sister college had such a department.[37] Nationally, enrollment in the fourteen elite "Division A" women's colleges exceeded that of enrollment in affiliated preparatory schools by more than two to one.[38] Campus preparatory schools declined more rapidly after 1909, when the National Association of

Collegiate Alumnae (the forerunner of the American Association of University Women) denied membership to institutions having such campus schools or "departments." The Girls' Latin School of Baltimore immediately left the Woman's College campus for another site. In its 1919 definition of an American college, the National Conference Committee and the American Council on Education included "the absence of any connecting preparatory school operated by the college."[39]

Even after the separate incorporation of preparatory schools, leading women's colleges maintained historic ties with these institutions. Some, like Wellesley College, benefited from two feeder schools in the immediate locale. Its founder, Henry Durant, had financed the establishment of the Dana Hall School in the town in 1881, and twelve years later President Helen Shafer persuaded two alumnae to found the Walnut Hill School in nearby Natick, noting that "its proximity to Wellesley enables students and instructors to keep in close touch with Wellesley activities." Founded in 1886, the Cambridge School for Girls (formerly the Gilman School) remained "closely connected with the development of Radcliffe College." In 1916, Harvard and Radcliffe faculty sat on its board of directors.[40]

Preparatory school campuses and their faculties, however, continued to be valuable resources for founders of Catholic colleges. In Baltimore, the School Sisters of Notre Dame, who already owned the Collegiate Institute's extensive campus and buildings, could open a college on the property at very low initial cost. In planning the college, founders could rely on the counsel and assistance of experienced Collegiate Institute faculty. Finally, proximity to a long-established preparatory school, patronized by Protestant as well as Catholic students, was certain to bring desirable publicity to new colleges in their early years. For many small Catholic women's campuses, the coveted institutional membership in the American Association of University Women was therefore slow to come. Removal of campus high schools would likely pose financial hurdles and might affect enrollment. According to a Notre Dame preparatory school graduate, in 1927, "most, two thirds of my high school class, went over to Notre Dame to college."[41]

The presence of preparatory schools on college campuses, however, posed serious social, psychological, and academic dilemmas. Although administrators made every effort to keep college and preparatory students separate, collegians increasingly resented having to share campus grounds and buildings with high school girls. The adverse effect of the high school on the college's public image and prestige had always concerned Notre Dame administrators. College Hall, the first building exclusively for college use, did not open until 1910. An imposing structure, it housed classrooms, a library, laboratories, a dining room, a dormitory, and social spaces. But it did not successfully resolve the "preparatory school problem," since college students continued to share the chapel, auditorium, gymnasium, and campus grounds with high school students who greatly outnumbered them.

While the campus was "just bulging" at this time, it was not bulging with collegians.[42] In 1920, they accounted for just 20 percent of students on campus, and in 1925 for 30 percent.[43] By the end of the 1930s, about one-third of students on campus were enrolled in the college. For the college to grow, administrators warned, it needed a larger physical plant. It seemed to them that the simplest solution was to move the preparatory school to another campus and then remodel its vacated facilities for college use. While leaders of the order acknowledged that such a step would greatly benefit the college, they were reluctant to take action. Not only would the plan require the order to assume considerable debt to acquire land and construct a high school building, but it would also offend traditionally generous preparatory school alumnae.

Like her predecessors, President Margaret Mary O'Connell faced a controversial internal issue that had simmered without resolution for decades. Since 1895, the college and a large preparatory boarding school had shared buildings and other campus facilities. By 1910, the situation was already affecting the college's academic standing. In that year, four women's colleges qualified for membership in the Association of Colleges and Preparatory Schools of the Southern States. Goucher College, the only Maryland representative in the group, had just severed legal ties with the Girls' Latin School, its preparatory department since 1890.[44] Because they did not yet comply with the association's regulation calling for "rigid separation of preparatory and college students," the other three institutions—the College of Notre Dame, Mount Saint Agnes College, and the Woman's College of Frederick—failed to gain membership.[45] The presence of a preparatory school and a lower school on the Notre Dame campus became an increasingly serious threat to the college's academic rating. In 1945, President Frances Smith again appealed to the board of trustees to take action on the matter: "All would greatly benefit by the removal of the Preparatory school to a separate campus," she stressed.[46] In 1950, the Association of Colleges and Secondary Schools of the Middle States and Maryland likewise urged its relocation.

Demand for college admission rose sharply nationwide after World War II, with a high proportion of applicants seeking to reside on campus. In 1946, however, the College of Notre Dame could accommodate only about 140 resident students, and "only 37 or 40 new Freshmen."[47] A college that for a half century had struggled to build its enrollment was now rejecting well-qualified applicants. A decade later, full-time enrollment, including day and resident students, numbered only 329, a situation caused entirely by insufficient resident housing.[48] For O'Connell, this was a compelling argument for moving the preparatory school to another campus as quickly as possible. Her top priority was to provide "increased accommodations for resident students."[49] The board of directors, however, was unwilling to act quickly. The purchase of real estate, construction of high school and convent buildings, and renovation of the former preparatory school facilities for college use would place a serious financial burden on the order.

The issue of the preparatory school remained at an impasse in 1956 when an impatient O'Connell took an unorthodox step. Convinced that the backing of the church hierarchy would greatly strengthen her case with the college's board of directors, she asked Baltimore archbishop Francis Keough, Michael Curley's successor, to take her side in the preparatory school matter. The maneuver worked. "I understand that your suggestion relative to the high school moving to another campus is being considered very seriously," a jubilant O'Connell wrote to Keough. "You have made it seem . . . imperative in your conversation with Sister Superior and me recently. For that one favor alone, I can never be grateful enough."[50] The move was not to occur, however, for another four years. In late 1958, the board of directors finally voted to relocate the high school.[51] The order purchased a sixty-six-acre campus in Towson, about eight miles from the college, and constructed a one-thousand-student high school, complete with athletic facilities and a residence for sister-faculty. The Notre Dame Preparatory School moved to its new home in 1960. For the first time in its nearly seven-decade history, the College of Notre Dame had a sixty-one-acre campus and its buildings to itself. After renovations, the original preparatory school building, now named Gibbons Hall, opened for college use in the 1961 fall term.

Episcopal intransigence had left the board of directors and the advisory board with few options for financing the college's long-desired dormitory project, even as the preparatory school issue was finally being resolved. Privately, the trustees hired a New York fundraising firm "on a consulting basis," alumnae organized "Hands across the Nation" card parties, and students and faculty held fundraising events on campus.[52] Results of these private efforts were predictably meager, and the $1.5 million goal for the building project seemed more remote than ever. Meanwhile, a new government program, the Federal College Housing Program (Title IV of the Housing Act of 1950), had begun to offer significant funding to assist institutions eager to accommodate more resident students. But the program did not cover religious organizations. As long as the religious order was its legal owner, the College of Notre Dame did not qualify for financial assistance under this program. This situation led O'Connell and the advisory board to request that the order establish the college as a separate corporation with its own board of trustees.

In February 1957, an act of the Maryland legislature "granted a separate charter to the College of Notre Dame of Maryland, Inc. for the education of women, the promotion of learning and 'general educational purposes' and to confer degrees upon any qualified person."[53] The college corporation was now legally "distinct from the 'School Sisters of Notre Dame in the City of Baltimore,' the original corporation set up in 1864."[54] Signers of the certificate of incorporation were Mother Vitalia Arnold, provincial superior, and Sisters Matrona Dougherty, superior of the campus convent; Margaret Mary O'Connell, president of the college; Bridget Marie Engelmeyer, dean of the college; and M. Gerald Maher. Officers of the college corporation were O'Connell, president; Engelmeyer, vice president and secretary; and Sister Redempta Ott, treasurer. The religious order, "for and in consideration of the sum of One Dollar," transferred to the College of Notre Dame of Maryland, Inc., all campus land and tangible personal property located on it, as well as all securities, cash, and bank accounts that had been held in the name of the College of Notre Dame of Maryland. The new corporation assumed the institution's "contracts, obligations, and commitments."[55]

Separate incorporation did not immediately diminish the order's influence on the college. Trustees had to be "members in good standing" of the order, college projects requiring the assumption of major debt could not proceed without prior permission from the order's general superiors in Rome, and provincial superiors, as in the past, continued to play decisive roles in faculty appointments. "The plant, personnel, curriculum, and entire operation will be continuous with the past," stressed George Constable. "The only change [is] the technical legal entity which operates it. . . . The legal entity is new but the institution and its operation is old."[56] Nonetheless, jurisdictional disputes lessened considerably. Now, according to Constable, "the whole leadership structure focused on the [college] president and the chairman of the board, who was the [order's] provincial head."[57] This change alone greatly strengthened the hand of the president.

At the time, the vast majority of Catholic college and university trustees were members of the clergy or religious orders. According to a 1960 review of 108 institutions, 84 percent had no lay trustees.[58] Soon after Notre Dame's separate incorporation, however, lay members of the advisory board proposed that it become "essentially a lay board."[59] The new board of trustees responded by adding two lay faculty members to the advisory board, Elizabeth Morrissy and Mildred Otenasek. On March 3,

1963, George Constable and Henry J. Knott became the first laypersons elected to Notre Dame's board of trustees. Constable had become a Roman Catholic shortly after graduating from Princeton in 1933; he earned his law degree at Yale and joined his father's law firm in 1940. He provided legal counsel for the College of Notre Dame and sat on its advisory board and then on its board of trustees from 1945 until 1992. Knott, a prominent figure in Maryland real estate and building development who had graduated from Loyola College in 1929, became renowned for his philanthropy toward Maryland colleges, schools, and hospitals. He was a major donor to the College of Notre Dame as well as a longtime member of its advisory board and board of trustees.

On August 31, 1957, the college's application for a $1.04 million long-term, low-interest federal loan to construct a 150-student residence hall, a dining hall, and a small student chapel was approved.[60] The total cost of the project was estimated at $1.5 million. President O'Connell immediately applied to Archbishop Keough for permission to undertake a public fundraising campaign to repay the government loan, but her letter went unanswered. Several months later, she tried again: "It is vital to our planning at this stage to know whether or not we may have a Drive, and if so, just when it may be."[61] In reply, Keough underscored the fact that several campaigns were presently underway in greater Baltimore, including one for Loyola College. "With all this in mind," he told O'Connell, "I wished to spare you and the Sisters embarrassment from the institution of a Drive which might very well end in humiliating failure. . . . If now, however, your Advisory Council deem [*sic*] this risk so negligible, you may be sure your Archbishop will refrain from prohibiting the conduct of a fund-raising Campaign."[62]

Despite the archbishop's feelings, the board of trustees authorized the college to issue "College of Notre Dame of Maryland, Inc. Dormitory Bonds of 1957," for the same amount as the federal loan. Dated November 1, 1958, the bonds would mature in serial installments until 1997. The trustees also agreed that the college could borrow up to $1.3 million at 5.5 percent from other sources, with mortgages on college property used to secure both types of loans.[63] But in light of the archbishop's negative reaction to the college's fundraising plans, and aware of his power, the trustees delayed launching a major public campaign. In late 1958, Henry Knott and his brothers contributed a "munificent gift" to allow the residence hall project to get underway.[64] Construction of residence and dining halls moved along quickly, and the trustees agreed to again seek the archbishop's permission to undertake a fundraising campaign. O'Connell's cautiously worded letter to Keough in August 1959 revealed their concern about his reaction: "We have been mindful of Your Excellency's advice. . . . This will not be a public Capital Funds Drive. We have not engaged a professional fund-raiser."[65]

At the time of its separate incorporation, the college admitted all qualified day applicants, but had to turn away many who wished to live on campus. Once Doyle Hall opened in the fall of 1959, enrollment began to rise. By the fall of 1960, it totaled 560, with 298 resident students (53 percent) and 262 day students (47 percent).[66] Four years later, the college's full-time enrollment was 979. "The 3 to 1 ratio of residents to commuters [for the freshman class] showed a gain over the 2 to 1 ratio of 1963 applications," O'Connell reported.[67] In early 1959, with the construction of Doyle Hall nearly completed and the relocation of the preparatory school imminent, O'Connell had sought permission to commence her next building project, a science center. Here she met with stiff resistance from her religious superiors. Provincial Superior Vitalia Arnold, chair of the board of trustees, was concerned about the debt liability the project might impose on the order. After all, Archbishop Keough remained opposed to public fundraising by the College of Notre Dame.[68] Until reduction of the outstanding debt on Doyle Hall was "well underway," she would not approve the science building project.[69]

This picture changed dramatically in 1962 when the Maryland state legislature approved a program of matching construction grants for Maryland colleges, private and public. The advisory board agreed that the college ought to apply for one of these "wholly unexpected and much-coveted" grants. The only board member to express reservations about this step was George Constable. "In asking [for] financial aid from the government, we are crossing an important policy bridge," he cautioned. There are "religious implications. . . . The [United States] constitution is clear on the matter."[70] The college, however, applied and received a matching grant of $750,000 to construct a science center, representing nearly one-third of the building's estimated cost. With preliminary building plans already in hand, O'Connell anticipated speedy completion of the science building.

Provincial Superior Arnold's doubts about the college's ability to repay the matching grant continued. Until matching funds were in hand or pledged, the project could not get underway. O'Connell applied unsuccessfully to General Superior Ambrosia Roecklein in Rome for permission to proceed without Arnold's approval.[71] Meanwhile, advisory board members Henry Knott and George Constable, whose judgment she valued, struggled to convince her that any delay in construction would damage the college, telling her that "the State will be reluctant to give again if the money is kept until the matching amount is raised."[72] In the fall of 1963, as the academic year opened, the science building project was at a standstill.

Sectarian Identity on Trial

Before the issue of the construction delay could be resolved, the College of Notre Dame encountered a momentous and unexpected challenge. On September 10, 1963, the Horace Mann League of the United States of America, joined by ten Maryland residents, filed a complaint in the Maryland Circuit Court of Anne Arundel County in Annapolis against the state of Maryland and four church-affiliated colleges. They contended that the state legislation of 1962 and 1963 that had awarded a total of $2.5 million in matching grants for building construction to "pervasively sectarian" institutions violated the constitutional doctrine of separation of church and state as set forth in the First and Fourteenth Amendments to the US Constitution. Defendants were the State Board of Public Works (the state governor, treasurer, and comptroller); Hood College in Frederick (United Church of Christ); Western Maryland College in Westminster (Methodist); Saint Joseph College in Emmitsburg (Catholic); and the College of Notre Dame. The American Jewish Congress and Protestants and Other Americans United for Separation of Church and State (POAU), among others, supported the suit.[73]

This lawsuit was part of a series of legal challenges to governmental support of religious institutions brought during the mid-twentieth century by an alliance of occasionally strange bedfellows, ranging from atheists to "outsider" religious groups to mainstream Protestants concerned about Catholic access to federal and state funds. As Catholic institutions sought to become more visibly "Catholic" during the anti-Communist postwar era, heated public debate, widely covered by the media, between Catholic and Protestant leaders on controversial religious questions rekindled old animosities. Mainstream citizens, uneasy that Catholics were undermining the nation's social fabric, sought legal as well as cultural redress.[74]

Legal cases, when they involved funding, were often decided by narrow majorities, and frequently turned on whether the money in question could be said to be used for secular purposes. POAU, for example, had been formed by a group of influential Protestant ministers and educators in response to the US Supreme Court's 5–4 decision in *Everson v. Board of Education* in 1947 (330 U.S. 1), allowing a school district to reimburse parents of children attending public and private religious (nearly all Catholic) schools for related public transportation costs.[75] Courts also established sometimes vague standards for who could access funds, inviting new challenges to force narrower definitions. Was the College of Notre Dame more like a diocesan seminary, which existed only for sectarian purposes and was by definition ineligible for government funding, or was it more like the private liberal arts colleges that had long ago severed cultural as well as legal ties with their founding denominations?

The two-week "Horace Mann trial" before Judge O. Bowie Duckett of the circuit court began on November 30, 1964. Since, at this time, more than two-thirds of the private colleges in the United States were church related, higher-education and religious circles nationwide followed the case closely.[76] College catalogs, student handbooks, corporation documents, and accreditation reports were placed in evidence during the trial, and the four college presidents and a number of faculty members were cross-examined. Leo Pfeffer, a constitutional lawyer and chief counsel for the Horace Mann League, represented the plaintiffs, while George Constable represented the College of Notre Dame.[77] At issue in the trial, in large part, was what it meant for the college to be (as nobody denied it was) "Catholic."

Religion and the College, 1895–1950s

The legal establishment of the college and the addition of laymen and laywomen to its board had changed the institution's governance, ultimately shifting the balance of power away from the religious order. But it had not changed its essential character. There was no question that its religious affiliation was central to its intellectual goals. Unless the college attended to the students' spiritual and moral development as well as to their academic success, its administrators believed, it would fail to fulfill its mission to develop exemplary female leaders in American society. The elemental vision of Notre Dame's founders was to give women the opportunity to benefit from a Catholic higher education. True education had a moral purpose, and religious values played a central role in cultivating the mind. The teachings of the Catholic Church provided the rationale for college regulations regarding student conduct, and Catholics valued the distinctive religious culture that marked their women's colleges. Organized religion played a role in every area of college life, not simply in official church services. It affected academic programs and course requirements, college rituals, social traditions, and extracurricular student organizations. While students in the Seven Sister colleges chose Greek goddesses like Athena, Daphne, and the Bacchae as patrons, their College of Notre Dame counterparts opted for the Virgin Mary.[78]

Most elite northern colleges at the turn of the twentieth century expected their students to attend religious services regularly. Although, in general, women's colleges had stricter obligations than men's colleges, there was considerable variation. Harvard ended its required daily chapel in 1886; Yale in 1926.[79] Since the 1880s, Mount Holyoke had expected students to attend daily prayers in the college chapel and Sunday worship in the village church. In 1904, monitors checked attendance at Vassar's "restful [weekday] chapel service after dinner,"[80] as well as at Sunday religious observances that included a morning worship service, a Bible lecture, and an evening prayer meeting led by the college president.[81] In 1911, the rector of a Northampton church close to the Smith campus overlooked their obligatory character when he concluded that "the religious life and activity are easily the most popular of all electives in our women's colleges."[82] By the 1930s, students observed Smith's daily chapel attendance rule on an honor basis.[83] While Bryn Mawr had no formal chapel attendance requirements, students in 1912 attended a brief daily chapel service. "This is voluntary, but almost everyone goes," students reported.[84] Radcliffe's traditional morning prayer service ended in 1932.[85]

At Notre Dame and other early Catholic women's colleges, religious values permeated campus life and found public expression not only in liturgical services but also in student religious clubs and social service organizations. In 1895 Catholic students attended daily weekday Mass, while Protestant students were free to engage in Bible study instead. In addition, students participated in daily morning and evening prayer services.[86] Sundays, however, were different. "For the maintenance of order," stated the college catalog, students of all faiths were expected to be present for "the public worship [Mass] on Sunday."[87] The expectation that Catholic students attend the weekday Mass soon disappeared, but the requirement to attend both Mass and an evening benediction service on Sundays remained obligatory for decades.[88]

Protestant as well as Catholic students belonged to the College of Notre Dame choir as singers and instrumentalists. In the college's early decades, the choir played a central role in religious services and important campus events. Diverse audiences testified to its ambitious repertoire and fine quality. At the dedication of the college chapel in 1896, a sixty-member choir, directed by Professor Lucien Odend'hal and accompanied by organist Sister Casilda Benning and student harpist Helen Burr '99, sang Alexandre-Charles Fessy's *Messe solennelle*. The college choir's high liturgical standards carried on a long tradition. In 1874, the choir of the Collegiate Institute had sung Haydn's *Mass in D* for the dedication of the school's original building. For Burr, participation in the choir was a high point of college life. "I received great benefit from playing in the choir at school and singing the vespers and Masses," she recalled five decades later. "The wonderful rhythms of those chants!"[89]

Notre Dame initially modeled its campus rituals and traditions on those of mainstream women's colleges, but gradually these events acquired a distinctly Catholic character. At Bryn Mawr, May Day celebrations in 1900 included a procession, a pageant with Maid Marian as May Queen, and dancing around maypoles.[90] Notre Dame's first May Day Festival in 1918, organized by the student social club Kymry, included "spring dances, crowning of the May Queen, and the May Pole dance."[91] The event had no religious content. Nor did a May Day event sponsored by Ye Merrie Masquers, the college drama club, the following decade. It was just "an old-fashioned May Day . . . with the Queen elected by secret ballot of the entire Association, with the exception of the Seniors."[92]

These May Day Festivals were not the same as the campus-wide May Procession (figure 10), a religious celebration held annually since 1873 to honor the institution's namesake. A student description depicts the 1925 May

FIGURE 10. May Procession, 1950. Photo from NDMA.

Procession as "a touching sight," winding around the campus, with students singing hymns and reciting the rosary, eventually reaching the campus shrine in honor of the Blessed Virgin Mary.[93] At midcentury, everyone on campus participated in this event, "from the tiniest first grader to the tallest college senior—college girls in cap and gown, high school girls in blue uniforms, grammar school girls in white."[94] After 1944, with Marian devotions on the rise in response to the global spread of Communism, the college added a ceremony incorporating "the bestowal of a miraculous medal by each sophomore on her [senior] 'big sister.'"[95]

A favorite commencement week tradition in turn-of-the-century women's colleges was Ivy Day. Smith College seniors, dressed in white gowns and flanked by juniors bearing daisy chains, processed through the campus singing their class song. The ivy song and the ivy oration by a senior followed. The 1898 orator emphasized that "there always have been and will be two fields for woman, as a mother and teacher, of which there are none other that are higher."[96] Colleges varied slightly on this program. At Pembroke College, for example, the senior class in caps and gowns processed behind "lines of white-robed undergraduates" bearing an ivy chain.[97] Ivy-planting ceremonies at Catholic women's colleges were variations on those of mainstream institutions. According to the school's archives, the College of Notre Dame modeled its first ivy planting in 1912 on that of the Woman's College of Baltimore, but added distinctive religious features. Faculty and students processed around the campus, ending at the entrance to College Hall. There, after the college chaplain blessed the ivy, each senior in turn planted an ivy branch in front of the building. The ritual ended with the graduating class singing a farewell hymn to the Virgin Mary. By the 1940s and 1950s, seniors wore long white dresses for Ivy Day; members of the other classes wore caps and gowns. Unless they were playing special roles, students customarily wore academic garb for such events.

In the 1890s, all Notre Dame students enrolled in at least one religious club, and this expectation continued through the 1950s.[98] Catholic values found informal public expression in these religious societies. At the same time, they enabled students to unite to address various social needs, local and national. The oldest of these clubs was the Sodality of the Sacred Heart of Jesus, later known as the League of the Sacred Heart. It had originated in the Collegiate Institute in 1876, and was carried into the college after 1895. At first, students engaged in prayer meetings, collected contributions for college needs, and supported a few charitable projects. In the 1910s, the group's interests expanded somewhat. Some members volunteered with the United War Mothers Campaign, while others sponsored book drives to build the college library.[99]

As Communism spread in the post–World War I years, church leaders encouraged numerous independent college mission clubs to collaborate in order to counteract this growing threat to religion. The National Catholic Students' Mission Crusade, established in 1918, modeled itself on the Student Volunteer Movement for Foreign Missions, a large Protestant organization founded in 1886. Within six years, it had enlisted 390,000 volunteers nationwide to promote the church's domestic and foreign missions.[100] In Baltimore, the Notre Dame Mission Society, known as Our Lady's Mission Unit, joined the national organization in 1919.[101] Over the next two decades, missionary enthusiasm ran high. Student "crusaders" distributed mite boxes, sponsored bazaars and mission days, and organized benefit lectures and plays in support of church missionary work. The college library featured Catholic missionary literature, and by 1923 carried eleven mission magazines. In 1925, the college hosted a Mass and all-day rally for five thousand, sponsored by the Mission Crusade's Baltimore Conference.[102]

The Sodality of the Blessed Virgin (Children of Mary Sodality) appeared in 1923. Although attendance was not obligatory, administrators took it for granted that Catholic students would join. In 1936, "all but 10 paid the activity fee of one dollar."[103] They raised money for flowers for the Blessed Virgin's altar in the chapel and a campus grotto and focused more on prayer meetings than did other campus religious clubs. Members recited the Office of the Blessed Virgin Mary on Mondays and attended Mass as a group on the third Sunday of the month and on Marian feast days. The Sodality remained consistently popular with students. By the 1950s it was still "a big thing at the time," an alumna remembered.[104]

In the 1930s, official college publications became more explicit about how the institution should witness publicly to its Catholic identity. Its "purpose and ideal," according to the 1935–36 catalog, was "to present a well-balanced program of study, one that will result, ultimately, in a cultured Catholic woman, capable of directing her own life to its high destiny, and equipped with the means of rendering service to others. The ideal Notre Dame graduate has a correct sense of values."[105] In its 1936–37 catalog, the college introduced a far more militant and openly religious statement composed by Professor Elizabeth Morrissy: "The intelligent presentation of the principles of Catholic teaching in all fields of thought may be demanded, so that Notre Dame students may take their place in bringing about sound recovery by helping to restore to first place the spiritual values. . . . Students must stand firm and play an active part in the coming battle of civilization that is even now gathering forces, where the division will be made on the answer to the question, 'What think ye of Christ?'"[106] In a 1937 radio address, Morrissy elaborated on the fundamental bond of the college and religion: "Our faith is the corner stone of our intellectual life as it is the final guide of our moral life. It is because we believe this that the College of Notre Dame exists."[107] Its graduates, as the college's 1941–42 catalog stated, must "not only be able but determined to fulfill their mission as Catholic leaders in the various walks of life."[108]

Student interest in connections among the intellectual, service, and religious aspects of life that Morrissy had articulated did not immediately coalesce. In the 1930s, the Catholic Action Movement and organizations like the Catholic Evidence Guild, founded in England in 1918, called on college students to abandon their "intellectual apathy" and promote the church's social and political agenda.[109] Before World War II, appeals like this did not arouse much enthusiasm on the Notre Dame campus.[110] For example, in 1939, a few students organized a campus cooperative store to counter "so much unchristian and erring capitalism and communism in the world,"[111] but they could not mobilize any support for the project. Students refused to volunteer to staff the store or to buy stock in it (at a dollar per share), and the cooperative quickly failed. The Depression years instead afforded students more exciting and tangible opportunities to assist those in need, and a variety of service groups flourished on campus. In Saint Francis Xavier's Colored Parish in East Baltimore, for example, students visited needy citizens in their homes and raised funds to educate their daughters so as "to bring about a more intelligent understanding of the Negro," although they expressed little indignation that their own college would not admit the girls.[112]

In the 1940s, leaders of Catholic colleges encouraged faculty and students to integrate Catholic values more widely into all areas of campus life. Especially in the aftermath of World War II, the Catholic Church in the United States, preoccupied by perceived threats of secularism and world Communism, became more boldly "Roman." Catholics held huge public rallies and religious celebrations. The College of Notre Dame continued to stress the comprehensive role of religion in every aspect of college life. "To train college students in Catholic doctrine is primarily the function of the religion classes, but the responsibility of developing a Catholic attitude towards every phase of life is shared by all departments of the college," wrote the dean, Sister Dominic Ramacciotti, in 1940.[113]

At the same time, in matters of religious observance, freedom of conscience was becoming the deciding factor, as it had over the preceding decades at elite Protestant colleges.[114] Jewish faculty member Regina Soria recalled, "I remember once one of the teachers of religion would ask the students whether they had gone to Holy Communion or not. Sister Dominic stopped that, said they had no right to ask the students what they do."[115] Students of all faiths sought ways to witness to them openly; a Jewish music major chose to sing Ravel's *Kaddisch* in Hebrew before "a large, enthusiastic audience" as part of her required public recital in 1947.[116] But strict Catholic observance remained normative, if not mandatory; Mass was "a focal point of many of the things that happened here. Lots of us went to daily Mass during Lent," recalled Jean Monier '53.[117]

Student militancy on social issues intensified in the post–World War II years. The College of Notre Dame reached beyond campus boundaries to join the National Federation of Catholic College Students, an organization with 179 institutional members established to prepare student leaders "for an effective lay apostolate."[118] The college also belonged to the nonsectarian National Student Association, established in 1947. Student delegates who attended its annual congresses saw themselves as missionaries: "As students of a small Catholic women's college we have our place in the breadth and the scope of this comprehensive student movement," explained an early delegate. "As Catholic students we have an obligation to share, explain, and promote our philosophy and thought and our religion—not so much to convert as to make known the truth that is ours."[119] From its founding, delegates and observers from Catholic women's colleges participated actively in this organization.[120]

By the 1950s, integrating religion into the life of the college had become a central goal. Administrators revised the college catalog format, placing "Religious Life," which traditionally had its own separate section, under the broader heading of "Student Life."[121] They called on faculty to include "fundamental principles or practices of the Catholic Church" in their courses "wherever . . . applicable."[122] The Art Department, for example, called on students to "learn and live on a small scale the life of a Christian artist,"[123] and to explore "the spirituality that a painting could have, or . . . a poem, a mathematical derivation, or a sonata."[124] By the end of the 1950s, President Margaret Mary O'Connell could say confidently that the "life and study and the atmosphere of the college are permeated, enlarged, and integrated by the Catholic way of life."[125] For many mainstream critics, her words described a sectarian institution. The stage was set for the court challenges of the 1960s and 1970s.

Responding to the *Horace Mann* Case

During the 1960s, the plaintiffs in the *Horace Mann* case based their claim that the College of Notre Dame was "sectarian" and thus ineligible for government funding in large measure on the role of the religious order in campus life. Gainer E. Bryan, editor of the *Maryland Baptist*, published a firsthand account of Leo Pfeffer's cross-examination of Margaret Mary O'Connell:

> He noted her statement that she is responsible to her board of directors "exactly as any other college president" but that the chairman of the board is the provincial superior of her order, the School Sisters of Notre Dame. Then he read from the Rule of Order [*sic*], which owns and operates the school: "In respect to intellect, obedience shall be blind." "Is that a correct statement of the rule?" he asked. She replied, "It has never precluded my freedom of action as administrator." Pfeffer attacked her statement that she consults with the archbishop only on "matters of magnitude," which she specified as finance campaigns. Five times he asked her the question, "To your knowledge does the local ordinary (the archbishop) have the authority to refuse to allow a particular priest to teach at a Catholic college in his diocese?" Each time she replied that as far as she knew, in her experience, "we have never applied to the archbishop for these priests to come." However, she had conceded earlier that the archbishop was consulted about the appointment of theology teachers. Court testimony brought out that 36 members of the faculty of Notre Dame are religious, 35 are lay, and only 8 (laymen) are non-Catholic.[126]

Plaintiffs saw this as clear proof that the college was part of a sectarian subculture. However, Judge Duckett considered the central issue in the case to be whether or not the four church-related colleges would agree to use state funds solely for secular purposes. He concluded that they would and found in favor of the State of Maryland and the colleges.

Pfeffer appealed the circuit court's decision to the Maryland Court of Appeals. For the appeals court, the central issue in the case was whether or not "a recipient college was so pervasively religious in its orientation and operations that it could be considered 'legally sectarian.'"[127] The appeals court reviewed the "stated purposes" of each college; its financial and religious relationships with "its sponsoring church"; the place of religion in its curriculum, extracurricular events, buildings, and campus; its requirements regarding student attendance at religious services and events; its accreditation status; and the college's image and contribution to its local community.[128] On June 2, 1966, the Maryland Court of Appeals, 4–3, reversed the circuit court decision in favor of the State of Maryland and Western Maryland, Saint Joseph, and Notre Dame Colleges. It allowed the grant to Hood

College to stand.[129] The appeals court majority found Notre Dame to be "sectarian" because most of its students, administrators, and faculty were Catholic; the religious order controlled its governing board; and its official publications attested to a campus environment "permeated . . . by the Catholic way of life."[130] The US Supreme Court refused to hear an appeal of this decision.

As the college struggled to defend its nonsectarian character in the courts, it had to wrestle with some relatively recent introductions of Catholic religious practice designed to stress Catholic identity vis-à-vis the celebration of citizenship. Notre Dame Day, celebrated annually on March 25, the Feast of the Annunciation, honored the college's founding and its patroness. It shared the date with Maryland Day, a state holiday until 1996. The college's first public celebration of Notre Dame Day had taken place in 1901 with students and faculty attending morning Mass. "Beautiful singing and the school sang a new hymn composed by one of the sisters & set to music," the college annalist recorded. "It is to be known as 'The Notre Dame Hymn,' and commemorates the First Mass celebrated in Maryland, the message of the angel, and the foundation of our beloved Notre Dame of Maryland."[131] In its early years, the college celebrated Maryland Day intermittently. In 1915, no religious ceremony marked the holiday. College students joined Dean Meletia Foley, an ardent nature lover, for a leisurely walk in the Garrett estate next door, "to study the birds and trees."[132] The 1926 program was typically simple. At a college assembly, two students read papers while a third sang a song to honor the college's founding and the state holiday.[133]

But as the Catholic Church encouraged a more visibly "Catholic" identity in the postwar era, academic ceremonies became more religious in content. The 1953 Maryland Day celebration began and concluded in the convent chapel with morning Mass, sung by the entire community, and a benediction service and consecration of students to the Virgin Mary. A pleased Margaret Mary O'Connell described the day's events: "In the morning, faculty members in each department prepared special lectures relating the work of that department to the Blessed Mother."[134] Topics included "The Biology of Virgin Birth and the Blessed Virgin Birth," "Our Lady in World Crises," "The Economics of Nazareth," "Our Lady was a Jew," "Our Lady in the Atomic Age," "The History of the Ave in Music," "The Mother of the Word," and "'Euclid Alone Has Looked on Beauty Bare?'" In the afternoon, Our Lady's Sodality students directed a dramatic reading of "an original sonnet sequence entitled 'The Seven Joys of the Blessed Mother and the Eighth' . . . interpreted by original dance pantomimes against a mural of the Seven Sorrows of our Blessed Mother executed . . . by [a] senior art major."[135] In style and content, Maryland Day programs had not changed much by 1963, the year the *Horace Mann* case was filed. Lawyers for the plaintiffs pointed to Maryland Day programs from the preceding decade as evidence of the college's sectarian character. The college's lawyers replied that Maryland Day was an extracurricular event. Faculty lecture topics of that day were not part of the regular curriculum, and students were free to choose those they wished to attend.

As the *Horace Mann* case continued, Notre Dame endeavored to deflect criticism by removing some religious content from Maryland Day programs. On May 25, 1965, the day was fairly routine. Following regular morning classes and a special Mass, a faculty member gave an afternoon piano concert in honor of the Virgin Mary.[136] The day passed unobserved in 1966. Noted the college annalist, "Annunciation Day and Maryland Day. Ordinary classes were held, with no exception to the day's routine."[137] In 1968, the holiday celebration returned, but with minimal religious reference. "Our College's annual celebration to recall our history and our ideals," wrote the annalist. "Members of the faculty are mingling with the students, enjoying the choice of two among several lectures running concurrently."[138] Lecture subjects that year included "Why College Physical Education?" and "The Challenge of Change in Art." A 1971 lecture by Ralph Nader on "environmental hazards" was the last Maryland Day observance for nearly two decades.[139]

Roemer v. Board of Public Works

The loss of the Maryland state matching grant for the science center in June 1966 was a serious setback for Notre Dame. However, in March 1964, while the grant remained in escrow pending the outcome of the trial, a gift of $200,000 from Henry Knott allowed the college to proceed with construction.[140] At the same time, Knott asked his friend Archbishop Lawrence Shehan, who had succeeded Archbishop Francis Keough in Baltimore, to persuade the School Sisters of Notre Dame to modify their traditionally conservative approach to financing major college projects.[141] Episcopal influence brought results. Unlike his predecessors, Shehan did not object to public fundraising by Notre Dame, and a major professional drive for the matching funds for the science building was soon underway. The Knott Science Center finally opened in October 1967.

In 1966, before the *Horace Mann* case was finally decided, the college had also received a federal loan of $955,000 under the Higher Education Facilities Act of 1963 (HEFA) to aid in the construction of the science center.[142]

George Constable found it ironic that the college had received this federal loan before the Maryland Court of Appeals decided that the college was ineligible for state funds "under the Federal Constitution."[143] No one had yet challenged this federal program in the courts, a situation that changed in 1968 when a group of taxpayers challenged the constitutionality of HEFA awards to four Connecticut Catholic colleges (Sacred Heart, Albertus Magnus, Fairfield, and Annhurst), claiming that they were "pervasively sectarian" and hence ineligible for federal monies. On June 28, 1971, in a 5–4 decision in *Tilton v. Richardson*, the US Supreme Court found the federal grants constitutional. Since buildings financed by HEFA awards were exclusively for secular use, the court's majority saw no "excessive entanglement" of religion and government.[144] Church-related colleges across the country breathed a collective sigh of relief.

At the College of Notre Dame, however, the relief was short lived. Only a month earlier, the State of Maryland had passed legislation to help the state's private colleges "wipe out deficits" through annual awards of $500 per graduating senior.[145] With 180 graduates, Notre Dame received a $90,000 state grant for the 1971–72 academic year. But early in 1972, John Roemer III, executive director of the American Civil Liberties Union (ACLU), joined by three other taxpayers and supported by the ACLU of Maryland,[146] as well as by POAU, filed suit against the State of Maryland and five church-related institutions. They asserted that awards of public funds to Saint Joseph College, Western Maryland College, Loyola College, Mount Saint Mary College, and the College of Notre Dame of Maryland violated the establishment clause of the First Amendment.

Using criteria similar to those employed in the *Horace Mann* case, the plaintiffs scrutinized the bylaws, catalogs, curricula, buildings, faculty, and funding sources of each institution for evidence that it was an arm of "sectarian religion." In 1974, the three judges of the US District Court for the District of Maryland upheld the state grants to the five colleges in a 2–1 decision and, following the US Supreme Court's 1971 decision in the *Tilton* case, denied the plaintiffs' request for an injunction against the state awards.[147] The plaintiffs appealed to the US Supreme Court. At this point, after Western Maryland College agreed to remove all religious symbols, even crosses, from its chapel and to loosen its ties to the Methodist Church, that institution was permitted to withdraw from the suit.

Two years later, *Roemer v. Board of Public Works*, another 5–4 decision, upheld the constitutionality of the Maryland state grants to the four Catholic colleges. The majority affirmed the judgment of the US District Court that intellectual freedom "without religious pressures" characterized the secular curricula of the institutions, that neither the Catholic Church nor ecclesiastics serving on governing boards dictated college policies, and that financial rather than religious motives dictated the colleges' preference for religious order members in hiring. The dissent argued that the institutions did not meet the "entanglement test" because required theology courses were essentially religion lessons.[148] In both the *Tilton* and *Roemer* cases, US Supreme Court majorities had found that Catholic colleges were, as historian Charles Wilson puts it, "constitutionally indistinguishable from other institutions in the independent sector of American higher education."[149] Eligible church-related colleges could now compete on equal terms for government programs that supported general institutional needs, with the exception of religious projects. As the *Roemer* case moved through the courts in the 1970s, the College of Notre Dame was under considerable stress, remembered Sister Francis Regis Carton, chair of Notre Dame's board of trustees during that time.[150] A negative court decision would have dealt a major blow to the college's ambitious expansion plans. Instead, in 1977, the college received a matching Maryland state grant of $343,000 to underwrite the renovation of the LeClerc gymnasium and auditorium.[151]

Decreasing "Sectarian" Identity after *Mann* and *Roemer*

The court cases of the 1960s and 1970s contributed to changes in religious life on campus, academic and extracurricular, but they were not the only factor. These decades saw growing student resistance to mandatory religious observances at church-related colleges nationally. When the *Horace Mann* suit commenced in the 1960s, compulsory attendance at campus religious observances and required religion courses were already under student siege at Notre Dame. "Religion, I feel, is not something one can be forced to practice" was the most common complaint. Other students objected to having to participate in religious processions, described by one as just "dragging, tiring, meaningless trails."[152] By early 1964, college administrators and faculty were discussing growing student resistance to the required annual retreat. "We are very much concerned about a spirit of indifference—even contrariety—that seems to become more prominent from year to year," one said. "Many students do not observe the silence requested of them during Retreat; and some few skipped not only exercises, but even Mass!"[153] Attempts by administrators to revive campus religious life often ended badly. When they made attendance at the 1965 annual retreat optional,[154] two-thirds of the student body elected not to make it, while many who signed up attended only "selected conferences."[155] The expectation that students would join at least one religious club disappeared. Within a few years, traditions of campus religious life at the College of Notre Dame had significantly changed.

Responding both to the legal challenges of these decades and to growing student wariness of compulsory religion, the college sought more socially inclusive ways to witness to its Catholic identity in the 1970s. It softened conspicuous religious elements in college rituals and celebrations, both academic and extracurricular. The college's mission statement now even avoided using the word "Catholic": "Founded as a Christian college, Notre Dame still expresses a commitment to the values and culture of the Christian heritage," stated the 1972–73 catalog. "It affirms the belief that a truly liberal arts college should expose students to a variety of approaches to the human experience—including the religious approach."[156]

But beyond shaping self-presentation and the minutiae of daily life on campus, the court cases also pressured Catholic colleges, among them the College of Notre Dame, into giving more control to lay boards and severing or significantly modifying relationships with founding orders. As late as 1959, the minutes of board meetings at Notre Dame reveal the extent of the order's authority: "Mother Provincial said she could assign a sister to the science and the English departments and [she] would try to provide a sister for mathematics. She recommended that we engage a lay teacher for history and another priest for religion."[157] The School Sisters of Notre Dame had recognized that the order's influence over the college, even after its separate incorporation, would be a priority interest for lawyers for the plaintiffs in the *Horace Mann* case. Hoping to minimize the charge that this made the college sectarian, the board of trustees removed the authority of the provincial superior and the superior of the campus convent over appointments of lay faculty. However, because religious superiors continued to control appointments of sisters, who made up a majority of the faculty, lawyers for the plaintiffs focused on the order's religious rule, a document they referred to as "an oath." They concluded that the rules of convent life denied sister-faculty the academic freedom enjoyed by faculty at accredited mainstream institutions.

In her deposition on December 10, 1964, the *Baltimore Sun* reported, President O'Connell had attempted, with limited success, to explain that "the rule on education which members of her order accept before teaching at the college is not a compulsory directive, but a statement of purpose and motivation. . . . 'It is not the type of obedience you're referring to,' she insisted. 'All of us feel this is a guide for personal life.' . . . [She] said that the rule of her order on education has no application to reading lists of books on the college level.'"[158] For Notre Dame faculty, sisters and lay, the allegation that they were not free to design their own courses and select their own texts attested to a perennial anti-Catholic bias. Four decades earlier, while a Notre Dame faculty member and Johns Hopkins graduate student, Elizabeth Morrissy had heard the same charge. When she casually commented to fellow university students that she chose her own textbooks at Notre Dame, "the men at Hopkins in the department . . . wouldn't believe it. They'd say, 'Well, have you used Haig?' . . . I said, 'Nobody ever questions what textbook I use.'" In fact, she said, "nobody ever interfered with anything I ever wanted to do, ever. I was given complete right-of-way. . . . I can't imagine more freedom than I had."[159]

But following the Maryland Court of Appeals' 1966 decision, a number of Catholic universities moved quickly to revise governing boards and corporate charters to establish greater legal independence from their founding religious orders. Governing boards of Saint Louis University and the University of Notre Dame, until then clerical in membership, now had significant lay representations. By reshaping its governing board, Fordham University hoped to improve its prospects of qualifying for New York State "Bundy funds," offering financial support to nonsectarian institutions. Webster College, a small women's institution in Saint Louis, established a lay board of trustees and, to the dismay of many, severed ties to its founding order, the Sisters of Loretto, and the Catholic Church.[160] While these boards were reconstructing themselves, on July 13, 1967, a panel chaired by Rev. Theodore Hesburgh, president of the University of Notre Dame, at a meeting of the North American Region of the International Federation of Catholic Universities in Land O' Lakes, Wisconsin, presented a "Statement of the Nature of the Contemporary Catholic University," a powerful call for "true autonomy and academic freedom in the face of authority of whatever kind, lay or clerical, external to the academic community itself."[161]

The *Horace Mann* case, along with contemporaneous developments, mobilized the College of Notre Dame's trustees to critically examine those areas of college life that had aroused the greatest controversy in court testimony. Mainstream arguments that the college was sectarian had focused heavily on the key role played by the religious order in its governance. Since five lay members and six religious sisters currently constituted the board of trustees, some members called for a restructuring. As long as the order effectively controlled the board, Henry Knott argued, the college would never be able to compete effectively with other private colleges. "I think the rope must be cut from the Religious Order and we must operate the same as Yale, Harvard or any other educational institution with the predominence [sic] of lay Trustees," Knott wrote to O'Connell.[162] Although they acknowledged that with a declining membership they would soon be unable to provide funds and contributed services of sisters for the college at past levels, the School Sisters of Notre Dame voiced serious reservations.

Before further action was taken on the matter of a majority-lay board, the internal politics of the SSNDs had to be worked through. When Sister Margaret Mary O'Connell became president of the college on September 17, 1950, the advisory board typically met only twice yearly with the president and trustees and had no real decision-making authority. Within the college, sisters still filled key administrative offices and dominated major college committees. Convinced that laity had much to offer the college, O'Connell advocated for the addition of prominent leaders from business, the professions, education, and politics to the advisory board, and even to the board of trustees itself.

In carrying out her vision for the college, O'Connell was often caught between a religious order reluctant to underwrite large loans for college expansion projects and trustees who viewed the need to negotiate with religious superiors in Europe as a serious deterrent to the college's development. Her strategy was to enlist members of the local hierarchy and prominent lay trustees to serve as mediators with her religious superiors on behalf of such college projects as the relocation of the preparatory school, the construction of the science center, and the approval of a joint library with Loyola College. While this unorthodox tactic certainly spurred the development of the college over her eighteen-year term as president, it did not win her universal approval. Early in 1968, Mother Provincial Mary Maurice Kelly, chair of the board of trustees, asked O'Connell to retire.[163] In June, Sister Elissa McGuire, a professor of economics, became acting president of the college, a position she held until the election of Sister Kathleen Feeley as president in 1971.[164]

In 1975, a group of trustees pressed for greater lay representation on the advisory board, "men of affluence" in particular. However, some sisters, noting that the bylaws of the college required that sisters hold a majority of seats on its board of trustees, considered such a step imprudent. "The Sisters should not jeopardize their ownership of the college, not only the property but the educational entity," argued Sister Bridget Marie Engelmeyer.[165] The impasse ended in 1977 when Provincial Superior Francis Regis Carton announced that a two-tiered model of a corporation and a board of trustees, currently popular at a number of Jesuit colleges, would allay the concerns of the religious congregation. The trustees amended the Articles of Incorporation to provide for a board numbering between five and twenty-five, and for a five-member corporation. The corporation "would have control over any change in the assets of the College, including sale, mortgage and gifts of property."[166] Corporation members included the chair of the board of trustees, the college president, the leader of the order's eastern province, the leader of the college's religious community, and additional trustees, sisters or lay, "to bring the total number of members up to five and to assure that at least three of the members shall be members of the said Congregation."[167]

But one area that both major court cases left untouched was the college's social code governing student behavior and the religious justifications for it. These issues came to center stage in the 1970s as students rallied to bring Notre Dame's social rules into conformity with those adopted by other institutions, Catholic and secular. Escalating social and political tumult accompanying the civil rights, antiwar, and women's movements, as well as internal disputes over traditional and contemporary religious values within the American Catholic community following the Second Vatican Council, sparked conflict on the campuses of women's colleges.[168] Like other American women pressing for social and professional equality in every area of life, students at Catholic women's colleges set out to gain the same autonomy over their personal and social lives on campus that their male peers enjoyed. The controversies that ensued, and their significance, are the subjects of the next chapter.

CHAPTER 6

"Convent Colleges"

Social Mores and Educated Women

Catholic higher education for women developed in a century marked not only by major political and economic changes but also by evolving social values. The first Catholic colleges for women came under intense scrutiny from misogynistic church officials and often suspicious laity, and administrators and faculty proceeded cautiously. In the sensitive areas of student conduct and campus social regulations they followed strict Catholic social values and practices. In the late nineteenth century, the cause of women's education was radical enough that unseemly student behavior could threaten institutional viability. The School Sisters of Notre Dame were likely relieved when the *Southern Review of Commerce* editorialized in the 1890s that "the atmosphere of Notre Dame College tends to develop . . . that sweet womanly character which has always been the chief charm of the mothers of the best of mankind."[1] Although as legal owners of the colleges the religious orders controlled their financial and physical resources, as Catholic institutions they remained under the close scrutiny of local bishops. Early administrators and faculty, therefore, proceeded cautiously, defending their academic programs in explicitly religious terms in official publications and protecting the colleges from harmful publicity by adopting strict student social codes based on Catholic standards of proper female behavior.

Administrators and faculty always had to contend, however, with a balance between parental and episcopal expectations and the reality of shifting social mores among the young women they taught. The Great Depression of the 1930s and two world wars widened women's professional ambitions, and by the 1950s, there was more social mixing of the sexes within collegiate youth culture. The temporal convergence of the feminist and civil rights movements in the 1950s and 1960s significantly shaped the thinking of American women in the areas of sexual morality and gender equality. The College of Notre Dame, like its peers, struggled to establish and enforce student behavioral codes against the backdrop of developments in other sectors of higher education. All types of American colleges shared some key questions during the twentieth century: in particular, were administrators to act *in loco parentis* toward students, most of whom were legal adults? Which areas of behavior were the province of student self-government, and which belonged to administrators and faculty? Catholic women's colleges, founded and conducted by orders of religious sisters, also had to reassess the current relevance of college behavioral rules historically shaped by the norms of the convents that sat at the heart of every campus.

Despite decades of student complaints, Notre Dame's "monastic" behavioral code of conduct remained staunchly in place well into the social and cultural upheavals of the 1960s. While violations of the code had begun to increase in the 1950s, students generally observed its norms. This changed in the early 1970s when well-organized student protests for more liberal parietal rules shook the campus and quickly engaged parents, alumnae, and local Catholics in strenuous debate over modern feminist values and the church's gender-specific moral prescriptions. Many viewed the social rules of a women's college as an indication of its commitment to Catholic moral values. Whether or not this commitment could flourish under less stringent behavioral prescriptions was the question. Student campaigns in this era sought to bring Notre Dame's social code into conformity with the social rules governing women students in other Catholic colleges. These student efforts played an important role in the emergence of the college as a public forum for women seeking equal rights within church-affiliated institutions. They also raised the looming question of whether Catholic women's colleges had the right to set their own standards, or whether they ought to reflect behavioral norms for women set by the male administrators of other colleges.

Governing Behavior at Early Women's Colleges

Founders and faculty of early women's colleges in England and the United States faced similar scrutiny from male clergy, prominent educators, and potential donors. Virtually all proceeded circumspectly, exhorting students to be "exemplars of femininity," ever dignified and ladylike. Any unseemly public behavior could very well threaten enrollments and even the long-term viability of female institutions.[2] Administrators of female institutions, secular and church affiliated, worked to protect their public image by monitoring both student and faculty behavior. In 1917, a Vassar College administrator rebuked faculty member Mabel Newcomer for chaperoning students at a suffrage rally, since "women's education was still on trial and must not be confused with other doubtful causes."[3] To allay concerns of conservative Catholics that the freedom of campus life, even under church auspices, might endanger the morals of young women, College of Notre Dame leaders gave close attention to student conduct from the beginning.

The School Sisters of Notre Dame drew on Catholic moral teachings to form the rationale for strict regulations governing the conduct of female students. While by the mid-1910s college catalogs declared that "the College is not governed by minute specific rules," students of the era vigorously disputed that claim, with some justification.[4] The 1910 catalog, for example, spelled out the dress code: "In order to preserve uniformity, the College requires students to wear simple black dresses; heavy texture for winter and lighter for summer."[5] By 1915 they could wear "dresses of any dark colored material." The mainstream press consistently described Catholic female colleges as "convent colleges" because they enforced stricter social regulations than mainstream women's colleges of the day. In color and fashion, student attire reinforced the convent image, and students complained about the similarity of their own dark dresses and the sisters' black religious habits. The US Catholic community, however, generally agreed that conservative attire was a way to protect young women from occasions of sin.

Conventual codes lingered in other ways. By 1900, Vassar had eliminated its 10 p.m. lights-out rule; similar colleges soon did likewise.[6] At Catholic women's colleges, by contrast, "lights out and mandatory silence after 10:00 p.m. in the rooms" remained the rule well into the 1920s.[7] In large measure, this was because administrators organized classes, meals, and study schedules around the convent horarium. Routine convent practices—such as, for example, calling nuns to obligations by the ringing of bells—were carried over directly to the colleges. In the 1930s, a bell system was still summoning Notre Dame students to rise in the morning and to shut off lights at night. Bells also called them to classes and religious and academic all-campus functions. The ubiquity of bells annoyed but also amused generations of students. As one wrote wryly in the 1936 college yearbook, "Their persistence is the very engine of our progress; their promptness, the essence of our meticulousness; their strength, the unit of our existence. . . . To prove this, one has but to ring a bell, and in less than five minutes the entire student body will assemble."[8] A bell system continued to signal class hours well into the 1960s.

During the college's early decades, enforcement of deportment was consistent, rigorous, and public. In a weekly assembly attended by the entire student body, the dean reviewed institutional policies and customs and made it clear that students were to honor them precisely. As directress of the Collegiate Institute from 1877 until it closed in 1895, Meletia Foley had conducted the weekly assembly. Later, as dean of the College of Notre Dame from 1895 until her death in 1917, she followed a similar agenda for the Sunday assembly. College students, like their Collegiate Institute predecessors, continued to call this event "Judgments."

The typical meeting lasted about ninety minutes. It commenced with all singing the dean's favorite hymn, "Abide with Me." After making some remarks on academic matters, Foley enumerated breaches of college rules, careless grammatical speech, and unladylike manners by individual students that she and the faculty had noticed during the past week.[9] The Sunday assembly always included a "good manners class."[10] For Foley and her colleagues, this was an essential component of the school's educational program: "It is as much the function of true education to develop the shy, awkward girl into the gracious, graceful woman, as to help a girl to master a mathematical problem or a law of science," stated the 1912 college catalog.[11]

Marie W. Smith, a 1904 preparatory school graduate, described a typical assembly in Dean Foley's era:

> Her most effective corrections were often given in very few words. Students obeyed. They feared to displease. I know—for I was one of them. To sit through a Sunday evening "Correction Class" conducted by Sister Mary Meletia was an unforgettable event. In some way every misdemeanor or discourtesy reached Sister's ears and even those only slightly guilty (and who was not?) trembled in expectation of what might be said. We were always "Miss" at "Correction Class" and "Miss Smith" or "Miss Brown" stood quaking at attention when her name was called. We might, in the secret recesses of some recreation nook, laugh heartily at the quaint unusual remarks by which corrections had been made, but there was never a smile during the ordeal.[12]

In 1923, forty-nine-year-old Sister Mary I. Dillon became dean of the college. Reserved in manner and a stickler for social propriety, she did not endear herself to students. Under her leadership, the college became decidedly more conservative and faculty-student interaction more formal. "College regulations were complied with or the student could find another college," recalled an alumna of the decade.[13] "Young people," Dean Engelmeyer recalled later, "objected to her quietly inflexible way of maintaining discipline."[14] Students now wore caps and gowns to the Friday assemblies that replaced the Sunday "Judgments." Although assembly agendas now focused on academic matters, they never omitted a review of social rules appropriate for true Catholic women.

Creating a Women's World

One of the ongoing tensions marking the first century of higher education for women was the dual societal imperative to protect students from potentially reputation-ruining contact with their male peers while simultaneously encouraging them to prefer matrimony and childbearing over lifetime careers as intellectuals and professionals. Both Catholic norms and mainstream America's spoken and unspoken fears about young women's sexual behavior shaped campus rules governing relationships during the early twentieth century.

In their earliest decades, both secular and Catholic women's colleges prioritized limiting contact between students and their male peers, creating a nearly entirely female social world designed to protect students on campus as they would have been at home. Student residences on turn-of-the-century secular and Protestant women's campuses increasingly favored a "domestic" structural design. According to Marion Talbot, dean of women at the University of Chicago, because society's welfare depended heavily on women, "it is essential that the college hall, in which the woman student spends a large part of her time, should be organized as much as possible like the family and the home."[15] Similarly, leading women's colleges in England adopted "domestic" motifs and resembled large country houses.[16] In order to "protect the femininity of young college women," trustees planning Scripps College instructed architects to "give to the dormitories the appearance and atmosphere of a beautiful home."[17] Smith College also used "the ties of family life" to justify its adoption of cottage-style student housing.[18]

The new Catholic women's colleges, however, preferred a conventual model to more "homelike" designs.[19] Students at the College of Notre Dame lived in a massive building, replete with wide corridors, high ceilings, elaborate parlors, a grand dining room, and a large chapel; in both form and function, it was the antithesis of a typical domestic design. The founders

FIGURE 11. Afternoon tea, balcony of College Hall, 1918. Photo from NDMA.

considered large buildings, like large convents, to be entirely fitting environments for female learning and living. Confident that nuns would closely supervise all aspects of student life, Catholic parents had few qualms about permitting their daughters to live away from home. A description of the Notre Dame of Maryland campus in the 1890s is representative of many later suburban Catholic women's colleges:

> In the midst of a smiling landscape on Charles Street avenue, about half way between Baltimore and Towson, the county seat, are the spacious grounds and lofty trees surrounding an imposing structure—the Convent of Notre Dame—attached to which is the famous Notre Dame of Maryland, a collegiate institute for young ladies. It is approached by a broad avenue. From the broad marble hall, up the wide stairs to drawing-rooms, study halls, music-rooms, chapel and dormitory, the twin goddesses of health and hygiene have fulfilled all the requirements. In an upper story, where the windows command a magnificent view of the Chesapeake Bay, are a dozen rooms, each one handsomely furnished. They are occupied by parlor boarders, and are presided over in each department by a sister. Besides the regular curriculum,

the scholars are given ample scope for proper physical development in calisthenics, boating, tennis, &c.[20]

Leaving campus was not easy for students at women's colleges. Without chaperones, one author wrote in 1900, they could not visit "places of public amusement or [go] to social entertainments in the evening, or to athletic games other than their own."[21] Socializing with men on campus was equally challenging. Church-sponsored colleges reflected denominational perspectives. While their rules varied, all were strict.[22] In 1900, a Smith College student could not lunch with a man at the college unless another student joined them.[23] The same year, students at Wesleyan Female College in Macon, Georgia, could not have male visitors or correspond with nonfamily males.[24] Eastern women's colleges, generally more liberal, permitted students to entertain male friends in public parlors until residence halls closed for the night, but they discouraged male visitors on Sundays.[25] With the warden's permission, Vassar College students in 1913 could entertain men in their rooms from one o'clock to four o'clock in the afternoon—as long as chaperones were present.[26]

Early rules for Catholic college women were similar. In Notre Dame's early years, students could have only "family and lady visitors" on Thursday afternoons from three to five, and even these visits were monitored by faculty—a regimen that, if slightly less strict than convent visitation rules of the era, at least approached them in severity.[27] Trips off campus were also rare; according to an 1899 College of Notre Dame graduate, "Every two weeks, if we managed to keep within the law, we could obtain a town permission to leave the campus from 11 a.m. till 5 p.m."[28] But these rules were far slower to change than those at secular women's colleges. When a writer for the *Woman's Journal* concluded in 1930 that "chaperonage in its old sense is dead" for the college woman, she did not take into account students at Catholic female colleges.[29] At Notre Dame, nuns supervised resident students at night until the 1940s, but they did not chaperone campus social events.[30] College administrators instead relied on lay faculty to accompany students to off-campus events—not only social functions like dances, but also concerts, academic lectures, and even religious celebrations. In 1923 the librarian, Miss Himmelhaber, chaperoned the senior class at the Federation of Catholic Alumnae Mass at the local cathedral.[31]

The small cadre of lay faculty and staff found themselves always on call. "I had to chaperone everything or they couldn't have it," remembered Professor Elizabeth Morrissy. Students particularly detested this college rule. The 1923 college yearbook lampooned the chaperone as "a noble exponent of a fast-dying cause. As reactionary and conservative as Metternich, and usually as welcome as cutworms. In an official role, usually found around seminaries and educational institutions of high order. Their popularity varies inversely with usefulness."[32] By the end of this decade, in a concession to rising complaints, the college permitted students to attend lectures at Johns Hopkins University chaperone free.

The strict contact rules meant that men continued to play a decidedly peripheral role in the social life of women's campuses at the turn of the twentieth century. Women's colleges developed strong traditions of their own, many of which transferred quickly from secular to Catholic colleges. The College of Notre Dame held its first Class Day exercises on June 13, 1899. The program included the presentation of awards, singing of the class song, and reading of the class history, the class prophecy, and the class ode, composed by Dorothea Kilkoff, a senior. Class Day at Vassar College in this era featured a daisy chain carried by "sixteen of the fairest members of the Junior class,"[33] and Notre Dame soon added a similar feature. Whereas at its 1902 Class Day, students wore caps and gowns "with long streamers of their class colors," by 1906, the celebration also featured a "beautiful daisy chain march . . . with all the college girls taking part in singing college glees & songs."[34]

At Notre Dame's first cap-and-gown investiture of freshmen in the fall of 1906,[35] the convent superior, who was the college's official president, granted a campus holiday "to be taken whenever the freshmen desire it."[36] This was reminiscent of Smith College's Mountain Day, an annual fall holiday since 1877; the president chose the date, and the ringing of the campus bells gave students the good news. Even after 1935 when a single individual no longer served as local convent superior and college president simultaneously, the superior represented the order at various college events. In the 1940s, she joined the college president in presenting graduates with "their usual parting gift of lovely copies of *The Following of Christ*,"[37] and in the 1950s she presided at senior honors awards ceremonies.

Commencement week festivities at Notre Dame had incorporated a lantern chain by 1930. This was a "sophomore lantern serenade to seniors," with scores and lyrics composed by students. Seniors gathered on the balcony of College Hall around nine o'clock at night, while sophomores, bearing lighted lanterns, formed a chain between juniors and freshmen. "Weav[ing] back and forth on the esplanade," they sang "regretful adieus" to their sister-class. Freshmen and juniors sang their goodbyes, and the senior class sang in response. All students joined in a song of "religious and school sentiments," and the event ended with a bugler's rendition of taps. The tradition lapsed in the 1960s, but reappeared two decades later "with less ceremony than the original."[38]

Student clubs proliferated in all colleges in the early twentieth century, and Notre Dame, despite its small size, reflected this trend. Numerous social, religious, and student departmental clubs, some short lived, provided a modest degree of student autonomy and added considerable vitality to campus life. By the mid-twentieth century, students typically joined at least two clubs: "One would have been a religious organization and one was maybe another kind," recalled a graduate from 1949.[39] College drama societies were especially popular for fostering campus spirit and offering varied entertainment.[40] The entire Notre Dame community, including students from the preparatory school, zealously attended the earliest student dramatic performances. Faculty served as coaches. About a 1907 outdoor performance of *As You Like It*, the annalist wrote, "It was the very best thing we have had here. The setting was perfect, and the girls read their lines faultlessly."[41] In 1916, students formed a drama club, the Play Folk, soon renamed Ye Merrie Masquers. Its inaugural performance was Augusta Gregory's comedy *Spreading the News*.[42] The club drew its casts for early productions from all four college classes, a decision necessitated by the college's small size. The senior class play, so popular at mainstream women's colleges at this time, did not take hold at Notre Dame until 1926.

Dances were another area where turn-of-the-century administrators vacillated between the desire to strictly control contact with the opposite sex and the necessity of allowing young women to develop social skills they would need once they left college. At Vassar, men were able to attend two large dances a year, while at Smith's house dances, held in the gymnasium, they were "not allowed on the floor."[43] On Catholic women's college campuses, students had even fewer opportunities to socialize with male friends. The purpose of campus dances and student teas was to familiarize students with rules of proper social behavior and etiquette. Administrators did not consider the presence of young men essential to this end. All-female class dances had disappeared in the elite eastern women's colleges by the turn of the century, but they continued at Notre Dame. "No one slept for a week before and after the Senior Dance," reported a 1924 student publication, "before, because they feared they wouldn't dance with all the Seniors—afterwards, because they hadn't." The freshmen class dance was also "a red-letter evening. Good orchestra, soft lights, everyone looking her best."[44]

Elizabeth Morrissy, who joined the Notre Dame faculty in this decade, recalled her astonishment when she first witnessed a college dance—a reaction that highlights how practices on Catholic campuses had fallen far behind those elsewhere. Students wore full evening dress, although short sleeves were off limits. "They had an orchestra, but no men," she marveled.[45] College administrators hired orchestras on the condition that they follow college directives regarding music and instruments. Not surprisingly, students complained that the music was passé. "The only fly in the festive ointment was that the 'jazziest' of music was strictly tabooed," wrote a student journalist of a 1923 dance.[46] A jazz musician hired for the Valentine Dance the next year was instructed not to play the saxophone. According to student lore, administrators feared the saxophone "aroused girls' passion."[47]

In this social context, close relationships between young women flourished. Neither public commentators nor college administrators in the late nineteenth century saw this as a serious threat to the wider social order, though it was a topic of concern for other reasons: in 1882, Alice Stone Blackwell, a leader of the Association of Collegiate Alumnae, criticized "crushes" and "smashing" in women's colleges because they kept students from studying, and noted that "smashes" were less common at coeducational institutions.[48] In the 1890s, Dean Meletia Foley was similarly casual in her attitude toward student friendships. Classes were small, and it was unsurprising that close alliances developed. Younger students in the campus preparatory school frequently had crushes on college students. In fact, Catholic women's college leaders viewed student social rituals based on courtship and marriage as useful ways to promote campus harmony. A faux wedding ceremony at the College of New Rochelle in the 1910s was "delightfully picturesque and an unforgettable scene," a witness reported. "In a setting of daintily costumed bridesmaids the bride, president of the Freshmen, is united to the groom, president of the Juniors, both vowing devotion to the ideals of New Rochelle in the name of their classes."[49]

But concern about women's relationships intensified in the early twentieth century, and social pressure gradually shifted attitudes on campus. Whereas nineteenth-century women's college students admired their instructors as pioneer professional women, their twentieth-century successors tended to view them as social failures. They "look at us with coldly critical eyes, and do not wish to be like us," remarked a Mount Holyoke College professor in 1913.[50] By this time, the popular press and speakers in public forums were harshly denouncing women's colleges, with their large faculties of unmarried women, as places that fostered lesbianism.[51] At Notre Dame in the 1910s, students who engaged in public displays of affection evoked the mockery of peers. A 1915 issue of a short-lived campus gossip sheet spoofed a student attracted to one of the nuns:

"The Reason"
Round the corridors she wanders,
Aimless as a brook in spring—
Ask you why she wanders thusly?
Ask you why the birdlets sing?
'Twas an arrow of Dan Cupid's
Turned her to this silly thing.
Hopes and heart-thrills never ending,
Love rejected, pain untold—
Standing hours before the Convent,
Just the loved one to behold.[52]

Among Sister Mary Dillon's first acts as dean of the college in 1923 was to outlaw as "unhealthy" any public display of affection between students or between students and faculty, especially "smashing" and crushes.[53] The "crush," according to that year's yearbook, was "an emotional attachment that impels one person towards another. It is usually accompanied by outward signs such as pallor of countenance, brilliancy of eye, palpitation of heart, and weakness about the section of the anatomy known as the 'patella.' . . . The word is derived from a Sanscrit stem—as are also ice-cream, candy, and flowers."[54]

Attacks on women's colleges became increasingly virulent in the 1920s, as conservative social critics assailed them for encouraging students to delay or forego marriage in favor of professional careers. As evidence, they pointed to lower marriage rates and smaller families among graduates of women's colleges relative to other American women. By encouraging celibacy in "intellectual women," these schools promoted "race suicide."[55] Of particular concern were colleges attended by daughters of upper-class families, since "no question is of greater importance to eugenics than that of the birth-rate among the eugenically superior parts of the population."[56] As the public campaign against women's colleges continued, leaders of the Seven Sister colleges issued a joint press statement to reassure the American public that at least in their colleges, "the proportion of married graduates . . . steadily if slowly increases. It has passed fifty per cent in almost all . . . and its trend is still upward."[57]

Despite the tradition of close Catholic female communities, by the 1920s the pressure was on to decrease romantic attachments between women. To dissuade public criticism in this area, Notre Dame authorities not only encouraged communal activities like sports and music over "crushing," but they also lifted the college's long-standing prohibition on mixed dances and parties on campus—an action enthusiastically welcomed by students. However, they continued to closely supervise such events, whether held on campus or at off-campus venues. In the 1920s, for example, a freshman class held a dance in a downtown hotel to raise funds to benefit the gymnasium project. A student who attended recalled the occasion vividly six decades later: "We had to leave the campus in the school bus, driven by the school chauffeur. We were taken to the Belvedere, we met the boys there, and we left them there and came home again by bus when the dance was over. So much for social life."[58] Mixed dances remained a particular concern during the Prohibition years (1919–33). "Everybody was being pretty careful about carrying flasks. . . . So they were very strict," Morrissy remembered. Male guests at campus dances had to remain in the hall for the entire evening; anyone who left could not reenter. Then, Morrissy said, "when the party ended, the girls said goodnight to the men in the gym and went back through the tunnel home [to the residence hall], and the men went on their way."[59]

Campus social life improved significantly in the late 1920s. In 1926, in a "very new departure," an informal campus tea included male guests. From all reports it was a "great success." Two months later, "for the first time [nearby Catholic men's college] Loyola and Notre Dame danced together to the strains of the Merry Widow Waltz." In February 1927, the LeClerc gymnasium became the setting for the first junior prom. This annual dance quickly became the foremost campus social event. Students donated net proceeds to benefit the college. Other Catholic women's colleges were also liberalizing their social policies; for College of New Rochelle students, all-female dances ended in 1929.[60]

Press criticism of women's colleges as places that encouraged female relationships to the detriment of marriage and child-rearing left Catholic women's colleges, with their overwhelmingly female boards of trustees, administrations, and faculty, feeling especially vulnerable.[61] The sisters' own renunciation of marriage could draw unwelcome press attention and affect enrollment, and their celibate lifestyle and full-time careers defied the prevailing social dictum that women's primary role was to marry and raise children. However, within the Catholic community, parishioners generally considered the life choice of nuns to be legitimate and honorable. Students in Catholic women's colleges, for the most part, took the high proportion of unmarried women on their faculties for granted. Sister-faculty in women's colleges deeply influenced students. Because they lived on campus, students could observe on a daily basis their celibate communities, religious

dedication, and scholarly commitment. At Notre Dame, their highly indi-
vidualistic personalities intrigued generations of students. An alumna of the
1940s recalled that she "didn't know what to make . . . [of] the individuality of
the SSNDs. Here they were in a religious community, and each one of them
was so remarkably different. . . . Somehow the order could accommodate
those differences."[62] The class of 1924 dedicated their yearbook to "All the
Sisters" who taught them "to go forth—unafraid—alone." The class of 1936
chose to honor Elizabeth Morrissy, an unmarried lay professor, "whom we
regard as the ideal woman."[63]

Some students did not just admire their celibate faculty; they emulated
them. Convent life dependably attracted a small but steady proportion of
college students until the 1960s. Between 1899 and 1950, 49 percent of
Notre Dame alumnae married; 40 percent engaged in professional careers;
and approximately 10 percent joined religious orders. This proportion was
representative of similar institutions.[64] In 1943, of seventy-five Notre Dame
students who responded to a Catholic Student Mission Crusade campus survey, one-fifth replied "yes" to the question, "Are you willing to sacrifice all
to serve Christ in the Religious state as a Sister?"[65] The proportion acting on
this sentiment was smaller, but nonetheless considerable. Students admired
peers who entered the religious life, and crowded the college chapel to witness "departure ceremonies" for classmates leaving for the novitiate. Until
midcentury, according to Patricia Wittberg, "it was not unusual for ten to fifteen percent of each graduating class at Catholic women's colleges to enter
the community of the sisters who taught there."[66]

Young men rarely appeared on the Notre Dame campus except on weekends and for special occasions, a situation that began to change in the 1940s
as student clubs sponsored small parties and mixers. The dramatics club
organized "a little dansant" in 1940 that "gentlemen from Loyola College and
Johns Hopkins University attended zealously."[67] Clubs also sponsored social
entertainments to follow college cultural programs. Following a 1948 concert by the Johns Hopkins Glee Club and Symphony Orchestra in LeClerc
Hall, the Kymry Club hosted an "informal dance" for students from both
colleges.[68] By including men from secular and Protestant colleges like Johns
Hopkins as well as Loyola in campus social events, Notre Dame differed from
a majority of Catholic women's colleges of the day, which typically restricted
social invitations to students from Catholic men's institutions.[69]

The proportion of college women opting to marry soon after graduation
rather than to embark on full-time professional careers rose in the postwar
era. According to a 1948 survey by the American Association of University
Women, one-quarter of respondents "felt that there should have been more

college preparation for one or another aspect of married life."[70] Many Notre Dame alumnae concurred. The college had prepared its students for graduate study and professional careers, but it had neglected the growing numbers who intended to marry and raise children. While it had nurtured their intellectual and professional goals, it had not done enough to prepare them for the challenges of domestic life. As a 1953 graduate put it, "The number must be very low of Catholic college women graduates who enter marriage and feel (honestly) that they are accomplishing any great goal or objective today." Alumnae called on the college to pay more attention to the intellectual struggles of young mothers in the home: "The good Sisters should be aware of the feelings of many, if not most, married graduates of Catholic colleges and possibly help us to answer or find that 'bridge between.'"[71]

Easing Regulations, Student Government, 1940s–50s

Despite a gradual easing of social contact rules governing relationships with men, College of Notre Dame administrators kept tight control over aspects of student life long after their secular counterparts had ceased to do so. As many of these colleges liberalized their dress regulations in the 1920s to accommodate the short-skirted fashions of the decade, Notre Dame did not follow suit. "Dress length, ten inches from the ground," read the 1921 college catalog. "Short sleeves and low necks are not permitted. . . . Colored sweaters are not permitted."[72] During Dean Mary Dillon's tenure (1923–31), the dress code remained tight. Students were to wear black or navy dresses; sleeveless dresses were specifically proscribed.[73] Dillon's successor relaxed these restrictions somewhat. Students could now wear "any decent clothing" of any dark color during class hours.

During the 1940s, thousands of young women across the United States wore pants while working in war production plants; by the 1950s, pants were ubiquitous as casual wear. By the early 1960s, Radcliffe College's dress code required only that students wear skirts to class. They were otherwise free to wear pants. At Notre Dame, however, students could not "appear in public in anything except skirts—no shorts, no long pants."[74] Despite their fierce protest that the dress code was evidence of a "convent mentality," modifications were slow to come. While eventually students were free to wear pants on the campus and in residence halls, the expectation that they wear skirts to class and in the college dining hall remained in force until the dress code ended in 1971.

Coeducational dramatic performances were acceptable at Radcliffe and Harvard by the early 1910s, and drama clubs at other Seven Sister colleges were recruiting actors from local men's colleges by the next decade.[75] Catholic female colleges were generally slower to allow this practice, although there were exceptions by the 1930s.[76] At the College of Notre Dame, however, students played both male and female roles in drama productions (see figure 6) until 1958, when, for the first time, Johns Hopkins and Loyola men joined them in a college play. The advisory board judged the men "a great asset" in the production, and Notre Dame's all-female casts finally disappeared.[77]

More than any other campus privilege, however, freedom to smoke signified female independence. Beginning in 1925, Vassar students were free to "smoke inconspicuously," at first outdoors, then in a designated "smoking room." Within a few years, most mainstream female colleges removed or modified their smoking rules. In 1929, Acting President Hans Froelicher decided to eliminate Goucher College's rule against smoking in public because "enforcement of the rule . . . required snooping and tattling, incompatible with the dignity of the college."[78] For Smith College president William Allan Neilson, smoking had nothing to do with morality; it was just a question of propriety.[79] By 1930, according to a *Woman's Journal* columnist, except for Mount Holyoke, students at the Seven Sister colleges were no longer "held up to the standards of the convent." A Vassar student described her sense of emancipation: "Thank Heaven, nowadays we can live like people and aren't expected to be nuns."[80]

Stung by invidious comparisons of their college to a convent, and themselves to nuns, Notre Dame students demanded the same smoking privileges enjoyed by their peers at other Catholic colleges. In 1934, administrators at Saint Mary's College in Indiana, despite faculty objection that this step signified "the breaking down of the sacrosanct tradition and respectability of Saint Mary's," had allowed students to smoke on campus. Similar colleges soon followed suit. Many restricted smoking to a specific campus site. In 1935, for example, New Rochelle College provided a campus "tearoom" for this purpose.[81] Leaders of the College of Notre Dame, however, refused to make any concession; smoking violated norms of appropriate female behavior. Disgruntled students responded by congregating to smoke in noisy groups in areas "on the fringe of the campus" and in local restaurants and stores.[82] As this drew undesirable publicity to the college, officials in 1940 reluctantly provided a "smoking room" in a residence hall basement that was open for an hour or two daily. A 1947 graduate described it as "a tiny little room." Students would "rush in there at lunchtime, play bridge, and have a cigarette. . . . I don't think it was very acceptable at that time, but it was tolerated."[83]

By the war decade of the 1940s, Notre Dame students had become more assertive in seeking autonomy over their extra-academic activities. The highlight of Field Day, the chief campus event of the year, was the presentation of the "Blazer Girl" award, at the Recreation Association (formerly the Athletic Association) banquet, to the student who had demonstrated the highest athletic and leadership achievement over three years at the college. Traditionally, the nominee of the student body received the college blazer, although the final decision lay with the association's board. As in the past, students at the 1945 event confidently expected their favored candidate, the vice president of the junior class, to receive the Blazer Girl honor. Thus when physical education instructor Anne Kean announced that "the R.A. Board did not find any candidate worthy of the blazer [that year], and therefore would not confer it," thirty-nine students rose in protest and marched noisily out of the hall.[84]

This demonstration, the first in the college's history, shook administrators and faculty, especially since nearly 40 percent of the protesters were freshmen. After consulting the sister- faculty, President Frances Smith deprived the Blazer Girl protesters of all honors, scholarships, faculty recommendations, and student offices for at least a semester. Most students believed the president's penalties to be unfairly punitive and blamed administrators, not the Recreation Association board, for denying their candidate the Blazer Girl Award. The campus was in turmoil. So much animosity and cutthroat competition marked the year's Sing Song production that administrators abolished the requirement that all students belong to the Recreation Association and participate in Sing Song.[85] For the first time, administrators and faculty appreciated the significant extent to which the Depression decade and World War II had bred a new cohort of independent-minded students. The Blazer Girl walkout of 1945 symbolized the beginning of a new era. Student willingness to organize in opposition to perceived injustices developed steadily after this incident.

Early student governments at Seven Sister colleges were simple organizations. Bryn Mawr's Self-Government Association, formed in 1885, was believed to be "the first of its kind" in the United States.[86] At Vassar College in 1900, leaders of the senior class, the Students' Association (formed in 1867), and the Young Women's Christian Association constituted the student government.[87] Smith College had limited self-government by 1904. The authority of student representatives there extended to informing a faculty committee of student concerns and then relaying that committee's verdicts to the student body. Students were unimpressed: "This is faculty rule, surely," a Smith student complained. [88] Wellesley lacked even this minimal structure.

According to a 1900 survey, "The system of government in Wellesley College is very definitely not a form of self-government. It rests in the hands of an academic council of the faculty, and more especially, and for everyday purposes, in the hands of the president and heads of houses."[89]

Southern colleges generally lagged in introducing student governments. In 1909 students at Sophie Newcomb College (Louisiana), objecting that their rudimentary student government was "practically useless," called for a Student Club with a board of representatives that would oversee the honor system and "be the mediator between the students and the faculty." They took pains to promise that this would not challenge faculty authority: "By student self-government is not meant opposition to faculty control, it means, rather, organization of the student body to co-operate with the faculty."[90]

Student governments at Catholic women's colleges also developed slowly. Students at several early institutions were electing quasi-official delegates between the student body and the faculty by the 1910s. At the College of New Rochelle, an elected student advisory board "represent[ed] the student interests in disciplinary affairs, and other matters of college management."[91] While in 1903 students at Trinity College (Washington, DC) drafted a detailed proposal for a student government, a decade passed before it was acted on.[92] In general, however, the relatively small size of Catholic women's colleges dampened student interest in developing student governments. In her memoir, President Madeleva Wolff of Saint Mary's College, a strong backer of student government, noted that on a small campus everyone knew everyone else, and "frankly, they did not want to take the blame for things."[93] At the College of Notre Dame, it was Frances Smith who introduced an honor system in 1936, although students, after the fact, took credit for the initiative: "An experiment which has succeeded in some schools and failed in others should unquestionably be put over by force of student opinion in a Catholic college," editorialized *Columns*. "The honor system dignifies the college just as it dignifies the students. It makes our minds more open and our hearts more beloved by the most honorable Judge of all."[94]

The development of student government at the College of Notre Dame was representative of that of the small Catholic female colleges that were increasing in number nationally in the 1930s. A rudimentary student government had appeared in 1931, with students commissioning class presidents to represent their interests with college administrators. But because they lacked "a set formula of student government," these class officers could not organize their fellow students effectively. In January 1936, sensing a degree of faculty support during an "open-floor" faculty-student discussion, students proposed to develop a formal student government.[95] When by late 1937 the faculty had not responded, the senior class president sought the assistance of Rev. Daniel Lord, SJ, a well-regarded figure in Catholic higher education circles and, at the time, a visiting lecturer at Notre Dame. He suggested that students form a Board of Student Organizations (BOSO), composed of class officers and heads of student organizations, to "control student activities and be responsible to the President of the College." At the same time, a Board of Resident Students (BRS), with representatives from the four classes, would "enforce the regulations governing resident students."[96] With Lord's backing, the plan won administrative and faculty approval, and in 1938 the student body elected its first student government president.

As a council of students, BOSO supervised the college's calendar of events and helped administer the fledgling honor system. Its overarching goal was "the promotion of a unified spirit throughout the entire student body."[97] But as BOSO answered directly to the college president, student independence developed only fitfully. Student proposals were often unfocused and unrealistic; for example, a petition to eliminate final examinations for the 1938 senior class so they could enjoy "the college farewell activities" predictably did not get far.[98] In the 1940s, a new Student Association, to which all students belonged, replaced BOSO. It was a more tightly structured student government, with three standing committees: a committee on government to make and enforce rules to protect the mutual rights of the college and students; a committee on social activities to oversee campus events; and a committee on residence to deal with the special concerns of resident students. An executive board with representatives from these committees "co-ordinate[d] all the activities of student life," and a student-faculty council dealt with disputed matters.[99] The collective power of students remained limited, however. At a 1948 college assembly, students voted for a new student-government constitution, but it could not take effect without faculty approval.[100]

In 1949–50, the Student Association executive board included a faculty adviser appointed by the administration, officers of the Student Association, class presidents and representatives, the president of the Resident Student Association, and delegates to the National Federation of Catholic College Students and the National Student Association. This reorganization strengthened the student government. By the 1950s, the student-faculty council was considering substantive proposals, among them that students attend faculty meetings, have representation on the board of trustees, and rate faculty and evaluate courses each semester. While these proposals were too radical to gain much administrative and faculty support in the conservative 1950s, they were to return in revised and stronger versions in the next decade.[101]

In the 1940s, student government functioned principally as an enforcement arm with regard to college rules and regulations, cooperating with the faculty "in building up and upholding the Honor System on which the discipline of the college is based."[102] The college's new honor system applied only to cheating on examinations. Students agreed to report cheating, whether by themselves or by others, to the Board of Student Organizations. BOSO set penalties for infractions, and the academic dean held final authority in imposing them. With the emergence of the Student Association in 1947, the honor system's domain widened to include student "conduct in general."[103] By essentially "redefining" campus boundaries, Notre Dame administrators extended the honor system's authority to off-campus activities. It now went far "beyond academic testing to include every aspect of student life."[104] By 1950, "administration of the honor system"[105]—that is, reviewing and setting punishments for honor code violations in all areas of campus life[106]—was the single most important function of the Student Association board.

The Push for Student Control, 1960s–70s

Overall, Catholic women's colleges had actively incorporated mainstream values into their curricula and academic standards, but drew a line at emulating secular colleges when it came to student behavior rules. Since their social codes were strict and slow to change, disparities between Catholic and secular female institutions were soon evident—and became more so in the postwar era. Students at Catholic women's colleges chafed under social regulations that they believed limited their autonomy as adult citizens and impaired the quality of their social lives on campus. By the 1950s and 1960s, conflicts between contemporary social mores and gender-specific Catholic social norms were rising.

Both mainstream and church-related women's campuses at midcentury tended to be politically inactive places. Bryn Mawr was "pervasively indifferent to politics, not just to 'women's rights,'" remembered a 1958 alumna.[107] This state of affairs changed rapidly in the 1960s. As students on secular women's campuses participated in political, feminist, and social reform movements in larger numbers, their College of Notre Dame contemporaries, for the most part, focused on internal campus reform. Relatively few participated in the October 15, 1969, national moratorium on college classes to protest the Vietnam War, or in the antiwar protests that swept campuses across the country on May 6, 1970.[108] Instead, students applied activist tactics to gaining control over campus decisions, particularly around which campus activities required their attendance and how much contact they could have with men.

"Cuts" and "Community Honor"

Among Notre Dame's academic rules, the most resented and long-standing was the requirement that students attend all classes—the famous "no cuts" policy. The 1923 college yearbook defined the "cut" as an obsolete term, "formerly spoken of in hushed whispers, now entirely disregarded in polite society. Implies a privilege, unheard of in the present regime."[109] College catalogs of the 1930s described the cuts policy in detail. If a student's absences from class in a course exceeded the number of times the course met weekly, she could not take the final examination in the course. Moreover, "absence immediately before or after a holiday will be counted as three times a regular absence" and "a cut will count as two absences."[110] These precise mathematical equivalencies continued during the war years of the 1940s: "Three instances of tardiness for any class are equivalent to an absence," read the 1943–44 catalog. Absences from important academic events, lectures, and weekly assemblies, as well as such nonacademic events as Sunday masses, retreats, and lectures, also resulted in the loss of academic quality points needed to graduate. "The idea that that would happen was enough of an incentive that students were present," commented a faculty member.[111] Students whose male and female friends were currently serving in the military considered these policies childish.

The no-cuts rule continued at most Catholic women's colleges longer than at their mainstream counterparts. Seeing little prospect for ending the broad policy at Notre Dame, students in 1960 settled on a more realistic goal. They would push for removal of the requirement that all students attend the weekly assembly, a tradition since the college's founding. Although their seemingly quixotic proposal that assembly attendance become optional for juniors and seniors failed in the short run, the strategy bore fruit two years later.[112] The college replaced weekly assemblies with a faculty-designed lecture series, chaired by the dean,[113] and permitted students to cut four of the lectures over the course of the academic year.[114] In 1965, the faculty approved a semester trial of unlimited cuts for seniors and honors students, and the college catalog that year stated that "students are given latitude for the exercise of judgment in class attendance."[115] By 1967, the academic cut system had ended.

The question of cuts was more complex than it appeared at first glance. Restricting cuts prioritized community life over individual choice, mandating that students consider their membership in the college and the class ahead of their own desires. Like all rules and laws, the cuts system also suggested a belief that externally imposed systems were important for keeping individuals and institutions alike on track. Increasingly, however, Notre Dame students themselves believed in prioritizing their own individual judgment. They took pains to distinguish between their academic experience—"a pleasure"—and residence hall life, which was marked by "hundreds of little rules." As one survey response summarized, "It is not the rules themselves, for we are all committed to high ideals in living if we come to a Catholic college in the first place, but the way in which these rules are administered can make everyone unhappy." With campus harmony eroding, "this family spirit that the school tries to cultivate only causes friction."[116] But while administrators, faculty, and parents remained wary, students' passive and active resistance to the honor system eventually made it impossible to maintain.

Even as most Notre Dame students in the 1960s agreed that the honor system was "one of the most prized possessions of this college," many found the concept of "community honor" in the area of the college's myriad social rules increasingly hard to accept.[117] A growing number refused to report social violations, whether their own or those of their peers, to the Student Association board. Why, they asked, was the observance of petty social rules on the same level of moral gravity as conformity to academic regulations? Why should infractions of a college honor code "extend to the trivial, such as walking on the grass"? Most viewed penalties for code breaches as decidedly disproportionate to the seriousness of offenses—as, for example, when "a student must report herself when she forgets to sign out, and for this she is penalized by a weekend campus" (that is, restriction to campus). The honor system, they agreed, was undermining Notre Dame's reputation as a progressive institution: "I'd like to be proud of my school and not have it referred to as a 'convent school,'" one student said.[118]

Student resistance to the "double reporting" obligation had led many colleges to modify or eliminate their honor codes. Pembroke College abandoned its code entirely in 1961, according to Louise M. Newman, "because students could no longer be relied upon to report their own or others' violations."[119] The double-reporting requirement undermined the ability of Notre Dame's Student Association to administer the honor system effectively. In 1966, neighboring Johns Hopkins University introduced a new "open dorm policy" for its undergraduate men's college, a turn of events that worried

Notre Dame leaders. They notified students that the standing college rule that "a student may not visit in a man's bedroom, nor is a man permitted to visit in hers" would now extend to "all dormitory rooms at Johns Hopkins and all apartments purchased by Johns Hopkins to be used as dormitories." Notre Dame students entering these premises would be in "severe violation" of the college's honor code and "subject to automatic suspension or expulsion."[120] This virtually unenforceable decree further eroded student respect for the honor system. Historically, at Notre Dame, "the honor code was really an academic honor code," commented Kathleen Feeley.[121] Broadening it over time to include social behavior had gravely weakened its character and influence.

In an effort "to give new vitality to the honor code . . . as an ideal apart from the regulations that had formerly been part of the old honor system," the Student Association board separated its judicial (judging violations) and legislative (student rules) branches.[122] By the early 1970s, the honor system itself had returned to its original focus on academic violations, a reversal that restored student respect for and pride in the honor code. Now a judicial board, with faculty representation, oversaw academic infractions of the honor code, while a separate student affairs committee, also with faculty representation, functioned as a hearing board for other violations.[123]

Sex and the Single (College) Girl

The women's movement called for equal rights for women in all areas of social life, and reforms introduced by the Second Vatican Council (1962–65) encouraged Catholic women, both lay and religious, to assume critical roles in the life, worship, and social leadership of the church. In the 1960s, Catholic women's college students took both calls seriously.[124] Many turned their eyes first toward gaining control over their own lives—specifically, over their ability to control their behavior on campus. Resistance to the cuts system and to the double-reporting obligation represented two aspects of Notre Dame students' campus activism. But they also joined in a nationwide student crusade for more liberal "parietals," the institutional rules governing visits by the opposite sex in dormitory rooms. In Catholic women's colleges, parietal privileges were still limited even in the 1970s, even as similar rules had fallen elsewhere. The campaign at Notre Dame for more liberal male visitation rules soon spread well beyond the triggering issue to engage the college and wider church communities in extended and contentious public debate over Catholic moral principles and student autonomy within church-related female colleges.

Although chaperonage was fading fast at most women's colleges by the 1920s, traditional curfew policies persisted. After World War II, with more social freedoms and economic opportunities opening to women, *in loco parentis* rules seemed to students to be decidedly behind the times. Curfew hours and obligatory "sign-in" and "sign-out" rules were especially onerous.[125] Elite eastern colleges led the way toward reform. By this time, Bryn Mawr's weekday curfew was 11:30 p.m., while Wellesley's was 10 p.m. on weekdays, midnight on weekends.[126] Curfews at Catholic women's colleges were earlier. In 1946, the weekday curfew at Chestnut Hill College in Philadelphia was 7 p.m. for freshmen and sophomores, 8 p.m. for juniors, and 9 p.m. for seniors, with later hours for weekends possible "with permissions."[127] At the College of Notre Dame, curfew regulations in the 1960s for all classes remained 7 p.m. on weekdays and midnight on weekends. These hours were stricter than those imposed by comparable women's institutions as well as former men's colleges that had recently become coeducational. In 1971, for example, Georgetown University, which had admitted women to its College of Arts and Sciences three years before, set curfew hours for freshmen at midnight during the week and 2 a.m. on weekends; its upper-class women, notes Susan L. Poulson, had an "optional check out privilege, allowing them to sign out for the evening if they returned by 9 a.m."[128]

On taking office in 1971, Notre Dame's new president, Kathleen Feeley, SSND, recognized that the curfew issue was a lost cause. Behavioral rules that applied only to resident students were inherently unjust, social expectations governing women's appropriate behavior were liberalizing, and *in loco parentis* rules were out at most mainstream colleges. Feeley immediately moved the weekend curfew to 2 a.m., and within two years abolished curfew regulations. "It was a major change," remembered Dean of Students Marie Michelle Walsh.[129] Students could now return to campus at any hour, and the institution took "no responsibility for supervising social activities off campus."[130]

The college's retreat from the *in loco parentis* doctrine in the matter of curfews encouraged students to organize for more liberal parietal rules. Parietals varied widely among institutions. Men's colleges liberalized their parietal policies earlier than women's institutions. In the 1930s, Harvard undergraduates could have female visitors in campus housing only with the written permission of college administrators twenty-four hours ahead, "unless the guests are mothers or sisters." As veterans in large numbers enrolled under the GI Bill following World War II, men's colleges relaxed their policies.[131] By 1968, visiting hours for Harvard students extended from 2 p.m. until midnight on weekdays, noon until 1 a.m. on Saturdays, and noon until midnight on Sundays.[132] These parietal restrictions ended altogether the following year.

In the 1950s, mainstream female colleges began to modify their regulations regarding male visitors. At Pembroke College, students could have male guests in dormitory lounges (but not in their private rooms) until 12:15 a.m. on Wednesdays through Fridays, and until 10:00 p.m. on other days. In the next decade, parietals in women's colleges expanded considerably. In accord with college guidelines, Wellesley students were free to set male visitation hours for their individual dormitories. In 1969, parietals for Vassar freshmen extended from 9 a.m. to 12 a.m. on weekdays, and from 9 a.m. to 2:30 a.m. on weekends.[133] At this time, students at the College of Notre Dame could not have male visitors in their dormitory rooms at any time. Gaining parietal privileges became their top priority. The struggle over parietals quickly engaged all campus constituencies, alumnae, parents, and the wider Baltimore community in a public battle that pitted modern feminist values against traditional gender-specific elements of Catholic moral doctrine and values.

The specific contours of the parietals controversy at Notre Dame reflected both parental and student assumptions about religious life in the post–Vatican II era. Like grassroots Catholics nationwide, the college's lay constituents had long taken it for granted that the collective works, religious dress, and cloistered lifestyle of nuns were immutable. However, encouraged by the decrees of Vatican II, female congregations across the world, but particularly in the United States, moved to reform the strict rules and customs that for centuries had regulated their lives. The radical changes in the dress, professional works, and personal autonomy of nuns generated considerable controversy within the Catholic community in the 1970s. Some laity and clergy applauded these reforms as long overdue, while others harshly condemned "radical feminist American nuns."[134] Opponents of change in Notre Dame's no-parietals position included many parents, alumnae, and local Catholics who contended that the concept flouted Catholic moral values. In their view, liberal nuns on the faculty had precipitated the parietals debate by promulgating feminist ideas among students.

Students, however, took an opposing position. They attributed the college's retention of strict social rules to the conservative perspectives of the School Sisters of Notre Dame, who, they assumed, shared neither their feminist views nor their commitment to gender equality. The warm rapport that had typically marked relations between sisters and students in the 1950s was dissolving. "Previous to that time, the sisters and the rest of the faculty were more or less friends of the students," recalled French professor Madeleine

Doyle, SSND. "In the sixties . . . we didn't have the friendliness."[135] Changes in student attitudes since her own college days amazed English professor Ruth Miriam Cary '48, SSND, who had joined the faculty in 1959. "They questioned everyone," she said. "They complained about everything. And they wanted to do everything. . . . They were completely self-confident. . . . They felt they were not free. Freedom was their big thing."[136] Student interaction with the dean of students, who oversaw the college's *in loco parentis* policies, deteriorated. Marie Michelle Walsh, SSND, who began her six-year term as dean of students in 1965, judged relations with students as "aloof, if not hostile."[137] The contentious spirit continued in the 1970s. According to Bernice Feilinger, SSND, dean of students between 1972 and 1978, students regarded her as just an agent of the administration.[138]

In contrast, Notre Dame's official catalogs in this era portrayed campus life in near-idyllic terms. "Notre Dame," stated the 1972 catalog, "is currently experiencing a real cohesiveness among the faculty and administration and the students. . . . At Notre Dame, friendships between the faculty and students are not inevitable—but almost."[139] Such rhetoric infuriated students who viewed college leaders as indifferent to their desire for reasonable parietal hours. In April 1970, students on the dorm committee appealed for help to the trustee committee on student affairs, composed of Henry Knott and George Constable. The response of the full board of trustees to this committee's report was emphatic: at no time were men to be permitted in student rooms.[140] Convinced that the trustees had not yet heard "the student point of view," campus leaders asked the board to establish a "viable channel of communication between the Student Association Board, as elected officers of the student body, and the Board of Trustees."[141] The board referred them back to its trustee committee on student affairs.

In February 1972, President Kathleen Feeley agreed to a four-week "experiment" with Saturday and Sunday afternoon parietals from 1 to 5 p.m.[142] The "experiment" stretched into the fall term of that year without much opposition, but the subject returned to center stage in December when students pressed for an extension of the hours to Saturday and Sunday evenings. Alarmed officers of the college called for an absolute ban on parietals. Among the signers of "The Statement on Parietals, 28 February 1973" were the academic dean, the treasurer, the director of admissions, the registrar, and the assistant dean of students.[143] Feeley denied the students' request for more parietal hours, and they again appealed to the board of trustees.

In March 1972, students regrouped at an Inter-Dormitory Council forum to devise new arguments and strategies for gaining parietal hours commensurate with those at comparable colleges. Neighboring Goucher allowed dormitory residents to set their own parietal hours, while Loyola students, female as well as male, could have visitors of the opposite sex in dormitory rooms from noon to midnight on Sunday through Thursday, and noon to 3:30 a.m. on Friday and Saturday. When compared to some eastern Catholic women's colleges, Notre Dame's visiting hours seemed positively ascetic. Newton College of the Sacred Heart (Massachusetts), for example, allowed twenty-three-hour parietals, seven days a week, while Trinity College (Washington, DC) set parietal hours for Sunday to Thursday, 7 a.m. to 12 a.m., and Friday and Saturday, 7 a.m. to 2 a.m.[144] Members of Notre Dame's Parents and Friends Association promptly drew up a much longer list of Catholic women's colleges that still prohibited male visitors in student dormitory rooms.

Students next requested permission "to entertain all visitors, male and female, in their rooms on weekend evenings," and organized a letter-writing campaign to Feeley to persuade her to act positively on their appeal.[145] They made three principal arguments. First, Notre Dame students were women who should have autonomy over their social lives. Second, trustees and administrators were refusing to allow parietals because they lacked confidence in the willingness of students to honor Catholic moral values. And third, students of the 1970s held healthier, more mature attitudes toward sexuality than earlier generations. Male students from Loyola, the Naval Academy, Johns Hopkins, and Towson energetically supported their Notre Dame peers in a "peaceful demonstration" for more liberal visitation hours and wrote to Feeley to impress on her the urgency of quick action. Without a parietals policy, advised a Loyola student, Notre Dame would soon be extinct.[146]

Lay and sister faculty took sides, and the controversy intensified. Some faculty contended that Notre Dame was far out of step with mainstream colleges and ought to adopt a reasonable parietals policy as soon as possible. Others vehemently disagreed. In their view, a parietals policy was a violation of Catholic moral standards. They reminded their colleagues that parents sent their daughters to Notre Dame rather than to other institutions precisely because it upheld Catholic religious values.[147] Accepted social standards were compromising Catholic moral standards. To these arguments, students rejoined, "What is the difference between Notre Dame girls and Loyola girls?"[148]

In early April 1973, Feeley informed the students' parents and guardians of the students' latest parietals petition, and asked for their views. She promised to present "any strong opinion for or against this proposal" to the trustees.[149] In August, parents and guardians received a second letter from the college. Dean of Students Bernice Feilinger outlined the college's current parietal rules and informed them that a Special Committee on Parietals would consider the question of changes to these rules.[150] Neither letter garnered many responses. But leaders of the Parents and Friends Association (PFA), offended that they had no representative on the college's Special Committee on Parietals, determined to conduct their own poll. "We are 100% opposed to any form of male entertainment in the college dormitory bedrooms," they wrote to parents and guardians. "We are interested in preserving the principles and moral stability of the oldest, Catholic, all girls [sic] college in America."[151] They would fight "to see that Notre Dame does not fall into the disrepute of so many other colleges who have decided to go along with 'the open bedroom policy.'"[152] As discord mounted, Feeley invited the PFA's executive director to report on the results of its poll at the September 21, 1973, board of trustees meeting.[153] And in an effort to mollify the PFA, the trustees added two PFA members, one of them its executive director, to the Special Committee on Parietals. The PFA executive director reported to the trustees that most of the approximately three hundred parents who had replied to its poll had emphatically rejected "the very thought of the 'open bedroom policy' at Notre Dame."[154] Respondents maintained that it was its Catholic identity that justified Notre Dame's existence and distinguished it from other institutions; indeed, the college might not survive if it relaxed its moral standards.[155]

The following month, Feeley publicized the results of the Special Committee's survey of college constituencies: 50 percent of the faculty, 93 percent of the student body, and 13 percent of parents and friends favored parietals.[156] The committee recommended that the trustees extend Notre Dame's parietal hours to Friday and Saturday evenings. At this point, for the first time, Feeley publicly presented her own position on the issue to the college community. As she saw it, introducing a visitation policy need not mean a decline in the college's moral standards. "In the social milieu of 1973, open house in the residence hall is a social condition, not a moral problem," she argued. "Are we giving the impression that young women are 'safe' at Notre Dame because it does not allow evening visitation, even though the young women have the freedom to leave campus at will and go where they like? Is the 'image' a positive contribution to the moral tone of Notre Dame, or is it a façade?"[157]

Stunned by Feeley's comments, the PFA's executive board called on the board of trustees to settle the question. On December 7, 1973, the board of trustees rejected the Special Committee's proposal to extend parietals,[158] and reinstated the severe 1972 policy: visiting hours for men in residence halls were on Saturdays and Sundays between 1 and 5 p.m. only. The protracted parietals battle had, however, convinced the board of trustees that settling conflicts over campus social rules was not its responsibility.[159] Thus when students raised the question again two years later, the minutes of the board of trustees meeting asserted simply that "this decision [will] be handled by the administration, where other dormitory issues are handled."[160] With this authorization in hand, Feeley moved quickly to bring Notre Dame's parietals policies into conformity with those of other Catholic women's colleges: weekdays, 4 p.m. to 1:30 a.m.; Saturdays, noon to 1:30 a.m.; and Sundays, noon to 9 p.m. The parietals war was over.

While Feeley's efforts to distinguish between parietal rules and the college's religious identity did not succeed in the short run, the controversy proved to be a watershed for Notre Dame. Alumnae generally viewed the social reforms of the 1970s positively. As a 1955 graduate put it, "A strong academic background with rules substituted for values and a lack of independence only weakens and frustrates the woman in the world she is facing today."[161] The myriad social rules that for so long had governed student life disappeared or were markedly relaxed. And the heated debate over male visiting hours became a historical curiosity within a remarkably short period of time.[162] "The College has come a long way," marveled a 1981 student.[163]

The extended parietals controversy had contributed to the development of more politically astute students seeking to play focal roles in most areas of life at Notre Dame. They soon gained seats on key college policy-making bodies, including the curriculum and long-range planning committees. Relative to mainstream college students, however, their campaign for representation on the board of trustees took longer. By 1973, the Goucher College board of trustees had added a member of the senior class, chosen from nominees of the student government, as a voting member for a three-year, nonrenewable term. Not until 1983, however, did Notre Dame's board of trustees approve the addition of a nonvoting student representative, elected by her peers, to its membership. Despite the relatively limited authority accorded the student representative, this was a decisive step for a Catholic women's college at this time.[164]

Reviewing decades of changes in behavioral codes for women's college students makes it clear how much those rules consistently addressed the social anxiety surrounding women's higher education from its inception to the present and, in particular, how much of that anxiety was articulated through both metaphorical and literal language about nuns. While "convent rules" protected young women from unapproved contact with men, they also contributed to critiques that women's colleges were promoting careerism over marriage and children. And, as early as the 1920s, Catholic women's colleges, which had evolved to address the persistent refusal of men to allow women into academic spaces, faced criticism that their behavioral codes were discouraging students from developing normal relationships with their future husbands. In fact, the popular stereotype that linked strict social rules with nuns and convents still flourishes, spanning both denominational and national boundaries. In 1992, for example, Lord Roy Jenkins, chancellor of Oxford University, in a reference to Somerville College's liberal social code, remarked, "So far from being run as a nunnery, Somerville has since 1980 allowed its students to have overnight male guests provided they are properly signed in."[165]

The extraordinary bilateral critique of the nuns in the Notre Dame parietals dispute reflected a rapidly shifting social ethos within the US Catholic community in the post–Vatican II era over feminist values, women's rights, and women's higher education. For conservative parishioners, the church was changing much too quickly, while for their liberal counterparts it was not changing quickly enough. It also signaled a serious conflict brewing during the same decade, as leaders of all-male Catholic colleges, who had long resisted admitting women, suddenly saw female students as a welcome solution to the enrollment woes of the late 1960s. The continued existence and independence of numerous female colleges conducted by nuns were a threat to these new coeducational plans. At the time of the parietals dispute, the College of Notre Dame was under severe pressure to merge with neighboring Loyola College, an arrangement its administrators felt would unacceptably erode the sisters' independence. While from many students' perspective the parietals dispute was about whether the nuns trusted them to manage their own behavior, from the perspective of the college's administration the key question of the early 1970s was whether and how a largely female board, administration, and faculty could resist male control via merger. How Notre Dame responded to this crisis, and how it continues to maintain its identity today, is the subject of the conclusion.

Conclusion
A Catholic Women's Liberal Arts College

The emphasis here has always been on women . . .
women's issues, women as an entity in life, women as
being equal with men. . . . Every opportunity was given
women to develop equally as men developed. . . . This
has been the saving grace.

—Mildred B. Otenasek '36

The blueprint for the building of the College of Notre
Dame detailed with principles of truth, spirit, and love,
was never rolled up gently and placed in a drawer. . . .
The plan was lived by all who once were here, by us who
are here now; and it will be carried on by those who are
yet to come. . . . The general design is complete.

—*Damozel*, 1949

As this book has argued, Catholic higher education for women emerged and took shape under a variety of cross-pressures. Catholic sisters followed Protestant and secular trends in creating colleges to form young women to succeed intellectually and spiritually, whether in marriage and motherhood, in a profession, or as a member of a religious order. Small female colleges proliferated in part because multiple orders established colleges to educate their own parochial schoolteachers and graduates. The Baltimore experience, with minor variations, was typical. The School Sisters of Notre Dame established the Institute of Notre Dame in 1863 and obtained a state charter the following year. Within four years, the Sisters of Mercy opened a second girls' school in the Mount Washington section of the city, Mount Saint Agnes Academy.[1] In 1890 they obtained a state charter for Mount Saint Agnes Collegiate Institute, with a clause giving it power to confer bachelor's degrees; it now competed for students with the Institute of Notre Dame and the Notre Dame Collegiate Institute. In 1896, as the College of Notre Dame completed its inaugural academic year, the Sisters of Mercy renamed their school Mount Saint Agnes College. Although small in size, Mount Saint Agnes College adversely affected the College of Notre

Dame by competing with it for students and philanthropic funds within the local Catholic community.[2] This soon became a common development pattern in dioceses nationally.

Bishops, for their part, believed that if higher education for women had to exist at all, nuns were obligated to provide it, both to keep young Catholic women out of secular institutions and increasingly to provide a legally qualified workforce of nuns for the church's parochial schools and hospitals. Since these institutions were essentially cost free to the episcopacy, and since they provided major benefits to local dioceses, bishops got over their initial reservations about women's higher education and encouraged their rapid expansion. As chapter 1 recounted, Cardinal Gibbons was vigorously promoting plans for Trinity College even before the College of Notre Dame had graduated its pioneer class in 1899. Catholic women's colleges multiplied as Gibbons's fellow bishops followed his example nationally. Although mainstream women's colleges were concentrated in the East, their Catholic counterparts spread to all parts of the country in order to accommodate the growing Catholic population. Since most of these families could not afford to send their daughters to established residential colleges like the College of Notre Dame, the College of New Rochelle, and Trinity College, local bishops encouraged, and occasionally ordered, sisterhoods to open colleges to accommodate day students.

Church-related men's colleges were fewer in number and had larger enrollments than women's colleges. By 1932–33, of eighty-nine regionally accredited Catholic colleges, thirty-nine men's institutions enrolled 55,587 students, an average of 1,425 students per school, whereas fifty women's colleges enrolled 10,450 students, an average of 209.[3] Of the seventy-four Catholic women's colleges operating nationwide in 1930, 62 percent did not meet the requirements of regional accrediting agencies.[4] Nevertheless, by the mid-1960s, Catholic women's colleges had expanded still further. From the late nineteenth century through the 1940s, teaching sisterhoods had responded to state and church demands by opening normal schools in their motherhouses for their young members. When the Sister Formation Movement of the 1950s called for young sisters to hold college degrees before commencing their work as parochial school teachers, a number of these normal schools developed into four-year colleges that admitted laywomen.

Expansion of these institutions soon grew beyond what could realistically be supported. According to Rev. Edward V. Stanford, a consultant for the Association of American Colleges, by 1950 "Pennsylvania had 18 senior Catholic colleges, nine for women, six for men and three partly coeducational institutions."[5] Between 1950 and 1964, five more women's colleges appeared, and plans for another male and two more female institutions were in the offing. Three of the new female colleges were in metropolitan Philadelphia, which according to a report in the *New York Times* "already had three Catholic colleges for women and three for men."[6] Typical of many of his peers, Archbishop John J. Krol was "unconvinced that nine colleges were too many."[7] Catholic women's colleges were smaller, on average, than their secular counterparts. In eastern states in 1970, their full-time enrollments averaged 685, while enrollments in Seven Sister colleges ranged from 2,336 at Smith to 790 at Bryn Mawr.[8]

But in 1964, the year Archbishop Krol hoped for yet more colleges to open in Philadelphia, the postwar educational expansion was already reaching its outer limits. Only a few years later, long-simmering financial, enrollment, and staffing crises erupted into full view, threatening the viability of Catholic institutions ranging from larger men's institutions to tiny women's colleges. The crisis was particularly acute in the latter. With their enrollments dropping and financial problems rising, many closed their doors or merged with local formerly men's colleges. Others turned quickly to coeducation. The total number of US women's colleges declined by nearly 70 percent, from 233 to 74, between 1960 and 2000; many of these were Catholic.[9] Only a small minority, among them the College of Notre Dame, were able to remain single-sex colleges. Meanwhile, in the 1960s and 1970s, the *Horace Mann* and *Roemer* cases had forced the College of Notre Dame to reexamine the links between its religious affiliation and its secular mission. As the presence of religious communities on campuses began to decline sharply in these decades, many colleges' long-held vision of their identity became a matter of campus-wide debates, and Notre Dame was no exception. How was it to honor Catholic values without being "sectarian"? Were its religious tradition and spirit affected by the struggle to qualify for government funding? What would be the consequences of the swift post-1970 transition from religious to lay leadership? The College of Notre Dame had to wrestle with its identity and viability as a Catholic women's college during the post–Vatican II decades as it faced external and internal challenges to both.

Loyola College and the Threat to Single-Sex Education

As earlier chapters have discussed, Catholic men's colleges, while they often allowed their faculty to lecture part time at nearby women's colleges, seldom saw those institutions as peers. In October 1899, a few months after the College of Notre Dame awarded its first bachelor's degrees, Mother Theophila Bauer applied to Rev. Thomas Conaty, rector of the Catholic University of

America in Washington, for official affiliation with the university: "Recognizing the Catholic university as the culmination of the Catholic educational system of America, . . . the Faculty of Notre Dame of Maryland respectfully ask of the University the same measure of recognition accorded to Colleges for men, that have fulfilled such conditions as are prescribed for affiliation."[10] Taken aback by this request, the university trustees discussed the matter two days later. Although the liberal bishops John Ireland of Saint Paul and John Lancaster Spalding of Peoria supported Bauer's request, Cardinal Gibbons adamantly opposed it. He insisted that the distinction of being the first female college to affiliate with Catholic University rightfully belonged to the projected Trinity College, "not only because of its proximity to the University, but also because of the sacrifices entailed in its founding."[11] Although the board rejected the College of Notre Dame's application, it formed an ad hoc committee of Conaty, Spalding, and Archbishop John J. Keane to explore "the matter of affiliation of female colleges and academies."[12]

In June 1900, the committee asked College of Notre Dame administrators for "a complete statement of your Collegiate work as leading to the A.B. degree."[13] Dean Meletia Foley seized this opportunity to press her views on the right of women to higher education on equal terms with men. In a remarkable document, she pointed to the successful affiliation of secular women's colleges with universities in England and the United States.[14] At Radcliffe College, she wrote, "the requirements for the degrees of Bachelor of Arts and Master of Arts [were] . . . the same as for the corresponding degrees in Harvard University." Barnard College women received a degree "of equal value with the degree of B.A." awarded Columbia University men. She concluded her case by quoting Saint Peter Fourier: "The elevation of a whole people is possible only through its women."[15] Despite its logic and eloquence, the letter did not sway the university's trustees. At their October 10, 1900, meeting, they denied affiliation to any women's college, "considering what it means and what it may imply."[16] Over the next few years, the university published requirements for colleges seeking affiliation, and "duly affiliated" three colleges, all female institutions.[17] Notre Dame, however, did not gain university affiliation for another decade, probably due to its persistently small size.

Much about the higher-education landscape had changed between 1899 and 1969, but men's institutions' reflexive sense that women's institutions existed only on sufferance had not. As a result, smaller and poorer Catholic women's colleges tended to catch the brunt of the fallout from decisions made by their all-male neighbors in the face of their own late-1960s enrollment crises. The experiences of the College of Notre Dame with its neighbor, a Catholic men's college, were representative.[18] The Jesuits, who established Loyola College in 1852 in downtown Baltimore, relocated their school in 1921 to property immediately adjacent to Notre Dame's campus. When Loyola opened its doors to women in 1971, the College of Notre Dame faced formidable challenges to its autonomy and long-term survival. The interaction of the School Sisters of Notre Dame and the Jesuits as they addressed the coeducation question provides exceptional insight into the gender dynamics of Catholic higher education in twentieth-century America.

In the 1920s and 1930s, the Jesuits took pains to distinguish themselves from the female institution next door. Even though the colleges were of comparable size in the 1930s, the Jesuits conveyed an attitude of male ascendancy in their dealings with the School Sisters of Notre Dame and their students.[19] In particular, they avoided the slightest hint of "coeducation." A testy exchange between the college presidents in 1928 concerning an advertisement placed by the College of Notre Dame in magazines and newspapers is revelatory. The notice described the college as "taught by the Sisters of Notre Dame and assisted by the Fathers of Loyola College." Loyola's president, Henri Wiesel, SJ, immediately protested to Notre Dame's president, Mother Philemon Doyle. The content of the advertisement was accurate, he conceded, but it gave the impression that Loyola's Jesuits were teaching "young girls," his term for Notre Dame students.

Wlodimir Ledochowski, SJ, superior general of the Jesuits at this time, adamantly opposed any form of coeducation in the order's schools, and Wiesel felt sure that he would not be pleased to hear that Jesuits were teaching women in Baltimore. "I am not going to be so sudden in action as to withdraw the Fathers," he told Doyle, "but I am going to ask that such advertising make no mention about the Jesuit Fathers being on the Faculty."[20] Wiesel made his views on women's education clear in the baccalaureate sermon he preached at Notre Dame in 1933 when he advised the graduates to "Learn the humble arts of cooking and sewing and mending," and "assume the responsibilities of child-bearing and child-rearing."[21] His attitude, as we have seen, was shared by many of his contemporaries.

Catholic undergraduate colleges, with few exceptions, remained single-sex institutions for many decades. Bishops and clergy particularly discouraged parents from enrolling their daughters in highly respected Protestant women's colleges. Catholic women's colleges offered special religious as well as academic and social benefits. Like his counterparts across the country, Rev. Martin Gamber, chaplain of the Notre Dame preparatory school, warned students in the 1940s, "You can't go to Vassar, you'll lose your religion."[22] As the number of middle-class Catholic youth eager to attend college rose swiftly in the twentieth century, bishops and clergy across the country reiterated the dangers of coeducation. While some Protestant churches, Barbara Solomon notes, "justified coeducation in ethical and religious terms of the equality of souls, male and female," the Catholic Church continued to maintain that mingling the sexes at the undergraduate college level posed moral dangers that outweighed any social benefits of gender equality.[23]

Nonetheless, the subject of coeducation remained important in Catholic educational circles. By the early 1900s, states were developing certification requirements for teachers at private as well as public schools, and parochial schools had to meet these state standards quickly. Catholic women's colleges were still few in number and scattered geographically. Some local bishops turned to the men's colleges in their dioceses for a solution. In 1909, Marquette University in Milwaukee set a precedent by introducing a summer program to prepare parochial school teachers on a part-time basis for state teaching certification. According to a contemporary report, the Milwaukee Jesuits, who conducted Marquette, took the step "only after persistent urging of the Ordinary, Archbishop Messmer."[24]

Marquette's 1912 summer school rules for nuns were strict. According to Pauline M. A. Tavardian, they could "sit in class, but they were not permitted to recite. Because Jesuits were not permitted to teach women, weekly papers and exams had to substitute for classroom participation."[25] Bishops nationally called on male religious orders that conducted colleges within their dioceses to launch similar part-time programs for parochial school faculties. Through "female programs," offered via part-time extension, evening, and summer courses, full-time teachers earned state certification.[26] By 1916, Marquette's evening and summer programs enrolled several hundred women, lay as well as religious sisters. None attended classes in the regular full-time college, which remained a male preserve.

An early exception to the strict single-sex policy that marked Catholic higher education occurred in the 1910s and 1920s. In 1891, Mother Katharine M. Drexel, heir to a large Philadelphia banking fortune, founded the Sisters of the Blessed Sacrament, a religious order devoted solely to the education of African Americans and Native Americans. Since no Catholic college in the nation, male or female, admitted African American students, Drexel determined to remedy that situation. In 1917, she expanded a New Orleans high school for girls that she had founded two years earlier into a teacher training school. She then proceeded to gain papal permission for religious sisters to teach male students at the college level and, with the members of her sisterhood, gradually developed the training school into a state-accredited, four-year Catholic liberal arts college. When Xavier College awarded its first bachelor's degrees in 1928, it became the nation's first Catholic college to admit African Americans and its first Catholic coeducational college.[27]

As young men entered military service during World War I, a sharp dip in college applicants brought the coeducation question to the fore in Catholic men's college circles. But since the enrollment impact of this war was short lived, 90 percent of Catholic colleges were still single-sex in the early 1940s. (The figure was about 30 percent for all US colleges.) When enrollments in men's colleges again plunged following the nation's entry into World War II, administrators at Catholic men's colleges prepared to make a case for coeducation with the national hierarchy. However, the passage of the Servicemen's Readjustment Act of 1944 (the GI Bill), which provided tuition and monthly stipends that enabled returning veterans to attend colleges and technical schools, addressed their enrollment concerns. Applications to Catholic men's colleges soared, and trustees and administrators responded by expanding faculties, academic and housing facilities, and campus real estate. "Overall in 1947," according to Elizabeth A. Edmondson, "Catholic schools reported enrollment increases ranging from 50 percent to more than 200 percent over prewar enrollment."[28]

Baltimore's Loyola College, like other men's colleges in the postwar era, was very eager to expand its enrollment. However, it was extremely land poor. Rev. Vincent Beatty, SJ, who became president of the college in 1955, saw in the campus of the College of Notre Dame next door an expedient solution to this problem.[29] In 1957, he approached Sister Matrona Dougherty, superior of the Notre Dame community and a member of the college's board of directors, to discuss his "property problem." He explained that he wanted to acquire a piece of land owned by Johns Hopkins University that lay between the Notre Dame and Loyola campuses. But at this time, Johns Hopkins did not wish to sell it. Beatty believed that Johns Hopkins very much wanted to acquire "a strip of Notre Dame property." If Notre Dame would sell this piece of land to Loyola, he would then proceed to offer it to Johns Hopkins in exchange for the Hopkins parcel he particularly wanted. Dougherty informed him that Notre Dame's board of directors had "decided not to sell any of our land."[30]

As the applicant pool of returning veterans declined in the 1950s and early 1960s, men's colleges, left with underutilized faculties and facilities, saw in coeducation a good strategy for survival and growth. At this time, all women's colleges were facing serious enrollment concerns as female high school graduates opted in rising numbers for coeducational colleges. A move to coeducation by Catholic men's colleges would pose a particularly severe challenge to the nation's 116 small Catholic women's colleges. In 1951, presidents and deans from sixty-six of these institutions attended a "special conference on the problems of women's colleges" convened by the National Catholic Educational Association. Their overriding concern was the prospective move to coeducation by Catholic men's colleges.[31] The long-standing policy of single-sex education at Catholic undergraduate colleges had long protected women's institutions from having to compete for students with the typically larger and richer men's colleges located near them. Although the Loyola and Notre Dame campuses had existed in close proximity since 1921, Notre Dame did little active recruiting. According to an early director of admissions, "We didn't go out and look for students; we just waited for them to come. We seemed to have enough at the time."[32]

This casual approach marked many Catholic women's colleges until the church's traditional opposition to coeducation evaporated in the postwar years. Leaders of men's colleges, by this time, had gained considerable support from the national church hierarchy. At the 1952 meeting of the National Catholic Educational Association, Archbishop Richard J. Cushing of Boston spoke for most of the church hierarchy when he announced that "coeducation is here to stay and there is nothing we can do about it." Instead of "bickering about the threat of coeducation to women's colleges," he said, Catholic colleges ought to be working to enroll the "60 percent of the Catholic student potential" currently attending secular institutions.[33]

Despite male impatience, women's college leaders raised the coeducation question again at the 1954 annual meeting of the National Catholic Educational Association. They noted that since Catholic colleges in the United States had been single-sex since the founding of Georgetown College in 1789, churchmen who advocated that these institutions shift to coeducation were dishonoring a 165-year tradition. This was too much for Rev. Edward Rooney, SJ, executive director of the Jesuit Educational Association, who dismissed this observation out of hand. The "Catholic tradition" of single-sex colleges was a fiction, he argued. The Catholic Church had never opposed coeducation. "Are we going against tradition in having coeducation in higher education?" he said. "I do not think you can talk about tradition in the education of women on the higher-level."[34]

Coeducational colleges were steadily attracting more female applicants, and leading mainstream men's colleges were debating whether to open their doors to women.[35] Catholic men's institutions recognized that if they did not follow suit, they would likely close. Once they had the green light from the national hierarchy and from leaders of male religious orders, these institutions began to take action in the 1960s. Many dioceses had at least one college for men and another for women. Larger urban archdioceses had more. Male colleges in these locations typically commenced their shift to coeducational status by seeking to merge with nearby women's campuses. If successful, they could boost their applicant pools virtually overnight and simultaneously acquire desirable real estate. Women's colleges refusing to merge would see their enrollments fall.

In Baltimore, Loyola president Vincent Beatty's aggressive campaign for land aroused concern that Loyola might have further designs on the College of Notre Dame's campus. Thus college leaders viewed with considerable ambivalence his 1964 proposal that the two colleges build a joint library. At this time, Notre Dame's Fourier Library, constructed in 1941, was judged adequate for the college's future needs. However, lack of funds had slowed development of its book collection, and in the 1960s, the collection ranked below American Library Association standards for a college of Notre Dame's size.[36] Some trustees viewed a joint library as a good solution to Notre Dame's library accreditation difficulties.[37] Provincial Superior Mother Vitalia Arnold, who chaired the board of trustees, worried about the financial implications of the library proposal. She urged the trustees to "reserve your judgement" until the completion of the new science building. Despite some concern that delay could mean the loss of a golden opportunity, the board agreed to withhold its approval until "a plan for the financing of a joint library can be developed which Notre Dame can handle."[38]

Impatient to move the library proposal forward, Notre Dame trustee Henry Knott appealed to Baltimore archbishop Lawrence Shehan for assistance. "We have run into a road-block here with Mother Vitalia," he told Shehan, "so I had Sister Margaret Mary O'Connell at the College call their Mother General (Ambrosia [Roecklein]), who happened to be in the United States, and discuss this with her, and ask her to tell the Mother [Vitalia] that you had told me you were in favor of this project." Shehan agreed to "prevail upon her to let the project proceed."[39] At a meeting with Mother Ambrosia, he argued that Notre Dame ought to put Fourier Library to another use and cooperate with Loyola on the joint library project: "The project has my whole-hearted approval," he said.[40]

Notre Dame's trustees approved the library project in 1966. The officers of the Loyola–Notre Dame Library Corporation were Truman Semans of Loyola (president) and Sister Mary Ian Stewart of Notre Dame (vice president). As part of its share of the project's estimated $5 million cost, Notre Dame agreed to contribute 4.6 acres of land bordering Loyola's campus as the site for the joint library.[41] Progress was slow for several years. Just as negotiations were about to be finalized, Loyola officially announced that it would begin to admit women in September 1971.[42] At this news, Notre Dame's trustees considered abandoning the cooperative library project, but "after tense discussion [with Loyola] . . . the decision to continue was affirmed."[43] When the Loyola Notre Dame Library opened in 1973, with expenses prorated according to institutional enrollments, it was the nation's only library built and jointly owned by two institutions of higher education.[44]

Relations between the two colleges had been deteriorating rapidly for nearly a decade when, in the early 1960s, the College of Notre Dame, Loyola College, and Mount Saint Agnes College, a women's institution in straitened financial circumstances, set up a narrowly focused "joint committee on cooperation to work toward internship collaboration." The group met routinely until 1967, when the Mount Saint Agnes committee member called for "a complete merger" of the three colleges. The idea stunned Notre Dame trustees.[45] With the exception of the joint library project, the colleges had always operated independently. Realizing that the term "merger" was a red flag for Notre Dame, Loyola officials thereafter referred to "federation." But for their Notre Dame counterparts, the terms were synonymous. The battle lines were drawn.

In March 1968, Loyola and Mount Saint Agnes proposed that the three colleges jointly petition the Association of Colleges and Secondary Schools of the Middle States and Maryland for a common evaluation at its scheduled 1970 reaccreditation visit. Notre Dame refused to join in the request. A few months later, Loyola and Mount Saint Agnes received a $100,000 grant from the US Department of Health, Education, and Welfare "to study the feasibility of merging their curricula and perhaps their administration."[46]

Like many men's colleges contemplating a move to coeducation, Loyola needed to acquire real estate and financial resources. With nearby Notre Dame and Mount Saint Agnes, it developed a "cooperation committee" that aimed to expand interinstitutional programs.[47] In March of 1970, a Tri-College Study Committee recommended that "the three colleges be federated by September 1971,"[48] and a month later, Loyola trustees unanimously resolved "to [join] our two sister institutions . . . in a federation."[49] Loyola also pledged to seek "the proper formula for the final federation of the three colleges."[50] By this time, rumors of a possible merger were spreading on the Notre Dame campus, but since high-level negotiations were as yet confidential, the atmosphere remained relatively calm. This ended in early June 1970 when Notre Dame's acting president, Sister Elissa McGuire, remarked at an alumnae event that a merger of Notre Dame and Loyola was a distinct possibility and that it "might be found more beneficial than simple cooperation."[51] The comment spread like wildfire.

These rapid developments alarmed Notre Dame's trustees and administrators. They commissioned Sister Kathleen Feeley, then a faculty member in the English Department, to draft a position paper detailing the college's position for use in future discussions with the other two institutions. She was particularly to indicate areas where Notre Dame might cooperate with Loyola and Mount Saint Agnes and specify areas that would be nonnegotiable.[52] On June 12, 1970, Mother Maurice Kelly, Acting President Elissa McGuire, and trustee George Constable met with representatives from Loyola and Mount Saint Agnes, and with Baltimore's Cardinal Lawrence Shehan, to discuss a possible merger of the institutions. The cardinal strongly favored the concept. Notre Dame's representatives, however, stated that Notre Dame would participate in coinstitutional programs but would not merge with Loyola and Mount Saint Agnes.

At the next meeting of Notre Dame's board of trustees, Henry Knott, an alumnus of Loyola and, concurrently, a trustee at both Loyola and Notre Dame, proposed that Notre Dame accept the merger proposal. The crucial consideration, in his view, was "what was best for Catholic higher education in Baltimore, not what was best for any individual college."[53] His fellow trustees, a majority of whom were sisters, overwhelmingly disagreed with his suggestion, and proceeded to ratify Feeley's position paper as Notre Dame's official Ten-Point Federation Plan. Its key points were that Notre Dame would agree to federation on two conditions: that the federated colleges would "continue with separate names, charters, boards of trustees, student bodies, and degrees," and that Notre Dame, in addition, would "continue with its separate administration, faculty, campus, girls' residence halls, and student government."[54]

Sentiment on the merger question within Notre Dame constituencies was solidly with the board of trustees. As part of its seventy-fifth anniversary celebration, Notre Dame convened a campus-wide conference (Quest '70) to consider the direction of the college over the next decade. However, Loyola's stunning merger proposal took center stage in the day's discussions. Attendance was very high, and George Constable confirmed that "all present at the program were opposed to [the] merger."[55] Mount Saint Agnes College, in significant financial difficulty, merged with Loyola on July 1, 1971.[56] History professor Charles Ritter recalled that Mount Saint Agnes's swift "absorption" by Loyola seemed to Notre Dame constituencies "a portent of what would happen to us if we 'merged' with Loyola."[57]

As in the 1950s, meanwhile, a shortage of land soon thwarted Loyola's ability to admit a substantial number of women while maintaining its desired male enrollment. Like Father Vincent Beatty, whom he succeeded in 1964, Loyola's president, Joseph Sellinger, SJ, saw in the Notre Dame campus next door an ideal solution to his space constraints. Notre Dame's lush sixty-two-acre campus included five residential buildings; four educational, administration, and library buildings; and four utility buildings.[58] Aware that Notre Dame's residence halls were underutilized, due in part to his own institution's recent move to coeducation, in 1973 Father Sellinger requested that Notre Dame rent dormitory space to house Loyola's female undergraduates. The college refused to consider this proposal.[59] Despite troubling enrollment and financial projections, Notre Dame trustees stood united when Sellinger returned two years later asking to purchase ten acres of Notre Dame's campus to use for Loyola's female sports programs. He also sought to lease a section of Notre Dame's new Knott Science Center or, alternatively, to append a "Loyola wing" to that building.[60] Again, Notre Dame's trustees dismissed these proposals.[61]

In 1975, Loyola suggested the formation of a joint Loyola–Notre Dame Committee to promote institutional cooperation "free from past experience."[62] Notre Dame's trustees formed an ad hoc committee to assess the proposal. While this group was deliberating, several prominent local citizens, among them the archbishop, again lobbied Notre Dame to sell land to Loyola. In a flurry of heated speeches and press releases, they accused Notre Dame of being behind the times and indifferent to the common interests of Catholic higher education in Baltimore. Notre Dame administrators and faculty resolved not to bend to "this kind of influence."[63] In its report to the board of trustees, the ad hoc committee maintained that Loyola's cooperation proposal was just another strategy in its campaign for land: "To sell or lease one of our basic assets to a competitor is simply to impede our possible growth and to extend Loyola's long arm around the edge of our campus, indeed into it. . . . The college should . . . say that the answer is 'no.'"[64] In February 1976, with one abstention, the board of trustees voted not to sell or lease any land to Loyola. An overwhelming majority of the wider campus community backed that decision.

Loyola's interest in Notre Dame's land remained high, however. In late October 1977, Henry Knott, now a former Notre Dame trustee, took up Loyola's cause. He apprised President Kathleen Feeley that a major Loyola benefactor was willing to pay $500,000 for ten acres that Loyola desired "in the rear of your property, adjacent to the library." In his opinion, this was a superb opportunity for Notre Dame to acquire badly needed funds. Again the college's trustees declined the offer. "It would be folly for Notre Dame to diminish its campus," Feeley informed Knott. "The sisters who bought this property in 1873 had much more land than they 'needed'; yet over the years the development of the College has led to the constructive use of almost all of its acreage. The present administrators should be equally farsighted."[65] Undeterred, Knott sent Feeley the proposal to purchase land for Loyola and requested her "considered judgment on same."[66] Again Notre Dame refused to sell any land to Loyola.[67]

President Sellinger, however, would not take no for an answer. Late in 1978, with no progress in sight, he made a dramatic public statement to the Baltimore press, Loyola alumni, and the wider Maryland Catholic community. Despite his best efforts, he announced, he had failed to acquire any land for Loyola by purchase or lease. As a result, Loyola's future was in jeopardy. As it was no secret that Sellinger wanted property owned by the College of Notre Dame, his remarks turned public sympathy against the women's college. Kathleen Feeley responded firmly, reminding Sellinger that when Loyola made the decision to become a coeducational college seven years earlier, it was well aware that it would need more real estate to expand its academic facilities, student housing, and athletic fields. It also knew that the College of Notre Dame intended "to plan its future as an independent women's college . . . [and] not to diminish its campus by selling or leasing acreage." Therefore, to suggest that "whoever did not sell or lease land to Loyola is responsible for its land shortage" was preposterous. She concluded that "with Robert Frost I believe 'good fences make good neighbors.'"[68] Tensions between the colleges eased somewhat thereafter, but Notre Dame remained vigilant.[69] As George Constable recalled in 1989, Loyola was always "desperate for land. . . . There was great pressure for us to either sell them land, or give them land, or lease them land, which we resisted. That went on for many years, and I guess is still going on, in a sense."[70]

In the 1960s and 1970s, Loyola's Jesuit leaders showed little sympathy for Notre Dame's decision to maintain its status as an independent women's institution. In their view, coeducation was both inevitable and desirable for Loyola, and annexing Notre Dame was a logical way to achieve that goal. The School Sisters of Notre Dame absolutely disagreed. Without doubt, the coeducation battle of the 1960s and 1970s was the greatest challenge in the history of the College of Notre Dame. It also had lasting benefits. As one faculty member of the era put it, "We came to a better sense of ourselves as unique, also a sense of ourselves as performing a service, the service of education, for people in a way which was necessary, useful, and which would not have continued had we merged."[71] In the half century since, relations between the two institutions and their sponsoring religious communities have become increasingly collegial. Today, their students freely cross-register, and schools and programs of Loyola University Maryland and Notre Dame of Maryland University are coeducational, with one exception: the undergraduate women's college of Notre Dame of Maryland University.[72]

Growing Professional Programs

The decision of the College of Notre Dame to remain a single-sex institution was countercultural in the 1970s. Popular sentiment was that Catholic women's colleges could not successfully compete with church-affiliated coeducational institutions. From exclusion to courtship to takeover was the common experience of most women's colleges in their interaction with formerly male institutions in their locales. The few that succeeded in remaining women's colleges, like Notre Dame, did so by identifying new student populations and taking bold steps to accommodate their needs.[73]

The College of Notre Dame's trustees had elected Sister Kathleen Feeley as president in 1971, the same year that Loyola began to admit women students. Feeley faced severe challenges. Over the previous five years, full-time enrollment had declined by 30 percent, to 549 students.[74] A study undertaken for the Maryland Council for Higher Education and the Maryland legislature, as well as audits for 1967–68 and 1971–72, revealed a "financially insecure" institution. At this time, over half the college's educational and general revenue was coming from the sisters' contributed services ($376,000) and a Maryland state grant of $90,000, and endowment income accounted for only 1 percent of total revenue.[75] The college was financially unstable and in debt, and the contributed services of the sisters were beginning a sharp decline.[76] Most critical, the college's enrollment prospects were bleak. Over the years 1967–72, revenue from tuition and fees had declined by 6 percent while expenditures had increased by 21 percent. The study projected that expenditures would rise by 6 percent annually and considered the $2.2 million debt outstanding on Doyle Hall and the Knott Science Center to be very high, given the college's contingent liability for the joint library.

Based on a projected total enrollment of six hundred and annual tuition and fees set at $1,600, the college faced a $380,000 deficit by 1976–77.[77] To avoid such a shortfall, and in the absence of other income, tuition and fees would have to rise by 10 percent annually. With enrollment declining, this was not an option. Feeley informed the trustees that if they would hold tuition and fees at $1,600 until 1976–77, she believed she could raise enrollment to 896 full-time equivalent students by that date. If successful, this strategy would produce a $94,000 budget surplus by that year. The trustees, with no other options, approved Feeley's proposal, although they considered her enrollment projection overly optimistic.[78]

Feeley saw in the introduction of innovative professional programs a promising solution to Notre Dame's survival as a women's college. Trustees, administrators, and faculty joined forces to develop the Weekend College, as recounted in chapter 4. The Weekend College became the leading factor in improving the college's financial and enrollment positions. By 1986–87, enrollment was nearly 40 percent higher than it had been a decade earlier.[79] Registration in the Weekend College was 953; in master's degree programs, 183; and in the regular undergraduate college, 753. By 2002, the Weekend College enrolled 2,400 students. The college's operating budget was in the black, and its endowment was slowly growing. Notre Dame students were cross-registering at six local institutions, including Johns Hopkins and Loyola.[80] The 1987 *U.S. News & World Report* survey ranked the College of Notre Dame fourth among smaller comprehensive institutions in the East.[81]

The Weekend College had emerged from an effort to meet a specific crisis: how to remain independent and female in competition with Notre Dame's neighbor, Loyola College. But its success had other positive effects, and they brought the institution badly needed publicity. "People started hearing Notre Dame, Notre Dame. . . . It lost some of its image that it had before of being exclusive. . . . We knew we had to do it on our own, we had to make Notre Dame someplace where young women wanted to go," recalled Sr. Dorothy Arthur, the college treasurer from 1969–75.[82] As the college became more visible and accessible to local women in the 1970s, it exerted a growing influence within the Baltimore community. It also saw rapid diversification of its student body. Although the college had admitted its first African American student in 1951, the number of minority students did not increase markedly for two decades. By 1984, however, African Americans constituted 11 percent of the student body.[83] A 2000 analysis of the percentage of black students at fifty-two women's colleges listed the College of Notre Dame in eleventh place, with 17.2 percent. Among eighteen Catholic colleges in the survey, Notre Dame ranked fourth.[84] By 2014, nearly one-fourth of its total enrollment was African American.

By most measures the Weekend College was a major success, both serving new populations of students and enabling the institution to stay afloat. In 1987 Feeley described it as "a unique mode of delivering education to a working population. . . . With 717 graduates and 953 students in its undergraduate degree programs and 183 students in its master's degree programs, the Weekend College has proved itself to be an educational service which has, indeed, 'made a difference' in metropolitan Baltimore and beyond. . . . In Notre Dame's Weekend College, the part-time student has been elevated to first-class status. . . . Notre Dame offers [them] all the support systems and amenities which one usually finds only in a full-time program."[85] But not everyone shared Feeley's enthusiasm about these developments. While the Weekend College enrollment had climbed notably, that of the day college had not, stagnating at about 800 by the turn of the twenty-first century. In fact, the regular undergraduate college enrollment in 1970 was higher than it was in 1983.[86]

As a result of these changes, the pattern of majors of Notre Dame students in the 1980s differed considerably from what it had been three decades earlier. Professional fields of study continued to increase in popularity at Notre Dame and other educational institutions nationally during the next few decades.[87] Although a five-year pre-engineering program allowed students to earn BA degrees from Notre Dame and BS degrees from the University of Maryland College of Engineering,[88] the college's long-standing emphasis on science was under siege. The formerly strong English and foreign language departments together enrolled only 6.3 percent of student majors in 1984, whereas communications attracted 16.5 percent. Three professionally oriented fields accounted for nearly half (47.1 percent) of all majors. As the college prepared for university status in 2011, it sought and received the approval of the Maryland Higher Education Commission for new undergraduate majors in nursing, marketing communications, international business, and environmental sustainability.[89] Faculty debated how Notre Dame could continue to be a quality liberal arts college when it enrolled a majority of its students in professional, career-focused programs. To meet this concern, general education requirements in the liberal arts increased between 1970 and 1990.[90] But ensuring that degrees earned via part-time programs equaled in quality those awarded in the full-time undergraduate women's college remained an ongoing concern.

Catholic Identity on Campus, 1970s–2000s

Catholic higher education for women developed in a century marked by momentous political and economic change and evolving social mores. Suffrage, a prolonged depression, and two world wars had widened women's professional ambitions and social independence; the civil rights and feminist movements mobilized women to demand equal opportunity with men in education and employment; and the Second Vatican Council of the 1960s motivated Catholic women's colleges to reassess their institutional identities. The College of Notre Dame of Maryland was a pioneer in the late twentieth-century movement to broaden the accepted definition of American collegians. No longer were they a demographic cohort of eighteen-to-twenty-one-year-olds who earned bachelor's degrees over four years of full-time study. Now their ranks included employed adults who enrolled on a part-time basis and took more than four years to earn their degrees. As a result, the 1970s saw increasing racial, ethnic, and religious diversity among faculty and students. The proportion of Catholic students and faculty at Notre Dame declined, as did the visibility of the religious order on campus. At the same time, the institution's local influence was rising as it enrolled relatively more students from greater Baltimore and the surrounding communities. Such changes raised several essential questions for a college seeking to witness to its religious identity and historic mission in American society.

The Collegiate Institute (1873–95) and, subsequently, the College of Notre Dame had enrolled Protestant and occasionally Jewish students. Catalogs made it clear that the college welcomed students of any or no religious faith, until an amended version appeared in 1921–22, stating that "students of Christian denominations are received."[91] Until the 1970s, despite early experiences with religious diversity, a largely Catholic student body and faculty shared perspectives about the religious identity and mission of the college. The court cases of the 1960s and 1970s discussed in chapter 5, however, caused significant change. Usually, historical treatment of church-state conflicts focuses on the state—that is, on the implications of aid to a church-related institution for the wider society—and not on the aftermath of a success or failure in a court challenge for the church-affiliated institution. The College of Notre Dame's experiences in the church-state cases reveal how mainstream challenges affected the direction of Catholic higher education for women.

The court cases had demonstrated that Notre Dame was a public as well as a church-related institution. The fear of more court tests of "pervasive sectarianism" caused some reluctance to state the college's strong ties to the Catholic Church. Adapting to this new reality caused uneasiness on campus. The purpose of the college was "to bring about intellectual growth in the student, based on Christian principles," declared Sister Virgina Geiger. "Once we have not fulfilled that I don't see any reason for us existing."[92] But while most members of the college community agreed that religion was central to the life of the college, it had become very clear not only that the college needed to broaden its ecumenical appeal, but also that its traditional ways of witnessing to Catholicism's importance on campus had become ineffective even to many Catholic students. By the 1980s, student involvement in college religious services and activities had considerably diminished. The Campus Service Organization, to which all students belonged, had no religious element. Many students were indifferent to the college's religious affiliation; some opposed publicizing it. In 1986, for example, *Columns* editors expressed misgivings "about the religious trend [that] an issue on Mother Teresa [of Calcutta] would indicate."[93] More than half the students surveyed at this time could not evaluate campus ministry programs because they did not feel familiar enough with them to do so.[94]

It was not only the wake of the *Horace Mann* and *Roemer* cases, then, that made the college, like many of its peers, become a more secular institution. As faculties and student bodies became more religiously diverse, institutions had to reassess how best to interpret and witness to their traditional religious missions. Notre Dame's official mission statements, published in its annual catalogs, attest to its struggle with this issue in the 1970s and 1980s. In 1974–76, "Judeo-Christian" replaced "Catholic" in a statement expressing the institution's commitment to "those beliefs upon which the college was founded: the belief in Judeo-Christian values; the belief in the value of women; and the belief in the value of education."[95] The word "Catholic" reappeared in the 1982–83 catalog statement, but only in a general sense: "The College of Notre Dame was inspired by and exists today in the Catholic tradition."[96] According to the 1984–85 catalog, the education offered "is values-oriented, an education that emphasizes the total development of the student—spiritual and moral as well as intellectual."[97]

Notre Dame's 1986–87 catalog acknowledged the institution's allegiance to its founding principles, including "a conviction in the value of a quality liberal arts curriculum, a dedication to the education of women, and a belief in Judeo-Christian values."[98] That year, there was considerable campus discussion about whether or not "Judeo-Christian" was a "more inclusive" term than "Catholic,"[99] and the Middle States Association's evaluating team suggested that the mission statement incorporate a fuller explanation of the meaning of the term "Judeo-Christian values."[100] In her response, President Feeley emphasized that at Notre Dame,

the Catholic educational tradition has provided a firm base on which to build a philosophy, a curriculum and a spirit of service. . . . To foster a holistic education, we give attention to the spiritual life as well as to the intellectual life. . . . We support traditional religious values. . . . The cross which tops the Merrick Tower of Gibbons Hall is visible from miles around the college. It signals to one and all the spiritual dimension of life and the spiritual dimension of a Notre Dame education. . . . It is a spirituality which excludes no one. . . . Whether muffled or clear, this spiritual note enriches the educational milieu of Baltimore."[101]

In her reply, Feeley situated a broadly appealing "spirituality" in the context of the College of Notre Dame's Catholic heritage without delineating theological or practical expectations for students and faculty. This was perhaps a necessity, because the identity of both groups was rapidly changing. Much of the burden for providing a Catholic campus environment for faculty as well as students had traditionally rested on the sisters, recalled a lay faculty member: "The sisters always have . . . provided both the spiritual background for what takes place in the education process here at the college, and also a very serious and devoted academic dedication which they transmit to the students and also to the lay faculty."[102]

The college's religious character was becoming a growing concern as the sisters' visibility on campus declined. A sustained national slump in the popularity of single-sex colleges had tested the staying power of American women's colleges in the 1970s and beyond. At the same time, a second viability challenge for Catholic institutions came from a sustained downward spiral in the number of young Catholic women joining the religious orders. Whereas these groups nationally reported a total of 32,433 candidates between 1958 and 1962, the corresponding total for 1971–75 was only 2,590.[103] This slump severely affected the capacity of sisterhoods to support the colleges they had founded.

Until this era, the sisters' services had spared Catholic women's colleges undue concern about a key budget item. Sisters on their faculties subsidized the college by working for minimal salaries. Their contributed services reduced the need to hire costlier lay faculty. As late as the 1960s, Notre Dame president Margaret Mary O'Connell casually requested that the order educate more sisters for the college faculty, proposing that superiors assign six junior sisters annually to earn PhDs. She reasoned that "the dividends for both College and Community, most of whose Sisters received their first undergraduate degree at this College, would far exceed the costs in personnel, time and money, over the long haul."[104] But such recommendations came too late.

The proportion of sisters holding full-time faculty and administrative positions at Notre Dame had held steady in the midcentury decades, at 58 percent in 1940 and 61 percent in 1960.[105] By 1987, however, of a total full-time faculty of sixty-six, School Sisters of Notre Dame accounted for only one-third.[106] Some colleges experienced far steeper declines. Between 1960 and 1980, the proportion of Sisters of Mercy on Chicago's Saint Xavier's College faculty dropped from 60 to 10 percent.[107] This falloff had an immediate effect on institutional budgets. At Notre Dame, the donated services of sisters accounted for 27 percent of total institutional income in 1956, but only 20 percent in 1971.[108] In 1978, Feeley, noting that "at present religious comprise 52% of the faculty," invoked anxiety about the college's financial position: "We have always considered the contributed services of the SSNDs to be our 'living endowment.' In recent years those services were the equivalent of the income from approximately $9.5 million. However, decreasing numbers of religious in our society means that we must look to the day when a greater portion of our faculty will be lay teachers."[109]

On March 19, 1992, the Notre Dame board of trustees elected one of their membership, the trustee and executive vice president Rosemarie Nassif, SSND, to succeed Kathleen Feeley as president of the college.[110] The new president's grace period was short. Feeley's success in addressing the challenges of coeducation and college finances had led many to consider her the savior of the college. At the same time, difficult battles for tenure, higher salaries, and participation in college governance decisions during her term of office had produced a faculty, sisters and lay alike, that was vigilant about its hard-won rights. Feeley was able to introduce the Weekend College in the 1970s quickly, and with minimal faculty involvement, because it was evident to all constituencies that the college's survival required immediate action. In the early 1990s, however, no comparable threat to institutional survival loomed, and both religious and lay faculty members had begun to play significant roles in college governance.[111]

Nassif's strategic plan included several ambitious initiatives that soon generated campus controversy. Faculty apprehension focused on her proposal to replace the college's traditional organizational structure with a five-vice-president model. While this was a common configuration among peer institutions, faculty questioned its usefulness for a college of Notre Dame's size. They called for more consultation about a restructuring that could adversely affect their authority in college governance. Campus tensions rose in 1995, and in February 1996, Nassif resigned.[112] Dorothy Brown, professor of history at Georgetown University, served as interim president during 1996–97.[113] In the spring of 1997, Mary Pat Seurkamp, vice president for institutional planning and research at Saint John Fisher College (Rochester, New York), became the first lay president of the College of Notre Dame, an office she held until her retirement in 2012. Following the 2013 resignation of President

James Conneely, formerly associate provost at Eastern Kentucky University, Joan Develin Cooley, president emerita of McDaniel College (Westminster, Maryland), served as interim president of the college until 2014. That year, the board of trustees elected Marylou Yam, provost and vice president for academic affairs at Saint Peter's College (Jersey City, New Jersey), as president of Notre Dame of Maryland University.

As at many comparable colleges, over the last fifty years Notre Dame's relationship with its founding order has moved from one of hierarchical dominance to one of affiliation—or as the School Sisters of Notre Dame term it, "sponsorship," defined as "the mutually beneficial and dynamic relationship between the congregation and an organization in which the SSND charism and educational vision . . . are defining characteristics of the organization's mission."[114] To implement this interpretation, leaders of the college and the order established a sponsorship review process, adding in 2001 a vice president for mission to the college's governing structure.[115] There is general agreement that this strategy has produced significant benefits. "It imparts to our sponsored colleges a culture that approaches education as more than individual enhancement," explained president emerita Mary Pat Seurkamp. "Sponsorship assumes a commitment to the Catholic intellectual tradition and to the values of the sponsoring religious congregation."[116]

125 Years of Catholic Women's Education

As their original rationale—the refusal of elite men's colleges to admit women—evaporated during the 1960s and 1970s, women's colleges began to face the question of whether they ought to continue at all, a question that persists today. For fifty years young women in general have preferred coeducational to single-sex colleges, and Catholic philanthropy flows disproportionately to institutions, now coeducational, that were originally founded by and for men. As student interest in attending coeducational colleges climbed inexorably, women's colleges continued to argue that female students benefited relatively more from the single-sex than from the coeducational college experience. In 1987, President Kathleen Feeley offered a representative explanation: the College of Notre Dame, she said, "offers to girls and women a choice to which they have a right: the choice to be educated in an atmosphere in which they are the singular object of the educational enterprise. . . . Today, women's colleges have a unique opportunity to nurture in women the special feminine qualities which have leavened our society even as they prepare women for a future of equality of influence through widely diverse channels."[117] In making this argument, Feeley departed from the position of the founders of the College of Notre Dame. Offering women the opportunity to attend a Catholic college was indeed their priority, but the sisters themselves did not oppose the concept of coeducation. They founded a college for women because at the time Catholic undergraduate colleges admitted only men.

Catholic women's colleges, in other words, may have been something of a historical accident. Yet their social impact on female citizens remains distinctive. They paved new roads in private higher education, adding diversity to the types of colleges flourishing in the United States. As a result of the church's long-term opposition to coeducation, Catholic women's colleges spread from the Atlantic to the Pacific, and opened in rural as well as urban settings, broadening access to higher education, especially for the daughters of working- and middle-class families. From their inception, they advanced women's roles in the wider society as their graduates moved into positions of authority and power in church and state. Historically, they have represented major commitments of Catholic resources, both financial and human, to women. In their own way, these colleges reconfigured the Catholic Church in the United States.

Collectively, the numerous Catholic colleges also played a significant and underrecognized role in the women's college movement in the United States. If Catholic college women saw themselves as entering formerly closed, elite male realms, this was an experience they shared with the nineteenth-century founders of the Seven Sisters and with their peers at secular colleges throughout the twentieth century. Although both lay and religious women were always constrained by the need for episcopal approval, like their secular and Protestant counterparts Catholic women's colleges were significant female-dominated spaces within an otherwise overwhelmingly masculine power structure. Their campuses became places where women often formed significant social and professional bonds away from the eyes of bishops, fathers, and husbands, and where they could hold positions of real responsibility unavailable in other institutions. The achievements of the women who taught in them have had real and lasting effects on their communities.

For over a century, then, Catholic women's colleges have advanced women's intellectual and professional opportunities in American society. They played a key role in democratizing Catholic higher education by incorporating women into the enterprise, widening opportunities for working- and lower-middle-class women to attend private colleges. Their story is the story of how women became agents in their own right as citizens of society and of the nation's largest church. These institutions were able to defy a century of male primacy in the church's colleges only because of the financial and labor support of religious orders of women sustained over many decades. However, female dominance in their governance and faculties also had the negative effect of marginalizing these colleges in mainstream and church educational circles. As a result, the historical importance of Catholic women's colleges is only now coming into view.

This book has evaluated the historical experiences, successes, failures, and long-term significance in the history of Catholic women's colleges, as exemplified in the development of the first of their number, the College of Notre Dame of Maryland, over the course of the twentieth century. Tense debates around single-sex education, the value and place of the liberal arts curriculum, and Catholic institutional identity have marked discussion at the college over recent decades, as they have at similar schools in an era of simultaneous expansion and constriction. Have the college's original vision, values, and goals remained essentially unchanged, even as the forms in which they revealed themselves altered significantly over the passing decades? Is Notre Dame's present situation simply a variation on the college's original theme, or is it, in fact, a wholly new theme?

As the history recounted here shows, by the turn of the twenty-first century Notre Dame had broadened its boundaries dramatically. Its student body was now heterogeneous in race, religion, and gender. Its original women's undergraduate college was joined over time by a Weekend College that welcomed men as well as women students. It expanded its curriculum to include professional fields of study as well as the liberal arts and offered graduate as well as bachelor's degree programs. Far from the protective restrictions it had long placed on students, it actively developed cross-registration opportunities for its students with other institutions.[118] By responding effectively to challenges from both mainstream society and the church community, Notre Dame transformed itself from an upper-middle-class, racially segregated institution to one of the most socially and racially diverse of the nation's private religiously affiliated colleges.

As in 1895, Notre Dame's focus on women and its commitment to the liberal arts remain fundamental to its character. Its determination to survive as an autonomous institution apart from Loyola explains, in large measure, its 1970s decision to remain a women's college. Its success in maintaining and developing its own identity and position in the intervening decades means that if Notre Dame moves to further coeducation in the future, it will do so on its own terms. Meanwhile, its undergraduate women's college remains the core of the institution. The liberal arts are integral to professional programs of study, while liberal arts majors enjoy unique opportunities to elect courses in a range of professional fields. Its emphasis on science, which dated from its 1895 foundation, took on new dimensions in its School of Nursing and School of Pharmacy, and its historic commitment to the study of education grew as well; its first PhD was awarded in that field. Four decades of coeducation and the expansion of professional programs in Notre Dame's Weekend College and graduate programs in many ways enriched its undergraduate women's college. Since 1895, Notre Dame has preserved its commitment to women's higher education in the face of critical tests from church and society. The extent to which it achieved its original purposes is the judgment of history.

ABBREVIATIONS AND ARCHIVES CONSULTED

Most primary sources for this history are located in the archives of Notre Dame of Maryland University, currently held in Archives and Special Collections at the Loyola Notre Dame Library. Because these sources were originally consulted before the archives were moved and recataloged, they are cited not by box and folder number, but by title and date along with the designation "NDMA" (Notre Dame of Maryland Archives) and, in some cases, an indication of subcollection.

AAU	Association of American Universities
AAUP	American Association of University Professors
ABA	Archives of the Archdiocese of Baltimore, Associated Archives at Saint Mary's Seminary & University, Baltimore, MD
ASEUT	American Society for the Extension of University Teaching
BMEP	Bridget Marie Engelmeyer Papers, NDMA
BOSO	Board of Student Organizations, College of Notre Dame
Chron.	*Annals and Chronicles of Notre Dame,* NDMA
CND	College of Notre Dame of Maryland (1895–2011)
HEFA	Higher Education Facilities Act of 1963
MSA	Association of Colleges and Secondary Schools of the Middle States and Maryland (later Middle States Association of Colleges and Schools)
NDM Catalog	*Catalogs of the College of Notre Dame*
NDMA	Archives of Notre Dame of Maryland University
OES	Oxford Extension Society
OHP	Oral History Project, NDMA
PFA	Parents and Friends Association, College of Notre Dame
PM	Patricia Murphy, SSND
POAU	Protestants and Other Americans United for Separation of Church and State

RC   "Reminiscences of Notre Dame" Collection, NDMA
SJ   Society of Jesus (Jesuits)
SSND   Congregation of the School Sisters of Notre Dame

Student Publications

Arras (yearbook)
Columns (newspaper)
Damozel (literary magazine)

A full bibliography for this book can be found at cornellpress.cornell.edu/book/9781501753794/pursuing-truth/.

Notes

Introduction

1. State charters awarded to mid-nineteenth-century girls' boarding academies often empowered them to confer "college" degrees. A number of women's colleges that emerged from academy roots argue that their foundings date to those of related lower schools. In 1955, Saint Mary's College in Indiana, founded under such a charter, challenged the temporal priority of the College of Notre Dame of Maryland on these grounds. See, for example, "Oldest Women's College to Mark Anniversary," *Catholic Free Press* (Worcester, MA), February 18, 1955; and "Underscorings," *America*, April 9, 1955, 33.

2. The term "Seven Sisters" emerged from the 1915 Seven Colleges Conference in Poughkeepsie, New York, a meeting of administrators of these institutions to discuss mutual concerns. On Catholic education, see Philip Gleason, "Bibliographic Essay on the History of Catholic Higher Education," in *Handbook of Research on Catholic Higher Education*, ed. Thomas C. Hunt, Ronald J. Nuzzi, Ellis A. Joseph, and John O. Geiger (Greenwich, CT: Information Age, 2003), 95–113. Gleason considers some features of female higher education in his excellent study, *Contending with Modernity: Catholic Higher Education in the Twentieth Century* (New York: Oxford University Press, 1995).

3. In her classic study *In the Company of Educated Women: A History of Women and Higher Education in America* (New Haven, CT: Yale University Press, 1985), Barbara Solomon addresses the emergence of Catholic institutions, but provides limited commentary on their development. In *Outside In: Minorities and the Transformation of American Education* (New York: Oxford University Press, 1989), Paula Fass curiously situates her discussion of Catholic women's colleges in a chapter on Catholic elementary and secondary schools rather than in the chapter dealing with women's higher education. Andrea Turpin's study *A New Moral Vision: Gender, Religion, and the Changing Purposes of American Higher Education, 1837–1917* (Ithaca, NY: Cornell University Press, 2016) explicitly excludes consideration of Catholic institutions. Linda Eisenmann's extensive review of studies of women's education published between 1985 and 1997 ("Reconsidering a Classic: Assessing the History of Women's Higher Education a Dozen Years after Barbara Solomon," *Harvard Educational Review* 67 [Winter 1997]: 689–717) further underscores the paucity of historical research on Catholic institutions.

4. See, for example, Sally Schwager, "Educating Women in America," *Signs: Journal of Women in Culture and Society* 12 (Winter 1987): 333–72; Lynn D. Gordon, "From Seminary to University: An Overview of Women's Higher Education, 1870–1920," in *The History of Higher Education*, 2nd ed., ed. Lester K. Goodchild and Harold S. Wechsler (Old Tappan, NJ: Pearson Custom, 1997), 473–98; and Ruben Donato and

Marvin Lazerson, "New Directions in American Educational History: Problems and Prospects," *Educational Researcher* 29 (November 2000): 4–15.

5. Studies of teachers and scholars, as opposed to institutions, that fully incorporate the Catholic experience include Geraldine J. Clifford, *Those Good Gertrudes: A Social History of Women Teachers in America* (Baltimore: Johns Hopkins University Press, 2014); and Margaret W. Rossiter, *Women Scientists in America*, 3 vols. (Baltimore: Johns Hopkins University Press, 1982–2012).

6. See William P. Leahy, *Adapting to America: Catholics, Jesuits and Higher Education in the Twentieth Century* (Washington, DC: Georgetown University Press, 1991), 71–72.

7. Among US women's colleges, it was the first Catholic representative, and among Catholic colleges, it was the first to admit women. Other works that tell a more general story about higher education through the lens of a single institutional history include Morton Keller and Phyllis Keller, *Making Harvard Modern: The Rise of America's University* (New York: Oxford University Press, 2001); and Rosalind Rosenberg, *Changing the Subject: How the Women of Columbia Shaped the Way We Think about Sex and Politics* (New York: Columbia University Press, 2004).

1. American Catholics and Female Higher Education

1. Patricia A. Palmieri, "*Incipit Vita Nuova*: Founding Ideals of the Wellesley College Community," *History of Higher Education Annual* 3 (1983): 66; Joan Marie Johnson, *Southern Women at the Seven Sister Colleges* (Athens: University of Georgia Press, 2008), 59; Ruth Bordin, *Alice Freeman Palmer: The Evolution of a New Woman* (Ann Arbor: University of Michigan Press, 1993), 271. See also Timothy E. W. Gloege, *Guaranteed Pure: The Moody Bible Institute: Business and the Making of Modern Evangelicalism* (Chapel Hill: University of North Carolina Press, 2015).

2. W. Bruce Nash, "Localism, Denominationalism, and Institutional Strategies in Urbanizing America: Three Pennsylvania Colleges, 1870–1915," *History of Education Quarterly* 17 (Fall 1977): 241.

3. Theresa Gerhardinger to Charles Augustus, Bishop of Munich, November 1852, in *Historical Dimensions: Letters of Mother M. Theresa Gerhardinger, SSND*, ed. M. Hester Valentine (Winona, MN: Saint Mary's College Press, 1977), 89–90.

4. Barbara Brumleve, "The Archives of the School Sisters of Notre Dame: A Profile," *American Catholic Studies Newsletter* 15, no. 2 (Fall 1988): 15. After over a century in Munich, the generalate moved to Rome in 1957.

5. Mary Theresa of Jesus to His Royal Highness, King Ludwig I of Bavaria, July 1847, in *The North American Foundations: Letters of Mother M. Theresa Gerhardinger, School Sister of Notre Dame*, ed. M. Hester Valentine (Winona, MN: Saint Mary's College Press, 1977), no. 725. See also Anne Philbin, *The Past and the Promised: A History of the Alumnae Association, College of Notre Dame of Maryland, Baltimore, Maryland* (Baltimore: Alumnae Association, College of Notre Dame of Maryland, 1959), 23. The pioneer sisters in Baltimore were Sisters Caroline Friess, Magdalen Steiner, Seraphina von Pronath, and Barbara Weinzierl, and a novice, Mary Emmanuel. On Ludwig's role in funding German Catholic religious orders in the United States, see Kathleen Curran, *The Romanesque Revival: Religion, Architecture, and Transnational Exchange* (University Park: Pennsylvania State University Press, 2003).

6. See A School Sister of Notre Dame [M. Dympna Flynn], *Mother Caroline and the School Sisters of Notre Dame in North America* (Saint Louis: Woodward & Tiernan, 1928), 1:289.

7. Community prayers continued to be said in German until 1887. See *Chron.*, July 1, 1887; July 4, 1887. For an account of Friess's 1850 trip, see A School Sister of Notre Dame, *Mother Caroline*, 1:48–49; and Mary David Cameron, *The College of Notre Dame of Maryland, 1895–1945* (New York: Declan X. McMullen, 1947), 27–28. For the origins and effects of cloister rules in religious communities of women in Europe in this era, see Susan O'Brien, "*Terra Incognita*: The Nun in Nineteenth-Century New England," *Past & Present* 121, no. 1 (November 1988): 110–40.

8. *Sadlier's Catholic Directory, 1877*, cited in Thomas W. Spalding, *The Premier See: A History of the Archdiocese of Baltimore, 1789–1980* (Baltimore: Johns Hopkins University Press, 1989), 238; "Taking Nuns' Veils: Thirty-One Young Women Received as Novices in Baltimore—Two Novices Take the Black Veil," *New York Times*, October 16, 1878.

9. See A School Sister of Notre Dame, *Mother Caroline*, 1:250.

10. Theresa Gerhardinger to Theophila Bauer, n.d. (ca. 1876), in Valentine, *Historical Dimensions*, 181. Gerhardinger was well aware that Bauer's small dog, Jacquelie, rarely left her side. See Cameron, *College of Notre Dame*, 40.

11. For more on Friess, see A School Sister of Notre Dame, *Mother Caroline*; and Peter M. Abbelen, *Venerable Mother M. Caroline Friess, First Commissary General of the School Sisters of Notre Dame in America: A Sketch of Her Life and Character* (Saint Louis: B. Herder, 1893).

12. Theresa Gerhardinger to Caroline Friess, March 14, 1870, in Valentine, *Historical Dimensions*, 141. For Wegman's experiences in Baltimore, see Bridget Marie Engelmeyer, *Sister Ildephonsa Wegman: Footnote to a Legend* (Baltimore: College of Notre Dame of Maryland and School Sisters of Notre Dame, 1996).

13. Theresa Gerhardinger to Caroline Friess, May 3, 1868, in Valentine, *Historical Dimensions*, 127–28.

14. Caroline Friess to Rev. P. M. Abbelen, January 2, 1880, in *The Letters of Mother Caroline Friess*, ed. Barbara Brumleve (St. Louis: School Sisters of Notre Dame, 1991), 269–70.

15. "Mr. [Thomas F.] Troxall died at 'Montrose,' December 10, 1871. His executors, Naomi E. Troxall and Wilson R. Troxall, sold the place to the School Sisters of Notre Dame for $25,584.50, subject to a yearly rental of $476.25 (i.e., to Dr. Benjamin W. Woods)." See William B. Marye, "Baltimore City Place Names, Part 4, Stony Run, Its Plantations, Farms, Country Seats and Mills," *Maryland Historical Magazine* 58 (December 1963): 377. Historical sources spell the name "Troxall" variously as Troxall, Troxell, and Truxell. Villa Montrose was among a number of "villas" built on Charles Street in the 1850s: "Rather than 'cottages' for the middle class, wealthy clients constructed 'villas,' which were the most 'refined' houses in the United States." Julia A. Sienkewicz, *Historic American Buildings Survey: Addendum to Evergreen (Evergreen Museum & Library)*, National Park Service (Washington, DC: U.S. Department of the Interior, 2009), 54, http://lcweb2.loc.gov/master/pnp/habshaer/md/md1600/md1633/data/md1633data.pdf.

16. *Chron.*, April 5, 1873. Following a 1914 typhoid epidemic in the area, the Baltimore Board of Health ordered the lake drained permanently. The description of the

lay sister is from Zerline Emilie Stauf, "In Retrospect and Reflection," handwritten account, n.d., RC. Stauf (1864–1958), a Protestant, became a Catholic after graduating from the Collegiate Institute in 1882. After several years as a translator at the US Bureau of Education, she returned to the College of Notre Dame as a German instructor and retired in 1945.

17. Sienkewicz, *Historic American Buildings Survey,* 64.

18. *Chron.,* April 17, 1871; December 29, 1872; February 21, 1873; Sienkewicz, *Historic American Buildings Survey*, 63–64.

19. *Chron.,* February 21, 1873. See also Grace Sherwood '35, "The Golden Jubilee of Notre Dame College," typescript, n.d., RC. SH & JF Adams, Builders, had gained regional recognition by the 1860s. See, for example, "The New Mount Hope Hospital," *Baltimore Sun,* December 14, 1861. In July 1882, the *American Architect and Building News* called Adams "a leading builder of Baltimore, Md" (see Sienkewicz, *Historic American Buildings Survey*, 8n8).

20. *Chron.,* July 2, 1874; December 6, 1874; February 1, 1876.

21. *Chron.,* July 18, 1876. Caroline Friess was sharply critical of her superiors in Munich for not responding effectively to the Baltimore crisis in the 1870s; see Caroline Friess to Rev. P. M. Abbelen, January 2, 1880, in Brumleve, *Letters,* 269–70.

22. For a detailed discussion, see Engelmeyer, *Sister Ildephonsa Wegman.*

23. Joshua Dorin, "College Hall (Wellesley College)," *Wellesley History* (blog), June 4, 2013, https://wellesleyhistory.wordpress.com/2013/06.

24. *Chron.,* December 24, 1872.

25. The directress and prefect of studies of the Institute of Notre Dame, Ildephonsa Wegman and Meletia Foley, respectively, governed both schools until 1877.

26. M. Theresa Stevens, "The Educational Policy of the Order of School Sisters of Notre Dame" (PhD diss., Saint Louis University, 1928), 103–4. See Grace H. Sherwood, "Genesis of Notre Dame: From Academy to College," *Baltimore Sun,* May 27, 1945. The Aisquith Street school admitted only day students after 1912 (Philbin, *Past and the Promised*, 35).

27. Sister Bridget Marie Engelmeyer, "The Faculty in Early Colleges for Women: The Notre Dame Experience," typescript, n.d., BMEP. "Lay" sisters were typically from a lower social class and had less formal education than "choir" sisters; the two-tier membership system persisted in many orders until the Second Vatican Council.

28. Engelmeyer, *Sister Ildephonsa Wegman*, 40–41.

29. At this time, Grant was enjoying little support among Catholic voters nationally. Not only did he favor taxation of church property but he also strongly supported a proposed federal amendment that would deny public funds to "any sectarian school." While the Blaine Amendment failed to pass, many states incorporated its provisions in their constitutions and the rancorous controversy continued. See Mark D. McGarvie, *Law and Religion in American History: Public Values and Private Conscience* (New York: Cambridge University Press, 2016), 86–88, 250; Timothy Walch, *Parish School: American Catholic Parochial Education from Colonial Times to the Present* (New York: Crossroad, 1996), 62–63; and James Hennesey, SJ, *American Catholics: A History of the Roman Catholic Community in the United States* (New York: Oxford University Press, 1981), 185.

30. Sister Mary Immaculata Dillon, untitled typescript, n.d. (ca. 1919), NDMA.

31. Margaret Mary O'Connell, "The Educational Contributions of the School Sisters of Notre Dame in America for the Century 1847 to 1947" (EdD diss., Johns Hopkins University, 1950), 103–4; *Chron.*, June 15, 1876.

32. Mary Augusta Hutton '76, "Recollections of NDM," 1939, RC.

33. Hutton, "Recollections of NDM."

34. See Virginia Wolf Briscoe, "Bryn Mawr College Traditions: Women's Rituals as Expressive Behavior" (PhD diss., University of Pennsylvania, 1981), 1:440–41.

35. Ildephonsa Wegman to Archbishop James Roosevelt Bayley, Baltimore, September 26, 1876, NDMA.

36. Caroline Friess to Theophila Bauer, June 29, 1877, in Brumleve, *Letters*, 209–10.

37. Wegman died in Montreal in 1886. She apparently never formally resigned from the order; see "Sister Ildephonsa's Death Card, May 17, 1886," NDMA.

38. Quoted in "History of Notre Dame, 1897," handwritten speech (by Mary I. Dillon, SSND?), RC. Aikin (1807–88) was a member of the medical school faculty from 1836 until his retirement in 1883.

39. Eugene Fauntleroy Cordell, *Historical Sketch of the University of Maryland, School of Medicine (1807–1890)* (Baltimore: Press of Isaac Friedenwald, 1891), 144.

40. Hutton, "Recollections of NDM." For early lay lecturers, see also Cameron, *College of Notre Dame*, 42–45.

41. Cordell, *Historical Sketch*, 149.

42. Robert Dorsey Coale (1857–1915) became dean of the University of Maryland Medical School. For his obituary, see the *Baltimore Sun*, May 19, 1915.

43. Regina Armstrong, "Richard Malcolm Johnston, Gentleman and Man-of-Letters," *Catholic World* 68 (November 1898): 264. See also Henry P. Goddard, "Richard Malcolm Johnston: Reminiscences of the Writer of Southern Dialect Stories Who Recently Died," *Saturday Review of Books and Art*, November 26, 1898; Zerline Stauf, "In Retrospect and Reflection," n.d., RC.

44. John C. French, *A History of the University Founded by Johns Hopkins* (Baltimore: Johns Hopkins Press, 1946), 308–9. Odend'hal died in 1946.

45. Engelmeyer, "Faculty in Early Colleges." On Lyman, see Franklin Ellis and Samuel Evans, *History of Lancaster County, Pennsylvania* (Philadelphia: Everts & Peck, 1883), 557.

46. *NDM Catalog*, 1877; *NDM Catalog*, 1885–86. Evangelista (Josephine) Meyer (1844–1909) was the Baltimore provincial superior from 1898 to 1907. Jeannette (Theresa) Duffy (1853–1901) joined the order in 1879 and taught at Notre Dame until her death.

47. Sherwood, "Golden Jubilee."

48. Louise Schutz Boas, *Woman's Education Begins: The Rise of the Women's Colleges* (Norton, MA: Wheaton College Press, 1935), 222.

49. Sherwood, "Golden Jubilee."

50. *NDM Catalog*, 1874.

51. "The World Belongs to the Energetic—The Class Motto," 1887 valedictory address, Scrapbook/Album 19th Century, NDMA.

52. Stevens, "Educational Policy," 112–13. See also *NDM Catalog*, 1893–94.

53. Theresa Gerhardinger, Superior General, Circular Letter #5333, January 20, 1879, in Valentine, *Historical Dimensions*, 172. Sisters at this time took a "fourth vow" to uphold the order's regulations on the instruction of students. Following the revision

of the Code of Canon Law in 1918, the "fourth vow" became part of the vow of obedience. See A School Sister of Notre Dame, *Mother Caroline*, 1:283.

54. Stevens, "Educational Policy," 103–4. Rosenthal attended the school for five years. See *Chron.*, June 19, 1890.

55. *NDM Catalog*, 1876; *NDM Catalog*, 1881.

56. Bettina Berch, *The Woman Behind the Lens: The Life and Work of Frances Benjamin Johnston, 1864–1952* (Charlottesville: University of Virginia Press, 2000), 10. In 1882–83, Johnston was classified as a "Collegiate A" student, and in 1883–84 as a member of the "senior class—graduating department." See also Pete Daniel and Raymond Smock, *A Talent for Detail: The Photographs of Miss Frances Benjamin Johnston, 1889–1910* (New York: Harmony Books, 1974); Sam Watters, *Gardens for a Beautiful America, 1895–1935: Photographs by Frances Benjamin Johnston* (New York: Acanthus, 2012).

57. *Chron.*, May 21, 1887.

58. See *NDM Catalog*, 1873.

59. Eva (Lockwood) Pearce '74 (left without degree), "Description of N.D.," n.d., RC.

60. Hutton, "Recollections of NDM."

61. A School Sister of Notre Dame, *Mother Caroline*, 2:281. In 1888, when Bauer's term as provincial superior ended, her successor, Mother Clara Heuck, reversed this step. Bauer remained at Charles Street as superior of the campus convent and president of the school.

62. Sister M. Frances Smith, "Notre Dame's Sister Mary Meletia," *Centenary Inter-Provincial News Letter*, April 1947, NDMA. Marie Wagner Smith (1886–1950) entered the order upon graduating from the Notre Dame of Maryland Preparatory School in 1904. She earned a PhD in English at the Catholic University of America in 1935. In the same year, she was appointed president of the College of Notre Dame of Maryland.

63. *NDM Catalog*, 1877.

64. *Baltimore Sun*, news clipping, n.d. (ca. 1890), Scrapbook/Album 19th Century.

65. Caroline Friess to Rev. P. M. Abbelen, Milwaukee, January 2, 1880, in Brumleve, *Letters*, 269–70.

66. Caroline Friess to Rev. Mother General Margaret of Cortona Wiedemann, February 8, 1891, in Brumleve, *Letters*, 478–79.

67. Caroline Friess to Theophila Bauer, May 29, 1884, in Brumleve, *Letters*, 361–62.

68. Caroline Friess to Theophila Bauer, December 21, 1886, in Brumleve, *Letters*, 412.

69. Caroline Friess to Rev. Mother General Margaret of Cortona Wiedemann, February 8, 1891, in Brumleve, *Letters*, 478–79.

70. "Gilman's Inaugural Address," February 22, 1876, Johns Hopkins University, https://www.jhu.edu/about/history/gilman-address.

71. French, *History of the University*, 75.

72. "Radcliffe College: Academic and Social," *Harvard Graduates' Magazine*, September 1894, reporting on President Charles W. Eliot's remarks at Radcliffe's June 26, 1894, commencement. Twenty-two students received bachelor's degrees and three received master's degrees.

73. Kathleen Sprows Cummings, *New Women of the Old Faith: Gender and American Catholicism in the Progressive Era* (Chapel Hill: University of North Carolina Press, 2009), 61–62.

74. Sherwood, "Golden Jubilee."

75. Merle Curti and Roderick Nash, *Philanthropy in the Shaping of American Higher Education* (New Brunswick, NJ: Rutgers University Press, 1965), 106; Mary J. Oates, *The Catholic Philanthropic Tradition in America* (Bloomington: Indiana University Press, 1995), 135–37.

76. Superiors of male religious orders, who conducted most US Catholic colleges, followed the bishops' lead publicly, whatever they may have privately thought about the merits of coeducation. Some were opposed on principle; others, especially during wartime, saw advantages in admitting women. Few were strongly sympathetic to the cause of women's higher education overall.

77. C. Joseph Nuesse, *The Catholic University of America: A Centennial History* (Washington, DC: Catholic University of America Press, 1990), 345. The undergraduate college, also for men, opened in 1904. For an interesting account of turn-of-the-century undergraduate life at Catholic University, see Frank Kuntz, *Undergraduate Days, 1904–1908: The Catholic University of America* (Washington, DC: Catholic University of America Press, 1958). Johns Hopkins admitted women to its graduate school in 1907.

78. The Congregation of the School Sisters of Notre Dame was not the only sisterhood interested in opening a women's college in the late nineteenth century. Plans of the Sisters of Saint Joseph in Saint Paul, Minnesota, who had acquired land for a college, were delayed by the economic depression of the 1890s. Other communities met episcopal opposition.

79. On the college's growth in the John Ireland era, see Carol K. Coburn and Martha Smith, *Spirited Lives: How Nuns Shaped Catholic Culture and American Life, 1836–1920* (Chapel Hill: University of North Carolina Press, 1999), 180–84.

80. Jay P. Dolan, *The American Catholic Experience: A History from Colonial Times to the Present* (Notre Dame, IN: University of Notre Dame Press, 1992), 302. Bishops of German origin made up about 15 percent of the total. On the ethnic, class, and educational background of bishops, see John Tracy Ellis, *American Catholics and the Intellectual Life* (Chicago: Heritage Foundation, 1956), 33–37.

81. Maryann Valiulis, "Neither Feminist nor Flapper: The Ecclesiastical Construction of the Ideal Irish Woman," in *Chattel, Servant or Citizen? Women's Status in Church, State and Society*, ed. Mary O'Dowd and Sabine Wichert (Belfast: Institute of Irish Studies, 1995), 168–78.

82. Michael M. O'Kane, *Woman's Place in the World* (Dublin: M. H. Gill, 1913), cited in Senia Paseta, *Before the Revolution: Nationalism, Social Change and Ireland's Catholic Elite, 1879–1922* (Cork: Cork University Press, 1999), 139–40. According to the *Irish Catholic Directory and Almanac* (Dublin: James Duffy, 1904), 231, O'Kane headed the Dominican house in Limerick. The Irish hierarchy established this monthly publication in 1864 to strengthen ties between Ireland and the Vatican.

83. David Barry, "Female Suffrage from a Catholic Standpoint," *Irish Ecclesiastical Record*, ser. 4, 26 (1909): 295–303.

84. See Cummings, *New Women*, 96.

85. Gibbons became the United States' second cardinal in 1886. John Tracy Ellis, *The Life of James Cardinal Gibbons, Archbishop of Baltimore, 1834–1921*, 2 vols. (Milwaukee: Bruce, 1952) remains the definitive biography of this churchman.

86. O'Connell, "Educational Contributions," 137.

87. Rev. Patrick C. Gavan, June 4, 1925, NDMA.

88. Bishop John Lancaster Spalding of Peoria, Illinois, had mentioned the idea of a college to the Sisters of Notre Dame de Namur in 1893, but they did not seriously consider it (Sister Mary Henretty, SND, "Trinity College, Washington D.C.: History of Foundation and Development," unpublished paper, April 1906, Archives, Trinity Washington University). Sister Julia McGroarty admitted in 1897 that "the undertaking [of a college] did not appeal to me," although she permitted Sister Mary Euphrasia to broach it with Cardinal Gibbons. See Cynthia Farr Brown, "Patterns of Leadership: The Impact of Female Authority in Four Women's Colleges, 1880–1910," in *Women Administrators in Higher Education: Historical and Contemporary Perspectives*, ed. Jana Nidiffer and Carolyn T. Bashaw (Albany: State University of New York Press, 2001), 47.

89. See Brown, "Patterns of Leadership," 37–65.

90. Elmer E. Brown, *The Making of Our Middle Schools* (repr., Manchester, NH: Ayer, [1905] 1969), 329.

91. *NDM Catalog*, 1895–96.

92. "Notre Dame of Maryland: Commencement," news clipping, n.d. (ca. June 1895), Scrapbook/Album 19th Century, NDMA.

93. O'Connell, "Educational Contributions," 119n141.

94. Sherwood, "Genesis of Notre Dame."

95. *NDM Catalog*, 1903.

96. *Chron.*, June 13–14, 1899.

97. See "College Honored by Gift of First Diploma," *Newsletter, Alumnae Association of the College of Notre Dame of Maryland* 31, no. 4 (April 1954): 2.

98. *Chron.*, June 14, 1899. Bonaparte later became US secretary of the navy (1905–6) and US attorney general (1906–9). See Robert D. Salie, "The Harvard Annex Experiment in the Higher Education of Women: Separate but Equal?" (PhD diss., Emory University, 1976), 318.

99. Adele (Mohlenrich) Hicks '17, untitled reminiscence of Notre Dame, n.d., RC.

100. *Morning Herald*, June 15, 1899; "Notre Dame: Famous College for Women and Preparatory School for Girls," *Baltimore Morning Herald*, August 28, 1900.

101. In 1951, Kilkoff was supervisor of communications and records at the US State Department. See Philbin, *Past and the Promised*, 54.

102. Arnold Sparr, *To Promote, Defend, and Redeem: The Catholic Literary Revival and the Cultural Transformation of American Catholicism, 1920–1960* (Westport, CT: Greenwood, 1990), 167n15; Philip Gleason, *Contending with Modernity: Catholic Higher Education in the Twentieth Century* (New York: Oxford University Press, 1995), 152; Mother Grace, OSB, "The Catholic Renascence Society: Its Past and Future," *Renascence* 1 (Autumn 1948/49): 3. Among the society's first major donors were the College of Notre Dame, Mount Mary College, and Mother Mary Myles, SSND, of the Baltimore Motherhouse. The society flourished nationally until about 1960. Marquette University continues to publish its journal, *Renascence: Essays on Values in Literature*.

103. Gleason, *Contending with Modernity*, 28.

104. A Sister of Notre Dame [M. Patricia Butler], *An Historical Sketch of Trinity College, Washington, D.C., 1897–1925* (Washington, DC: Trinity College, 1925), n.p. According to Kathleen Sprows Cummings, the idea for a female college may have originated with Sister Julia McGroarty, although "whether she took the initiative . . . or whether the opportunity was presented to her remains a matter of some dispute" (*New Women*, 67).

105. James Cardinal Gibbons to Sister Julia McGroarty, Baltimore, June 21, 1897, ABA.

106. "Dedicated: Trinity College at Washington a Triumph for Mother Julia," *Kentucky Irish American*, October 13, 1900. The actual dedication date was November 22.

107. Sister Superior Julia to Sister Mary Euphrasia, September 2, 1897, quoted in Sister of Notre Dame, *An Historical Sketch*, n.p.

108. James Cardinal Gibbons to Cardinal Francesco Satolli, September 5, 1897; James Cardinal Gibbons to Archbishop Sebastiano Martinelli, August 25, 1897, ABA. See also Paul G. Robichaud, "The Resident Church: Middle Class Catholics and the Shaping of American Catholic Identity, 1889 to 1899" (PhD diss., University of California, Los Angeles, 1989), 236.

109. MCM, "The Columbian Reading Union," *Catholic World* 65 (September 1897): 861–62. The hierarchy viewed the absence of a preparatory school as especially noteworthy, although colleges founded by Protestant denominations routinely developed from such schools. On Presbyterian women's colleges, for example, see Patricia Wittberg, *From Piety to Professionalism—and Back? Transformations of Organized Religious Virtuosity* (Lanham, MD: Lexington Books, 2006), 29n25, citing Page Putnam Miller, *A Claim to New Roles* (Metuchen, NJ: Scarecrow, 1985), 184. Large sisterhoods owning tuition academies generally had more property and other assets than communities lacking such schools. Like other private female colleges, boarding academies also provided essential resources for the development of Catholic colleges.

110. "College for Young Women Catholics: Meeting Held to Further the Building of an Annex to the University at Washington," *San Francisco Call*, April 30, 1899; "Catholics Plan a Woman's College," *New York Herald*, April 30, 1899.

111. *New York Times*, June 16, 1897.

112. "College Plan Opposed: German Catholics Object to the Project for Higher Education of Women," *Baltimore Sun*, August 30, 1897.

113. Quoted in Sister Columba Mullaly, *Trinity College, Washington, D.C.: The First Eighty Years, 1897–1977* (Westminster, MD: Christian Classics, 1987), 31.

114. *Chron.*, July 12, 1897.

115. Henretty, "Trinity College, Washington, D.C."

116. See Annie P. Toler Hilliard, "An Investigation of Selected Events and Forces That Contributed to the Growth and Development of Trinity College, Washington, D.C. from 1897 to 1982" (EdD diss., George Washington University, 1984), 91.

117. See, for example, Robert J. Brugger, *Maryland: A Middle Temperament, 1834–1980* (Baltimore: Johns Hopkins University Press, 1988), 410; and Karen M. Kennelly, "Catholic Women's Colleges: A Review of the Record," *Current Issues in Catholic Higher Education* 10 (Summer 1989): 12n11.

118. Bridget Marie Engelmeyer, "From the Archives, July 1976," BMEP.

119. Historians perpetuated the confusion in the twentieth century. Nuesse referred to the college in 1900 as a collegiate institute, while Brugger stated that "the School Sisters of Notre Dame had founded their institution, the first Catholic women's college in the country, in 1873." See Nuesse, *Catholic University of America*, 120; Brugger, *Maryland*, 410. In 1875, the Sisters of the Holy Cross established Saint Catherine's Normal Institute in Baltimore.

120. See A School Sister of Notre Dame, *Mother Caroline*, 2:113.

121. Mullaly, *Trinity College*, 55.

122. Quoted in Mullaly, *Trinity College*, 60.

123. "Solemn Opening of Trinity College," *Catholic University Bulletin* 7 (January 1901): 122. In 2004, Trinity College was renamed Trinity Washington University.

124. L. J. [Lucian Johnston], handwritten draft of letter, n.d., NDMA.

125. "Important Correspondence," *Catholic World* 58 (January 1899): 575. See Austin O'Malley, "College Work for Catholic Girls," *Catholic World* 68 (November 1898): 161–67.

2. Women Educating Women

1. James H. Plough, "Catholic Colleges and the Catholic Educational Association: The Foundation and Early Years of the CEA, 1899–1919" (PhD diss., University of Notre Dame, 1967), 183. The Catholic Educational Association became the National Catholic Educational Association in 1927.

2. See Jana Nidiffer and Carolyn Terry Bashaw, eds., *Women Administrators in Higher Education: Historical and Contemporary Perspectives* (Albany: State University of New York Press, 2001).

3. Lavinia Hart, "Women as College Presidents," *Cosmopolitan*, May 1902. At this time, men served as the presidents of Vassar and Smith Colleges.

4. For more on Scripps College, see Helen Lefkowitz Horowitz, "Designing for the Genders: Curricula and Architecture at Scripps College and the California Institute of Technology," *Pacific Historical Review* 54 (November 1985): 439–61.

5. This governing structure also marked Catholic men's colleges. Jesuit-run colleges did not separate the offices of college president and local religious superior until the 1930s. See Paul A. FitzGerald, *The Governance of Jesuit Colleges in the United States, 1920–1970* (Notre Dame, IN: University of Notre Dame Press, 1984), x–xi.

6. See Mary E. Friel, "History of Emmanuel College, 1919–1974" (PhD diss., Boston College, 1980), 135.

7. Bridget Marie Engelmeyer, "A Half-Hour Sketch of the History of NDM," typescript of talk given at Mission '87, July 7, 1987, BMEP.

8. Adele M. (Mohlenrich) Hicks '17 to President Kathleen Feeley, January 3, 1983, NDMA.

9. Elizabeth Morrissy, interview by Barbara Gross, May 2, 1973, transcript, OHP.

10. Bridget Marie Engelmeyer, SSND, interview by Mary Jo Maloney, April 8, 1973, transcript, OHP.

11. *Chron.*, September 18, 1923; September 20, 1927. See also Virgina Geiger, SSND, interview by Patricia Murphy, SSND (henceforth PM), March 8, 1989, transcript, OHP.

12. Sister M. David Cameron to Sister M. Claudine Vincent, January 16, 1959, NDMA. Cameron (b. 1906) was a 1927 Notre Dame graduate; she held master's and bachelor's degrees in library science from Catholic University (1943, 1938).

13. Other Catholic women's colleges were also taking this step. See Sister Columba Mullaly, *Trinity College, Washington, D.C.: The First Eighty Years, 1897–1977* (Westminster, MD: Christian Classics, 1987), 118. On Doyle, see Rev. William K.

Dunn, *Eulogy for Mother Philemon Doyle, S.S.N.D., Dec. 8, 1874–Dec. 23, 1961*, pamphlet, n.p., NDMA. At Notre Dame, the superior of the campus convent remained a member of the board of trustees until 1981. See *Chron.*, May 14, 1981.

14. Andrea Turpin, *A New Moral Vision: Gender, Religion, and the Changing Purposes of American Higher Education, 1837–1917* (Ithaca, NY: Cornell University Press, 2016), 146.

15. *NDM Catalog*, 1924–25.

16. Patricia Byrne, "A Tradition of Educating Women: The Religious of the Sacred Heart in Higher Education," *U.S. Catholic Historian* 13 (Fall 1995): 59.

17. "General Resolutions," *Catholic Educational Association Bulletin* 11 (November 1914): 34, cited in William P. Leahy, *Adapting to America: Catholics, Jesuits and Higher Education in the Twentieth Century* (Washington, DC: Georgetown University Press, 1991), 88n30.

18. Sisters of Saint Joseph at the College of Saint Catherine (Saint Paul, Minnesota) earned graduate degrees at the University of Wisconsin, the University of Chicago, and Columbia University, while Religious of the Sacred Heart at the College of the Sacred Heart (Menlo Park, California) attended the University of California, Berkeley, and Stanford University in this decade. Holy Cross sister Madeleva Wolff, later president of Saint Mary's College (Notre Dame, Indiana), earned her PhD at the University of California, Berkeley, in this era. See Byrne, "Tradition of Educating Women," 54, 60.

19. The Panics of 1873 and 1893 each lasted six years. Evelyn functioned as a "quasi-coordinate" college of Princeton University, from which it drew lecturers and trustees. Many of its students were daughters of Princeton faculty. Alexander Leitch, *A Princeton Companion* (Princeton, NJ: Princeton University Press, 1978), 170–71, 528. For more on Evelyn College and Ingham University, see Frances P. Healy, "A History of Evelyn College for Women, Princeton, New Jersey, 1887 to 1897" (PhD diss., Ohio State University, 1967), 170–71; Patricia A. Graham, *Community and Class in American Education, 1865–1918* (New York: John Wiley, 1974), 195; "Ingham University Closed," *New York Times*, February 10, 1895.

20. See Y. E. Lofeanna, "Wellesley College in Transition," *American Educational Review* 28 (February 1907): 894–95.

21. *NDM Catalog*, 1895–96.

22. Louisa Carroll Jenkins, chairman, Alumnae of Notre Dame of Maryland Committee, et al., to Oliver Adams, n.d. (ca. 1900), NDMA. The permanent scholarship was fully funded in 1912. Separatist feelings between graduates of the two schools did not abate, and Dean Foley's 1910 appeal for them to rally as one body to recruit students for the college bore little fruit. Despite the organization's motto, *gradu diverso via una* (the same way by different steps), the rift continued to widen. Finally, "after heated discussion," attendees at the Alumnae Association's 1929 annual meeting voted that high school graduates, starting with the class of 1929, would separate to form the High School Alumnae (*Chron.*, June 3, 1929).

23. Minutes, Sister Mary Meletia Memorial Fund Committee, February 15, 1921; January 9, 1922; May 9, 1922; June 12, 1922; College of Notre Dame Alumnae Association to Alumnae, May 19, 1924, NDMA. Wehage died at age thirty-six in 1912.

24. *NDM Catalog*, 1922–23; *NDM Catalog*, 1936–37.

25. Gail Apperson Kilman, "Southern Collegiate Women: Higher Education at Wesleyan Female College and Randolph-Macon Woman's College, 1893–1907" (PhD diss., University of Delaware, 1984), 83–84, citing *Report of the United States Commissioner of Education for the Year 1906–1907*, 840–47.

26. Barbara H. Palmer, "Lace Bonnets and Academic Gowns: Faculty Development in Four Women's Colleges, 1875–1915" (PhD diss., Boston College, 1980), 242, table 2; Alice K. Fallows, "Working One's Way through Women's Colleges," *Century Magazine*, July 1901; *Catalogue of Mount Holyoke College, 1899–1900.*

27. Anne S. Philbin, interview by PM, May 24, 1989, transcript, OHP.

28. Day students at the College of Saint Angela paid $125 in 1904. See James T. Schleifer, *The College of New Rochelle: An Extraordinary Story* (Virginia Beach, VA: Donning, 1994), 19.

29. *NDM Catalog*, 1920–21; *NDM Catalog*, 1929–30; copy of the Association of Colleges and Secondary Schools of the Middle States and Maryland (MSA) information form, April 26, 1930, prepared by Dean Mary I. Dillon, NDMA; "Undergraduate Courses," *Bryn Mawr College Calendar, 1932*, cited in Sarah Manekin, "Gender, Markets, and the Expansion of Women's Education at the University of Pennsylvania, 1913–40," *History of Education Quarterly* 50 (August 2010): 311.

30. Catherine E. Beecher, *Woman's Professions as Mother and Educator: With Views in Opposition to Woman Suffrage* (Philadelphia: G. Maclean, 1872), 54.

31. See Margaret M. McGuinness, *Called to Serve: A History of Nuns in America* (New York: New York University Press, 2013).

32. Sister Mary (Mary Immaculata Dillon), untitled typescript, n.d. (ca. 1919), NDMA.

33. On "contributed service" and endowment, see Mary J. Oates, "Sisterhoods and Catholic Higher Education, 1890–1960," in *Catholic Women's Colleges in America*, ed. Tracy Schier and Cynthia Russett (Baltimore: Johns Hopkins University Press, 2002), 190–93. The "vocations crisis" is often dated after Vatican II, but in fact a national decline in applications began somewhat earlier.

34. Caroline Friess to Theophila Bauer, October 9, 1891, in *The Letters of Mother Caroline Friess*, ed. Barbara Brumleve (St. Louis: School Sisters of Notre Dame, 1991), 487.

35. "Villa Marie, Vacation Retreat of Notre Dame Sisters Dedicated," *Baltimore Sun*, November 28, 1909; *NDM Catalog*, 1910–11; A School Sister of Notre Dame [M. Dympna Flynn], *Mother Caroline and the School Sisters of Notre Dame in North America* (Saint Louis: Woodward & Tiernan, 1928), 2:105.

36. "Notch Cliff," *Notre Dame Quarterly*, November 1916. The farm was also a popular venue for alumnae reunions in this era; see "Fair Guests at Notch Cliff: Notre Dame Alumnae Close Reunion with Picnic," *Baltimore Sun*, June 15, 1909.

37. *NDM Catalog*, 1936–37.

38. *NDM Catalog*, 1935–36.

39. Caroline Friess to Theophila Bauer, April 15, 1885, and April 27, 1885, in Brumleve, *Letters*, 379–81.

40. "The Death of a Remarkable Nun [Theophila Bauer]," news clipping, n.d. [July 13, 1904], NDMA.

41. *Chron.*, July 11, 1904; Mary David Cameron, *The College of Notre Dame of Maryland, 1895–1945* (New York: Declan X. McMullen, 1947), 62. On October 4, 1896, the

Baltimore American published a full-page report on the new building. See also Grace H. Sherwood, "Genesis of Notre Dame: From Academy to College," *Baltimore Sun*, May 27, 1945.

42. *Chron.*, November 17, 1897. She reaffirmed that judgment on a second visit in 1905; see *Chron.*, March 11, 1905.

43. School Sisters of Notre Dame, Baltimore, MD, letter to the editor, *Catholic World* 68 (January 1899): 575.

44. *Chron.*, April 10, 1905. Bridget Marie Engelmeyer provides illustrated descriptions of the campus and early buildings in "A Maryland First," *Maryland Historical Magazine* 78 (Fall 1983): 186–204.

45. [Meletia Foley?], "Notre Dame College," early notebook, n.d., NDMA. Other sisterhoods also acquired funds to open colleges by taking mortgages on their other properties.

46. "Mr. Carnegie's Discrimination against Denominational Colleges," *Literary Digest*, June 10, 1905.

47. "The Carnegie Foundation," *Independent*, July 6, 1914. See also David C. Hammack, "Toward a Political History of American Foundations," in *History of Higher Education Annual: 1990*, ed. Roger L. Geiger (Piscataway, NJ: Transaction, 1990), 91–101.

48. Report of Inspection of College of Notre Dame of Maryland, Baltimore, Md., for MSA, February 13–14, 1950, NDMA. See Gladyce H. Bradley, "Negro Higher and Professional Education in Maryland," *Journal of Negro Education* 17 (Summer 1948): 309, table 4.

49. Frederic O. Musser, *The History of Goucher College, 1930–1985* (Baltimore: Johns Hopkins University Press, 1990), 100, table 6, "Median Goucher Faculty Salaries, 1950–51 and 1964–65."

50. Margaret Mary O'Connell, "Data Presented for Consideration of the Commission on Institutions of Higher Education, MSA, 4 December 1959," NDMA.

51. President's Report, 1960–61, NDMA.

52. President's Report, 1961–62, NDMA.

53. Revised Report of the Faculty Committee on Rank, Tenure, and Salary, 1965–1966; "Salary Scales for 1966–67," NDMA.

54. Bridget Marie Engelmeyer, unsigned sheet, September 1968, BMEP; "Annual Institutional Summary—College of Notre Dame of Maryland, October 1, 1968" (submitted to MSA), NDMA.

55. Minutes, board of trustees, February 17, 1971, NDMA; minutes, board of directors, July 29, 1971, NDMA; *Chron.*, February 5, 1981.

56. The College Council for Faculty Research and Development emerged from this initiative.

57. Minutes, board of trustees, November 21, 1975, NDMA. See Rank, Tenure, and Salary Committee, *Up by Our Boot Straps: A Report on the State of Faculty Salaries at the College of Notre Dame of Maryland*, approved by Faculty Senate, November 16, 1976, NDMA.

58. Rank, Tenure, and Salary Committee, *Up by Our Boot Straps*.

59. Minutes, President's (Advisory) Council, March 15, 1978, NDMA. Henry J. Knott Sr. established the Marion I. & Henry J. Knott Foundation in 1977. For more on this Catholic family foundation, see http://www.knottfoundation.org.

60. *Chron.*, March 8, 1981.

61. *Chron.*, April 5, 1981.

62. *Chron.*, October 2, 1981; October 24, 1981. See "Vassar's Hopes and Needs," *New York Times*, January 31, 1892. Eberstadt left the College of Notre Dame without a degree but earned a bachelor of music degree at New York University.

63. Mary A. Jordan, "The College for Women," *Atlantic Monthly*, October 1892.

64. Leta S. Hollingworth, "Phi Beta Kappa and Women Students," *School and Society* 4 (December 16, 1916): 932–33.

65. "Mount Holyoke Seminary to Become a College for Women," *Boston Journal*, December 2, 1887.

66. Henrietta E. Hooker, "Mount Holyoke College," *New England Magazine*, January 1897.

67. For an examination of a predominantly female faculty that moved to a predominantly male one at this time, see Patricia A. Palmieri, *In Adamless Eden: The Community of Women Faculty at Wellesley* (New Haven, CT: Yale University Press, 1995).

68. Margaret Farrand Thorp, *Neilson of Smith* (New York: Oxford University Press, 1956), 150, 166.

69. President Rufus Harris of Tulane University, quoted in Charles L. Mohr and Joseph W. Gordon, *Tulane: The Emergence of a Modern University, 1945–1980* (Baton Rouge: Louisiana State University Press, 2001), 23; Robert A. McCaughey, *Scholars and Teachers: The Faculties of Select Liberal Arts Colleges and Their Place in American Higher Learning* (New York: Barnard College, 1994), 29.

70. Rosalind Rosenberg, *Changing the Subject: How the Women of Columbia Shaped the Way We Think about Sex and Politics* (New York: Columbia University Press, 2004), 207–8. Gildersleeve was the dean of Barnard College from 1911 until 1947.

71. Susan Rieger, "Women's Colleges: A Debate; 'Time Has Run Out,'" *Boston Sunday Globe*, April 7, 1991.

72. M. Madeleva Wolff, *My First Seventy Years* (New York: Macmillan, 1959), 127.

73. M. Alice Joseph Moore, "Catholic College Student Retention in the United States" (PhD diss., Catholic University of America, 1957), 79. Clergy accounted for 10 percent of faculties surveyed.

74. "Students—Suggestions & Opinions 1960s—(Response Rate Not Indicated)," n.d., NDMA. Emphasis added.

75. *Baltimore Sun*, December 28, 1987.

76. Cameron, *College of Notre Dame*, 60.

77. *Chron.*, September 14, 1897.

78. Mullaly, *Trinity College*, 87, 89.

79. Edmund Shanahan, "Old Notre Dame, 1873–1923," 1923, RC. See also Rev. Lucian Johnston, "Sister Mary Meletia: An Eloquent Appreciation," *Baltimore Catholic Review*, May 19, 1917.

80. Sister M. Frances Smith, "Notre Dame's Sister Mary Meletia," *Centenary Inter-Provincial News Letter*, April 1947, NDMA.

81. "Sister Meletia, as Remembered by Louise Balls (Class of 1901)," n.d., NDMA.

82. Adele (Mohlenrich) Hicks, untitled reminiscence of Notre Dame, n.d., RC. Hicks was an alumna of the preparatory school (1913) and the college (1917).

83. Margaret Mary O'Connell, "The Educational Contributions of the School Sisters of Notre Dame in America for the Century 1847 to 1947" (EdD diss., Johns

Hopkins University, 1950), 151; John C. French, *A History of the University Founded by Johns Hopkins* (Baltimore: Johns Hopkins Press, 1946), 147–57.

84. Fortier joined the Columbia University faculty in 1910 (*Columbia University, Bulletin of Information, 1911–1912,* 7). In 1860, Yale pioneered the offering of graduate courses, and in 1872, both Yale and Harvard established graduate schools.

85. *NDM Catalog,* 1899; "Notre Dame of Maryland College for Women," press release, 1904, NDMA.

86. Mullaly, *Trinity College,* 90.

87. Carr E. Worland, "American Catholic Women and the Church to 1920" (PhD diss., Saint Louis University, 1982), 87; *Trinity College Circular,* July 15, 1897.

88. See Cameron, *College of Notre Dame,* 69, and app. D, 171–79. For much of this time, the Jesuit order disapproved of members teaching women. Secular clergy were not similarly restricted.

89. See Cameron, *College of Notre Dame,* app. D, 171–79. Rev. Lucian Johnston was the son of the southern novelist Richard Malcolm Johnston. Rev. Francis Pennington Mackall, a convert to Catholicism and former Episcopal deacon, served the longest term as chaplain in this era (1915–30).

90. *Chron.,* January 10, 1899. Shattuck received his PhD from Johns Hopkins University (1897) and joined the Vassar faculty in 1902 (*Graduates and Fellows of the Johns Hopkins University, 1876–1913* [Baltimore: Johns Hopkins Press, 1914], 18, 109). See also R. Louise Balls '01 to M. David Cameron, SSND, December 2, 1946, hand-printed reminiscences of "Sister Jeannette (1853–1901)," NDMA.

91. Mary Agnes Klug, SSND, interview by PM, February 14, 1989, transcript, OHP.

92. Maura Eichner, SSND, interview by Barbara Gross, April 9, 1973. Eichner studied part time while teaching in the campus preparatory school. She was twenty-six when she received her BA in 1941.

93. See Cameron, *College of Notre Dame,* 82.

94. Shanahan, "Old Notre Dame."

95. *NDM Catalog,* 1910–11.

96. Helen Burr-Brand to Sister M. David Cameron, November 9, 1944, NDMA. By 1915, elective courses in art and music carried credit toward the bachelor's degree, and in 1937, the college introduced an art major.

97. ASEUT joined the Philadelphia Forum in 1916. See A. Stephen Stephan, "Background and Beginnings of University Extension in America," *Harvard Educational Review* 18 (Spring 1948): 107.

98. On Sykes, see *Chron.,* September 18, 1900; February 3, 1901; and February 21, 1902. See also Connecticut College, "Connecticut College News Vol. 3 No. 1," 1917, paper 15, http://digitalcommons.conncoll.edu/ccnews_1917_1918/15. Harvard and Boston University extension school courses met locally and attracted mainly Boston-area residents. However, if at least forty citizens residing outside suburban Boston signed up for a course, the extension school would send a professor to them. In 1926, with demand for education courses high, extension school faculty met classes weekly in suburban locations in Massachusetts, New Hampshire, Connecticut, and New York. See "Harvard—B.U. Extension Courses, Thirty to Be Offered This Year," *Boston Daily Globe,* October 1, 1926.

99. Michael Shinagel, *"The Gates Unbarred": A History of University Extension at Harvard, 1910–2009* (Cambridge, MA: Harvard University Extension School, 2009), 24.

100. Shinagel, *"Gates Unbarred,"* 42.

101. "Cardinal Confers Degrees," *Baltimore Sun*, June 5, 1919. Spaeth (1868–1954) was a member of the Princeton University English Department faculty from 1905 until 1935, and the first president of the University of Kansas City, Missouri, from 1935 until 1938.

102. John Cowper Powys, *Autobiography* (New York: Simon & Schuster, 1934), 427–28, 475. Powys (1872–1963) held an MA from Cambridge University. In the United States, he was affiliated with ASEUT from 1904 until 1911, and then with the University Lecturers Association of New York. He lectured on "classical and modern literature." See Morine Krissdottir, *Descents of Memory: The Life of John Cowper Powys* (New York: Overlook Duckworth, 2007).

103. *Susurrus*, March 29, 1915, NDMA. *Susurrus* was a short-lived campus gossip newsletter.

104. Dean Foley endeavored to schedule lectures for late afternoons so that teachers from local Catholic schools could attend. See "Lectures on Science," news clipping, n.d. (ca. 1896–1900), Scrapbook/Album 19th Century, NDMA. On Munson, see Arnold Genthe, *As I Remember: The Sources of Modern Photography* (New York: Reynal & Hitchcock, 1936), 128.

105. See "Robert B. White Dead," *Red Bank (NJ) Register*, February 25, 1903. Lecture fields were unrestricted.

106. *Chron.*, March 2, 1905.

107. *NDM Catalog*, 1913–14. See "Women to Ask Treaty Giving Them Equality: They Will Urge at Havana That They Be Admitted to Pan-American Conferences," *New York Times*, January 15, 1928; "Feminism Making Progress in Cuba at Rapid Strides," *Milwaukee Journal*, February 19, 1928; and Instituto de Literatura y Lingüística de la Academia de Ciencias de Cuba, "Martinez y Martinez, Julia," *Diccionario de la literatura cubana* (Alicante, Spain: Biblioteca Virtual Miguel de Cervantes, 1999), http://www.cervantesvirtual.com/obra/diccionario-de-la-literatura-cubana--0/.

108. The 1920 lecture series included the Goucher College historian Katherine J. Gallagher, who spoke on Russia. See *Chron.*, April 13, 1920.

109. Elizabeth Morrissy, interview by Barbara Gross, May 2, 1973, transcript, OHP. See French, *History of the University*, 335, on the Johns Hopkins University Appointments Bureau, which opened in 1913.

110. *Chron.*, March 16, 1953. Morrissy, who joined the Notre Dame faculty in 1920, earned a BA from Beloit College (1908) and an MA (1922) and PhD (economics, 1932) from Johns Hopkins University. On Morrissy, see Mary J. Oates, "Morrissy, Elizabeth," in *Notable American Women: A Biographical Dictionary*, vol. 5, *Completing the Twentieth Century, 1976–2000*, ed. Susan Ware (Cambridge, MA: Harvard University Press, 2004), 455–56.

111. Ruth Bordin, *Alice Freeman Palmer: The Evolution of a New Woman* (Ann Arbor: University of Michigan Press, 1993), 271–72. See also Lofeanna, "Wellesley College in Transition," 894.

112. Carrie A. Harper, "A Feminine Professorial Viewpoint," *Educational Review* 46 (June 1913): 47–48, 50–51.

113. Elizabeth P. Hoisington, interview by PM, May 31, 1989, transcript, OHP.

114. Elizabeth Morrissy, interview by Barbara Gross, May 2, 1973, transcript, OHP. Among early full-time lay faculty, only Zerline Stauf opted for long-term campus housing.

115. Regina Soria, interview by PM, February 20, 1989, transcript, OHP; Lavinia C. Wenger, interview by Mary Jo Maloney, April 10, 1973, transcript, OHP.

116. Adam Leroy Jones, chairman, Commission on Institutions of Higher Education, MSA, to President Philemon Doyle, College of Notre Dame, November 17, 1925, NDMA.

117. Elizabeth Morrissy, interview by Barbara Gross, May 2, 1973, transcript, OHP.

118. *Chron.*, June 23–29, 1935; September 10, 1935; June 29, 1936; September 23, 1936.

119. See [President Frances Smith], "Needs of the College of Notre Dame of Maryland," single typed sheet, n.d. (ca. May 23, 1949), NDMA. Smith (1886–1950) held an MA (1922) from Fordham University and a PhD in English from Catholic University (1935).

120. [Sister Denise Dooley?], "History of the College, Early Faculty, Rev. Dr. John J. Griffin," typescript, n.d. (ca. 1962), NDMA. Dooley (1891–1972) held a BA (1921) and MA (1922) from Fordham University and a PhD from Johns Hopkins University (1934). She joined the chemistry faculty in 1921 and served as dean of the college between 1931 and 1941. Sister Cordia Karl (1893–1984) held a BA from Hunter College (1916) and an MA (1927) and PhD (1931) in mathematics from Johns Hopkins University.

121. *Chron.*, June 30, 1930; Summer 1932.

122. Thomas E. Shields, "The Need of the Catholic Sisters College and the Scope of Its Work," *Catholic Educational Review* 17 (September 1919): 424. See also John Murphy, "Professional Preparation of Catholic Teachers in the Nineteen Hundreds," *Notre Dame Journal of Education* 7 (Summer 1976): 128.

123. Other communities attempted to imitate this strategy. See Professor Joseph J. Walsh, MD, Fordham University, to Mother Rose Meagher, July 6, 1917, Motherhouse Archives, Sisters of Charity of Nazareth, Nazareth, KY.

124. See Sisters, Servants of the Immaculate Heart of Mary, Monroe, Michigan, *Building Sisterhood: A Feminist History of the Sisters, Servants of the Immaculate Heart of Mary* (Syracuse, NY: Syracuse University Press, 1997), 286–87; and Byrne, "Tradition of Educating Women," 56–63. Karen M. Kennelly, "Women Religious, the Intellectual Life, and Anti-intellectualism: History and Present Situation," in *Women Religious and the Intellectual Life: The North American Achievement*, ed. Bridget Puzon (San Francisco: International Scholars, 1996), 43–72, provides an excellent survey of diverse efforts of sisterhoods across the country to educate members for college faculties.

125. FitzGerald, *Governance of Jesuit Colleges*, 10–11. See also Plough, "Catholic Colleges," 436–39.

126. C. Joseph Nuesse, *The Catholic University of America: A Centennial History* (Washington, DC: Catholic University of America Press, 1990), 257–58.

127. *Chron.*, June 7, 1937. Staab (1906–97), a Catholic University graduate (BMus, 1934; MMus, 1940), joined the Notre Dame faculty in 1935.

128. Walter Crosby Eells and Austin Carl Cleveland, "Faculty Inbreeding," *Journal of Higher Education* 70 (September/October 1999): 580–81. Reprinted from *Journal of Higher Education* 6, no. 6 (June 1935): 323–28.

129. See *Chron.*, September 20, 1937; *NDM Catalog*, 1921–22.

130. O'Connell, "Data Presented for Consideration."

131. *Chron.*, September 24, 1938; September 26, 1938; June 12, 1940.

132. Baltimore archbishop Michael Curley, like many of his compatriots, found it difficult to acknowledge professional competence in women religious. In 1937 he

instructed College of Notre Dame president Frances Smith to compose for his signature a letter announcing the college's new advisory board. His comments on her draft betrayed his discomfort: "It may be a little long, but it is a very well written letter. . . . I suppose when women, consecrated or otherwise, get a chance at writing, they have to be enthusiastic about it and express it in length. Anyway, we shall let the letter stand as it is." Frances Smith to Michael J. Curley, January 30, 1937; Curley to Smith, February 2, 1937, NDMA.

133. See "Education Notes and News," *Catholic School Interests* 3 (January 1925): 325; "The Washington Sessions of the Sections and Societies, AAAS Fifth Washington Meeting, 29 December 1924–3 January 1925," *Science*, February 6, 1925.

134. "Phi Beta Kappa Unit Picks 50 at Hunter," *New York Times*, April 28, 1948; *Chron.*, April 28, 1948; June 15, 1948. For more on Cordia Karl, see Judy Green and Jeanne LaDuke, *Pioneering Women in American Mathematics: The Pre-1940 PhDs* (Providence, RI: American Mathematical Society and London Mathematical Society, 2009), 316–17.

135. Bridget Marie Engelmeyer, SSND, interview by Mary Jo Maloney, April 8, 1973, transcript, OHP.

136. Dorothy Brown, interview by PM, May 16, 1989, transcript, OHP.

137. Bridget Marie Engelmeyer, SSND, interview by Mary Jo Maloney, April 8, 1973, transcript, OHP. After retiring as dean, Engelmeyer became the college archivist (1973–88).

138. Dorothy Brown, interview by PM, May 16, 1989, transcript, OHP.

139. *Chron.*, February 27, 1925; March 27, 1926.

140. *Chron.*, March 29, 1937.

141. *Chron.*, November 8, 1944; August 30, 1947. Sister Dominic (Louise) Ramacciotti, a graduate of Fordham University (BA, 1926; MA, 1929) and of Catholic University (PhD, romance languages, 1936), joined the Notre Dame faculty in 1935. By the mid-1950s she had left Notre Dame and the religious order to establish a Girls' Town near Rome, Italy, to prepare adolescent orphans for careers as governesses and social workers. See Regina Soria, *Educare Alla Vita: Mother Dominic Ramacciotti e la sua Citta delle Ragazze Quaderno, 1* (Perugia: Guerra Edizioni, 2006); "Religion: The Nun in Tweeds," *Time*, March 10, 1958; and Anna Brady, "Italy's Girls' Town Founder," *Baltimore Sun*, September 7, 1958.

142. *Sister Mary Noreen: Catalog of an Exhibition Held Dec. 30, 1949–Jan. 31, 1950* (New York: Demotte, 1950); Helen Foss, "News Reports," *College Art Journal* 9 (Winter 1949–50): 210–23; *Chron.*, December 29, 1949. Margaret Gormley (1892–1960), a Bostonian, was a prize-winning student and a 1913 graduate of the Eric Pape School of Art (see "Eric Pape School Awards: Scholarship Prizes for the Season of 1912—An Interesting Exhibit of Students' Work," *Boston Evening Transcript*, June 12, 1912). She then studied with Charles Jay Connick, noted stained-glass artist and designer, who had just opened his Boston studio-workshop. After entering the order in 1918, she joined Notre Dame's art faculty in 1921. A Notre Dame graduate (1929), she also held an MA in history from Fordham University (1932).

143. Glenn McNutt, "A Change of Scenery," *Baltimore Sun*, December 20, 1999.

144. "Dramatics," *Damozel*, 1924; Mary Noreen Gormley, SSND, to Archbishop Michael Curley, October 1, 1938; Curley to Gormley, October 6, 1938, ABA. The Catholic Art Association's journal, the *Catholic Art Quarterly*, appeared from 1937 to 1970.

Until 1941, it was titled the *Christian Social Art Quarterly*, and from 1959 to 1970, *Good Work*. The association disbanded in 1970.

145. Regina Soria, interview by PM, February 20, 1989, transcript, OHP. Soria (1911–2006) founded the Circolo Culturale Italiano di Baltimora in 1955. See also "100 Years of Art at the College of Notre Dame of Maryland—A Faculty Retrospective," *Catalogue for the Gormley Gallery Exhibition*, College of Notre Dame of Maryland, ca. 1996, n.p., NDMA.

146. His last listing on the faculty roster was in 1949–50. See *NDM Catalog*, 1949–50. Pierre-Charles-Marie Couturier was born in France in 1897 and died in Paris in 1954. He entered the Dominican order in 1925 and took Marie-Alain as his religious name. For more on his connection to Notre Dame, see "Rev. M. A. Couturier to Conduct Saturday Classes at Notre Dame," *Baltimore Sun*, September 13, 1941; and Francoise Caussé, "Couturier Marie-Alain," *Dictionnaire biographique des frères prêcheurs* (2015), http://dominicains.revues.org/1867. On Couturier's social and political views, see Robert Schwartzwald, "Father Marie-Alain Couturier, O.P., and the Refutation of Anti-Semitism in Vichy France," in *Textures and Meaning: Thirty Years of Judaic Studies at the University of Massachusetts Amherst*, ed. Leonard H. Ehrlich, Shmuel Bolozky, Robert A. Rothstein, Murray Schwartz, Jay R. Berkovitz, and James E. Young (Amherst, MA: Department of Judaic and Near Eastern Studies, University of Massachusetts, 2004), 140–56. Thomas F. O'Meara, "Modern Art and the Sacred: The Prophetic Ministry of Alain Couturier, O.P.," *Spirituality Today* 38 (Spring 1986): 31–40, explores his influence on modern religious art and architecture. On his link to the de Menils, see Calvin Tomkins, "The Benefactor," *New Yorker*, June 8, 1998. See also "The Father Marie-Alain Couturier, O.P. (1897–1954) Papers," Couturier Collection, Yale Institute of Sacred Music, Worship and the Arts, Yale University, Archival Register, compiled by Joanna Weber, June 1994.

147. This meeting occurred on June 25, 1942. Ruth S. Riley to Bridget Marie Engelmeyer, June 25, 1974; Engelmeyer to Riley, July 2, 1974, BMEP. Green's public lectures were given in March and July of 1942.

148. Mary Lou McNeal '50, interview with the author, May 21, 1996.

3. Divided or Diverse?

1. These included the twelve Ursulines from Rouen, France, who traveled to New Orleans, Louisiana Territory, in 1727 to establish a Catholic girls' school, the first such institution of its kind in what is now the United States. For a good analysis of the impact of this class distinction on US sisterhoods, see Margaret S. Thompson, "Sisterhood and Power: Class, Culture, and Ethnicity in the American Convent," *Colby Quarterly* 23 (September 1989): 149–75. On dowries, social origins, and duties of Ursuline choir and converse (lay) nuns in eighteenth-century New Orleans, see Emily Clark, *Masterless Mistresses: The New Orleans Ursulines and the Development of a New World Society, 1727–1834* (Chapel Hill: University of North Carolina Press, 2007), 67–74. See also Christine Trimingham Jack, "The Lay Sister in Educational History and Memory," *History of Education* 29, no. 3 (2000): 181–94.

2. M. Hester Valentine, ed., *Historical Dimensions: Letters of Mother M. Theresa Gerhardinger, SSND* (Winona, MN: Saint Mary's College Press, 1977), 184–86. Sisters who taught academic subjects enjoyed more prestige and privileges than "piano,

drawing, and needlework teachers," who were able to vote in community elections but could not stand for office.

3. Caroline Friess to Rev. P. M. Abbelen, November 21, 1879, in *The Letters of Mother Caroline Friess*, ed. Barbara Brumleve (St. Louis: School Sisters of Notre Dame, 1991), 252–55.

4. Kathleen Feeley, *That Deeper Knowing: School Sisters of Notre Dame, Baltimore Province, 1847–2005* (Baltimore: School Sisters of Notre Dame, 2013), 27, quoting *Chronicles of the Baltimore* [SSND] *Province*, July 7, 1889.

5. Theresa Gerhardinger to an unidentified Baltimore priest, n.d. (ca. 1876), in Valentine, *Historical Dimensions*, 184–86.

6. Theresa Gerhardinger to Theophila Bauer, n.d. (ca. 1876), in Valentine, *Historical Dimensions*, 181.

7. Caroline Friess to "Dear Sisters," February 12, 1890, in Brumleve, *Letters*, 470.

8. *Chron.*, October 15, 1936.

9. Sarah Mulhall Adelman, "Empowerment and Submission: The Political Culture of Catholic Women's Religious Communities in Nineteenth-Century America," *Journal of Women's History* 23 (Fall 2011): 151–52. By this time, house sisters were able to vote in community elections but could not yet stand for office. For more on the experience of the School Sisters of Notre Dame relative to this issue, see Florence J. Deacon, "Handmaids or Autonomous Women: The Charitable Activities, Institution Building and Communal Relationships of Catholic Sisters in Nineteenth Century Wisconsin" (PhD diss., University of Wisconsin, Madison, 1989), chaps. 2, 5, and 6; and Thompson, "Sisterhood and Power," 157. See also Feeley, *That Deeper Knowing*, 136.

10. "History of the College of Notre Dame of Maryland," *Arras*, 1954; *NDM Catalog*, 1902.

11. Anne Philbin, *The Past and the Promised: A History of the Alumnae Association, College of Notre Dame of Maryland, Baltimore, Maryland* (Baltimore: Alumnae Association, College of Notre Dame of Maryland, 1959), 34–35.

12. *NDM Catalog*, 1916–17.

13. "Woman's College," *Baltimore Morning Herald*, August 28, 1900; Helen Lefkowitz Horowitz, *Alma Mater: Design and Experience in the Women's Colleges from Their Nineteenth-Century Beginnings to the 1930s* (New York: Alfred A. Knopf, 1984), 83; "Radcliffe College: Special Students," *Harvard Graduates' Magazine*, December 1894; *Catalogue of Mount Holyoke College, 1899–1900*.

14. Bridget Marie Engelmeyer, SSND, interview by Mary Jo Maloney and Charles Ritter, April 8, 1973, transcript, OHP.

15. "Notre Dame of Maryland: Prospectus for Day Pupils," n.d. (ca. 1896); "History of the College, Early Faculty, Rev. Dr. John J. Griffin," typescript, n.d. (ca. 1962), NDMA.

16. Mary Trinitas Bochini, SSND, interview by PM, April 6, 1989, transcript, OHP. Bochini, a 1949 Notre Dame graduate, joined its faculty in 1962. She held a PhD in psychology from Catholic University (1977).

17. *NDM Catalog*, 1910–11.

18. *Chron.*, September 14, 1920; September 1929.

19. Grace E. Hawk, *Pembroke College in Brown University: The First Seventy-Five Years, 1891–1966* (Providence, RI: Brown University Press, 1967), 152.

20. *Chron.*, September 21, 1932; September 20, 1933; September 24, 1934; September 22, 1937. Of twenty-two graduates in 1936, twenty were day students. See Philbin, *Past and the Promised*, 127.

21. Adele M. (Mohlenrich) Hicks, '17, untitled reminiscence of Notre Dame, n.d., RC.

22. "Kappa Rho Sigma," *Notre Dame Quarterly*, November 1916. Alexander Pope, in *Imitations of Horace* (ii, 1), wrote of a "feast of reason and flow of soul."

23. Photo of Kappa Rho Sigma members, n.d. (ca. 1916), NDMA. The home state of one student is not provided.

24. Tracy Mitrano, "The Rise and Fall of Catholic Women's Higher Education in New York State, 1890–1985" (PhD diss., State University of New York, Binghamton, 1989), 159.

25. Elizabeth Gudrais, "The Undergraduate: The Sorority Scene," *Harvard Magazine*, November–December 2000.

26. "Kappa Rho Sigma Banquet," *Notre Dame Quarterly*, March 1917.

27. *NDM Catalog*, 1918–19.

28. The annalist notes the "Birthday Party of the Kymry Club, the successor to the KPE Fraternity." See *Chron.*, November 2, 1917.

29. "Kymry Klub," *Damozel*, 1923; "Kymry Notes," *Damozel*, 1925.

30. Mary Louis Whalen, SSND, interview by PM, March 3, 1989, transcript, OHP.

31. Elizabeth P. Hoisington, interview by PM, May 31, 1989, transcript, OHP. Hoisington was a day student for three years, and a resident student in her senior year, 1939–40.

32. "Kymry—I.R.C.—F.T.A. (Future Teachers of America)," *Arras*, 1950.

33. Virgina Geiger, SSND, interview by Barbara Gross, March 3, 1973, transcript, OHP.

34. Anne S. Philbin, interview by PM, May 24, 1989, transcript, OHP.

35. Miriam Kivlighan, SSND, March 26, 1973, transcript, OHP.

36. Bridget Marie Engelmeyer, handwritten notes, December 13, 1942, BMEP.

37. Bridget Marie Engelmeyer, handwritten notes, December 17, 1946, BMEP.

38. See ". . . and memories to keep the past alive," *Today: College of Notre Dame of Maryland* 8, no. 1 (Winter 1981): 13.

39. *Chron.*, December 18, 1951. See also *Chron.*, December 16, 1953.

40. "Boarders Frolic at Poverty Party," *Columns*, February 25, 1938.

41. "To the Editor," *Columns*, December 15, 1942. Elizabeth Hoisington (1918–2007) enlisted in in the Women's Army Auxiliary Corps immediately upon graduating from Notre Dame in 1942. By 1965, she was director of the Women's Army Corps. In 1971, she and Anna Mae Hays, chief of the Army Nurse Corps, were the first women promoted to the rank of brigadier general in the US Armed Forces.

42. Minutes, directors, March 23, 1959, NDMA.

43. President's Report, 1964–65, NDMA; *Chron.*, October 9, 1964.

44. "Students—Suggestions & Opinions 1960s—(Response Rate Not Indicated)," n.d., NDMA.

45. See Office of Research and Planning and Strategic Planning Committee, "Executive Summary of Student Satisfaction Survey, 1984 Day Program Students," NDMA.

46. *Notre Dame Quarterly*, Spring 1917; see also "Recreation Association—Dance Group—Masquers," *Arras*, 1950.

47. "Games at Notre Dame," *Baltimore Sun*, June 5, 1904; Christina Carroll, "Field Day," *Vassar Encyclopedia*, 2005, http://vcencyclopedia.vassar.edu/student-organizations/athletics/field-day.html. Field Day ended at Vassar in 1937.

48. "Athletics," *Damozel*, 1923; "History of the College of Notre Dame of Maryland," *Arras*, 1954.

49. "Recreation Association," *Arras*, 1951.

50. See Hicks '17, untitled reminiscence of Notre Dame; "Women Riders to Exhibit Skill at College Kermis: Horse Show with 25 Equestrians Will Be Held Friday at Notre Dame," *Baltimore Sun*, May 26, 1924; "2,000 Gather at Opening of Notre Dame Kermis," *Baltimore Sun*, May 29, 1924. See also "Field Day Features Riding Exhibition," *Columns*, April 30, 1938; *Chron.*, May 17, 1938. See also Recreation Association, "Programs of Field Day," NDMA.

51. "SA Assembly—Founded in a Great Tradition," n.d. (ca. November 1953), BMEP.

52. *Chron.*, May 14, 1969; May 13, 1970.

53. "Cardinal to Give Diplomas: Commencement Will Be Held at Notre Dame This Week," *Baltimore Sun*, June 1, 1913.

54. *Sing Song School Songs* (Baltimore: College of Notre Dame of Maryland, Student Association, 1960), 1.

55. "Sing Song Draws Enthusiastic Audience," *Columns*, May 1934.

56. Virgina Geiger, SSND, interview by Barbara Gross, March 27, 1973, transcript, OHP. Kean (b. 1895) held diplomas from the Finch Conservatory of Music (1914) and the Sargent College of Physical Education (1919), and a BA from Western Maryland College (1936).

57. *Columns*, March 23, 1937.

58. "Letter to the Editor," *Columns*, March 23, 1939.

59. Frances Baker Waldron '32, quoted in *Sing Song School Songs*, 12.

60. Bridget Marie Engelmeyer, handwritten notes, April 14, 1943, BMEP.

61. Marie Augustine Dowling, SSND, interview by PM, March 21 and April 18, 1989, transcript, OHP.

62. Dot Brown '54, quoted in *Sing Song School Songs*, 12–13.

63. Bridget Marie Engelmeyer, SSND, interview by PM, May 30, 1989, transcript, OHP.

64. The original alma mater, "A Blue Strand," had emerged from the 1933 Sing Song program. Students set its verses to music from the 1929 film *The Desert Song*. Copyright issues led to its replacement in 1951. The students Lucie Beal Collins and Ann Connor composed both words and music for a new alma mater, "We Raise Our Voices Proudly." See *Sing Song School Songs*, 1.

65. *Chron.*, March 10, 1956; April 2, 1965.

66. *Chron.*, March 7, 1970.

67. *NDM Catalog*, 1986–87.

68. Coralie Ullrich, SSND, interview by PM, March 2, 1989, transcript, OHP.

69. *Chron.*, February 28, 1987; April 7, 1987; March 26, 1988.

70. Ruth Miriam Carey, SSND, interview by PM, March 22, 1989, transcript, OHP. Since 1989, Notre Dame Preparatory School has carried on the Sing Song tradition. See "Notre Dame Prep Gym Meet," *Catholic Review*, March 7, 2013.

71. For discussions of race and religious life in the United States, see Diane Batts Morrow, *Persons of Color and Religious at the Same Time: The Oblate Sisters of Providence, 1828–1860* (Chapel Hill: University of North Carolina Press, 2002); Clark, *Masterless Mistresses*; Shannen Dee Williams, "Subversive Habits: Black Nuns and the Struggle to Desegregate Catholic America after World War I" (PhD diss., Rutgers University, 2013); and Cyprian Davis, *A History of Black Catholics in the United States* (New York: Crossroad, 1990).

72. See, for example, Mary Beth Fraser Connolly, *Women of Faith: The Chicago Sisters of Mercy and the Evolution of a Religious Community* (New York: Fordham University Press, 2014), 189–90, 314n69. This state of affairs persisted into the 1960s.

73. On Drexel, see Consuela Marie Duffy, *Katharine Drexel: A Biography* (Cornwall Heights, PA: Mother Katharine Drexel Guild, 1965); Suellen Hoy, *Good Hearts: Catholic Sisters in Chicago's Past* (Urbana: University of Illinois Press, 2006), 87–89, 190n9; Mary J. Oates, "Mother Mary Katharine Drexel," in *Women Educators in the United States, 1820–1993: A Bio-Bibliographical Sourcebook*, ed. Maxine Schwartz Seller (Westport, CT: Greenwood, 1994), 209–17.

74. An excellent comparative survey of the intentional admission of blacks by Seven Sister colleges is Linda Perkins, "The African American Female Elite: The Early History of African American Women in the Seven Sister Colleges, 1880–1960," *Harvard Educational Review* 67, no. 4 (1997): 718–56.

75. *Chronicle*, February 1931. This publication became the *Interracial Review* in 1932. On racially discriminatory policies at Catholic women's colleges in the 1930s, see George K. Hunton, as told to Gary MacEoin, *All of Which I Saw, Part of Which I Was: The Autobiography of George K. Hunton* (New York: Doubleday, 1967), chap. 5. On the development of the Catholic Interracial Council of New York, see Martin A. Zielinski, "Working for Interracial Justice: The Catholic Interracial Council of New York, 1934–1964," *U.S. Catholic Historian* 7 (Spring/Summer 1988): 233–62.

76. Michael F. Rouse, *A Study of the Development of Negro Education under Catholic Auspices in Maryland and the District of Columbia* (Baltimore: Johns Hopkins University Press, 1935), 107–8.

77. R. Louise Balls '01, "Sister Jeannette," NDMA. On Goessmann, see Georgina Pell Curtis, ed., *The American Catholic Who's Who* (Saint Louis: B. Herder, 1911), 248. Goessmann later headed the Goessmann School for Girls, a preparatory school in Amherst, Massachusetts. At this time, faculty members at leading colleges and universities whose views on controversial social issues offended college trustees faced dismissal. On disputes at Stanford University, the University of Wisconsin, and the University of Chicago in the years 1894–1900, see Louis Menand, *The Metaphysical Club: A Story of Ideas in America* (New York: Farrar, Straus and Giroux, 2001), 411–12.

78. "150th Anniversary—Oblate Sisters of Providence," pamphlet, n.d. (ca. 1979), ABA.

79. *Chron.*, January 31, 1949. See also *Chron.*, August 26, 1951. In 1924, Villanova University, twelve miles from Philadelphia, was the first Catholic college to admit the Oblate Sisters. For an excellent history of the early years of this community, see Morrow, *Persons of Color*. See Williams, "Subversive Habits," for a study of black sisterhoods after World War I.

80. Gregory Nelson Hite, "The Hottest Places in Hell: The Catholic Church and Civil Rights in Selma, Alabama, 1937–1965" (PhD diss., University of Virginia, 2002), 31–36. In the 1930s, the number of African Americans earning degrees from Catholic

colleges was still extremely small. See David W. Southern, *John LaFarge and the Limits of Catholic Interracialism, 1911–1963* (Baton Rouge: Louisiana State University Press, 1996), 191.

81. Mother Grace Dammann, "Principles versus Prejudices: A Talk Given to the Alumnae on Class Day, May 31st, 1938," *Tower Postscript*, Summer 1938, 1–20. See also Mitrano, "Rise and Fall," 143.

82. Richard J. Roche, *Catholic Colleges and the Negro Student* (Washington, DC: Catholic University of America Press, 1948), 108, cited in Philip Gleason, *Contending with Modernity: Catholic Higher Education in the Twentieth Century* (New York: Oxford University Press, 1995), 390n7.

83. Bridget Marie Engelmeyer, handwritten notes, December 9, 1942, BMEP.

84. See "Fight on Bias Reviewed: Catholic Foundation for Human Brotherhood Tells of Progress," *New York Times*, April 13, 1945. Hartmann, a 1936 Notre Dame graduate, joined the Notre Dame faculty in 1943. She held an MSW from Loyola University, Chicago.

85. Minutes of meeting, January 19, 1944, Children of Mary Sodality, Secretary's Record, 1923–44, NDMA.

86. Episcopal support or opprobrium was often critical to such decisions. Grace Dammann's determination to admit blacks to Manhattanville College had the support of New York's Cardinal Patrick Hayes. In 1943, Archbishop Samuel Stritch, who headed the Archdiocese of Chicago, encouraged Saint Mary's College in Indiana and its neighbor, the University of Notre Dame, to admit black students; Saint Xavier College in Chicago followed the next year. On the other hand, in Saint Louis, Archbishop John Glennon, who governed from 1903 to 1946, resisted efforts in this area. His successor, Archbishop Joseph Ritter (1946–67), made racial integration a priority, and despite resistance from many quarters, significant reform ensued.

87. Gladyce H. Bradley, "Negro Higher and Professional Education in Maryland," *Journal of Negro Education* 17 (Summer 1948): 303.

88. On Baltimore's racial climate in this era, see Kenneth D. Durr, *Behind the Backlash: White Working-Class Politics in Baltimore, 1940–1980* (Chapel Hill: University of North Carolina Press, 2003).

89. Michael J. Curley to Henry W. Weismann, May 10, 1932, quoted in Stephen J. Ochs, *Desegregating the Altar: The Josephites and the Struggle for Black Priests, 1871–1960* (Baton Rouge: Louisiana State University Press, 1990), 243.

90. The Archdiocese of Washington was created in 1939, but Curley, very unusually, continued to govern both Baltimore and Washington until his death in 1947.

91. Ochs, *Desegregating the Altar*, 243; "Celebrating the Promise of Racial Justice," *Josephite Harvest*, September 2004. An exception was made for a group of "colored sisters" in 1932. See C. Joseph Nuesse, *The Catholic University of America: A Centennial History* (Washington, DC: Catholic University of America Press, 1990), 321–22.

92. Diary of Monsignor Joseph Nelligan, May 16, 1942, quoted in Thomas W. Spalding, *The Premier See: A History of the Archdiocese of Baltimore, 1789–1980* (Baltimore: Johns Hopkins University Press, 1989), 378. In 1936, Nelligan was chancellor of the Baltimore and Washington Archdiocese.

93. See Davis, *History of Black Catholics*, 314n85.

94. Two students were admitted that year. See Sister Columba Mullaly, *Trinity College, Washington, D.C.: The First Eighty Years, 1897–1977* (Westminster, MD: Christian Classics, 1987), 353.

95. Jay P. Dolan, *The American Catholic Experience: A History from Colonial Times to the Present* (Notre Dame, IN: University of Notre Dame Press, 1992), 368.

96. James Hennesey, SJ, *American Catholics: A History of the Roman Catholic Community in the United States* (New York: Oxford University Press, 1981), 285, quoting Ritter to Sister Matthew Marie, March 28, 1947, Archives, Archdiocese of Saint Louis. See also Dolan, *American Catholic Experience*, 368.

97. University v. Murray, 169 Md. 497 (1936).

98. Bradley, "Negro Higher and Professional Education," 303–11; Nicholas Varga, *Baltimore's Loyola, Loyola's Baltimore, 1851–1986* (Baltimore: Maryland Historical Society, 1990), 358.

99. *Chron.*, February 20, 1948; February 27, 1948. A secret ballot would very likely have produced fewer favorable votes.

100. Maura Eichner, SSND, interview by PM, February 3, 1989, transcript, OHP.

101. Bridget Marie Engelmeyer, "Notes on the History of the College, February, 1948," BMEP; Rosamond Randall Beirne, *Let's Pick the Daisies: The History of the Bryn Mawr School, 1885–1967* (Baltimore: Bryn Mawr School, 1970), 101–2, 107.

102. G. James Fleming, "Racial Integration in Education in Maryland," *Journal of Negro Education* 25 (Summer 1956): 283n15.

103. Frances Smith to Mrs. (Caroline) Putnam, March 20, 1948; Roy J. Deferrari to Smith, March 11, 1948; Smith to Deferrari, March 20, 1948, NDMA; *Chron.*, April 10, 1948.

104. Liberata Dedeaux to Frances Smith, June 25, 1948, NDMA. Established in 1870 as an orphanage, Saint Frances Academy was a boarding school between 1926 and 1972. See Liberata Dedeaux, OSP, "The Influence of Saint Frances Academy on Negro Catholic Education in the Nineteenth Century" (MA thesis, Villanova University, 1944).

105. Frances Smith to Francis Keough, July 2, 1948, NDMA.

106. Frances Smith to Liberata Dedeaux, OSP, August 9, 1948, NDMA.

107. Rev. Arthur C. Winters, SVD, to Frances Smith, March 16, 1949, NDMA.

108. Bridget Marie Engelmeyer, November 7, 1949, handwritten notes, BMEP.

109. Frances Smith to Rev. Clarence J. Howard, SVD, March 27, 1950, NDMA. *Saint Augustine's Messenger* was an African American magazine published in Bay Saint Louis. Smith died later that year; the college was still segregated.

110. "The Class of 1950," *Arras*, 1950.

111. "Mrs. Roger Putnam Opened Door to Scholarships for 51 Youths," *Afro-American*, December 9, 1950.

112. "Announcement," typed sheet, May 22, 1968, NDMA. Margaret Mary O'Connell (1906–95) earned a BA at the College of Notre Dame (1926), an MA in biology at Catholic University (1938), and an EdD at Johns Hopkins University (1950). Mrs. Roger L. (Caroline) Putnam to Sr. Margaret Mary O'Connell, January 2, 1951, NDMA.

113. Minutes, advisory board, May 19, 1952, NDMA.

114. Bridget Marie Engelmeyer to Mike Mahoney (director of admissions), January 8, 1985, NDMA.

115. *Chron.*, January 18, 1959.

116. *Chron.*, June 3, 1962.

117. *Chron.*, June 22, 1961.

118. *Chron.*, August 21, 1966.

119. See History of Marygrove, accessed April 8, 2020, https://www.marygrove.edu/history-of-marygrove.html. Marygrove became coeducational in 1971.

120. "March on Washington Affirms Beliefs of Sister Maria Mercedes," *Columns*, November 11, 1963.

121. See Martha Biondi, *The Black Revolution on Campus* (Berkeley: University of California Press, 2014); and Ibram H. Rogers [Ibram X. Kendi], *The Black Campus Movement: Black Students and the Racial Reconstitution of Higher Education, 1965–1972* (New York: Palgrave Macmillan, 2012).

122. "Julian Bond: Politics and Black Power," *Columns*, November 11, 1968; "Sociology Staffs Combine; Offer Black Power Course," *Columns*, May 21, 1969.

123. Linda Levi, "Campus Action for Racial Equality: Educational Aspects of Problem Emphasized," *Baltimore Sun*, March 31, 1969.

124. Jeanette J. Lim, US Department of Education, to Kathleen Feeley, April 16, 1986, NDMA; Mary Pat Seurkamp, "Changing Student Demographics," *University Business Magazine*, October 1, 2007.

125. *Chron.*, May 5, 1988.

126. *Hopes and Dreams*, 1989, NDMA.

127. *Hopes and Dreams*, 1993, NDMA.

128. *Chron.*, May 26, 1948.

129. *Chron.*, October 14, 1953. Men on the faculty were not among the dinner guests.

130. Regina Soria, interview by PM, February 20, 1989, transcript, OHP.

131. Anne Cullen, interview by PM, May 3, 1989, transcript, OHP.

132. *Chron.*, May 21, 1961. The reason given for excluding lay faculty was "lack of room."

133. *Chron.*, June 4, 1961.

134. *Chron.*, September 29, 1962.

135. *Chron.*, September 1939; *Report of Inspection of the College of Notre Dame of Maryland, Baltimore, Md., for MSA*, February 13–14, 1950, NDMA.

136. Mary Oliver Hudon, SSND, interview by PM, May 3, 1989, transcript, OHP.

137. *Chron.*, November 14, 1968.

138. Minutes, Advisory Council, November 9, 1947, NDMA.

139. "Description of Advisory Council," typescript, n.d. (ca. fall 1947), NDMA. Carton (1895–1952) headed the order's eastern province from 1947 until 1952.

140. *Chron.*, September 21, 1947.

141. "Description of Advisory Council"; agenda for the December 1947 meeting of the Advisory Council, NDMA.

142. Minutes, Advisory Council, October 10, 1948, NDMA.

143. Mother Myles Carton, chair, Advisory Council, to Bridget Marie Engelmeyer, November 12, 1948, NDMA; *Chron.*, November 14, 1948; August 26, 1951.

144. There was no connection between Mother Carton's 1947–51 Advisory Council and the President's Advisory Council, organized in 1964 at the initiative of

advisory board member Henry J. Knott to assist in fundraising and provide "top volunteer leadership for College programs and projects, including Trustee appointments." See *Chron.*, August 28, 1964; and "College of Notre Dame Council: Statutes and By-Laws," Article 2: Purpose (1964), NDMA. In 1968, the advisory board of the college merged with the President's Advisory Council. See Sr. Margaret Mary O'Connell to Herbert J. Watt, June 5, 1968, NDMA. After 1975, the President's Advisory Council became known as the President's Council of the College of Notre Dame.

145. Coralie Ullrich, SSND, interview by PM, March 2, 1989, transcript, OHP. Ullrich was a 1935 graduate of the college.

146. Bridget Marie Engelmeyer, SSND, interview by PM, May 30, 1989, transcript, OHP. Watkins, a 1937 graduate of the University of California, Los Angeles, held an MEd from Johns Hopkins University. She was a member of the Art Department faculty from 1959 to 1981.

147. "Proposal of the Committee on the Establishment of a Faculty Senate," n.d. (ca. March 1967), NDMA. See also "First Report of the Faculty Senate," January 1968, NDMA.

148. Mary Trinitas Bochini, SSND, interview by PM, April 6, 1989, transcript, OHP.

149. Minutes, board of trustees, October 20, 1969, NDMA.

150. Minutes, board of trustees, June 3, 1970, NDMA.

151. Sister Marie Augustine Dowling, secretary, Faculty Senate, to Sister Mary Maurice Kelly, Provincial Leader, SSND, December 16, 1970, NDMA. Kelly was the chair of the board of trustees.

152. Ruth Nagle Watkins, interview by PM, May 9, 1989, transcript, OHP.

153. Minutes, board of trustees, February 17, 1971, NDMA.

154. Ruth Nagle Watkins, chair, Faculty Senate, to Sister Francis Regis Carton, SSND, chair, board of trustees, September 20, 1972, NDMA. The five Catholic women's institutions surveyed were Trinity College, Saint Elizabeth College, Marymount College, Manhattanville College, and New Rochelle College.

155. Minutes, board of trustees, September 29, 1972, NDMA.

156. See *Chron.*, September 10, 1985; September 17, 1985; April 11, 1989.

157. Minutes, board of directors, April 7, 1967, NDMA.

158. Kathleen Feeley to members of the board of trustees, regarding meeting of the board's Budget Committee, July 19, 1972; minutes, board of trustees, September 29, 1972, NDMA.

159. Kathleen Feeley to Sister Francis Regis Carton and the board of trustees, February 25, 1974, NDMA.

160. Minutes, board of trustees, March 15, 1974, NDMA.

161. See *Report of the Faculty Committee on Rank, Tenure, and Salary, 1965–1966* and Rank, Tenure, and Salary Committee, *Up by Our Boot Straps: A Report on the State of Faculty Salaries at the College of Notre Dame of Maryland*, approved by the Faculty Senate, November 16, 1976, NDMA.

162. Minutes, board of trustees, December 10, 1976, NDMA; "Proposed Budget, 1978–1979," NDMA.

163. *Chron.*, June 29, 1979. At the time, the Baltimore Archdiocese was paying an annual stipend of $4,264 for sister-faculty in its parochial schools.

164. *Chron.*, April 3, 1986; September 19, 1986.

165. See Joe Ingalls, "Colleges Run by Nuns Forced to Change as Fewer Women Enter Religious Orders," *Chronicle of Higher Education*, March 25, 1987.

166. Kathleen Feeley, "White Paper on SSND Contributed Services to the College of Notre Dame of Maryland," August 20, 1991, typescript, BMEP.

167. *Chron.*, February 24, 1987.

168. Minutes, board of trustees, September 22, 1988, NDMA.

169. "Highlight of Operations," n.d. (1993–94), NDMA.

170. "When Diversity Is Foundational," Notre Dame of Maryland University, October 12, 2017, https://www.ndm.edu/news-and-events/news/when-diversity-foundational.

171. "Fall 2018 Enrollment," Notre Dame of Maryland University, accessed April 8, 2020, https://www.ndm.edu/sites/default/files/IR_dash/fact_sheet_fall_2018_09302019.pdf.

4. Educating Catholic Women

1. "Cardinal Gibbons Says Women Should Keep from the Polls," *New York Globe*, June 22, 1911. See also "Gibbons Flays Suffragists," *New York Times*, November 26, 1910; Cardinal Gibbons, "Pure Womanhood," *Cosmopolitan*, September 1905.

2. Lucian Johnston, "Alumnae Address, Notre Dame, June 1911," typescript, NDMA. Johnston had taught religion and served as chaplain at Notre Dame from 1899 to 1904.

3. Henri J. Wiesel, SJ, "Baccalaureate Sermon," *Damozel*, Senior Supplement, 1933, 15–20.

4. Hunter Ross Guthrie, "Woman's Role in the Modern World," *Catholic Mind* 38 (December 8, 1940): 490; Mary David Cameron, *The College of Notre Dame of Maryland, 1895–1945* (New York: Declan X. McMullen, 1947), 107.

5. "Fr. Burghardt Stresses Ideals of Womanhood in Cap and Gown Address," *Columns*, December 9, 1944. When a more seasoned Burghardt returned to Notre Dame fifteen years later to preach the baccalaureate sermon at commencement, he selected a gender-neutral topic: "the nature of true wisdom, for which humane studies are a preparation." See *Chron.*, May 31, 1959.

6. Mother General Mary Almeda, "My Dear Young Friends," *Damozel*, Senior Supplement, 1933.

7. Bridget Marie Engelmeyer, handwritten notes, December 1968, BMEP.

8. School Sisters of Notre Dame [Sister Meletia Foley] to Right Rev. T. J. Conaty, rector, Catholic University of America, October 9, 1899, NDMA.

9. Mary A. Jordan, "The College for Women," *Atlantic Monthly*, October 1892.

10. Charlotte King Shea, "Mount Holyoke College, 1875–1910: The Passing of the Old Order" (PhD diss., Cornell University, 1983), 176.

11. Henrietta E. Hooker, "Mount Holyoke College," *New England Magazine*, January 1897; Mabel L. Robinson, *The Curriculum of the Women's College* (Washington, DC: Government Printing Office, 1918), 55; Grace R. Foster, *Social Change in Relation to Curricular Development in Collegiate Education for Women* (Waterville, ME: Galahad, 1934), 98, 125; "This Month in Harvard History," *Harvard University Gazette*, December 7, 2006.

12. *NDM Catalog*, 1895–96; Annie P. Toler Hilliard, "An Investigation of Selected Events and Forces That Contributed to the Growth and Development of Trinity

College, Washington, D.C. from 1897 to 1982" (EdD diss., George Washington University, 1984), 113.

13. *NDM Catalog*, 1903.

14. Margaret Mary O'Connell, "The Educational Contributions of the School Sisters of Notre Dame in America for the Century 1847 to 1947" (EdD diss., Johns Hopkins University, 1950), 147n69.

15. Grace Sherwood '35, "The Golden Jubilee of Notre Dame College," typescript, n.d., RC.

16. *NDM Catalog*, 1899; *NDM Catalog*, 1964–65; *Catalogue of Mount Holyoke College, 1899–1900*. By the 1920s, Notre Dame offered a Latin major. On the classics, see O'Connell, "Educational Contributions," 139–40.

17. Transcript of Helen Burr '99, NDMA.

18. *NDM Catalog*, 1895–96.

19. Gail Apperson Kilman, "Southern Collegiate Women: Higher Education at Wesleyan Female College and Randolph-Macon Woman's College, 1893–1907" (PhD diss., University of Delaware, 1984), 175–78.

20. Shea, "Mount Holyoke College," 176.

21. Alice K. Fallows, "The Practical Religion of the College Girl," *Outlook*, August 1, 1903. See also Andrea Turpin, *A New Moral Vision: Gender, Religion, and the Changing Purposes of American Higher Education, 1837–1917* (Ithaca, NY: Cornell University Press, 2016), 182.

22. *NDM Catalog*, 1899.

23. *Chron.*, September 30, 1902.

24. Edmund Shanahan, "Old Notre Dame, 1873–1923," 1923, RC.

25. Bridget Marie Engelmeyer, "Talk on Development of Curriculum of College NDM," typescript of speech to alumnae, October 13, 1972, BMEP. For a detailed discussion of the college's first curriculum, see O'Connell, "Educational Contributions," 139–41.

26. O'Connell, "Educational Contributions," 149.

27. [Sister Denise Dooley?], "History of the College, Early Faculty, Rev. Dr. John J. Griffin," typescript, n.d. (ca. 1962), NDMA.

28. Mary Agnes Klug, SSND, interview by Mary Jo Maloney, April 3, 1973, transcript, OHP. Science programs at many Catholic women's colleges in the 1930s focused more on teacher preparation than on pure science. See Tracy Mitrano, "The Rise and Fall of Catholic Women's Higher Education in New York State, 1890–1985" (PhD diss., State University of New York, Binghamton, 1989), 153.

29. Mary Alma McNicholas, SSND, interview by PM, March 9, 1989, transcript, OHP. McNicholas (1902–98), a 1926 Notre Dame alumna, held an MS from Fordham University (1933) and a PhD in biochemistry from Catholic University (1937).

30. "American Association of College Registrars, Enrollment Reports," 1.20 1994–2950, Registration, NDM, 1898–1955, NDMA.

31. Mabel Newcomer, *A Century of Higher Education for American Women* (New York: Harper & Brothers, 1959), 93, table 5.

32. Robert H. Knapp, *The Origins of American Humanistic Scholars* (Englewood Cliffs, NJ: Prentice Hall, 1964), 62, table 3; M. Alice Joseph Moore, "Catholic College Student Retention in the United States" (PhD diss., Catholic University of America,

1957), 70–71, table 23. On average, 35 percent of students in graduating classes between 1942 and 1949 majored in mathematics and natural sciences. See *Damozel*, various years.

33. Jean Schramm Monier, interview by PM, April 27, 1989, transcript, OHP. Monier, a 1953 Notre Dame alumna, taught biology (1962–88) and was director of alumnae relations (1989–92). See also "Biological Sciences—Chemistry," *Arras*, 1950.

34. *NDM Catalog*, 1912–13.

35. See folder "History of the College—Philosophy Dept.," NDMA.

36. *Annual Calendar of Notre Dame of Maryland, College for Women, 1910–1911*, 36, NDMA.

37. Adele M. (Mohlenrich) Hicks '17 to President Kathleen Feeley, January 3, 1983, NDMA. Protestant students were exempt from the religion requirement but not the philosophy requirement.

38. *NDM Catalog*, 1931–32.

39. Interview, Jane F. Scheurich Tacka '50, May 10, 1989, transcript, OHP. Notre Dame's 128-point (including religion) requirement for the degree prevailed until 1989, when, acknowledging that times had changed, it was set at 120 points.

40. M. Madeleva Wolff, "Religion in Education," in *The Catholic Mind through Fifty Years, 1903–1953*, ed. Benjamin L. Masse (New York: America Press, 1952), 213–14. On Harvard, see Ann Hall, "A History of the Committee on the Study of Religion," *Colloquy, Graduate School of Arts and Sciences, Harvard University*, Spring 2015, 23–25. The Harvard Divinity School did not enroll women until 1955.

41. Cameron, *College of Notre Dame*, 100–101.

42. Francis Regis Carton, SSND, interview by PM, April 4, 1989, transcript, OHP. Carton joined Notre Dame's Religious Studies Department in 1954 and earned her PhD at Catholic University in 1963. She was chair of the board of trustees (1971–75) and later vice chair (1975–79). For an excellent discussion of the dominant place of Thomistic philosophy and theology in the curriculum of Catholic colleges in the United States from the 1920s to the 1960s, see Philip Gleason, *Contending with Modernity: Catholic Higher Education in the Twentieth Century* (New York: Oxford University Press, 1995), 105–23.

43. Virgina Geiger, SSND, interview by Barbara Gross, March 27, 1973, transcript, OHP. Geiger (1915–2004), a longtime faculty member, held an MA (1941) and a PhD (1943) in history and philosophy from Catholic University.

44. *NDM Catalog*, 1918–19.

45. Mary F. Eastman, "The Education of Woman in the Eastern States," in *Woman's Work in America*, ed. Annie Nathan Meyer (New York: Henry Holt & Co., 1891), 45.

46. Christine Ladd Franklin, "The Education of Woman in the Southern States," in *Woman's Work in America*, ed. Annie Nathan Meyer (New York: Henry Holt & Co., 1891), 96. The Woman's College of Baltimore opened in 1885.

47. *Baltimore American*, October 4, 1896.

48. Drew C. Pendergrass, "'Ladies Armed with Clubs,'" *Harvard Crimson*, December 1, 2016.

49. "Baseball in Convent," untitled handwritten draft, signed "an eye-witness" [Lucian Johnston], n.d. (ca. 1897–1910), n.p.; *Chron.*, September 1, 1906. On the 1890s

debate over the merits of gymnastics versus team athletics for female college students, see Sherrie A. Inness, *Intimate Communities: Representation and Social Transformation in Women's College Fiction, 1895–1910* (Bowling Green, OH: Bowling Green State University Popular Press, 1995), 69–95.

50. See "An Imposing College Edifice," *Baltimore Sun,* June 5, 1910, for a description of College Hall; *NDM Catalog*, 1913–14. Bowling was very popular among college women in this era. See Polly Welts Kaufman, ed., *The Search for Equity: Women at Brown University, 1891–1991* (Providence, RI: Brown University Press, 1991), 20.

51. Lavinia Hart, "A Girl's College Life," *Cosmopolitan*, June 1901.

52. "Athletics," *Damozel*, 1923.

53. Frances T. Marburg, "The Social Life of Vassar Students," *Vassar Miscellany*, October 1915; Judith Ann Schiff, "Fore!," *Yale Alumni Magazine*, April 2001; "Appetite for Betterments," *Notre Dame Quarterly*, November 1916; "Golf for Notre Dame," *Baltimore Sun*, March 20, 1917; "Athletics," *Notre Dame Quarterly*, March 1917.

54. *Chron.*, November 4, 1921; Elizabeth P. Hoisington, interview by PM, May 31, 1989, transcript, OHP. The College of William & Mary admitted women in 1918.

55. Bridget Marie Engelmeyer, "Early P.E.," typescript, n.d. (ca. 1993), RC.

56. *NDM Catalog*, 1929–30.

57. Founded in 1887, the organization has been known as the Middle States Association of Colleges and Schools (MSA) since 1975. In 1919 it created a division, known since 1969 as the Middle States Commission on Higher Education (MSCHE), to set accreditation policies and accredit MSA member colleges. Adam Leroy Jones, associate professor of philosophy and director of admissions at Columbia University, was its first chair (1919–34). See Adam Leroy Jones to President Philemon Doyle, November 17, 1925, NDMA.

58. "Calendar of Events," *Damozel*, 1927; *NDM Catalog*, 1927–28. See also "SA Assembly—Founded in a Great Tradition," n.d. (ca. November 1953), BMEP.

59. See *NDM Catalog*, 1931–32; *NDM Catalog*, 1938–39; Ruth L. Crawford, "An Evaluation of the Physical Education Program at the College of NDM," typescript, May 18, 1946, NDMA; President's Report, 1959–60, NDMA.

60. *NDM Catalog*, 1912–13.

61. See Jana Nidiffer, "Morrill Land-Grant Act of 1862," in *Historical Dictionary of Women's Education in the United States*, ed. Linda Eisenmann (Westport, CT: Greenwood, 1998), 275–77.

62. Hart, "Girl's College Life."

63. G. Stanley Hall, "What College for My Daughter?," *Good Housekeeping*, May 1909.

64. Helen Lefkowitz Horowitz, "Designing for the Genders: Curricula and Architecture at Scripps College and the California Institute of Technology," *Pacific Historical Review* 54 (November 1985): 446.

65. Rose C. Feld, "Vassar Girls to Study Home-Making as Career," *New York Times*, May 23, 1926; "Education: Euthenics," *Time*, July 19, 1926. Euthenics is the study of improving the human environment in order to improve the human. It covers topics like nutrition and the arrangement and decoration of buildings.

66. Lynn Townsend White, *Educating Our Daughters* (New York: Harper & Brothers, 1950), 72, 161–62. White (1907–87) headed Mills College between 1943 and 1958.

Curricula in women's colleges, including Catholic institutions, in the quarter century following 1930 showed a distinct increase in health and hygiene requirements. On this development, see Newcomer, *Century of Higher Education*, 96–98, especially table 7, "Required Courses in Women's Colleges 1931–1932 and 1956–1957."

67. Ernest Havemann and Patricia Salter West, *They Went to College: The College Graduate in America Today* (New York: Harcourt, Brace, 1952), 54–56. The sample of 9,064 included graduates from most of the nation's accredited colleges.

68. Pius XII, "Women's Duties in Social and Political Life," reprinted in *Catholic Mind* 43, no. 996 (December 1945): 705–26.

69. Mary B. Syron, "A History of Four Catholic Women's Colleges" (MA thesis, University of Detroit, 1956), 59. To advance its liberal arts curriculum, the college ultimately terminated career-oriented programs like domestic science (1936) and commerce (1951). See James T. Schleifer, *The College of New Rochelle: An Extraordinary Story* (Virginia Beach, VA: Donning, 1994), 24–27, 54–55.

70. Sister Columba Mullaly, *Trinity College, Washington, D.C.: The First Eighty Years, 1897–1977* (Westminster, MD: Christian Classics, 1987), 250. This program was short lived.

71. *The First Fifteen Years of the College of Saint Scholastica: A Report on the Effectiveness of Catholic Education for Women* (New York: Declan X. McMullen, 1947), 21.

72. *NDM Catalog*, 1957–58; *NDM Catalog*, 1958–59.

73. For a discussion of Wellesley's thinking on the place of music and art in the liberal arts curriculum, see Helen Lefkowitz Horowitz, *Alma Mater: Design and Experience in the Women's Colleges from Their Nineteenth-Century Beginnings to the 1930s* (New York: Alfred A. Knopf, 1984), 84.

74. *NDM Catalog*, 1910–11; *NDM Catalog*, 1902. An elective course in stenography and typewriting was an "extra," not part of the 1910 curriculum, and students seeking private instruction in music, needlework, and elocution had to pay separately.

75. "142 Get Diplomas at New Rochelle," *New York Times*, June 4, 1936. Notre Dame's total enrollment in 1936 was 173; nearly two-thirds were day students. See Sister Frances Smith to Alumnae of the College of Notre Dame, draft of letter, n.d. (ca. September 1936), NDMA.

76. Lucy M. Salmon, "Progress in Education at Vassar College," *Vassar Quarterly*, November 1919.

77. Margaret Farrand Thorp, *Neilson of Smith* (New York: Oxford University Press, 1956), 202.

78. Jeanette Eaton, "The College Girl of 1930," *Woman's Journal*, May 1930.

79. See Frances Smith to Alumnae; "Rev. Philip Burkett, S.J. Teaches Sociology," *Notre Dame Quarterly*, November 1916.

80. Frances Smith to Alumnae.

81. Bridget Marie Engelmeyer, "B.S. Degree Evolution," typed notes, single sheet, November 17, 1976, BMEP. Overall, the college awarded only nine BS degrees between 1899 and 1974, seven of them during the Depression decade. The BS degree was reintroduced in 1978 in the Weekend College BS in Nursing program.

82. Carole B. Shmurak and Bonnie S. Handler, "'Castle of Science': Mount Holyoke College and the Preparation of Women in Chemistry, 1837–1941," *History*

of Education Quarterly 32 (Fall 1992): 331. Southern female seminaries also typically offered pedagogical training at this time (see Kilman, "Southern Collegiate Women," 175–78).

83. Frances M. Abbott, "College Women and Matrimony, Again," *Century Magazine*, March 1896; Frances M. Abbott, "Three Decades of College Women," *Popular Science Monthly*, August 1904; Jo Anne Preston, "Negotiating Work and Family: Aspirations of Early Radcliffe Graduates," in *Yards and Gates: Gender in Harvard and Radcliffe History*, ed. Laurel Thatcher Ulrich (New York: Palgrave Macmillan, 2004), 176.

84. Geraldine Joncich Clifford, "'Shaking Dangerous Questions from the Crease': Gender and American Higher Education," *Feminist Issues* 3 (Fall 1983): 28, citing Robinson, *Curriculum of the Women's College*, 120. Teaching was also a top career choice of female collegians in England. About two-thirds of the 1920s graduates of Saint Mary's College in Durham became schoolteachers, a typical proportion. See Jane Robinson, *Bluestockings: The Remarkable Story of the First Women to Fight for an Education* (London: Viking, 2009), 211.

85. Mary Van Kleeck, "A Census of College Women," *Journal of the Association of Collegiate Alumnae* 11 (May 1918): 557–91.

86. William Allan Neilson, "The Inaugural Address of the President of Smith College," *School and Society*, July 20, 1918, 61–68. On the feminization of teaching in this era, see "Of Feminine Achievement," *New Republic*, April 20, 1918; and Debra Herman, "College and After: The Vassar Experiment in Women's Education, 1861–1924" (PhD diss., Stanford University, 1979), 206–7.

87. Mary Clough Cain, *The Historical Development of State Normal Schools for White Teachers in Maryland* (New York: Teachers College Bureau of Publications, 1941), 102–3, citing "Teaching as a Profession," *Baltimore Sun*, December 28, 1903.

88. "Teachers' Course 1910–11: Johns Hopkins and Goucher College to Co-Operate; To Be Open for Both Sexes," *Baltimore Sun*, June 4, 1910.

89. *Chron.*, March 28, 1923.

90. *NDM Catalog*, 1922–23; *Chron.*, June 9, 1926; O'Connell, "Educational Contributions," 149. New York State and Washington, DC, recognized Maryland and Pennsylvania teaching certificates.

91. "Girls at College No Longer Blasé," *New York Times*, February 14, 1933, quoting Barnard College dean Virginia Gildersleeve.

92. The Maryland State Normal School became Towson State College in 1963, Towson State University in 1976, and Towson University in 1997. See Cain, *Historical Development*, 128–29.

93. Merrill E. Jarchow, *Private Liberal Arts Colleges in Minnesota: Their History and Contributions* (Saint Paul: Minnesota Historical Society, 1973), 123.

94. Theresine Staab, SSND, interview by Mary Jo Maloney, March 29, 1973, transcript, OHP. The major flourished until student interest in teaching careers declined in the 1970s.

95. Patricia W. Cautley, *AAUW Members Look at College Education: An Interim Report* (Washington, DC: American Association of University Women, 1949), 5.

96. Margaret Mary O'Connell, "Role of Private Colleges in Higher Education in Maryland," typescript of statement, Maryland Parent Teacher Association Congress, November 11, 1964, NDMA.

97. *NDM Catalog*, 1959–60.

98. Margaret Mary O'Connell, "Data Presented for Consideration of the Commission on Institutions of Higher Education, MSA, 4 December 1959," NDMA.

99. Jarchow, *Private Liberal Arts Colleges*, 136.

100. John Lancaster Spalding, "Normal School for Catholics," *Catholic World* 51 (April 1890): 88–97; Thomas E. Shields, "The Need of the Catholic Sisters College and the Scope of Its Work," *Catholic Educational Review* 17 (September 1919): 420–29. The Sisters' College closed in 1963.

101. Greg Rienzi, "100 Years of Educating Educators," *Johns Hopkins Gazette*, February 9, 2009.

102. See Schleifer, *College of New Rochelle*, 25.

103. "A Documentary Chronicle of Vassar College: 1949," *Vassar Historian*, accessed June 3, 2020, http://chronology.vassar.edu/records/1949.

104. *Chron.*, July 31, 1897

105. O'Connell, "Educational Contributions," 144.

106. *Chron.*, July 5, 1922.

107. Of sixteen young women entering the Sisters of Saint Joseph in Baden, Pennsylvania, in 1931, five held high school diplomas. See Jay P. Dolan, R. Scott Appleby, Patricia Byrne, and Debra Campbell, *Transforming Parish Ministry: The Changing Roles of Catholic Clergy, Laity, and Women Religious* (New York: Crossroad, 1989), 124.

108. See A School Sister of Notre Dame [M. Dympna Flynn], *Mother Caroline and the School Sisters of Notre Dame in North America* (Saint Louis: Woodward & Tiernan, 1928), 2:159. A similar program at Loyola College in Baltimore became part of its evening division in 1945.

109. *Chron.*, September 1929.

110. The training school offered eight winter sessions and nineteen summer school courses in 1935–36, and awarded its first certificates in 1937. See O'Connell, "Educational Contributions," 214–16.

111. *Chron.*, June 26, 1959.

112. "Student-Teachers Complete Requirements," *Columns*, May 1934.

113. Mary Dempsey, interview by PM, April 18, 1989, transcript, OHP; Lavinia Wenger, interview by Mary Jo Maloney, April 10, 1973, transcript, OHP. After graduating in 1914 from Western Maryland College, Wenger (1893–1976) earned an MRE (1922) from Bethany Biblical Seminary, Chicago, and an MA (1929) from the University of Pennsylvania. She joined Notre Dame's Education Department faculty in 1944.

114. Margaret Mary O'Connell, SSND, interview by Charles Ritter, April 10, 1973, transcript, OHP.

115. See Marie Xavier Looymans, SSND, interview by PM, March 13, 1989, transcript, OHP. Looymans (1914–2005) attended Towson Normal School and taught in Baltimore public schools before entering the order in 1941. She earned degrees at the College of Notre Dame (BA, 1946) and Catholic University (MEd, 1956), and was a member of the Education Department faculty from 1958 until 1987.

116. Zellers v. Huff, 55 N.M. 501, 236 P.2d 949 (1951). For an excellent analysis of the history and significance of this controversy, see Kathleen Holscher, *Religious Lessons: Catholic Sisters and the Captured Schools Crisis in New Mexico* (New York: Oxford University Press, 2012).

117. See Bertrande Meyers, *The Education of Sisters: A Plan for Integrating the Religious, Social, Cultural and Professional Training of Sisters* (New York: Sheed & Ward, 1941).

118. See Madeleva Wolff, CSC, *The Education of Sister Lucy: A Symposium on Teacher Education and Teacher Training*, National Catholic Educational Association, Philadelphia, April 21, 1949 (Notre Dame, IN: Saint Mary's College, 1949); M. Madeleva Wolff, "Academic Preparation of Religious Teachers," *Catholic School Journal* 48 (June 1948): 202–3; Gail Porter Mandell, *Madeleva: A Biography* (Albany: State University of New York Press, 1997), 189. On the Sister Formation Movement, see Dolan et al., *Transforming Parish Ministry*, 141–47; Mary Schneider, OSF, "American Sisters and the Roots of Change: The 1950s," *U.S. Catholic Historian* 7 (Winter 1988): 55–72; Marjorie Noterman Beane, *From Framework to Freedom: A History of the Sister Formation Conference* (Lanham, MD: University Press of America, 1993); Karen M. Kennelly, *The Religious Formation Conference, 1954–2004* (Saint Paul, MN: Good Ground, 2009); and Darra D. Mulderry, "Educating 'Sister Lucy': The Experiential Sources of the Movement to Improve Higher Education for Catholic Teaching Sisters, 1949–1964," *U.S. Catholic Historian* 33, no. 1 (Winter 2015): 55–79.

119. Cited in C. Joseph Nuesse, *The Catholic University of America: A Centennial History* (Washington, DC: Catholic University of America Press, 1990), 390–91n60.

120. "Sister Criticizes Poetry by Nuns," *New York Times*, October 11, 1959. Eichner (1915–2009) entered the order in 1933 and graduated from the College of Notre Dame in 1941. See Jacques Kelly, "Sister Maura, Poet and English Professor," *Baltimore Sun*, November 18, 2009.

121. Minutes, advisory board, May 23, 1955, NDMA.

122. Bridget Marie Engelmeyer, "Talk to Heritage Group July 1983," typescript, BMEP.

123. Mother Arnold's proposal was hardly novel. By the 1930s, according to Roger Geiger, "a growing number of students prepared for careers in education in regular colleges and universities" (*To Advance Knowledge: The Growth of American Research Universities, 1900–1940* [New York: Oxford University Press, 1986], 110).

124. Bridget Marie Engelmeyer, "Draft Notes for Interview with Sister Patricia Murphy, 30 May 1989," copy provided to the author by Delia Dowling, SSND, academic dean, 1995.

125. Minutes, advisory board, May 27, 1957, NDMA.

126. Delia Dowling, interview with the author, May 13, 1996.

127. *NDM Catalog*, 1969–70.

128. In 1904, the Education Conference of Catholic Seminary Faculties (est. 1898), the Association of Catholic Colleges (est. 1899), and the Parish School Conference (est. 1902) joined to form the Catholic Educational Association. Notre Dame was on the CEA's first list of accredited Catholic women's colleges, published in 1904. The CEA became the National Catholic Educational Association in 1927. See O'Connell, "Educational Contributions," 148.

129. This took place at the meeting of the directors of the Maryland State Board of Education, December 22, 1920. See *Chron.*, January 6, 1921.

130. The preparatory school had been registered and accredited by the New York State Board of Regents in 1902.

131. Adam Leroy Jones, chairman, Commission on Institutions of Higher Education, MSA, to Philemon Doyle, November 17, 1925, NDMA.

132. *Chron.*, January 11, 1926; *NDM Catalog*, 1927–28.

133. George Constable, interview by PM, April 25, 1989, transcript, OHP.

134. On the AAU program, see William K. Selden, "The AAU and Accreditation," *Graduate Journal* 2 (Fall 1959): 325–33.

135. William Allison Shimer, Phi Beta Kappa, New York, to Dean Denise Dooley, February 21, 1934, NDMA. See also Oscar M. Voorhees, secretary, Committee on Scholarship, Phi Beta Kappa Foundation, to Ethelbert Roche, March 14, 1931; Dean Mary Immaculata Dillon to Oscar M. Voorhees, March 31, 1931; and Denise Dooley to Gentlemen, Phi Beta Kappa, New York, February 19, 1934, NDMA. By 1940, the college had chapters of two national honor societies: Kappa Gamma Pi, for Catholic women's colleges, in 1926, and Delta Epsilon Sigma, for Catholic colleges and universities, in 1939. After the discontinuance of the AAU's accrediting program in 1951, the college gained membership in the American Association of University Women. It never gained a chapter of Phi Beta Kappa.

136. Adam Leroy Jones to Philemon Doyle, September 9, 1926; Mary I. Dillon to Adam Leroy Jones, April 1, 1930; Adam Leroy Jones to Mary I. Dillon, July 10, 1930, NDMA.

137. Ethelbert Roche to Adam Leroy Jones, February 10, 1932, NDMA.

138. Adam Leroy Jones to Ethelbert Roche, November 15, 1932; Ethelbert Roche to Adam Leroy Jones, November 26, 1932; Adam Leroy Jones to Ethelbert Roche, December 1, 1932, NDMA. Dempster's report also noted an insufficient number of "properly qualified faculty." See *Chron.*, October 11, 1932.

139. *Chron.*, March 6, 1939; Frank H. Bowles to Frances Smith, October 30, 1939, NDMA; Frank H. Bowles to Frances Smith, November 4, 1942, NDMA.

140. Roy J. Deferrari, "The Nature and Function of the Catholic College for Women," in *Fifty Golden Years: A Series of Lectures on the Liberal Arts College, Commemorating the Golden Jubilee of the College of Notre Dame of Maryland* (Baltimore: College of Notre Dame of Maryland, 1946), 56.

141. "Dr. Deferrari Stresses Aims for Education," *Columns*, April 19, 1945. See also Deferrari, "Nature and the Function."

142. Frank H. Bowles to Roy J. Deferrari, November 19, 1943, NDMA. A poll of alumnae conducted in response to these remarks found that the college was doing better than Bowles thought: 12 percent held graduate degrees, 3 percent were currently enrolled, and 13 percent had at some point taken graduate courses.

143. William H. Lichte to Frances Smith, November 15, 1947, NDMA.

144. The approved Catholic women's institutions at this time were Marygrove College (Michigan); Chestnut Hill College (Pennsylvania); Mount Saint Vincent College (New York); New Rochelle College (New York); Sacred Heart College (New York); Incarnate Word College (Texas); Our Lady of the Lake College (Louisiana); Rosary College (Illinois); Seton Hill College (Pennsylvania); the College of Saint Catherine (Minnesota); Saint Elizabeth College (New Jersey); Saint Teresa College (Minnesota); Dominican College (California); Rosemont College (Pennsylvania); and Trinity College (Washington, DC).

145. William H. Lichte to Frances Smith, December 16, 1947, NDMA.

146. Frances Smith to William Lichte, July 31, 1948, NDMA.

147. William H. Lichte to Frances Smith, November 18, 1948, NDMA.

148. See "Outcomes Study, Graduates, 1949–1958, College of Notre Dame, 1959," NDMA. This survey of the college's 653 graduates between 1949 and 1958 was undertaken at the initiative of the faculty prior to the January 1960 MSA reaccreditation visit. Although the final survey report was summary in character, a review of individual responses yielded additional useful data.

149. *Chron.*, April 1, 1954. Over the years, the small college consistently produced Fulbright scholars. In 2004–5 and 2009–10, it ranked among the top master's institutions nationally in receiving Fulbright awards (*Chronicle of Higher Education*, October 22, 2004; September 15, 2009). In the latter year, it was the only Maryland institution in this category to achieve this distinction. See "College of Notre Dame Named a Top Producer of U.S. Fulbright Students," Greater Baltimore Committee, October 21, 2009, https://gbc.org/college-of-notre-dame-named-a-top-producer-of-u-s-fulbright-students.

150. Polly Weaver and Barbara Witten, "Where Do the Top Students Go?," *Mademoiselle*, January 15, 1953. The authors based their report on the recently released book by Robert H. Knapp and Joseph J. Greenbaum, *The Younger American Scholar: His Collegiate Origins* (Chicago: University of Chicago Press, 1953). The number of students an institution sent on to graduate school indicated its production of "scholars." See also *Chron.*, January 7, 1953.

151. *Chron.*, May 17, 1944.

152. *Chron.*, January 9, 1952.

153. "Department of Classical Languages and Literature, 1945–1946," NDMA.

154. See Jacques Kelly, "Sister Maura, Poet and English Professor," *Baltimore Sun*, November 18, 2009.

155. *Chron.*, June 1, 1953. CND students were not the first Catholic women's college students to test themselves in these competitions. For example, in the 1930s a senior at the College of Saint Catherine "took top honors" in the *Atlantic Monthly* competition as well as first prize in the *Forum*'s national poetry contest. In the next decade, students of the award-winning writer Sister Mariella Gable, OSB, at the College of Saint Benedict "consistently placed" in the *Atlantic Monthly* contest, with "two of them winning the top prizes in 1942 and 1944." See Jarchow, *Private Liberal Arts Colleges*, 111; Nancy Hynes, OSB, introduction to Mariella Gable, OSB, *The Literature of Spiritual Values and Catholic Fiction*, ed. Nancy Hynes, OSB (Lanham, MD: University Press of America, 1996).

156. *Chron.*, April 23, 1955.

157. *Chron.*, April 25, 1957; *Chron.*, April 23, 1955; *Arras*, 1957.

158. Office of the President, (Acting President) Mary Elissa McGuire, 1968–71, NDMA.

159. Maura Eichner, SSND, interview by PM, February 3, 1989, transcript, OHP. In 2007, the *Atlantic Monthly* was renamed the *Atlantic*.

160. Eleanora A. Baer and Salvatore G. Dimichael, "Catholic Women's Colleges and the War," *Journal of Higher Education* 16 (December 1945): 481.

161. *Chron.*, February 10, 1942.

162. "118 Receive Degrees at Vassar Ceremony," *New York Times*, July 2, 1948.

163. "Notre Dame Takes Active Part in Defense Program," *Columns*, February 13, 1942; "Science Schedule Accelerated," *Columns*, March 31, 1942; "Biology Department Prepares M.T.s," *Columns*, March 17, 1943.

164. Margaret Mary O'Connell, SSND, interview by Charles Ritter, April 10, 1973, transcript, OHP.

165. Mary Agnes Klug, SSND, interview by Mary Jo Maloney, April 3, 1973, transcript, OHP. Klug (1909–2009), a 1931 Notre Dame graduate, earned an MS in chemistry in 1946 at Catholic University. She was successively a member of Notre Dame's Chemistry Department faculty (1942–57), director of admissions (1957–72), and director of planned giving (1972–81).

166. Report of Inspection of College of Notre Dame of Maryland, Baltimore, Md., for MSA, February 13–14, 1950, NDMA.

167. "Specialized Study for Women Scored," *New York Times*, November 19, 1950.

168. Moore, "Catholic College Student Retention," 70–71, table 23.

169. See "Outcomes Study." Seven percent of respondents were nuns, most of them teachers.

170. O'Connell, "Role of Private Colleges."

171. Mary Agnes Klug, SSND, interview by Mary Jo Maloney, April 3, 1973, transcript, OHP.

172. Engelmeyer, "Talk on Development of Curriculum."

173. President's Report, minutes, advisory board, May 22, 1950, NDMA. See also "Italian Department Opens Evening Class," *Columns*, October 17, 1940.

174. *NDM Catalog*, 1972–73, 10.

175. *Chron.*, November 7, 1973; minutes, board of trustees, November 7, 1974, NDMA; *Chron.*, September 24, 1975; Mary Oliver Hudon, SSND, interview by PM, May 3, 1989, transcript, OHP. Hudon had recently earned her PhD in educational administration from the University of Maryland.

176. Helen S. Astin, "Interview with Rosemary Park," in *The Higher Education of Women: Essays in Honor of Rosemary Park*, ed. Helen S. Astin and Werner Z. Hirsch (New York: Praeger, 1978), xxiii.

177. *Goddard College, 2011 Academic Catalog.*

178. In 2002, the program registered about seventy nondegree special students and thirty degree special students. See Mark Alden Branch, "Degree of Commitment," *Yale Alumni Magazine*, March 2002.

179. *Chron.*, December 12, 1974.

180. "Weekend College, Spring Semester, 1975" fact sheet, NDMA; minutes, board of trustees, September 5, 1975, NDMA. In 1984, Trinity College opened a Weekend College that initially admitted only women.

181. On the Weekend College experience, see Mary Griffin, "Reinventing Mundelein: Birthing the Weekend College, 1974," in *Mundelein Voices: The Women's College Experience, 1930–1991*, ed. Ann M. Harrington and Prudence Moylan (Chicago: Loyola Press, 2001), 215–24. The organizational structure of the Weekend College at CND was straightforward. There were three Weekend College terms annually, one of them in the summer. The fall and spring terms coincided with the college's regular fourteen-week term calendar. During regular terms, students enrolled in one to three courses on five weekends as they worked toward a bachelor's degree. Classes were

held every third weekend, commencing on Friday evening at six o'clock and concluding on Sunday at noon. During the three-week hiatus separating weekends of classes, students were free to engage in library research and consult with faculty. See *NDM Catalog*, 1978–79.

182. President's Report, 1964–65, NDMA. See also O'Connell, "Role of Private Colleges."

183. *CND Classbook*, 1966; Bridget Marie Engelmeyer, "Report of the Dean to the President for the Year 1966–67," July 18, 1967, NDMA; *Chanson, Class Book, 1964*, n.p.

184. "A Comeback for Women's Colleges," *Baltimore Sun*, September 12, 1975.

185. Mary Oliver Hudon, SSND, interview by PM, May 3, 1989, transcript, OHP.

186. Mary Lou McNeal '50, interview with the author, May 21, 1996. The 1980s saw the expansion of ancillary programs for the general public and for students enrolled in other institutions. An English Language Institute offered English as a second language and instruction in American culture. An Accelerated Certification for Teaching (ACT) program prepared students for certification as Maryland high school teachers. Students from other colleges could enroll in two-year pre-dental-hygiene, pre-medical-technology, pre-nursing, and pre-physical-therapy programs. Retired and semiretired citizens benefited from Renaissance Institute programs. See *Chron.*, March 19, 1980; *NDM Catalogs* 1981–82; 1984–85; 1985–86; 1987–88; 1989–90.

187. *NDM Catalog*, 1973–74.

188. *Chron.*, May 24, 1978; March 1, 1979.

189. Mary Oliver Hudon, SSND, interview by PM, May 3, 1989, transcript, OHP; *Chron.*, May 24, 1978; *Chron.*, March 1, 1979; *NDM Catalog*, 1979–80. The BS degree had not been offered for four decades.

190. *Chron.*, April 27, 1973; September 5, 1974. See also *Chron.*, September 1979. Students were free to major in either field.

191. *Chron.*, March 2, 1980.

192. *Chron.*, November 12, 1985.

193. *Chron.*, January 23, 1985.

194. "America's Best Colleges," *U.S. News & World Report*, November 25, 1985, 46–49. The Weekend College's large nursing program contributed significantly to this figure.

195. *Chron.*, November 25, 1985.

196. Kathleen Feeley, "Case Statement for the College of Notre Dame of Maryland," typescript draft, January 12, 1987, NDMA.

5. Sectarian or Free?

1. Horace Mann League v. Board of Public Works of Maryland, 242 Md. 645, 220 A.2d 51 (Ct. App. 1966); Roemer v. Board of Public Works, 426 U.S. 736 (1976).

2. Fred J. Kelly, Benjamin W. Frazier, John H. McNeely, and Ella B. Ratcliffe, *Collegiate Accreditation by Agencies within States* (Washington, DC: Government Printing Office, 1940), 31. The New York Regents could not prevent a college in another state from operating; however, inclusion on its list brought both credibility and prestige. As an early history of the College of Notre Dame pointed out, the power to grant degrees was separate from "affiliation" with the Regents: "The school was incorporated and

chartered as a college [by the State of Maryland], while at the same time the Academic Classes were affiliated with the Board of Regents of New York." "History of Notre Dame of Maryland," *Notre Dame Quarterly* 3 (March 1917): 3, NDMA.

3. "Sister Mary Meletia Foley," typescript notes, n.d., NDMA.

4. Carnegie Foundation for the Advancement of Teaching, *Annual Report*, 1906, 66, 79, cited in Frederick Rudolph, *Curriculum: A History of the American Undergraduate Course of Study since 1636* (San Francisco: Jossey-Bass, 1977), 222.

5. In 1921, the estimated value of the contributed services of thirteen sister-faculty and staff at Notre Dame totaled $18,000. Since at an average interest rate of 6 percent an endowment of $300,000 would generate $18,000 in income, the college estimated its "permanent" endowment to be $300,000. As the number of sisters employed at the college rose, so did the permanent endowment. In 1930, with twenty-four sisters working at Notre Dame, the institution estimated a permanent endowment of $875,000. Commission Information Sheet, submitted by Sister Mary Immaculata Dillon, dean, to Adam Leroy Jones, chairman, Commission on Institutions of Higher Education, April 26, 1930, NDMA.

6. Sister Mary Immaculata Dillon, dean, to Adam Leroy Jones, chairman, Commission on Institutions of Higher Education, May 29, 1930, NDMA.

7. Most Catholic women's colleges had groups of women volunteers to assist them. In 1898, before Trinity College opened its doors, a Ladies Auxiliary Board of Regents was soliciting funds nationally for the school. On the ladies' auxiliary's early efforts on behalf of Trinity, see Kathleen Sprows Cummings, "'We Owe It to Our Sex as Well as Our Religion': The Sisters of Notre Dame de Namur, the Ladies Auxiliary, and the Founding of Trinity College, 1898–1904," *American Catholic Studies* 115, no. 4 (2004): 21–36. In 1901, Trinity established an advisory board of prominent laity to advise its trustees. Inactive by 1926, the advisory board ended in 1935. See Sister Columba Mullaly, *Trinity College, Washington, D.C.: The First Eighty Years, 1897–1977* (Westminster, MD: Christian Classics, 1987), 652–55. For the most part, formal lay advisory boards of the type proposed by President Smith remained uncommon in the 1930s. While Saint Benedict's College in Minnesota introduced one in 1934, Emmanuel College in Massachusetts, Saint Mary's College in Indiana, and Saint Angela's (later New Rochelle) College in New York did not do so until 1948, 1952, and 1954, respectively. See Trinity College catalog, 1905–9; Merrill E. Jarchow, *Private Liberal Arts Colleges in Minnesota: Their History and Contributions* (Saint Paul: Minnesota Historical Society, 1973), 123; Mary E. Friel, "History of Emmanuel College, 1919–1974" (PhD diss., Boston College, 1980), 141; Gail Porter Mandell, *Madeleva: A Biography* (Albany: State University of New York Press, 1997), 193; and James T. Schleifer, *The College of New Rochelle: An Extraordinary Story* (Virginia Beach, VA: Donning, 1994), 67.

8. George W. Constable, interview by PM, April 25, 1989, transcript, OHP.

9. See minutes, advisory board, October 30, 1936, NDMA.

10. Minutes, advisory board, October 30, 1936, NDMA; *Chron.*, May 26, 1941.

11. See minutes, advisory board, October 30, 1936, NDMA.

12. Minutes, advisory board, October 30, 1936, NDMA. A few years later, Mother Doyle again proposed Morrissy for the advisory board, this time with success.

13. School Sisters of Notre Dame, "A Talk with Our Friends: Endowment?," *Damozel*, 1937.

14. "History of the Triangle Bookshop and Origin of the Notre Dame College Endowment Fund," typescript, n.d., NDMA.

15. James Almond to Frances Smith, December 22, 1944, ABA.

16. Archbishop Michael J. Curley to James Almond, December 26, 1944, ABA.

17. Minutes, advisory board, May 25, 1945; minutes, advisory board, May 21, 1946, NDMA.

18. Frances Smith to Joseph Nelligan, chancellor, January 16, 1947; Archbishop Michael J. Curley to Frances Smith, January 31, 1947, folder 158, Nelligan Collection, ABA.

19. "Notre Dame Sets Golden Jubilee Fund Drive," *Evening Sun* (Baltimore), February 6, 1947.

20. *Chron.*, March 9, 1947.

21. See Frances Smith, "Report of the Golden Jubilee Campaign," minutes, advisory board, May 23, 1949, NDMA.

22. "List of Colleges Receiving Aid; Institutions Aided by the Ford Foundation," *New York Times*, December 13, 1955; "Survey on the Use of Ford Foundation Endowment Grants," n.d. (ca. 1959), NDMA. The average salaries of professors at some colleges lagged behind those of teachers in local public schools.

23. With the exception of graduate tuition support for two sister-faculty, the Ford monies benefited only lay faculty. See Dorothy Brown, interview by PM, May 16, 1989, transcript, OHP; "Survey on the Use of Ford Foundation Endowment Grants."

24. Minutes, advisory board, May 28, 1956, NDMA.

25. In the late 1960s, the college also established a "quasi-endowment" fund of $85,000 from "operating surplus."

26. Minutes, advisory board, May 23, 1955; minutes, advisory board, May 28, 1956, NDMA.

27. Minutes, advisory board, May 28, 1956, NDMA. Not all colleges joined. Goucher, for one, believed it could raise more funds by independent solicitation.

28. Bridget Marie Engelmeyer, handwritten notes, May 20, 1957, BMEP.

29. It was an amendment to the charter (Acts of 1896, Chapter 124) that permitted the granting of college degrees as well as honorary degrees. See *Minute Book No. 1 of CND, Inc. (A Maryland Corporation)*, NDMA.

30. Report of Inspection of College of Notre Dame of Maryland, Baltimore, Md., for MSA, February 13–14, 1950, NDMA.

31. Minutes, advisory board, May 18, 1953, NDMA.

32. George W. Constable, interview by PM, April 25, 1989, transcript, OHP; "By-Laws of CND, Inc., 1963," art. 4, para. 2, NDMA.

33. See Notre Dame University advertisement in the *Independent*, July 6, 1914. The Gilman Country School for Boys moved to its own campus in 1910.

34. Baltimore educators agreed that the city's two public girls' high schools "were still, in 1900, unable to prepare girls for college." Marion Talbot and Lois K. M. Rosenberry, *The History of the American Association of University Women, 1881–1931* (Boston: Houghton Mifflin, 1931), 3n3.

35. "Woman's College," *Baltimore Morning Herald*, August 28, 1900.

36. *NDM Catalog*, 1896–97.

37. Virginia Wolf Briscoe, "Bryn Mawr College Traditions: Women's Rituals as Expressive Behavior" (PhD diss., University of Pennsylvania, 1981), 1:424; Joan Marie Johnson, *Southern Women at the Seven Sister Colleges* (Athens: University of Georgia Press, 2008), 42–43.

38. Briscoe, "Bryn Mawr College Traditions," 1:424.

39. Rudolph, *Curriculum*, 226.

40. Porter E. Sargent, *A Handbook of American Private Schools* (Boston: Porter E. Sargent, 1916), 158–59.

41. Mary Agnes Klug, SSND, interview by Mary Jo Maloney, April 3, 1973, transcript, OHP.

42. Miriam Kivlighan, SSND, interview by Barbara Gross, March 26, 1973, transcript, OHP.

43. *Chron.*, September 14, 1920; September 16, 1925.

44. Porter E. Sargent, *A Handbook of the Best Private Schools of the United States and Canada, Sixth Edition, 1920–1921* (Boston: Porter E. Sargent, 1920), 258–59.

45. Elizabeth A. Colton, "Standards of Southern Colleges for Women," *School Review* 20 (September 1912): 460.

46. President's Report, 1945–46, NDMA. The preparatory school admitted boarding students until 1939.

47. "Resident Student Department," single-page typescript, n.d. (ca. 1946–47), NDMA; President's Report, 1945–46, NDMA; *Chron.*, September 19, 1946.

48. President's Report, 1950–51; minutes, advisory board, May 21, 1951, NDMA; minutes, advisory board, May 27, 1957, NDMA; *Chron.*, October 15, 1954.

49. President's Report, 1960–61.

50. Margaret Mary O'Connell to Archbishop Francis Keough, March 19, 1956, ABA.

51. Minutes, board of directors, September 8, 1958, NDMA.

52. See Margaret Mary O'Connell, *Report of the CND of MD for the Year 1956–57*, NDMA.

53. *NDM Catalog*, 1969–70.

54. "Regarding College Corporation," typescript, October 19, 1964, NDMA.

55. Minutes, board of directors, March 2, 1957. Filed with the minutes are a "bill of sale"; a Thompson, Grace and Mays survey of the "Property of Notre Dame College, Baltimore, Md., 17 April 1954"; and "Notes and Comments to Accompany Pro Forma Balance Sheet as at April 30, 1957," NDMA.

56. George W. Constable to district director of the Internal Revenue Service, Baltimore, May 23, 1957, NDMA.

57. George W. Constable, interview by PM, April 25, 1989, transcript, OHP.

58. The 1960s and 1970s brought significant change. A 1977 poll of 119 institutions reported that laity constituted 62 percent of the total membership of their boards of trustees. See William P. Leahy, *Adapting to America: Catholics, Jesuits and Higher Education in the Twentieth Century* (Washington, DC: Georgetown University Press, 1991), 105–6.

59. Minutes, advisory board, May 27, 1957, NDMA.

60. *Chron.*, August 31, 1957. The loan came through the Housing and Home Finance Agency (HHFA). The Department of Housing and Urban Development superseded the HHFA in 1965.

61. Margaret Mary O'Connell to Archbishop Francis Keough, December 10, 1957, NDMA.

62. Archbishop Francis Keough to Margaret Mary O'Connell, December 13, 1957, NDMA.

63. Minutes, board of trustees, March 31, 1958, NDMA.

64. *Chron.*, November 20, 1958.

65. Margaret Mary O'Connell to Archbishop Francis Keough, February 24, 1959, NDMA.

66. *Chron.*, October 15, 1960. This figure excludes 82 novices and junior sisters who were full-time day students residing at the Bellona Avenue motherhouse, and 321 part-time students, most of them sisters, enrolled in Saturday and summer extension programs. The full-time equivalent enrollment in October 1960 for all categories of students was 706.

67. President's Report, 1963–64, NDMA.

68. Margaret Mary O'Connell to Archbishop Francis Keough, February 24, 1959; minutes, advisory board, May 25, 1959, NDMA.

69. Minutes, board of directors, March 23, 1959, NDMA.

70. President's Report, 1961–62, minutes, advisory board, November 29, 1961, NDMA.

71. Minutes, board of directors, February 13, 1962, NDMA.

72. Minutes, board of directors, November 5, 1962; minutes, advisory board, November 21, 1962, NDMA.

73. "Church Colleges Target in Aid Suit," *New York Times*, September 11, 1963.

74. For more on conflicts in the decades 1930–60, see John McGreevy, "Thinking on One's Own: Catholicism in the American Intellectual Imagination, 1928–1960," *Journal of American History* 84 (June 1997): 97–131.

75. A second POAU concern at this time related to President Truman's public support for a US representative to the Vatican. See "Religion: The Wall of Separation," *Time*, February 7, 1949: "Last week a militant group of U.S. clergymen and laymen met in Washington and set out to raise $1,000,000 'to resist the declared purposes of the Roman Catholic Church further to breach the wall of separation between church and state.' The organization, called Protestants and Other Americans United (for the Separation of Church and State), was holding its first big meeting since its founding a year ago (*Time*, Jan. 19, 1948). Main purpose of the conference was to launch a nationwide drive for members, with pamphlets, radio broadcasts and mass meetings scheduled for Atlanta, Cincinnati, St. Louis and other cities."

76. President's Report, 1963–64, minutes, advisory board, November 25, 1964, NDMA; "Suit Challenges State Aid to 4 Colleges," *Baltimore Evening Sun*, September 10, 1963; "817 Colleges Found to Have Church Ties," *New York Times*, December 8, 1964.

77. Pfeffer (1910–93) had gained national recognition for his book *Church, State, and Freedom* (Boston: Beacon, 1953). See Joseph R. Preville, "Leo Pfeffer and the American Church-State Debate: A Confrontation with Catholicism," *Journal of Church and State* 33, no. 1 (1991): 37–53.

78. Briscoe, "Bryn Mawr College Traditions," 2:913.

79. Hugh Hawkins, "Charles W. Eliot, University Reform, and Religious Faith in America, 1869–1909," *Journal of American History* 51 (September 1964): 210.

80. Alice K. Fallows, "Self-Government for College Girls," *Harper's Bazaar*, July 1904.

81. Nancy V. McClelland, "College Life at Vassar," *National Magazine*, October 1897.

82. Lyman P. Powell, "Religious Influences in College Life at Smith, Vassar, Bryn Mawr and Wellesley," *Good Housekeeping*, April 1911.

83. See Margaret Farrand Thorp, *Neilson of Smith* (New York: Oxford University Press, 1956), 264; Harriet M. Allyn, "The Trend of Mount Holyoke's Educational Policy," *Mount Holyoke Alumnae Quarterly*, April 1930; Jeanette Eaton, "The College Girl of 1930," *Woman's Journal*, May 1930; Grace E. Hawk, *Pembroke College in Brown University: The First Seventy-Five Years, 1891–1966* (Providence, RI: Brown University Press, 1967), 161, 241.

84. "Bryn Mawr Girls Tell Why They Chose This School in Preference to Others—How They Study and Play," *New York Times*, March 10, 1912.

85. On Radcliffe, see Andrea Turpin, *A New Moral Vision: Gender, Religion, and the Changing Purposes of American Higher Education, 1837–1917* (Ithaca, NY: Cornell University Press, 2016), 301n23.

86. *NDM Catalog*, 1895–96, 43.

87. *NDM Catalog*, 1910–11, 36.

88. Virgina Geiger, SSND, interview by Barbara Gross, March 27, 1973, transcript, OHP.

89. Helen Burr-Brand to Sister David, November 9, 1944, NDMA. See also Dorothy Brown, Margaret Steinhagen, and Josephine Trueschler, "Marikle Chapel of the Annunciation: College of Notre Dame of Maryland," December 2002, NDMA. In 1903, a papal decree threatened that cherished benefit. "Singers in church have a real liturgical office," declared Pope Pius X. "Therefore women, being incapable of exercising such office, cannot be admitted to form part of the choir" (*Inter sollicitudines*, para. 13). Mixed congregational singing was not affected by the edict. Yet no one could remember when women and girls had not sung in Catholic churches worldwide. In the 1820s, Caroline Gerhardinger (later Mother Theresa) taught in a girls' school in Stadtamhof, Bavaria, where "three times a week the student choir sang the High Mass in the Church of Saint Magnus" (Mary David Cameron, *The College of Notre Dame of Maryland, 1895–1945* [New York: Declan X. McMullen, 1947], 14). By the turn of the twentieth century, however, mixed choirs were commonplace in the United States, and the ban on women stunned bishops, clergy, and parishioners alike. In 1908, Rome emphatically rejected Pittsburgh bishop Regis Canevin's modest suggestion that Rome allow separate women's choirs. "The Holy Father has not given permission for women to form part of the church choirs in the United States," replied Cardinal Merry Del Val (Canevin to Vatican Secretary of State Cardinal Merry Del Val, November 14, 1908; Del Val to Canevin, November 29, 1908, reprinted in Carlo Rossini, "Women in Church Choirs," *The Caecilia: Monthly Magazine of Catholic Church and School Music* 61 [June 1935]: 325–26). With no support for the decree at the grassroots level, few bishops in the United States tried to enforce it. However, it remained in place until 1955 when Pope Pius XII reversed it: "A group of men and women or girls, located in a place outside the sanctuary set apart for the exclusive use of the group, can sing the liturgical texts at Solemn Mass, as long as the men are completely separated from the women and girls" (Pius XII, *Musicae sacrae disciplina*, 74). On the question of

women's "proper place" in church music in other religious denominations, see Sophie Drinker, *Music and Women: The Story of Women in Their Relation to Music* (New York: Coward-McCann, 1948).

90. Briscoe, "Bryn Mawr College Traditions," 2:873.

91. *Chron.*, May 2, 1918.

92. "Dramatics," *Damozel*, 1926.

93. "As It's Told Unofficially," *Damozel*, 1925.

94. "SA Assembly—Founded in a Great Tradition," n.d. (ca. November 1953), BMEP.

95. [Bridget Marie Engelmeyer?], "Commencement Traditions," typescript, n.d. (ca. 1953), BMEP; *Arras*, 1959. For an interesting discussion of the rise in popularity of Marian devotions in the midcentury United States, see Thomas A. Kselman and Steven Avella, "Marian Piety and the Cold War in the United States," *Catholic Historical Review* 72, no. 3 (July 1986): 403–24.

96. "Class Day at Smith College," *Republican* (Springfield, MA), June 21, 1898.

97. Hawk, *Pembroke College*, 62–63.

98. Bridget Marie Engelmeyer, handwritten notes, n.d. (ca. 1951–55), BMEP.

99. "Sacred Heart Sodality Notes," *Damozel*, 1924.

100. *Chron.*, October 2, 1930; "Delegates Report Mission Convention," *Columns*, October 27, 1937. The National Catholic Students' Mission Crusade ended in 1970. See David J. Endres, *American Crusade: Catholic Youth in the World Mission Movement from World War I through Vatican II* (Eugene, OR: Pickwick, 2010). The Student Volunteer Movement declined after World War I. See Nathan D. Showalter, *The End of a Crusade: The Student Volunteer Movement for Foreign Missions and the Great War* (Lanham, MD: Scarecrow, 1997).

101. Minutes, Our Lady's Mission Unit, May 16, 1919, NDMA. See John T. Gillard, "The Work of the Baltimore Crusaders," *Shield*, March 1927.

102. Minutes, Our Lady's Mission Unit, May 16, 1919; February 8, 1920; April 25, 1920; March 14, 1921; Report of Literature Committee, Mission Society of Notre Dame of Maryland, May 1920, all in NDMA; "Mission Notes," *Damozel*, 1924; "5,000 Attend Mass and All-Day Rally," *Baltimore Sun*, May 22, 1925.

103. Sister Mary David Cameron, Sodality of Our Lady, Report to the President, 1936–1937, June 21, 1937, NDMA.

104. Dorothy Brown, interview by PM, May 16, 1989, transcript, OHP. However, when student interest in campus clubs, religious clubs in particular, plummeted in the 1960s, Our Lady's Sodality ceased to exist. Encounter, a religion club focused on social action that replaced the Sodality and the Mission Unit, attracted few members. See *Chron.*, November 11, 1965; December 14, 1965.

105. *NDM Catalog*, 1935–36.

106. *NDM Catalog*, 1936–37.

107. Elizabeth Morrissy, *CND: Its History, Curriculum and Academic Standing*, pamphlet reprint of WCBM radio speech, May 20, 1937, NDMA.

108. *NDM Catalog*, 1941–42.

109. *Chron.*, October 26, 1934.

110. For a valuable discussion of the development of Catholic Action in the mid-twentieth century, see Debra Campbell, "The Heyday of Catholic Action and the Lay

Apostolate, 1929–1959," in *Transforming Parish Ministry: The Changing Roles of Catholic Clergy, Laity, and Women Religious*, by Jay P. Dolan, R. Scott Appleby, Patricia Byrne, and Debra Campbell (New York: Crossroad, 1989), 222–52. Unlike at the College of Notre Dame, students at Trinity College (Washington, DC) and Rosary College (Illinois) participated actively in Catholic Evidence Guild activities (Campbell, "Heyday," 235).

111. "Co-op Functions for Democracy," *Columns*, February 21, 1939.

112. "Traditions," typescript, n.d., BMEP.

113. Sister M. Dominic Ramacciotti, "The Correlation of Italian and Religion," typescript, June 4, 1940, NDMA.

114. For an interesting account of how the secularization of elite Protestant colleges affected the place and role of campus "sacred spaces," see Margaret Grubiak, *White Elephants on Campus: The Decline of the University Chapel in America, 1920–1960* (Notre Dame, IN: University of Notre Dame Press, 2014).

115. Regina Soria, interview by PM, February 20, 1989, transcript, OHP.

116. *Chron.*, April 20, 1947.

117. Jean Schramm Monier, interview by PM, April 27, 1989, transcript, OHP.

118. "Student Associations," *Arras*, 1950.

119. Mary Lou (Schroeder) McNeal '50, interview with the author, May 21, 1996. McNeal later directed the college's Ethel Clay Price Continuing Education Program (1972) and its Renaissance Institute (1989).

120. See Joan Long Lynch, "The Catholic Women's Colleges and the NSA," in *American Students Organize: Founding the National Student Association after World War II*, ed. Eugene G. Schwartz (Westport, CT: Greenwood, 2006), 493–95.

121. *NDM Catalog*, 1952–53.

122. "Curriculum," *Arras*, 1951.

123. "Outcomes Study, Graduates, 1949–1958, College of Notre Dame, 1959," NDMA.

124. "Outcomes Study."

125. Margaret Mary O'Connell, "Data Presented for Consideration of the Commission on Institutions of Higher Education, MSA, 4 December 1959," NDMA.

126. Gainer E. Bryan Jr., "Church Colleges Deny Control by Religion," *Baptist Press* (news service of the Southern Baptist Convention), December 11, 1964.

127. Charles H. Wilson, "Catholic Colleges and Civil Law, Benefits and Burdens," in *Trying Times: Essays on Catholic Higher Education in the 20th Century*, ed. William M. Shea and Daniel Van Slyke (Atlanta: Scholars Press, 1999), 9.

128. Peter J. Harrington, "Civil and Canon Law Issues Affecting American Catholic Higher Education, 1948–1998: An Overview and the ACCU Perspective," *Journal of College and University Law* 26 (Summer 1999): 74.

129. *Horace Mann League*. Saint Joseph in Emmitsburg, a women's college, closed in 1973. Hood, a women's college, became coeducational in 2003. See Joseph B. Robison, "Summary and Analysis of Maryland Court of Appeals Decision on State Aid to Church Colleges: Horace Mann League v. Board of Public Works of Maryland," *Journal of Church and State* 3 (1966): 401–14.

130. Margaret Mary O'Connell, "Data Presented for Consideration."

131. *Chron.*, March 25, 1901.

132. *Susurrus*, March 29, 1915.

133. *Collegian*, March 29, 1926.

134. President's Report, minutes, advisory board, May 18, 1953, NDMA.

135. President's Report, minutes, advisory board, May 18, 1953, NDMA; "Annunciation Day, 1953 Program," BMEP.

136. *Chron.*, March 25, 1965.

137. *Chron.*, March 25, 1966.

138. *Chron.*, March 25, 1968; "Notre Dame Day Program, March 25, 1968," Scrapbook (Art Department) Album, 1957–69, NDMA.

139. The revival of the holiday came at faculty initiative. See *Chron.*, October 18, 1988.

140. Minutes, advisory board, joint meeting of advisory board and the College Science Council, March 15, 1964, NDMA.

141. Henry J. Knott to Archbishop Lawrence Shehan, November 16, 1964, ABA. This episcopal intervention was successful.

142. *Chron.*, January 8, 1966.

143. George W. Constable, interview by PM, April 25, 1989, transcript, OHP.

144. Tilton v. Richardson, 403 U.S. 672 (1971). See Joseph R. Preville, "Catholic Colleges, the Courts, and the Constitution: A Tale of Two Cases," *Church History* 58 (June 1989): 197–210. On Catholic institutions and the GI Bill, see Elizabeth A. Edmondson, "Without Comment or Controversy: The G.I. Bill and Catholic Colleges," *Church History* 71 (December 2002): 820–47.

145. *Chron.*, May 28, 1971.

146. The ACLU of Maryland, formed in 1931, was an affiliate of the national ACLU, established in 1920.

147. Roemer et al. v. Board of Public Works of Maryland et al., 387 F.Supp. 1282 (D. Md. 1974).

148. Harrington, "Civil and Canon Law Issues," 101.

149. Wilson, "Catholic Colleges and Civil Law," 29–30.

150. Francis Regis Carton, SSND, interview by PM, April 4, 1989, transcript, OHP.

151. *Chron.*, April 29, 1977.

152. "Students—Suggestions & Opinions 1960s—(Response Rate Not Indicated)," n.d., NDMA.

153. *Chron.*, February 14, 1964.

154. President's Report, 1964–65, NDMA.

155. *Chron.*, March 6, 1965.

156. *NDM Catalog*, 1972–73.

157. Minutes, board of directors, March 23, 1959, NDMA.

158. Donald Bremner, "Notre Dame Head Says Oath Not a Directive," *Baltimore Sun*, December 11, 1964; Donald Bremner, "Teachers at Trial Deny Religious Bias," *Baltimore Sun*, December 8, 1964.

159. Elizabeth Morrissy, interview by Barbara Gross, May 2, 1973, transcript, OHP.

160. William W. Bassett, "The American Civil Corporation, the 'Incorporation Movement' and the Canon Law of the Catholic Church," *Journal of College and University Law* 25, no. 4 (1999): 721–50; "Roman Catholicism: A Louder Voice for Laymen," *Time*, February 3, 1967. On the Webster College case, see "Freeing the Catholic College from Juridical Control by the Church," *Journal of Higher Education* 40 (February 1969): 101–7; Philip Gleason, *Contending with Modernity: Catholic Higher Education in*

the Twentieth Century (New York: Oxford University Press, 1995), 314–15; and Anthony J. Dosen, "The Intentional Secularization of a Denominational College: The Case of Webster College," *Journal of Research on Christian Education* 10 (Fall 2001): 379–408.

161. Quoted in Gleason, *Contending with Modernity*, 317. See also Paul A. FitzGerald, *The Governance of Jesuit Colleges in the United States, 1920–1970* (Notre Dame, IN: University of Notre Dame Press, 1984), 213; and Bassett, "American Civil Corporation," 721–50. For a useful discussion of the impact of the Land O' Lakes Statement, see Patricia Wittberg, *From Piety to Professionalism—and Back? Transformations of Organized Religious Virtuosity* (Lanham, MD: Lexington Books, 2006), 118–21.

162. Henry J. Knott to Margaret Mary O'Connell, March 27, 1967, NDMA.

163. In her letter of resignation, submitted to the full board of trustees on April 22, 1968, O'Connell gave poor health as the reason for her decision. Privately, she confessed that the decision "was determined" for her. Margaret Mary O'Connell, SSND, interview by Charles Ritter, April 10, 1973, transcript, OHP. See also Margaret Mary O'Connell to Mother Provincial Mary Maurice Kelly, March 30, 1968, NDMA.

164. *Chron.*, July 5, 1968; minutes, board of trustees, February 17, 1971, NDMA. Elissa McGuire (1912–2005) entered the order in 1938 and earned degrees from the College of Notre Dame (BA, 1945), Johns Hopkins University (MA, 1952) and Fordham University (PhD, 1963). She managed the college endowment fund (1943–82) and retired from the faculty in 1988.

165. *Chron.*, February 14, 1975.

166. Minutes, board of trustees, February 25, 1977; *Chron.*, February 28, 1977, NDMA; minutes, President's Council, December 12, 1977, NDMA.

167. "CND, Inc., Articles of Amendment, October 25, 1977," NDMA. By 1981, the local leader of the religious community no longer sat on the board of trustees. See *Chron.*, May 14, 1981. By this time, the title "leader" had replaced the traditional title "superior."

168. Harrington, "Civil and Canon Law Issues," 68. For a full account of this exceptional event, see John W. O'Malley, *What Happened at Vatican II* (Cambridge, MA: Harvard University Press, 2008).

6. "Convent Colleges"

1. "Editorial Copy: The Education of Girls," *Southern Review of Commerce*, news clipping, n.d. (ca. 1890s), NDMA.

2. On British women's colleges in this era, see Elizabeth Edwards, "Educational Institutions or Extended Families? The Reconstruction of Gender in Women's Colleges in the Late Nineteenth and Early Twentieth Centuries," *Gender and Education* 2, no. 1 (1990): 23.

3. Mabel Newcomer, *A Century of Higher Education for American Women* (New York: Harper & Brothers, 1959), 18.

4. *NDM Catalog*, 1913–14; *NDM Catalog*, 1915–16.

5. *NDM Catalog*, 1910–11.

6. Debra Herman, "College and After: The Vassar Experiment in Women's Education, 1861–1924" (PhD diss., Stanford University, 1979), 166.

7. John Lukacs, *A Sketch of the History of Chestnut Hill College, 1924–1974* (Philadelphia: Chestnut Hill College, 1975), 10n4.

8. Ave M. Burns, "On Bells," *Damozel*, 1936.

9. Zerline Stauf, "In Retrospect and Reflection," n.d., RC.

10. Adele (Mohlenrich) Hicks '17, untitled reminiscence of Notre Dame, n.d., RC; "One Week," *Damozel*, 1925.

11. *NDM Catalog*, 1912–13.

12. Sister Frances Smith, "Notre Dame's Sister Mary Meletia," *Centenary Inter-Provincial News Letter*, April 1947.

13. Ruth (Jenkins) Bristor, interview by PM, April 13, 1989, transcript, OHP. Jenkins, who arrived at Notre Dame as a fifth grader in 1915, attended the preparatory school and graduated from the college in 1926.

14. Bridget Marie Engelmeyer, "For Announcement of a Scholarship to Be Named for Sister Mary," typescript, November 3, 1978, BMEP.

15. Maron Talbot, "Dormitory Life for College Women," *Journal of Home Economics* 2 (November 1910): 491. See Sherrie A. Inness, *Intimate Communities: Representation and Social Transformation in Women's College Fiction, 1895–1910* (Bowling Green, OH: Bowling Green State University Popular Press, 1995), 23–30.

16. Margaret B. Vickery, *Buildings for Bluestockings: The Architecture and Social History of Women's Colleges in Late Victorian England* (Newark: University of Delaware Press, 2000).

17. Helen Lefkowitz Horowitz, "Designing for the Genders: Curricula and Architecture at Scripps College and the California Institute of Technology," *Pacific Historical Review* 54 (November 1985): 454, 461. See also Helen Lefkowitz Horowitz, *Alma Mater: Design and Experience in the Women's Colleges from Their Nineteenth-Century Beginnings to the 1930s* (New York: Alfred A. Knopf, 1984).

18. "Narrative History of Campus Landscape Master Plan, Smith College," Historic Campus Architecture Project, Council of Independent Colleges, 2006, Artstor.

19. Although the College of Saint Angela, renamed the College of New Rochelle (New York) in 1910, developed a "cottage system," this was only because it did not yet have the funds to build a suitable large residence hall. Tracy Mitrano, "Against the Odds: Mother Irene Gill and the Founding of the College of New Rochelle," *History of Higher Education Annual* 7 (1987): 87.

20. J. Thomas Scharf, *The Natural & Industrial Resources and Advantages of Maryland* (Annapolis, MD: C. H. Baughman, 1892), 26. Scharf, a real estate broker and local historian, had aided the Adams brothers in finding and buying the Charles Street property for the School Sisters of Notre Dame. See Julia A. Sienkewicz, *Historic American Buildings Survey: Addendum to Evergreen (Evergreen Museum & Library)*, National Park Service (Washington, DC: U.S. Department of the Interior, 2009), 72n150, http://lcweb2.loc.gov/master/pnp/habshaer/md/md1600/md1633/data/md1633data.pdf.

21. Louise S. B. Saunders, "Government of Women Students in Colleges and Universities," *Educational Review* 20 (December 1900): 493–95.

22. Saunders, "Government of Women Students," 497.

23. "Unwritten Laws at Smith: Rules Which Govern the Attitude of the Students in Various Matters of Importance," news clipping, unknown publication, ca. 1900, Social Regulations File No. 34, Smith College Archives, Northampton, MA.

24. Gail Apperson Kilman, "Southern Collegiate Women: Higher Education at Wesleyan Female College and Randolph-Macon Woman's College, 1893–1907" (PhD diss., University of Delaware, 1984), 67. Wesleyan Female College became Wesleyan College in 1917.

25. Alice K. Fallows, "Self-Government for College Girls," *Harper's Bazaar*, July 1904.

26. Frances T. Marburg, "The Social Life of Vassar Students," Special Number, *Vassar Miscellany*, October 1915.

27. Until 1904 this rule was printed in the college catalog.

28. Doris Kilkoff (Butler) '99, quoted in Anne Philbin, *The Past and the Promised: A History of the Alumnae Association, College of Notre Dame of Maryland, Baltimore, Maryland* (Baltimore: Alumnae Association, College of Notre Dame of Maryland, 1959), 53.

29. Jeanette Eaton, "The College Girl of 1930," *Woman's Journal*, May 1930.

30. In 1944, the college hired a former house mother at Smith College "to supervise the College resident students at night." See *Chron.*, September 17, 1944.

31. *Chron.*, November 11, 1923. For other examples of lay chaperoning in this decade, see *Chron.*, November 12, 1923; February 7, 1924; February 18, 1924; March 14, 1924; March 17, 1924.

32. "N.D.C. Dictionary," *Damozel*, 1923.

33. Margaret H. Welch, "Life at Vassar College," *Harper's Bazar*, December 8, 1900.

34. *Chron.*, June 13, 1899; "Class Day at Notre Dame: Gold Medals and Prizes Awarded in Various Studies," *Baltimore Sun*, June 11, 1902; *Chron.*, June 4, 1906.

35. *Chron.*, November 3, 1906.

36. "Class of 1940 Receives Caps and Gowns," *Columns*, January 22, 1937.

37. Bridget Marie Engelmeyer, handwritten notes, n.d. (ca. 1942), BMEP.

38. "Dominican to Deliver Baccalaureate Sermon," *Columns*, May 27, 1936; "Sophomores," *Arras*, 1950; [Bridget Marie Engelmeyer?], "Commencement Traditions," typescript, n.d. (ca. 1953), BMEP; *Chron.*, May 18, 1982.

39. Josephine Trueschler '49, interview by PM, May 11, 1989, transcript, OHP. Trueschler (MEd, Johns Hopkins University, 1954) later joined the Notre Dame faculty.

40. Ken Gewertz, "Women Wearing Beards," *Harvard University Gazette*, November 21, 2002.

41. *Chron.*, May 31, 1907.

42. "Dramatics: 'The Play Folk,'" *Notre Dame Quarterly*, November 1916; "Notre Dame Ends First Fifty Years," *Columns*, April 19, 1945; Kathleen Marie Engers, SSND, interview by PM, May 30, 1989, transcript, OHP.

43. Saunders, "Government of Women Students," 497.

44. "Calendar for 1923–24," *Damozel*, 1924.

45. Elizabeth Morrissy, interview by Barbara Gross, May 2, 1973, transcript, OHP.

46. "Society News, May 30, 1923," *Damozel*, 1923; "Calendar of Events," *Damozel*, 1927.

47. "Emily Travers Welsh, 25 October 1992, Part I," 72, RC.

48. Nancy Sahli, "Smashing: Women's Relationships before the Fall," *Chrysalis* 17 (Summer 1979): 22.

49. Margaret Kelly, "Traditions of New Rochelle," in *Souvenir of the Silver Jubilee, College of New Rochelle, June 1929* (Albany, NY: Brandow, 1929), 23.

50. Carrie A. Harper, "A Feminine Professorial Viewpoint," *Educational Review* 46 (June 1913): 47.

51. See Horowitz, *Alma Mater*, 282–83.

52. *Susurrus*, March 29, 1915, NDMA.

53. Ruth (Jenkins) Bristor, interview by PM, April 13, 1989, transcript, OHP.

54. "N.D.C. Dictionary." For more on this subject, see Inness, *Intimate Communities*, 45–67.

55. William L. Felter, "The Education of Women," *Educational Review* 31 (April 1906): 360; Patricia A. Palmieri, "From Republican Motherhood to Race Suicide: Arguments on the Higher Education of Women in the United States, 1820–1920," in *Educating Men and Women Together: Coeducation in a Changing World*, ed. Carol Lasser (Champaign: University of Illinois Press, 1987), 49–64.

56. Roswell Johnson and Bertha Stutzmann, "Wellesley's Birth-Rate," *Journal of Heredity* 6 (June 1915): 250.

57. Virginia Crocheron Gildersleeve, Marion Edwards Park, Mary E. Woolley, Ada L. Comstock, William Allan Neilson, Henry Noble MacCracken, and Ellen F. Pendleton, "The Question of the Women's Colleges," *Atlantic Monthly*, November 1927. On the marriage question in the 1870–1920 era, see Barbara Solomon, *In the Company of Educated Women: A History of Women and Higher Education in America* (New Haven, CT: Yale University Press, 1985), 115–40.

58. Mary Louis Whalen, SSND, interview by PM, March 3, 1989, transcript, OHP.

59. Elizabeth Morrissy, interview by Barbara Gross, May 2, 1973, transcript, OHP.

60. *Chron.*, January 11, 1926; *Collegian*, March 18, 1926; "Traditions," typescript, n.d., BMEP; Cynthia Farr Brown, "Leading Women: Female Leadership in American Women's Higher Education" (PhD diss., Brandeis University, 1992), 366.

61. Horowitz, "Designing for the Genders," 439–61.

62. Josephine Trueschler, interview by PM, May 11, 1989, transcript, OHP.

63. *Damozel*, 1924; *Damozel*, 1936.

64. Report of Inspection of College of Notre Dame of Maryland, Baltimore, Md., for MSA, February 13–14, 1950, NDMA. Some married women may also have had professional careers.

65. "Survey Reveals Wide Views on Religious Vocation Idea," *Columns*, April 20, 1943. The survey response rate was 38 percent.

66. "Features," *Arras*, 1951; Patricia Wittberg, *From Piety to Professionalism—and Back? Transformations of Organized Religious Virtuosity* (Lanham, MD: Lexington Books, 2006), 76.

67. *Chron.*, October 27, 1940; Sheila D. F. Haskell, interview by PM, May 15, 1989, transcript, OHP.

68. *Chron.*, April 9, 1948.

69. David R. Contosta, "The Philadelphia Story: Life at Immaculata, Rosemont, and Chestnut Hill," in *Catholic Women's Colleges in America*, ed. Tracy Schier and Cynthia Russett (Baltimore: Johns Hopkins University Press, 2002), 150, attributes the policy to qualms about "mixed marriages."

70. Newcomer, *Century of Higher Education*, 218, citing Patricia W. Cautley, *AAUW Members Look at College Education: An Interim Report* (Washington, DC: American Association of University Women, 1949). Notre Dame graduates were not part of this study, since the college was not admitted to AAUW membership until 1951.

71. "Outcomes Study, Graduates, 1949–1958, College of Notre Dame, 1959," NDMA.

72. *NDM Catalog*, 1921–22.

73. *NDM Catalog*, 1925–26.

74. See "Students—Suggestions & Opinions 1960s—(Response Rate Not Indicated)," n.d., NDMA. See also Marie Michelle Walsh, SSND, interview by PM, April 4, 1989, transcript, OHP; and Alexandra Stanley, "The Way It Was at Radcliffe," *New York Times*, June 7, 1992.

75. Eaton, "College Girl of 1930." On Radcliffe and Harvard, see Karen Lepri, "'Clothes Make the Man': Cross-Dressing on the Radcliffe Stage," in *Yards and Gates*, ed. Laurel Thatcher Ulrich (New York: Palgrave Macmillan, 2004), 153–54.

76. In the 1930s, women from Rosemont College near Philadelphia were playing female roles in productions at local Catholic men's colleges; the arrangement was reciprocal. See Contosta, "Philadelphia Story," 150.

77. President's Report, 1957–58, minutes, advisory board, May 26, 1958, NDMA.

78. "Education: Goucher's Dignity," *Time*, December 16, 1929.

79. Margaret Farrand Thorp, *Neilson of Smith* (New York: Oxford University Press, 1956), 249.

80. Eaton, "College Girl of 1930." See Grace E. Hawk, *Pembroke College in Brown University: The First Seventy-Five Years, 1891–1966* (Providence, RI: Brown University Press, 1967), 121, 161.

81. See M. Madeleva Wolff, *My First Seventy Years* (New York: Macmillan, 1959), 97; Brown, "Leading Women," 371.

82. *Chron.*, September 23, 1940. See also Miriam Kivlighan, SSND, interview by Barbara Gross, March 26, 1973, transcript, OHP.

83. Kathleen Marie Engers, SSND, interview by PM, May 30, 1989, transcript, OHP.

84. *Chron.*, May 17, 1945; May 21, 1945.

85. See "Sing Song," *Columns*, April 19, 1945.

86. Virginia Wolf Briscoe, "Bryn Mawr College Traditions: Women's Rituals as Expressive Behavior" (PhD diss., University of Pennsylvania, 1981), 2:504–5.

87. Welch, "Life at Vassar College." See also Mary E. Ross, "The Students' Association of Vassar College: An Experiment in Democracy," Special Number, *Vassar Miscellany*, October 1915.

88. Alice K. Fallows, "Self-Government for College Girls," *Harper's Bazaar*, July 1904.

89. Saunders, "Government of Women Students," 49.

90. "Student Self-Government," *Newcomb Arcade*, January 1909.

91. Kelly, "Traditions of New Rochelle," 28–29.

92. Mary B. Syron, "A History of Four Catholic Women's Colleges," (MA thesis, University of Detroit, 1956), 77; Sister Columba Mullaly, *Trinity College, Washington, D.C.: The First Eighty Years, 1897–1977* (Westminster, MD: Christian Classics, 1987), 324, 563–70.

93. Wolff, *My First Seventy Years*, 96. See also Mary E. Friel, "History of Emmanuel College, 1919–1974" (PhD diss., Boston College, 1980), 31.

94. "On Your Honor," *Columns*, May 27, 1936.

95. "Editorial," *Columns*, January 24, 1936.

96. *Chron.*, September 24, 1937. See *NDM Catalog*, 1940–41. On Daniel Lord's life and career, see Stephen Werner, "Daniel A. Lord, SJ: A Forgotten Catholic Dynamo of the Early Twentieth Century," *American Catholic Studies* 129, no. 2 (2018): 39–58. Lord,

who had introduced student government at Saint Louis University late in the 1910s, lent considerable weight to the campaign of Notre Dame student leaders.

97. "N.D. Leaders Form Student Council," *Columns*, October 27, 1937; "History of the College of Notre Dame of Maryland," *Arras*, 1954.

98. "Editorial," *Columns*, April 30, 1938.

99. *NDM Catalog*, 1946–47; *NDM Catalog*, 1949–50.

100. "SA Assembly—Founded in a Great Tradition," n.d. (ca. November 1953), BMEP; *Chron.*, March 19, 1948; May 14, 1948.

101. See Bridget Marie Engelmeyer, handwritten notes, February 8, 1952 (on honor system); May 15, 1952 (on student rating of courses), BMEP. See also "Students—Suggestions & Opinions."

102. *NDM Catalog*, 1944–45.

103. Bridget Marie Engelmeyer, SSND, interview by PM, May 5, 1989, transcript, OHP.

104. "This College in Our Hearts," student assembly presentation, November 1955, 20, BMEP.

105. "Student Associations," *Arras*, 1950.

106. Bridget Marie Engelmeyer, SSND, interview by PM, May 30, 1989, transcript, OHP. College administrators settled problematic cases.

107. Catharine Stimpson, "Women at Bryn Mawr," *Change*, April 1974; Dorothy Brown, interview by PM, May 16, 1989, transcript, OHP.

108. *Chron.*, October 15, 1969; May 6, 1970.

109. "N.D.C. Dictionary."

110. *NDM Catalog*, 1937–38; *NDM Catalog*, 1938–39.

111. Marie Xavier Looymans, SSND, interview by PM, March 13, 1989, transcript, OHP. Yale College had a no-cuts policy during the war years; in 1945 it allowed students to cut three classes in each subject per semester.

112. See "Summary of Senior Curriculum Suggestions, 1960," typescript, filed with "Students—Suggestions & Opinions."

113. President's Report, 1962–63, minutes, advisory board, NDMA.

114. *Chron.*, November 14, 1962.

115. *Chron.*, January 21, 1965; *NDM Catalog*, 1965–66.

116. "Students—Suggestions & Opinions."

117. "Students—Suggestions & Opinions."

118. "Students—Suggestions & Opinions."

119. Louise M. Newman, "From Coordination to Coeducation: Pembrokers' Struggle for Social Equality," in *The Search for Equity: Women at Brown University, 1891–1991*, ed. Polly Welts Kaufman (Providence, RI: Brown University Press, 1991), 100.

120. "Statement from the Judicial Board, re Johns Hopkins University 'Open Dorm Policy,' 13 November 1966," BMEP. Johns Hopkins admitted women in 1970. See Julia B. Morgan, *Women at the Johns Hopkins University: A History* (Baltimore: Johns Hopkins University Press, 1986), 19.

121. Kathleen Feeley, interview with the author, April 16, 1996.

122. Sister Marie Michelle, dean of students, Annual Departmental Report, 1966–67; Report to the President, July 15, 1967, NDMA.

123. Bernice Feilinger, SSND, interview by PM, May 25, 1989, transcript, OHP. Most honor codes now focus on academic integrity, although they vary in regard to requiring proctored examinations and student reporting of observed infractions by

peers. Harvard College's first honor code, adopted in 2015, expects students to, as John S. Rosenberg puts it, "'affirm their *awareness*' (emphasis added) of the code, but not take an oath to accept the values it embodies or conform to its standards. . . . Students will not be compelled, or asked, to report on apparent violations by their peers." John S. Rosenberg, "On My Honor," *Harvard Magazine*, May–June 2014, 2.

124. See Mary J. Henold, *Catholic and Feminist: The Surprising History of the American Catholic Feminist Movement* (Chapel Hill: University of North Carolina Press, 2008).

125. Charles L. Mohr and Joseph W. Gordon, *Tulane: The Emergence of a Modern University, 1945–1980* (Baton Rouge: Louisiana State University Press, 2001), 46–47. Coeducational institutions regulated the social lives of female resident undergraduates to varying degrees. The University of Michigan did not officially eliminate curfew rules until 1970. See Ruth Bordin, *Women at Michigan: The 'Dangerous Experiment,' 1870s to the Present* (Ann Arbor: University of Michigan Press, 1999), 70–71.

126. Ann Blackman, *Seasons of Her Life: A Biography of Madeleine Korbel Albright* (New York: Simon & Schuster, 1998), 118.

127. Contosta, "Philadelphia Story," 145–46.

128. Susan L. Poulson, "From Single-Sex to Coeducation: The Advent of Coeducation at Georgetown, 1965–1975," *U.S. Catholic Historian* 13 (Fall 1995): 131.

129. Marie Michelle Walsh, SSND, interview by PM, April 4, 1989, transcript, OHP.

130. Bernice Feilinger, dean of students, to parents and guardians of resident students, August 1973, NDMA.

131. "Yesterday's News," *Harvard Magazine*, November–December 2011; Madeline W. Lissner, "Meet Me in My Room . . . but Not Past 7 p.m.," *Harvard Crimson*, June 3, 2006.

132. See Richard P. Edmonds, "College Increases Parietals," *Harvard Crimson*, June 13, 1968.

133. Donna Camiano, "Administration's View Accepted: Senate Sets Frosh Parietals," *Vassar Miscellany News*, May 2, 1969.

134. See *Chron.*, January 20, 1974; April 4, 1981.

135. Madeleine Doyle, SSND, interview by PM, February 9, 1989, transcript, OHP.

136. Ruth Miriam Carey, SSND, interview by PM, March 22, 1989, transcript, OHP.

137. "Students—Suggestions & Opinions."

138. Bernice Feilinger, SSND, interview by PM, May 25, 1989, transcript, OHP.

139. *NDM Catalog*, 1972–73.

140. Minutes, board of trustees, March 4, 1970, NDMA.

141. Student Association president to board of trustees, February 9, 1971, NDMA.

142. Kathleen Feeley to resident students, February 21, 1972, NDMA.

143. Parietals Question, 1972–73, NDMA.

144. Report on Parietal Forum, March 1, 1973; Parietals Question, 1972–73, NDMA. See also Frederic O. Musser, *The History of Goucher College, 1930–1985* (Baltimore: Johns Hopkins University Press, 1990), 159–60.

145. Kathleen Feeley to Francis Regis Carton, SSND, chairman, and members of the board of trustees, March 30, 1973, NDMA.

146. Letters File, March 1973, Parietals Question, 1972–73, NDMA. See also ". . . And Memories to Keep the Past Alive," *Today: College of Notre Dame of Maryland*, Winter 1981.

147. *Chron.*, April 13, 1973; Letters File, April 1973, Parietals Question, 1972–73, NDMA.

148. Report on Parietal Forum, March 1, 1973.

149. Kathleen Feeley to parents and guardians of students, April 6, 1973; minutes, board of trustees, April 27, 1973, NDMA.

150. Bernice Feilinger, SSND, dean of students, to parents and guardians of resident students, August 1973, NDMA.

151. Executive board, Parents and Friends Association, to Dear Parents, August 17, 1973, Parietals Question, 1972–73, NDMA.

152. Executive committee, Parents and Friends Association, to Kathleen Feeley, September 12, 1973, NDMA.

153. Kathleen Feeley to executive director, Parents and Friends Association, September 17, 1973, NDMA.

154. Parents and Friends Association executive committee to Francis Regis Carton, SSND, chair of the board of trustees; Kathleen Feeley, president; and members of the board of trustees, n.d. (ca. September 1973), Parietals Question, 1972–73, NDMA.

155. Letter to executive director, Parents and Friends Association, n.d. (ca. September 1973), Parietals Question, 1972–73, NDMA.

156. Progress Report of Parietals Committee, to Notre Dame Community—Faculty, Students, Parents of Students, from Kathleen Feeley, October 29, 1973, Parietals Question, 1972–73, NDMA.

157. Progress Report of Parietals Committee.

158. Executive board, Parents and Friends Association, to the board of trustees, December 4, 1973, NDMA; *Chron.*, December 7, 1973; Kathleen Feeley to parents and guardians of Notre Dame students, February 1, 1974, Parietals Question, 1972–73, NDMA.

159. Minutes, board of trustees, March 15, 1974, NDMA.

160. Minutes, board of trustees, December 10, 1976, NDMA.

161. Maureen Larkin Watson '55 to Kathleen Feeley, November 28, 1973, NDMA.

162. Minutes, board of trustees, September 6, 1974, NDMA.

163. *Arras*, 1981.

164. Minutes, board of trustees, March 24, 1983, NDMA; Musser, *History of Goucher College*, 160.

165. "Female College at Oxford Overrules Students to Admit Men," *Boston Globe*, June 5, 1992.

Conclusion

1. Mount Saint Agnes College was located on the sixty-eight-acre campus of the Sisters of Mercy Provincial House in Baltimore's Mount Washington section. The order sold the property in 1982 to the US Fidelity & Guarantee Company, a firm that later merged with the Saint Paul Companies. In 2003, Johns Hopkins University purchased the property. It is now known as Johns Hopkins at Mount Washington.

2. Chronically low enrollment forced Mount Saint Agnes College to close in 1918; the girls' academy remained open. When demand for two-year women's colleges rose in the 1930s, the defunct "college" reopened as Mount Saint Agnes Junior College.

A four-year program was developed in 1946, and three years later Mount Saint Agnes again awarded bachelor's degrees. By the 1970s, the college had merged with Loyola College. For more on Mount Saint Agnes, see Mary Jeremy Daigler, *Through the Windows: A History of the Work of Higher Education among the Sisters of Mercy of the Americas* (Scranton, PA: University of Scranton Press, 2000); M. Magdala Thompson, "A Brief History of Mount Saint Agnes College" (MA thesis, Loyola College Baltimore, 1959), esp. 49–51, 60–64. Joy Clough disputes Daigler's claim that Mount Saint Agnes was the first college founded by the Sisters of Mercy in the United States, maintaining that the distinction belongs to Georgian Court College (New Jersey, 1908). See Daigler, app. 2, 245; Joy Clough, *First in Chicago: A History of Saint Xavier University* (Chicago: Saint Xavier University, 1997), E-13, chap. 10, n. 6. For more on Mount Saint Agnes Academy, see Mary Loretto Costello, *The Sisters of Mercy in Maryland (1855–1930)* (Saint Louis, MO: Herder, 1931).

3. See W. Ray Smittle, "Catholic Colleges," *Journal of Higher Education* 7 (February 1936): 90. According to M. Mariella Bowler, "A History of Catholic Colleges for Women in the United States of America" (PhD diss., Catholic University of America, 1933), 90, women's colleges' average enrollment in 1932 was 185. Catholic women's colleges had an average enrollment of 117 in 1921. Most enrolled under 200 students; only one had at least 500 students in 1926. "College Survey Shows Women's Schools in Gain," *New World* (Chicago), December 3, 1926.

4. William P. Leahy, *Adapting to America: Catholics, Jesuits and Higher Education in the Twentieth Century* (Washington, DC: Georgetown University Press, 1991), 72. The College of Notre Dame had no trouble with accreditors, but it was roughly average in enrollment; in the fall of 1938, it had 215 students, while in 1943 the annalist excitedly proclaimed that "there are 100 freshmen!" *Chron.*, September 21, 1938; September 22, 1943.

5. Gene Currivan, "Catholics Debating Unplanned Growth of Small Colleges," *New York Times*, June 8, 1964.

6. Currivan, "Catholics Debating Unplanned Growth."

7. Currivan, "Catholics Debating Unplanned Growth."

8. Joanne Munoz, "The Adaptation of Catholic Women's Colleges to Changes in the Environment, 1970–1985" (PhD diss., University of Maryland, 1989), 1:76, referring to eastern institutions; Stacey Jones, "Dynamic Social Norms and the Unexpected Transformation of Women's Higher Education, 1965–75," *Social Science History* 33 (Fall 2009): 276–77, table 3, on Seven Sister enrollments.

9. Emily A. Langdon, "Women's Colleges Then and Now: Access Then, Equity Now," *Peabody Journal of Education* 76, no. 1 (2001): 8.

10. School Sisters of Notre Dame to T.J. Conaty, Rector, Catholic University, October 9, 1899, NDMA. Dean Meletia Foley drafted the letter.

11. Rita Watrin, *The Founding and Development of the Program of Affiliation of the CUA: 1912 to 1939* (Washington, DC: Catholic University of America Press, 1966), 18, quoting minutes, Catholic University of America trustees, October 11, 1899, Archives, Catholic University of America.

12. Thomas J. Conaty to Mother Superior (Theophila Bauer), October 28, 1899, NDMA.

13. Thomas J. Conaty to Theophila Bauer, June 13, 1900, NDMA.

14. Foley relied on the *Report of the United States Commissioner of Education, 1894–1895*; W. T. Harris, "Editor's Preface," in *Higher Education of Women in Europe*, ed. Helene Lange (New York: D. Appleton, 1890), v–xvii; and catalogs of prominent colleges.

15. [Meletia Foley] to Mgr. T. J. Conaty, n.d. (ca. June–July 1900), NDMA.

16. Watrin, *Founding and Development*, 18, quoting minutes, Catholic University of America trustees, October 10, 1900, Archives, Catholic University of America. See also "Colleges and High Schools Affiliated with the University," *Catholic Educational Review* 5 (May 1913): 417.

17. *Catholic Educational Review* 5 (May 1912): 445.

18. Loyola College became Loyola University Maryland in 2009; the College of Notre Dame became Notre Dame of Maryland University in 2011. See Nicholas Varga, *Baltimore's Loyola, Loyola's Baltimore, 1851–1986* (Baltimore: Maryland Historical Society, 1990), for a detailed history of the Jesuit institution.

19. "34 Are Graduated at Notre Dame," *Baltimore Sun*, June 4, 1931; "Loyola College to Graduate Class of 35 at Evergreen," *Baltimore Sun*, June 6, 1933.

20. Henri J. Wiesel to M. Philemon Doyle, October 14, 1928, BMEP. On Ledochowski's conservative position, see Paul A. FitzGerald, *The Governance of Jesuit Colleges in the United States, 1920–1970* (Notre Dame, IN: University of Notre Dame Press, 1984), 23; and Leahy, *Adapting to America*, 79–86.

21. Henri J. Wiesel, SJ, "Baccalaureate Sermon," *Damozel*, Senior Supplement, 1933, 15–20.

22. Dorothy Brown, interview by PM, May 16, 1989, transcript, OHP.

23. Barbara Solomon, *In the Company of Educated Women: A History of Women and Higher Education in America* (New Haven, CT: Yale University Press, 1985, 50.

24. Leahy, *Adapting to America*, 88n26. Milwaukee archbishop Sebastian Messmer (1847–1930), a leading conservative within the US hierarchy, pushed for a nationwide system of Catholic schools. He headed the archdiocese of Milwaukee from 1903 until his death. For more on his views, see Robert Cross, *The Emergence of Liberal Catholicism in America* (Cambridge, MA: Harvard University Press, 1967), 134.

25. Pauline M. A. Tavardian, "An Uncompromising Commitment to Mission: Mundelein College and the Advancement of Women's Higher Education, 1930–1950" (PhD diss., Loyola University, Chicago, 1990), 42. Chicago's DePaul University, conducted by the Congregation of the Mission (the Vincentians), set a precedent in 1916 when it made its College of Arts and Sciences coeducational. See Lizzy Boden, "Women at DePaul," *Bygone DePaul* (blog), April 7, 2010, http://news.library.depaul.press/full-text/2010/04/07/bygone-depaul-women-at-depaul.

26. Leahy, *Adapting to America*, 74–75, 83; Thomas J. Jablonsky, *Milwaukee's Jesuit University: Marquette, 1881–1981* (Milwaukee: Marquette University Press, 2007), 120–22. Courses offered were generally in education and social work. On women's experiences at Chicago institutions in this era, see Ann Marie Ryan, "Meeting Multiple Demands: Catholic Higher Education for Women in Chicago, 1911–1939," *American Catholic Studies* 120, no. 1 (2009): 1–26. Georgetown University admitted women undergraduates to the schools of foreign service, business administration, nursing, and languages and linguistics before its largest school, the College of Arts and Sciences, took that step in 1969. See Susan L. Poulson, "From Single-Sex to Coeducation:

The Advent of Coeducation at Georgetown, 1965–1975," *U.S. Catholic Historian* 13 (Fall 1995): 117–37.

27. See Mary J. Oates, "Mother Mary Katharine Drexel," in *Women Educators in the United States, 1820–1993: A Bio-Bibliographical Sourcebook,* ed. Maxine Schwartz Seller (Westport, CT: Greenwood, 1994), 209–17. Xavier's College of Pharmacy opened in 1927.

28. Elizabeth A. Edmondson, "Without Comment or Controversy: The G.I. Bill and Catholic Colleges," *Church History* 71 (December 2002): 833.

29. Vincent Beatty, SJ, was president of Loyola from 1955 to 1964.

30. Mary Matrona Dougherty to Vincent F. Beatty, February 7, 1957, NDMA. Johns Hopkins University had owned Evergreen, the residence of John Work Garrett (1872–1942) and his wife, Alice Warder Garrett (1877–1952), since 1942. By 1961, Beatty had acquired ten acres of land from Johns Hopkins, a transaction that made the Notre Dame and Loyola campuses contiguous. See also Julia A. Sienkewicz, *Historic American Buildings Survey: Addendum to Evergreen (Evergreen Museum & Library),* National Park Service (Washington, DC: U.S. Department of the Interior, 2009), 72n150, http://lcweb2.loc.gov/master/pnp/habshaer/md/md1600/md1633/data/md1633data.pdf.

31. See "Study Women's Colleges: Catholics Assert Institutions May Become Coeducational," *New York Times,* April 1, 1951. When in 1953 the Sisters of Mercy proposed to add a "cooperating" men's college to Saint Xavier College, their Chicago female institution, Cardinal Samuel Stritch summarily rejected the proposal. See Clough, *First in Chicago,* 149–50. Saint Xavier College admitted men in 1968; it gained university status in 1992.

32. Mary Agnes Klug, SSND, interview by Mary Jo Maloney, April 3, 1973, transcript, OHP.

33. "Co-education Is Upheld: Cushing Backs Trend to System in the Catholic Colleges," *New York Times,* December 14, 1952.

34. Quoted in Margaret Mary O'Connell, SSND, "Coeducation and the Education of Women—Eastern Regional Unit," *National Catholic Educational Association Bulletin* 51 (August 1954): 299. Rooney's jibe that "the oldest Catholic women's colleges in America are not old enough to talk about tradition" dismayed women in the audience. Rooney headed the Jesuit Educational Association from 1937 to 1966.

35. For a detailed account of the transition to coeducation at elite single-sex colleges in the United States and the United Kingdom in the 1960s, see Nancy Weiss Malkiel, *"Keep the Damned Women Out": The Struggle for Coeducation* (Princeton, NJ: Princeton University Press, 2016).

36. See President's Reports, 1961–62; 1964–65, NDMA.

37. Draft of minutes, advisory board, November 5, 1962, NDMA.

38. Minutes, board of directors, June 2, 1964, NDMA.

39. Henry J. Knott to Lawrence J. Shehan, October 9, 1964, ABA.

40. Lawrence J. Shehan to Henry J. Knott, November 8, 1964, ABA. Wisconsin native Mother General Ambrosia Roecklein (1893–1973), the first American elected to the order's highest office, governed from 1956 to 1968.

41. Minutes, advisory board, October 24, 1966; *Chron.,* June 28, 1967; *Chron.,* November 20, 1967; *Chron.,* November 22, 1967; minutes, board of trustees, October 20, 1969, NDMA; Varga, *Baltimore's Loyola, Loyola's Baltimore,* 478.

42. By the end of that year, all Jesuit colleges in the country were admitting women. See Poulson, "From Single-Sex to Coeducation," 117.

43. *Chron.*, September 29, 1970.

44. Minutes, board of trustees, November 19, 1987, NDMA.

45. Minutes, board of trustees, June 28, 1967, NDMA.

46. *Chron.*, March 19, 1968; May 23, 1968.

47. For a description of cooperative efforts in the Notre Dame and Loyola education departments in the early 1970s, see Margaret Steinhagen, interview by PM, May 15, 1989, transcript, OHP. At that time, 350 Loyola men and 150 Notre Dame women were taking courses in the cooperating institution. "Students—Suggestions & Opinions 1960s—(Response Rate Not Indicated)," n.d., NDMA; *Chron.*, July 19, 1971; *NDM Catalog*, 1972–73.

48. "Assumptions and Recommendations of the Tri-College Study Committee, March 24, 1970," NDMA. On the committee, William Kelly, SJ, represented Loyola; Marie Judith Foley, SSND, Notre Dame; and Elizabeth Geen, Mount Saint Agnes. Geen, recently retired as dean and vice president of Goucher College, was serving for a year as president of Mount Saint Agnes as it implemented its merger with Loyola.

49. "Resolution of the Board of Trustees of Loyola College—Passed Unanimously at the Meeting of the Board on April 25, 1970," NDMA; *Chron.*, May 14, 1970.

50. "Draft Proposal for a Co-institutional Arrangement between Loyola and Mount Saint Agnes, June 10, 1970," NDMA.

51. *Chron.*, June 3, 1970, NDMA.

52. "Position Paper of the Administration of the College of Notre Dame of Maryland on Its Relationship with Loyola College and Mount Saint Agnes College," n.d. (June 1970), NDMA. Feeley, a 1950 Notre Dame alumna, held a PhD in English from Rutgers University (1970). She was an American Council on Education Fellow in Academic Administration at the College of Notre Dame in 1970–71. Elected president of the college in 1971, she served until 1991.

53. *Chron.*, July 15, 1970.

54. Minutes, board of trustees, July 13, 1970, NDMA; "Resolution Passed by the Board of Trustees of the College of Notre Dame of Maryland, July 13, 1970," NDMA.

55. Minutes, board of trustees, September 23, 1970, NDMA.

56. See Thomas W. Spalding, *The Premier See: A History of the Archdiocese of Baltimore, 1789–1980* (Baltimore: Johns Hopkins University Press, 1989), 460; and Varga, *Baltimore's Loyola, Loyola's Baltimore*, 475.

57. Charles Ritter, interview by PM, May 26, 1989, transcript, OHP.

58. See "Annual Institutional Summary—College of Notre Dame of Maryland, October 1, 1968," NDMA. Before becoming president of Loyola, Sellinger had been dean of the college at Georgetown University (1957–64).

59. *Chron.*, January 16, 1973; minutes, board of trustees, February 16, 1973. Notre Dame housed female graduate students from local universities at this time. See minutes, board of trustees, September 6, 1974, NDMA.

60. Joseph A. Sellinger, SJ, to Kathleen Feeley, March 21, 1975, NDMA.

61. Joseph A. Sellinger, SJ, to Kathleen Feeley, SSND, March 21, 1975, NDMA; minutes, board of trustees, April 25, 1975, NDMA.

62. *Chron.*, November 21, 1975.

63. See Linelle LaBonte, SSND, director of photography, to Kathleen Feeley, February 19, 1976, NDMA. See also Marie Judith Foley, Department of Biology, to Kathleen Feeley, February 19, 1976, NDMA.

64. "Report of the Ad Hoc Committee to Study Question of a Joint Loyola-Notre Dame Committee to Deal with Matters of Cooperation," n.d., filed with minutes, board of trustees, February 20, 1976, NDMA.

65. Kathleen Feeley to Henry J. Knott, October 24, 1977, NDMA.

66. Henry J. Knott to Kathleen Feeley, November 17, 1977, NDMA.

67. Minutes, board of trustees, December 9, 1977, NDMA.

68. Kathleen Feeley to Joseph A. Sellinger, November 27, 1978, NDMA.

69. See *Chron.*, February 23, 1981; May 6, 1981; October 20, 1982.

70. George W. Constable, interview by PM, April 25, 1989, transcript, OHP.

71. Trinitas Bochini, interview by PM, April 6, 1989, transcript, OHP.

72. Notre Dame's Women's College enrolls traditional-aged undergraduates. Its College of Adult Undergraduate Studies developed from the Weekend College. In 2014, Notre Dame of Maryland University enrolled 1,250 undergraduate students; Loyola University Maryland enrolled 4,004 students, 59 percent of whom were women, and 1,650 graduate students.

73. For an overview of the movement to coeducation in the United States, see Rosalind Rosenberg, "The Limits of Access: The History of Coeducation in America," in *Women and Higher Education in American History*, ed. John Mack Faragher and Florence Howe (New York: Norton, 1988), 107–29. On Jesuit colleges and universities, see Leahy, *Adapting to America*, 67–92.

74. Registration figures from the Higher Education General Information Survey (HEGIS) reports, 1966–75, typed sheet, NDMA.

75. "Information from Touche-Ross & Co.'s Report for Maryland Council for Higher Education and the Maryland Legislature," n.d. (ca. 1973), filed with minutes, board of trustees, February 16, 1973, NDMA.

76. See "Information from Touche-Ross & Co.'s Report"; registration figures from the HEGIS reports, 1966–75.

77. "Information from Touche-Ross & Co.'s Report." See also [Elissa McGuire?], "Endowment of the College of Notre Dame," n.d. (ca. May 17, 1974), NDMA.

78. Kathleen Feeley to members of the board of trustees, August 21, 1974, NDMA. The receipt of $261,000 in Maryland state funds, released by the Supreme Court in December 1974 following the settlement of the ACLU suit, permitted the 1974–75 fiscal year to close with a small surplus.

79. Kathleen Feeley, "Case Statement for the College of Notre Dame of Maryland," typescript draft, January 12, 1987, NDMA. Other curricular initiatives followed, among them a school of nursing, a school of education, and a school of pharmacy.

80. Feeley, "Case Statement."

81. "America's Best Colleges," *U.S. News & World Report*, October 26, 1987.

82. Dorothy Arthur, SSND, interview by PM, March 2, 1989, transcript, OHP.

83. Jeanette J. Lim, US Department of Education, to Kathleen Feeley, April 16, 1986, NDMA; *Chron.*, May 5, 1988.

84. The median for all institutions was 7.2 percent. See "News and Views: It's Not True That Black Women Stay Away from Single-Sex Colleges," *Journal of Blacks in Higher Education* 30 (Winter 2000–2001): 12–13.

85. Feeley, "Case Statement."

86. *Chron.*, October 1, 1983. The college enrollment was 594 in 1970 and 568 in 1983.

87. In 2010, nearly 60 percent of students in traditional four-year colleges nationwide majored in professional fields.

88. *NDM Catalog*, 1988–89.

89. "College of Notre Dame Adds Majors to Prep for University Status," *Baltimore Business Journal*, March 25, 2011.

90. Stephen Vicchio, "Some Comments on the 'Uses' of the Liberal Arts," typescript of talk to New York City alumnae, February 24, 1990, NDMA.

91. *NDM Catalog*, 1921–22. The same qualifying words appear in the 1940–41 catalog.

92. Virgina Geiger, SSND, interview by Barbara Gross, March 27, 1973, transcript, OHP.

93. *Chron.*, April 24, 1986.

94. Office of Research and Planning and Strategic Planning Committee, "Executive Summary of Student Satisfaction Survey, 1984 Day Program Students," n.d., NDMA.

95. *NDM Catalog*, 1974–76.

96. *NDM Catalog*, 1982–83.

97. *NDM Catalog*, 1984–85.

98. *NDM Catalog*, 1986–87.

99. Minutes, board of trustees, September 22, 1994, NDMA.

100. "Report to the Faculty, Administration, Trustees, Students of the College of Notre Dame of Maryland by an Evaluation Team representing the Commission on Higher Education of the Middle States Association of Colleges and Schools. Prepared after study of the institution's self-study report and a visit to the campus on November 9–12, 1986," 2, NDMA.

101. Feeley, "Case Statement," 8.

102. Anne Cullen, interview by PM, May 3, 1989, transcript, OHP. Cullen joined the modern languages faculty in 1959.

103. Patricia Byrne, "In the Parish but Not of It: Sisters," in *Transforming Parish Ministry: The Changing Roles of Catholic Clergy, Laity, and Women Religious*, by Jay P. Dolan, R. Scott Appleby, Patricia Byrne, and Debra Campbell (New York: Crossroad, 1989), 173n75.

104. President's Report, 1963–64, NDMA.

105. *Chron.*, September 15–16, 1940; October 15, 1960.

106. Kathleen Feeley, "Expanded Mission Statement," January 12, 1987, appended to Feeley, "Case Statement," 2. At this time, most of the college's fifty-two adjunct faculty members staffed the Weekend College.

107. Clough, *First in Chicago*, 312.

108. See financial statements (assets, liabilities, reserves, capital, income, and expense) for fiscal year ended August 31, 1956; "CND, Statement of Income and

Expense, Fiscal Year Ended June 30, 1971," minutes, board of directors, July 29, 1971, NDMA.

109. Kathleen Feeley, "First Draft," typescript, 6–8, February 24, 1978, NDMA.

110. Jay Merwin, "Notre Dame Names New President: Sr. Rosemarie Nassif Says She Will Continue College's Tradition," *Baltimore Sun*, March 20, 1992. Nassif, who graduated from Notre Dame College in Missouri (closed 1977), held a PhD in chemistry from Catholic University (1972). At the time of her election, she was a 1991–92 American Council on Education Fellow in Higher Education at Bryn Mawr College.

111. Anne Cullen, interview by PM, May 3, 1989, transcript, OHP.

112. David Folkenflik, "College Head's Resignation Followed Faculty Unrest: Notre Dame Changes Sparked Opposition," *Baltimore Sun*, March 4, 1996. See also David Folkenflik, "Notre Dame's President to Leave," *Baltimore Sun*, February 29, 1996. On the Nassif presidency (1992–96), see Dorothy M. Brown and Eileen O'Dea, "'Trust and Dare': Adaptations and Innovations at the College of Notre Dame," in *Challenged by Coeducation: Women's Colleges since the 1960s*, ed. Leslie Miller-Bernal and Susan L. Poulson (Nashville, TN: Vanderbilt University Press, 2006), 276–79. Nassif later became president of Holy Names University in Oakland, California.

113. Brown, a 1954 Notre Dame alumna, earned a PhD from Georgetown University (1962). After teaching at Notre Dame (1958–66), she joined Georgetown's history faculty, retiring as professor and university provost in 2002.

114. *You Are Sent: Constitutions and General Directory of the School Sisters of Notre Dame* (Milwaukee: School Sisters of Notre Dame, 1986), 22, quoted in Mary Pat Seurkamp, "Who Will Bear This Identity? One Model of Sponsorship," *Current Issues in Catholic Higher Education* 26. no. 1 (2007): 88.

115. Eileen O'Dea, SSND, vice president for institutional planning, became the first vice president for mission.

116. Seurkamp, "Who Will Bear This Identity?," 95. Since 1993, an annual Community Day brings all campus constituencies together to reflect on Notre Dame's historic mission and identity in the light of Catholic intellectual tradition and social teaching. Christine DeVinne, "A Catholic Campus in Reflective Action: A Co-curricular Event Highlighting Identity and Mission," *Journal of Catholic Higher Education* 34 (May 2015): 91–106, describes Community Day programs and assesses their effectiveness over time.

117. Feeley, "Case Statement," 2–3. A number of scholarly studies in the 1970s and 1980s examined the collegiate origins of notable American women. On the record of women's versus coeducational colleges in producing female achievers, see M. Elizabeth Tidball and Vera Kistiakowsky, "Baccalaureate Origins of American Scientists and Scholars," *Science* 193 (1976): 642–52; Mary J. Oates and Suan Williamson, "Women's Colleges and Women Achievers," *Signs* 3 (Summer 1978): 795–806; Joy K. Rice and Annette Hemmings, "Women's Colleges and Women Achievers: An Update," *Signs* 13, no. 3 (1988): 546–49; and Daryl G. Smith, "Women's Colleges and Coed Colleges: Is There a Difference for Women?," *Journal of Higher Education* 61 (March–April 1990): 181–97.

118. Cross-registration represented another way that Notre Dame sought to alleviate women students' anxiety during a period of expanding coeducation. In

1972, students could take one course per semester at Goucher, Morgan State, Coppin State, or Towson State Colleges (*NDM Catalog*, 1972–73); by 1979, a consortium among Notre Dame, Loyola, Goucher, and Johns Hopkins was in place, with "faculty from Goucher and Notre Dame shar[ing] responsibility for instruction of senior students from all four colleges during the fall semester" (Marie Xavier Looymans, SSND, interview by PM, March 13, 1989, transcript, OHP). By the close of the 1970s, Notre Dame students were able to participate in "a dual degree program in engineering with the School of Engineering, University of Maryland, College Park" (*NDM Catalog*, 1978–79).

Index

Page numbers in italics refer to figures.

CPSIA information can be obtained
at www.ICGtesting.com
Printed in the USA
LVHW031936260221
680051LV00003B/199